Hitler's
MOTOR RACING BATTLES

Hitler's

MOTOR RACING BATTLES

The Silver Arrows under the Swastika

EBERHARD REUSS

Translated by Angus McGeoch

Haynes Publishing

Published with Aufbau; 'Aufbau' is a trademark of Aufbau Verlagsgruppe GmbH
Negotiated by Aufbau Media GmbH, Berlin

First published in April 2008

A catalogue record for this book is available from the British Library

ISBN 978 1 84425 476 7

Library of Congress control no: 2007943092

Published by Haynes Publishing, Sparkford, Yeovil, Somerset BA22 7JJ, UK
Tel: 01963 442030 Fax: 01963 440001
Int. tel: +44 1963 442030 Int. fax: +44 1963 440001
E-mail: sales@haynes.co.uk
Website: www.haynes.co.uk

Haynes North America Inc.
861 Lawrence Drive, Newbury Park,
California 91320, USA

Printed and bound in Great Britain by J. H. Haynes & Co. Ltd, Sparkford

CONTENTS

Motorsport professionals • Benz and
Daimler in financial straits • The racing
and rearmament expert • Death on the
AVUS circuit • The wonderful life of
a racing driver • A matter of national
importance • Mass production and
a slump in sales • Routes out of the
Depression • The national racing car
with the Porsche badge • The national
racing car with the Mercedes-Benz
badge • The race for subsidies •
Hitler's car dealer • A loyal customer of
Daimler-Benz • Hitler at home to racing
drivers • On the final straight

ACKNOWLEDGEMENTS

During the research for my books on the history of Grand Prix racing and the associated filming of my television documentary for South-West German Broadcasting, *Die Helden der Rennschlacht – Der Nationalsozialismus und die Silberpfeile* ('The Battle-Heroes of the Racetrack – Nazism and the Silver Arrows'), first broadcast on 7 July 1999, I had the opportunity to conduct interviews with Manfred von Brauchitsch, Georg Meier, Paul Pietsch and Dr Peter Lang, the son of Hermann Lang. Since then, in the course of journalistic work for the SWR and ARD channels on radio and TV, as well as in contributions to specialist magazines and daily newspapers, I have tackled this subject time and again and have been able to question and interview countless surviving witnesses from that period.

Sadly there is not the space to mention by name everyone who has helped me and provided information. I offer my thanks to them all, but will name here only a representative selection: Günther Molter, former chief press officer for Daimler-Benz AG; Harvey T. Rowe, co-author of the memoirs of Alfred Neubauer; Mariele Müller, widow of Hermann Paul Müller; Emmy Herzog, widow of the motorcyclist Leo Steinweg; Edith Meier, widow of Georg Meier; Professor Bernd Rosemeyer, son of the Auto Union works driver; Bernd Sebastian, the son of Ludwig Sebastian, who was Bernd Rosemeyer's mechanic at Auto Union; Dieter and Heinz Herz, sons of the NSU world record rider and friend of Rosemeyer, Wilhelm Herz; Jörg Reichle, departmental head with *Süddeutscher Zeitung* and son of the former Mercedes-Benz racing mechanic Eugen Reichle; Hansjörg Götzl, editor of *Motor-Klassik*; Tobias Aichele, biographer of Huschke von Hanstein; and Winfried Seidel, expert collector of vintage cars and well-informed connoisseur of the historical racing scene at Mercedes-Benz. Not least, I could always count on friendly support from Dr Harry Niemann, former head of group archives at DaimlerChrysler AG, and Professor Dr Peter Kirchberg, scientific adviser to

Audi Tradition. My thanks also go to my German publisher Aufbau Verlag and my editor Andreas Paschedag.

Finally, I thank Haynes Publishing, and am very glad that their Editorial Director, Mark Hughes, decided to include my book – which has since been selected as Germany's 'Motor Book of 2007' – in his publishing programme. I also owe considerable thanks to my knowledgeable translator, Angus McGeoch, who also added some new explanatory endnotes for this English edition. And I especially thank Claudia and Charlotte, who have lived with the creation of this book over many years with extraordinary patience.

Bernd Rosemeyer finishes a record run on the Frankfurt–Darmstadt autobahn in 1937. Waiting for the modified Auto Union Grand Prix car is its designer, Ferdinand Porsche. (Porsche AG)

CHAPTER ONE

INTRODUCTION: NAZI BROWN BENEATH THE SILVER

'Who speaks of victories? Survival is everything.'
Rainer Maria Rilke

Today Silver Arrows are once again making motor racing history. The most successful Grand Prix thoroughbreds of the late 1990s came from the McLaren-Mercedes stable. When their drivers – such as Mika Häkkinen and David Coulthard in earlier days, or, more recently, Lewis Hamilton and Fernando Alonso – were on the grid at Monte Carlo, Monza, Spa-Francorchamps or the Nürburgring, the headlines trumpeted the great and lesser triumphs of the Silver Arrows as though times had never changed.

The Daimler corporation calls its modern racing cars 'Silver Arrows' and even claims exclusive use of this trademark, as well as of the colour silver (although from 1934 to 1939 Auto Union also turned out its racing cars in silver, and did so demonstrably *earlier* than Daimler-Benz). But latterly this has all been due to sponsorship. At the start of the 1997 Formula One season the Reemtsma tobacco group replaced the crimson-and-white Philip Morris livery, and advertising slogans for West cigarettes were placed on the bodywork in place of Marlboro logos. Even after the change of principal sponsor to Vodafone in the course of the 2007 season, the silver background colour has remained, which of course provides all that is needed to trigger wonderful reminiscences of an age long past.

When the first of the *new* Silver Arrows, driven by David Coulthard, took to the track in Melbourne in 1997 it won the race. This was the first success for McLaren after 49 fruitless races – and the first triumph

The legend starts here. Manfred von Brauchitsch, winner of the Eifel Race at the Nürburgring in 1934. (Daimler AG)

for Mercedes-Benz as engine supplier since its Grand Prix comeback in 1993. And was it not true that at the Nürburgring in 1934 Manfred von Brauchitsch, in the very first outing for a silver Mercedes-Benz racing car, shot straight to victory and by doing so laid the foundation of all the legends?

This was certainly a stroke of luck for modern marketing strategists and canny sponsors. Indeed, those sorts of people were already around in Grand Prix racing in the 1930s, in the form of the Nazi regime[1] and its propagandists. They laid the foundation stone for the successes of the Silver Arrows that still raise a cheer today. And they did so with government subsidies, bonuses for winning, and adoration as national heroes – until their dying day. Wheels had to roll for victory. And on especially important occasions the seemingly unbeatable national racing cars were even adorned with the trademark of their patrons and exploiters – the swastika.

The memory of this particular form of mutual advertising has not been recalled for a long time. It was suppressed, concealed, played down, for after 1945 the majority of the people involved returned to their factories or to the racing circuits. They all regarded themselves as profoundly non-political. But doubtless that was why they allowed themselves to be harnessed to the Nazi bandwagon. And even decades after Germany's catastrophic defeat, quite a number would still be citing the victories of the Silver Arrows and the building of autobahns as proof that things were not all bad in those days.

In 1958, former Mercedes-Benz racing manager Alfred Neubauer made the bestseller lists with his memoirs, co-written with journalist Harvey T. Rowe under the title *Men, Women and Engines*. This was followed in 1959 by a second volume, *Master of a Thousand Horsepower*. The memoirs, which Rowe reworked in 1970 and abridged heavily to make a single volume, simultaneously influenced and transformed the image of the race-track heroes in their Silver Arrows: 'Every one of these names has become history today – a part of the history of international motor racing in its greatest and finest era.'[2]

In this way the myths and legends have remained alive, and are being cultivated as part of the marketing image, although by now Daimler, and Audi too, are being more frank about the history of their companies in the days of the Nazi dictatorship. Yet on the fringes of modern motorsport events, whenever the original cars or even just authentic replicas from the Silver Arrow era are rolled out and make their ear-splitting entrance as in days of old, then once again people are swept up by the fascination which these engineering wonders of the 1930s still evoke. What must it have been like for contemporary observers when cars from Mercedes-Benz and Auto Union raced from victory to victory, proclaiming supposed German superiority?

The shining hero and the leader of German motorsport. Bernd Rosemeyer and NSKK-Führer Adolf Hühnlein at the winner's ceremony after the 1937 Eifel Race. (Kirchberg)

This is not a Nazi rally but the official reception at the Mercedes-Benz factory in Untertürkheim after the Eifel Race in 1934. Behind the swastika-adorned rostrum is CEO Dr Wilhelm Kissel and on his left is Manfred von Brauchitsch. (Daimler AG)

'Nazism cultivated all forms of sport, and from a purely linguistic point of view it was more influenced by boxing than by all the other sports put together; but the most frequent and most memorable image of heroism is that provided in the mid-1930s by the racing drivers: after his fatal crash, Bernd Rosemeyer was for a while almost on a par with Horst Wessel[3] in the popular imagination.' That was the comment of Victor Klemperer in 1946 in *Lingua Tertii Imperii*, his study of the language of the Third Reich.[4] He goes on: 'For a while the victors in international motor racing, behind the wheel of their competition cars, leaning up against them or working underneath them, were the most photographed heroes of the day. If a young man did not take his heroic image from the muscle-bound warriors, naked or clad in a stormtrooper's uniform, as seen on posters and commemorative coins, then he certainly did so from racing drivers; what both embodiments of heroism share is the fixed stare, expressing tough, forward-looking determination and the will to conquer.'

But let us review the history of Hitler's motor racing battles once more. Let us question the last remaining eyewitnesses, draw on biographical memoirs, contemporary sources and documents. Let us correct the myths and perforce scratch the gloss of the racing legends. For beneath the silver that outshines everything there is a kind of brown stain, which can be attributed not to rust, but to suppressed history.

Notes

1 The word 'Nazi' was originally the popular German abbreviation of *Nationalsozialist*. The full name of the party was *Nationalsozialistische Deutsche Arbeiterpartei* (National Socialist German Workers' Party), more usually referred to by its initials NSDAP. In this book the terms Nazi and NSDAP will be used interchangeably where appropriate.

2 Alfred Neubauer, *Speed Was My Life*, London 1960.

3 Horst Wessel (1907–30) was a low-life young member of the SA who was shot dead in a street fight, ostensibly against Communists but probably a gangland brawl. Goebbels seized on his death as a propaganda coup and had a trivial poem by Wessel turned into a rousing anthem, the Horst Wessel Song, which was frequently sung on official occasions.

4 Victor Klemperer (1881–1960), a cousin of the conductor Otto Klemperer, was the son of a rabbi but converted to Protestantism in 1912. He served in the German Army in the First World War and in 1920 was appointed Professor of Literature in Dresden. When the Nazis came to power he was persecuted as a Jew and in 1935 was dismissed from his post but, with his wife, managed to survive in a series of hiding-places. Klemperer always kept a diary as well as making notes for *Lingua Tertii Imperii*. In February 1945 he survived the devastating Allied bombing raid on Dresden.

CHAPTER TWO

MOTORSPORT IN PRE-NAZI GERMANY

E very age creates the heroes it requires. In the decade following the First World War, Germany, like other countries, saw a boom in sports idols. One might say it was the continuation of hostilities by other means. Or perhaps it was sublimation. Or a case of capitalising on the nation's assets. Football, boxing, athletics and motor racing (with cars and motorcycles) all enthralled the masses; the daily press and specialist publications cashed in. They turned spectator sports into headline news.

As the great left-wing playwright Bertold Brecht commented in 1928: 'Sport starts getting big long after it has ceased to be healthy.' Fritz Kortner,[1] another prominent man of the theatre, was a boxing fan and had training sessions with Max Schmeling.[2] Kortner declared: 'These are the times we live in. What happens in the ring is a reflection of life. The pitiless fury with which they assault each other is like the bitter struggle we all have for our existence.'

Boxing became a metaphor for the ebb and flow of events in the 1920s and Max Schmeling was transformed into the perfect national sporting hero who, for a few rounds, united the strife-torn German people – from intellectuals of the far left, through to the revanchist German nationalists and hate-filled Nazis. To those on the right this sporting idol set an example to a nation prostrated by a world war and humiliated by the Treaty of Versailles. For those on the left, on the other hand, the pugilist's capacity to take risks and win through was anti-bourgeois and thoroughly liberating.

The sporting heroes themselves may well have found these interpretations

Capacity crowd at the Nürburgring: the Eifel Race in 1928, one year after the opening of this fabled race track. (Reuss)

rather alien, hard to live up to and quite possibly a matter of complete indifference. They wanted to win, to be successful – at any price, if need be – whether in the boxing ring or on the racetrack.

Motorsport professionals

Admittedly, in the period of the Weimar Republic[3] motorsport was a highly exclusive pastime. The spectacle might entertain the masses, but that was still far from making motor racing a mass sport. This was in sharp contrast to conditions beyond the borders of the German Reich, where not only big stadiums and sports halls but also permanent racing circuits were being built. True, the AVUS[4] circuit was opened in 1921, yet this urban motorway, which was originally intended to generate toll revenue for its private investors, was temporarily used as a racetrack due to the lack of paying traffic. There was a 9km straight, then a tight bend at the southern end, and another 9km straight leading to the wide northern bend, then the whole circuit started again. In those days the AVUS was the modest German variant of an international trend towards shifting dangerous racing away from closed public roads to permanent circuits. Between 1925 and 1927 the Nürburgring was built as a job-creation scheme in the barren Eifel region near the Belgian border. At the outset the cost was estimated at 4 million Reichsmarks (RM), but the racetrack eventually cost 14.5 million. However, the government was the majority shareholder, so tax revenues continued to flow in to support the racing business.

Even before the First World War national automobile clubs and their lobbyists – who typically ranged from aristocratic motorists, through influential captains of industry to well-disposed representatives of officialdom – were getting projects of this kind under way. Brooklands in the United Kingdom (1907) and the Indianapolis Motor Speedway in the USA (1911) were examples that, after the end of the war in 1918, were copied in mainland Europe at Monza on the outskirts of Milan and Montlhéry near Paris. These 'autodromes' were bounded by grandstands because, after all, the new racing arenas were intended to attract mass audiences.

It was particularly in France and Italy that the business began to flourish in the 1920s, when France's blue Bugattis and Delages vied for motorsport supremacy with the red Alfa Romeos and Maseratis of Italy. It was in those years that the single-seat racing car, the Grand Prix *monoposto*, developed into the fastest and most spectacular formula on the continent of Europe. The class of blue-blooded or well-heeled gentlemen, who before the Great War still competed with 'running-in' drivers paid by the factory – in other words racing mechanics – still took part in Grand Prix events in the 1920s and '30s, but faced with ever more complex racing car technology they gradually lost out to the driving skills of the specialists. In France, the Monegasque Louis Chiron, and in Mussolini's Italy Tazio Nuvolari and Achille Varzi, ended up by the early 1930s as the highest-paid artistes at the wheel, national idols and entrepreneurs on their own account. They were the perfect embodiment of egocentric commercialism, always looking to their own advantage, constantly haggling over the best works contracts and the top starting money, and anxious to enhance their own social status. In short: they foreshadowed today's sporting super-rich.

The only man to achieve this status in German-speaking countries before 1933 was Rudolf Caracciola. The slightly-built son of a hotelier from Remagen in the Rhineland, he worked his way up from being a car salesman and weekend racer to signing a works contract with Mercedes. At the age of 25 he won the first German Grand Prix in 1926 on the AVUS

Rudolf Caracciola at the AVUS in 1926 before the first German Grand Prix. Standing behind him are his riding mechanic, Eugen Salzer, and – with bow tie – Dr Fritz Nallinger, who later became Technical Director of the merged Daimler-Benz company. (Daimler AG)

circuit, and from then on was affectionately dubbed 'Caratsch' by press and public.

'It was the first time that I had matched myself against drivers of international class, not the very greatest of all, but top drivers all the same,' mused Caracciola in 1939, in the twilight of his career and after the German invasion of Poland. 'Of course, I was proud of that victory, but I realised that one win like that meant nothing, that you had to prove yourself ten times, a hundred times over, in order to really stay at the top. Only a few knew how to do that. Most of them, after a brief rise, sank back into the anonymity of private life, or else were swept from the track by the bony hand of death. But how did those few make it? On what terms did the Iron Guard of great drivers fight their way through, and what was the secret of their success? Answering these questions led me to modesty about myself: I recognised that every driver was merely part of a large organisation, namely the manufacturer that was behind him. The works created the conditions for victory. The sophisticated brains of the engineers, their staff of mechanics trained in precision work, the financial muscle of big business that carried them through periods of defeat – these were all the driver's invisible helpmates who had a decisive influence over victory or defeat.'

So the triumphant racing driver was just a cog in a vast wheel. Really?

Benz and Daimler in financial straits

In the 1920s the motor car was still the luxury toy and means of transport of a well-heeled few. And in Germany, compared with other industrialised nations, there were only very few of these well-placed 'motorists'. In raw statistical terms, the homeland of Herr Benz and Herr Daimler boasted only one car per 100 inhabitants in 1926, while the ratio in France and Britain was 3.2 per 100 and in the USA an amazing 21.7 per 100. Defeat in war followed by rampant hyperinflation had put the skids under German car makers.

Before 1914 two German companies in particular had gained success in motorsport and at the same time won fame and honour for the Fatherland – Daimler in Stuttgart under the Mercedes badge, and Benz in Mannheim. In 1911 the *Blitzen* (lightning) Benz, designed under the direction of Dr Hans Nibel, and with the American Bob Burman at the wheel, achieved the world absolute record speed of 228kph (141.7mph), while Christian

A forgotten but far-sighted revolution in car design: Nallinger's and Nibel's underpowered and underfinanced Benz Tropfenwagen at its Monza debut in 1923. (Daimler AG)

Lautenschlager led the victorious Mercedes team that triumphed in the last pre-war French Grand Prix in 1914. In those days, wins and records on the racetrack were crucial selling points, since they provided much more tangible proof of technical competence in series production. Thus it was only logical that after the First World War both companies would attempt to position themselves in the market by participating in international motorsport.

However, under the Weimar Republic, too, success in motorsport was a matter of money. The revolutionary Benz *Tropfenwagen* (a streamlined, teardrop-shaped car) with a mid-mounted engine and floating axles, developed by racing manager Willy Walb and his designers Fritz Nallinger and Hans Nibel, made a promising debut in the 1923 Italian Grand Prix at Monza. Driving their non-supercharged Benz racing cars, with only 90bhp under the bonnet, Fernando Minoia and Fritz Hörner came fourth and fifth respectively. Yet in the wake of the 1923 inflation crisis and an acute shortage of capital, the men from Mannheim, under pressure from the banks, had no choice but to join in an *Interessengemeinschaft* (commercial alliance) with the equally cash-strapped Daimler-Motoren-Gesellschaft. Under the decisive influence of Deutsche Bank the two hitherto competing companies completed a full merger in the summer of 1926. But as early as 1924 the sole responsibility for motor-sport activities already lay with the Daimler branch of the new twin concern. In the Stuttgart suburb of Untertürkheim more emphasis was placed at that time on the design of supercharged engines than on the niceties of bodywork design. Since 1923, the man in charge of racing on the Daimler side was Ferdinand Porsche, the then 47-year-old Technical Director. He had been appointed to succeed Paul Daimler, because the son of the firm's founder, after violent disagreements in the boardroom, had moved to the Horch car company in the eastern German town of Zwickau.

The racing and rearmament expert

Many considered Ferdinand Porsche a brilliant 'engine man', while others complained about his penchant for sophisticated but hair-raisingly expensive designs. Since beginning his career with the Austrian firms of Lohner and Austro-Daimler, this engineer, who always thought in large-scale terms, was in fact dreaming of producing a simple car that a large section of the population could afford – yet at the same time he was building giant artillery transporters, with which he made his name in the First World War as an armaments specialist with a company in Wiener Neustadt. Porsche's move to Daimler came at the right moment, since he was able to combine motor racing and series car production with development contracts for the Army Weapons Office. The latter was all top secret of course, since the Versailles Treaty banned German companies from involvement in the arms business that had once been so lucrative. In this way, under Porsche's direction, the company developed armoured combat and all-terrain vehicles, tracked vehicles and a 300hp aero engine. However, prior to this Porsche had been allowed to build one more Grand Prix racing car for Daimler in the then prevailing 2-Litre formula.

On 29 October 1924, at the Gran Premio d'Italia on the Monza circuit, Porsche's new Mercedes eight-cylinder supercharged M218 made its debut. Four cars were entered for the race and their output of about 170hp at 7,000rpm made them serious contenders for victory right from the outset. But the tricky handling characteristics of these monsters created problems, and Count Louis Zborowski had a fatal accident on the Lesmo bend. Was it faulty brakes? A patch of oil? A burst tyre? The cause was never established. Earlier, top Mercedes driver Giulio Masetti had already retired with a fractured fuel-pipe, and after Zborowski's accident Max Sailer, the director, withdrew the two remaining cars of Christian Werner and Alfred Neubauer/Otto Merz. The new design would never again be seen on the starting grid of an international Grand Prix; and any further ambitions Porsche cherished to build another racing car for the newly formed company of Daimler-Benz AG were shattered in 1926–7, when a majority vote of the Board vetoed it on grounds of cost.

Christian Werner at Monza testing the Mercedes M218, its designer standing at the side watching his new Grand Prix car. This was a typical Ferdinand Porsche product of the 1920s – very sophisticated, very expensive and very unsuccessful. (Porsche AG)

The remaining M218 Grand Prix models were nevertheless converted into sports cars. Two of them showed up in 1926 at the first German Grand Prix on the AVUS track, which, with a view to participation by German works teams, had been opened exclusively to sports cars. The two enclosed Mercedes racing cars were driven by Adolf Rosenberger and Rudolf Caracciola. In the final phase of the race Sailer, Porsche and Alfred Neubauer, the future Mercedes-Benz racing manager, watched as Caracciola, in pouring rain, maintained a rock-solid 200kph (125mph) in the supercharged eight-cylinder and pushed through to victory.

'It takes a death-defying nerve to drive at such high speed round an old-fashioned circuit like that,' wrote the magazine *Das Auto* admiringly. But it was scarcely ten years later that a completely new generation of German racing cars, initiated by Porsche and Nibel, would be tearing round the AVUS at speeds of 340kph (over 210mph) with more than 600hp on tap, and sending an entire nation into a frenzy of enthusiasm.

Yet that spectacle had hidden risks. Even the practice laps for this first

Opposite: Disaster at the AVUS in 1926. Three race stewards were killed when Adolf Rosenberger's Mercedes M218 crashed into a timekeepers' cabin. The car had been modified into a sports car version to meet the regulations of the first German Grand Prix. (Reuss)

Right: Adolf Rosenberger – the Jewish racing driver and businessman who financed the origins of the Porsche factory. (Daimler AG)

German Grand Prix were marred by a death, and on the Sunday of the race itself further serious accidents occurred. Adolf Rosenberger came off the track at about 150kph (90mph): his car slammed into a timekeepers' cabin and three race stewards were killed instantly. The unfortunate driver and his mechanic Curt Coquelline, who was also on board, got away with severe injuries. We will meet Rosenberger, the motor racing businessman from Pforzheim, again in the early 1930s in a different role – as Ferdinand Porsche's business partner.

Although Porsche was made Technical Director of the merged Daimler-Benz AG, post-merger he began to lose out in a power struggle against Nibel, his opposite number from the Benz side, and after violent differences he was forced to leave the group. In 1928 his contract expired and was not renewed, an additional factor having been disputes over his sometimes faulty but, in the main, far too costly and loss-making car and truck models. In the end Porsche was taken to court over his financial obligations to Daimler-Benz AG. In a bitter frame of mind, the disgraced

technician moved to the Austrian Steyr works. But in the wake of the
Wall Street Crash, Steyr's bankers collapsed and the stricken car maker
was bought out by its direct competitor, Austro-Daimler. However, Porsche
was not keen to work for Austro-Daimler again following his earlier
disagreements with them. He was therefore forced by circumstances to
go independent and founded the firm of 'Dr Ing. h.c. F. Porsche GmbH,
Design and Consultancy in Engine and Vehicle Building'.

By this time the age of the founding fathers of the Benz and Daimler
automobile marques was long past; even before the beginning of the 20th
century it was the banks and the big financiers who decided who would build
cars. The investment needed was just too great for a private individual. Yet
thanks to political events in Germany and Porsche's personal involvement
with the top men of the Nazi regime, his modest Stuttgart garage firm
grew into a major automobile group. The initial share capital in 1930 was
30,000 RM. As founder, Porsche then held 70 per cent of the equity, his
son-in-law Anton Piëch 15 per cent, and the remaining 15 per cent was
bought by Adolf Rosenberger, who also acted as Commercial Director of
the company. At that time the fact that the former Mercedes-Benz works
driver was Jewish did not present a problem.

Death on the AVUS circuit
Critical public opinion during the years of the Weimar Republic had much
more of a problem with the point of motor racing – particularly after the
four deaths at the very first German Grand Prix: 'AVUS Caesar – morituri
te salutant!' ('Those about to die salute you!') quipped the daily press,
but the supporters of the doomed gladiators were not going to let their
racing and their racetrack be spoiled. In the Allgemeine Automobil-Zeitung
('General Automobile Times') of 31 July 1926, Baron Ernst Günther
von Wentzel-Mosau, who had himself raced successfully in Benz and
Mercedes sports cars, wrote: 'A certain group of people, and also a section
of the press (which never changes) have felt constrained, following the
recent accidents, to indulge in some unpleasant polemic and to compose
headlines of a tendentious nature. Indeed the race management has even
been reproached for not calling off the race, and it has been proclaimed
to the world that the AVUS is totally unsuitable for racing. Even though
in the new Germany we may have lost the habit of taking a firm line on

anything, it should nonetheless be clear today that all these moaners have made their judgement uninvited and lacking any technical knowledge. Of course, the accidents that have occurred are deeply to be regretted, and none will do so more than the race management and the directors of the AVUS. However, neither party could have guessed in advance that such accidents could happen at all. Those who are today sounding off about fatal accidents and the like, would have been better advised to raise their voices beforehand, if they considered the AVUS unfit for racing, since anyone can be wise after the event.'

That was how the battle-hardened elite of the equally elitist world of motor racing thought and wrote scarcely eight years after the end of the Great War. And they praised the race organisers of the exclusive 'Automobile Club of Germany' for the fact that 'despite all the events assaulting them and the calls for the race to be abandoned, they had enough sense of responsibility and nerve to carry the contest through to the end.' Nearly three years after the first German Grand Prix, Baron von Wentzel-Mosau himself died as a result of an accident during the Stendal kilometre race. Legend has it that the Herr Baron, at the wheel of his Mercedes-Benz SSK, had already clocked the day's best time and an average of 173kph (107.5mph), had shot past the finishing post and was slowing down when an incautious spectator crossed the track. The blue-blooded driver took abrupt and selfless avoiding action, turned his car over and so met his end.

The wonderful life of a racing driver

'Kai spent every day in the pits. Everything here was arranged in a narrow arc and easy to take in at a glance. If you stretched out your hand you had everything within reach and it was just a matter of grabbing it. There was a car there with a rumbling engine that had to be observed and tamed, in order to get the best performance from it. That was a solid, honest, economical job without the shimmer and uncertainty of elusive feelings. You could stake your ambition on it and not go wrong.'

So wrote Erich Maria Remarque in his story *Station am Horizont* ('Next Stop, the Horizon') about Kai, the racing driver and *bon vivant*. It was serialised fortnightly in 1927–8 in the illustrated magazine *Sport im Bild* ('Sport Illustrated'), rather grandly subtitled 'The Paper of High Society'. Less than two years later Remarque's anti-war novel *All Quiet*

A society outing – a day of motor racing at the AVUS was an upper-class event during the 1920s and early '30s. (Perckhammer)

on the Western Front would make him instantly famous but reviled by the Nazis. At that time Remarque was editor of *Sport im Bild*, published by the Scherl Verlag, which was owned by the nationalist conservative Alfred Hugenberg.[5] The magazine covered fashion and society, literature and art – and motor racing. In those days there was no contradiction in that, since cars were still a luxury item and racing them still a 'sport for gentlemen'. Remarque's hero Kai typifies a deeply lethargic and pampered society; he is restlessly torn hither and thither between the rivalry of the racetrack and his simultaneous passion for three women. In places a dreadful piece of writing, it is at the same time an atmospheric portrait of the age, which lends colour to the archetypal playboy racing professional. The drivers were upper crust, from the top echelons of society. Eccentric figures like that are not really the stuff of which governments are made, and certainly not the crudely nationalistic state of Nazi ideology. However, while those fashionable gentlemen could never for a moment be confused with the low-life thugs of the SA[6] (Brownshirt militia), their courage, daring and death-defying brilliance had great propaganda value. At the same time, the ambition and vanity of these pampered stars had much in common with that of the Nazi bigwigs and their hangers-on.

So it was that after 1933 the aristocratic heroes of the circuit became the popular idols of their day. Fans who preferred something more folksy and down-to-earth tended to seek their heroes among motorcyclists, whose public appeal was no less great, but whose manner and speech were rather more demotic. The riders were recruited almost exclusively from a simpler social background, but in the end Nazi propaganda removed the difference and they were embraced, corrupted and promoted as national exemplars and 'heroes of the racetrack battle' alongside such fashionable racing drivers of the Weimar period as Rudolf Caracciola, Hans Stuck and Manfred von Brauchitsch – all of whom, incidentally, had become personally acquainted with the car-loving Nazi leaders long before the National Socialists seized power. After 1933 a younger generation of top drivers from far humbler origins, such as Bernd Rosemeyer, Hermann Lang and Georg 'Schorsch' Meier, achieved or even – in the case of Rosemeyer – far exceeded the same degree of fame, success and popularity. It was no coincidence that Rosemeyer, Lang and Meier served their motor racing apprenticeship on motorcycles.

But whether before 1933 or after, racetrack idols all over the world were and are stars who live on another plane altogether: in 1932, when Hans Stuck married the successful tennis player and journalist Paula von Reznicek, the witnesses at their wedding were the flying ace Ernst Udet and Crown Prince Wilhelm of Prussia.[7] And the money flowed in as well: for example, Rudolf Caracciola was contractually entitled to half the winner's prize at the German Grand Prix on the AVUS. That came to 8,000 RM, which he invested in setting up his own Mercedes-Benz dealership on Berlin's fashionable Kurfürstendamm. To put this in perspective, a skilled worker at the Daimler-Benz factory in Untertürkheim was paid rather less than 1 RM per hour and had to work a 52- or 54-hour week, so that his annual pay was around 2,500 RM. From the early 1930s Caracciola lived in a villa in the Swiss resort of Arosa. 'Caratsch' followed his first big victory for Mercedes-Benz with a continuous sequence of further wins; in 1927 he won the inaugural race at the Nürburgring, a further race there in 1928 and the German Grand Prix in 1931, but most importantly he also won international motorsport classics such as the Irish Tourist Trophy in 1929, and in 1931 the Italian Mille Miglia – the first foreigner ever to do so. In the same year, according to the racing boss Alfred Neubauer, Caracciola's income totalled 180,000 RM.

Nevertheless, in the wake of the economic slump and mass redundancies even the most eminent representatives of the Untertürkheim company lost their jobs: in 1932 Daimler-Benz AG closed down its works-based motor-sport activities for financial reasons, causing Caracciola to move to Alfa Romeo. That year he won the German Grand Prix in the Italian *monoposto*. This was a signal for motoring clubs and the automobile industry to seek subsidies *en bloc* for the construction of a 'German national racing car'.

A matter of national importance

Caracciola's defection to Alfa Romeo seemed to ordinary German motor racing fans like some kind of affront to the nation. Consequently at the AVUS on 22 May 1932 they booed 'Caratsch' and cheered 26-year-old Manfred von Brauchitsch. Driving an ungainly and heavyweight Mercedes-Benz SSK fitted with streamlined bodywork, von Brauchitsch stole a march on his fellow-countryman in the graceful Italian machine and beat the renegade into second place. The abbreviation SSK had no political overtones but stood for '*Super-Sport kurz* [short]'; in other words it was a variant, reworked for Hans Nibel, of the legendary and notoriously expensive SS six-cylinder sports car that Ferdinand Porsche had originally developed for the Untertürkheim firm. Thanks to a supercharger the

Left: The first non-Italian winner of the Mille Miglia: Rudolf Caracciola receiving congratulations from his wife 'Charly' and Mercedes-Benz race director Alfred Neubauer in 1931. (Daimler AG)

Opposite: Manfred von Brauchitsch and his silver, streamlined car that conquered the AVUS Race in 1932 – the real birth of the 'Silver Arrow'. (Daimler AG)

machine produced 300bhp, yet even in its lightest version weighed 1.4 tonnes. On demanding courses with many bends and under normal conditions it could not compete with the racing designs of Alfa Romeo, Maserati and Bugatti, all nearly 600kg lighter.

Von Brauchitsch's winning mount, which the Berliners affectionately nicknamed the 'cigar' and the 'cucumber', gleamed in a silver racing livery. It was a 'Zeppelin on wheels', whose torpedo-shaped body had been designed by Baron Reinhard von Koenig-Fachsenfeld. It was a shapeless projectile that radio commentator Paul Laven, in his summing-up of the AVUS Race, nevertheless described in an outburst of emotion as a 'silver arrow', and thus unknowingly coined an enduring epithet.

The fact that von Brauchitsch won in a Mercedes-Benz would be all the more significant as Daimler-Benz AG at that time had no cause for rejoicing. The only German car company that still took part in motorsport on a fairly large scale for promotional reasons, it now found itself, six years after the merger, once again in crisis. Half a century after its invention by Carl Benz, the automobile remained a luxury item in German-speaking countries. In relation to their small but wealthy clientele, motor cars were being manufactured by far too many companies at far too high a cost, and their market – modest at best – had collapsed completely in the worldwide economic slump. Even the International Car and Motorcycle Exhibition in Berlin was cancelled, while in the month of July 1932 alone 132,000

vehicles in Germany were de-registered by their owners for reasons of cost. The same year saw only 43,340 private cars and 36,272 motorcycles produced in Germany, compared with the peak figures in 1928 of 108,029 and 160,782 respectively. The number of people employed in the industry dropped to 34,392 from a peak in 1928 of 83,751. World tariffs, and in some cases a total ban on imports, limited export opportunities, and where once there had been 64 car and motorcycle manufacturers in Germany, by 1932 only 26 survived.

Mass production and a slump in sales

In order for us to understand, given this background, the ever greater rejoicing of company bosses over the benevolent attitude of the Nazi party towards the car and motorcycle industries, a small digression into earlier economic history is necessary. The economic depression hit German car makers all the harder because they had slept through technical innovations that had revolutionised the production of private cars elsewhere. Their American competitors produced far more cheaply and efficiently. In 1925 the Ford Motor Company took 400 man-hours to manufacture a standard model, whereas in Germany it took *fifty* times longer.

Building up a Mercedes chassis at Daimler's Untertürkheim factory in 1921: mass production was still a long way off. (Daimler AG)

In the wake of Germany's hyperinflation in the early 1920s, the only car firm to react was Opel: after a temporary factory closure its existing series of models was axed and all involvement in motor racing was abandoned. In May 1924 volume production of the new 4-PS (4hp) model was launched in their place. Initially, this car was available only in green with a pointed rear-end, at an aggressively low price of 4,500 RM – at a time when the cheapest of the big Mercedes cars was priced around 20,000 RM. The little green Opel was soon dubbed the 'tree-frog' and sold in such sensational numbers that, despite the successful rationalisation of its production, Opel was obliged within three years to increase its workforce from 2,400 to 7,600 in order to satisfy demand. Gradually model variants were developed, so that at the end of its seven-year production period the total number of 4-PS cars built was 119,484, a huge success given the conditions at the time.

By the end of the 1920s Opel was Germany's biggest motor manufacturer, with a 40 per cent market share. It was a clarion call to traditional German engineering technology in its struggle with Ford-style mass production. In 1928–9, when the Opel family sold their now publicly quoted company to the American General Motors Corporation – to intense outrage in Germany – Henry Ford rapidly made a move. On 2 October 1930 the American motor mogul appeared in person alongside the Chief Burgomaster of Cologne, Konrad Adenauer, to lay the foundation stone of a Ford factory near the Rhineland city. As had earlier been the case at Opel's Rüsselsheim plant, the Americans provided the model for standardised assembly-line production.

By contrast, the majority of German car manufacturers continued to seek their salvation in turning out expensively customised vehicles with an eye to the individual tastes of well-heeled clients. Until well into the 1930s production remained a hybrid of assembly-line and workshop. 'The Americans, on the other hand,' as Werner Oswald, the great chronicler of German car making, wrote in 2001, 'had for a long time been driving popular cars, modestly priced, cheap to run, reliable, durable, comfortable, nice to look at and easy to handle. They did have their weaknesses, of course, but all in all they were superior to the run-of-the-mill output of the German car industry. It was no use appealing to national pride or calling for higher tariffs, and certainly no purpose was served by the wretched tax on cubic capacity, which has remained with us until today.'

Initially Daimler-Benz AG benefited from the consequences of the

merger of 1926. The spokesman for the board of Deutsche Bank, Dr Emil
Georg von Stauss, who sat on the Supervisory Board of the Daimler-
Motoren-Gesellschaft, had, together with Dr Wilhelm Kissel, Finance
Director of Benz & Cie, laid down the foundations for the merging of the
two companies. From then on the two managers determined the strategic
decisions for the group. From 1926 Kissel acted as *de facto* chief executive
of Daimler-Benz AG, though he was not formally appointed until 1933.
The corporation's chief shareholder was Deutsche Bank, which, along
with Dresdner Bank and Commerzbank, dominated the Supervisory Board
and also provided its chairman in the person of von Stauss. The banker
additionally served as chairman of the Supervisory Board of the Bayerische
Motoren-Werke (BMW), which had signed a 'Treaty of Friendship' with
the former commercial alliance of Benz and Daimler. The founder and
managing director of BMW, Franz Josef Popp, wanted to add cars to his
output of aero engines and motorcycles, and with the help of Deutsche Bank
he succeeded in doing this by buying up vehicle builders Fahrzeugfabrik
Eisenach. This company produced the small 'Dixi' car under licence
from Austin. Under BMW ownership the bodies for this car were soon
also being manufactured in the Daimler-Benz plant at Sindelfingen. The
securing of facilities through co-operation and interlocking shareholdings
was a tradition in the German automobile industry long before the term
'Deutschland AG' (Germany plc) was coined for it.

True, there was competition between Munich and Untertürkheim in
the development of aero engines, but under the pressure of economic and
political events Daimler-Benz and BMW would even manage to achieve
co-ordination in their private car production. BMW boss Popp already sat
on the Supervisory Board of Daimler-Benz AG, whose Finance Director,
Kissel, was in turn a member of the BMW Supervisory Board. Both men
mixed in the same social circles, which naturally included Emil Georg von
Stauss. Together they were active in an apparently harmless movement to
'keep the car industry German'. It was under this banner that Kissel, Popp
and von Stauss planned to commit their linked companies to motorsport
– both in their own business interests and in the national interest. The
clientele and the brand image both required and furthered this policy even
in difficult times.

The steady reduction in manpower and the high prices of luxury cars

had admittedly produced sales revenue for Daimler-Benz of 26.85 million
RM and 27.76 million RM in 1928 and 1929 respectively. Yet the output
figures remained relatively modest: just over 10,000 cars were manufactured
annually, and the group's widely scattered production facilities were working
at scarcely half their capacity. In 1927 the number of manual and white-
collar workers in Daimler-Benz AG was 18,124. Two years later the workforce
numbered only 14,281, and then the world slump increased the extent and
pace of dismissals in a wholly unexpected manner. By the end of 1930 the
company's statistics showed a mere 9,786 on the payroll, and in March 1932
the all-time low of 4,958 was reached. Something *had* to happen.

Routes out of the Depression

The banker von Stauss represented his own interests and those of Deutsche
Bank as a member of the supervisory boards not only of Daimler-Benz and
BMW, but also of Lufthansa and the UFA film corporation. Furthermore,
since the elections of September 1930 he had been a member of the liberal
and nationalist German People's Party in the Reichstag (National Assembly),

*German Grand Prix, 1927. Surrounded by a crowd are Ferdinand Porsche and race winners
Rudolf Caracciola and Christian Werner.*

in which capacity he fought for subsidies and tax relief for German industry. He lobbied tirelessly for a programme of 'national motorisation', which was to achieve the salvation of the German vehicle industry with the help of state support through road-building and measures to promote the sales of private cars, but mainly by the dismantling of taxes targeting vehicles and fuel. At the same time the building of commercial vehicles and aircraft was to be strengthened in the national interest through government defence contracts. This is precisely the same policy that Mussolini and his Fascists had previously put into practice in Italy.

And the National Socialist Party drummed up support for similar objectives. In the Reichstag elections of September 1930 the Nazi Party succeeded in increasing their share of the national vote from 2.6 per cent to 18.3 per cent. Von Stauss had no compunction about associating with them, and was one of the first business leaders to establish contact with the top Nazis, particularly with Hermann Göring, to whom he was soon even making financial donations. And from his first personal meeting with Hitler in the early summer of 1931 von Stauss was so enthused that he immediately wanted to join the NSDAP. But Göring dissuaded him on the grounds that he would be much more valuable to the National Socialist movement as a member of the German People's Party. And this remained the case even in the years after the Nazis seized power. Thus von Stauss, who died in 1942, was one of the 'reactionary group of industrialists and powerful financiers who gave Hitler financial support before his rise to power and then helped him into the saddle': such was the verdict of the Finance Division of the US Office of Military Government for Germany, in its 1946 investigation into Deutsche Bank.

Herr von Stauss's social network included not only captains of industry and prominent Nazis, but also UFA film stars and German motor racing personalities. After his victory in the AVUS Race, up-and-coming driver Manfred von Brauchitsch numbered among the banker's circle of friends.[8] And for Ferdinand Porsche, von Stauss negotiated an out-of-court settlement with Daimler-Benz AG. What is more, in spite of everything, the banker advised his friend and corporate boss Wilhelm Kissel to hitch Porsche to the Mercedes star in an advisory function, if only to keep the gifted designer out of the hands of the competition. It was a piece of advice that initially foundered on the objections of Dr Hans Nibel, Porsche's successor as Chief Designer with Daimler-Benz AG. Von Stauss may in fact have urged Porsche to go independent with his own design bureau. At all events, as early as the summer of 1930 the man who later created Hitler's *Volkswagen*, or 'People's Car', took it upon himself, on behalf of Stauss and Kissel, to solve 'the problem of an appropriately sized inexpensive car designed for the masses'. Yet suitable projects of the kind that his bureau later urged on Zündapp and NSU do not come along every day.

How fortunate, then, that Adolf Rosenberger, the cosmopolitan businessman, shareholder and General Manager of Porsche's Stuttgart design office, belonged to an exclusive Berlin gentlemen's club where, among others, he got to know Baron Klaus Detlof von Oertzen. The latter was chief executive of the Wanderer car company in Chemnitz and, through Rosenberger, went into business with Porsche. The 30-strong Porsche design team was to upgrade a production model into a sports coupé, and because the car division of a conglomerate better known for its office machinery needed a compelling new image, in 1931 Porsche's people were also asked to embark on a racing car project for the new Grand Prix formula.

The racing car that changed his life – Ferdinand Porsche and the Auto Union P-type. (Porsche AG)

The national racing car with the Porsche badge

As luck would have it Ferdinand Porsche belonged to the circle of handpicked experts who in late 1931 were commissioned by the International Association of Recognised Automobile Clubs, the AIACR, to draw up a new set of rules. Starting with the 1934 season Grand Prix racing cars were not permitted to weigh more than 750kg. Before each race the weighing of vehicles was to be carried out at the trackside, and the limit to be observed referred to the weight of the empty car (*ie* without fuel, oil, water and tyres). The Grand Prix monsters of the time were significantly heavier than 750kg, which is why, given the state of technology, the officials believed that the new designs would need to make use of much smaller

Porsche's Auto Union predecessor – the Benz Tropfenwagen. Accompanied by his mechanic, Wilhelm Sebastian, Adolf Rosenberger has just won the Kassel Herkules Bergrennen in 1925. Sebastian and his brother, Ludwig, would later join Auto Union's racing division, but Rosenberger had to sever his partnership with Porsche because of his Jewish antecedents. (Walter)

and lighter engines in order to keep within the weight limit. In theory this meant a smaller cubic capacity and a maximum output of around 250bhp. The fact that German racing cars were able to mobilise almost double that power even in the first season of this 750kg formula, thanks to lightweight construction and supercharger technology, lay completely beyond the scope of contemporary imagination and helped to establish the success and thus the myth of the Silver Arrows.

The rough design for his new racing car, which Porsche finally submitted in 1932, closely resembled the Benz 'teardrop' car from 1923. This was no surprise, since his business partner Adolf Rosenberger had himself driven that unusual mid-engined racer and even won the 1925 Solitude mountain climb in it. It was no coincidence that Porsche now positioned the driver in front of the racing car's engine. Rosenberger, who had excellent contacts in big business circles, may indeed have been 'neither a designer nor an inventor', but 'his experience as a racing driver was nevertheless valuable to Dr Porsche. This experience is what provided … [Rosenberger's] contribution to the development of the racing car.'[9]

Meanwhile, Porsche and Rosenberger had once again to go around hawking the plans for their revolutionary mid-engined racing car, because the Wanderer group had gone belly-up. The principal shareholder of the Chemnitz company, Deutsche Bank (in the person of Daimler-Benz board member von Stauss), pleaded for sale or liquidation, although the Wanderer factory and likewise the crisis-battered competitors Horch and Adler, to add a further complication, were forcing their attentions on Daimler-Benz AG as merger partners. However, it seems that in this crisis von Stauss and company were unwilling to burden themselves with any more clapped-out car makers. Daimler-Benz AG and the closely associated BMW would alone survive on the German market against the 'American competition' of Opel and Ford.

However, the history of the German motor industry took a quite different turn, because the *Landtag* (provincial assembly) of Saxony leaped into the breach and in mid-February 1932 put up a guarantee of 6 million RM in order to save over 8,000 jobs at the stricken Saxon car makers Audi, DKW, Horch and Wanderer. On 28 June 1932 – with retrospective effect from 1 November 1931 – the four companies were merged under a holding company that was given the name Auto Union AG and adopted four interlocking circles as its corporate symbol. At a stroke the new Auto Union was thus to become

Daimler-Benz's most aggressive competitor within Germany. And the future rivalry between the two companies would find its most intense expression in motorsport, where the Silver Arrows from Zwickau and Untertürkheim henceforth competed for victories and subsidies.

With a certain piquancy, the blueprints for the Auto Union racing cars would be provided by the former Technical Director of Daimler-Benz AG. Ferdinand Porsche's racing car project conceived for Wanderer was transferred to the newly formed motor group in Saxony.

The national racing car with the Mercedes-Benz badge

Only a few kilometres from Porsche's design office, the executive corridors of the crisis-stricken Daimler-Benz AG were also inspired by the future racing car formula. Here too the construction of a German Grand Prix machine was also intended to serve as an advertising medium – and for this purpose government subsidies had to be organised. Von Brauchitsch's spectacular victory in the AVUS Race was a perfect pretext for Nibel, the Chief Designer, there and then to approach the Reich Minister of Transport, Gottfried Treviranus. Three days later the two men had a telephone conversation about financial assistance.

Dr Hans Nibel, the man who created the Blitzen Benz and the Benz Tropfenwagen before the merger with Daimler in 1926, followed Porsche as Technical Director of the Daimler-Benz company and designed the new Mercedes-Benz race car for the 750kg formula. (Daimler AG)

At this stage the intention was only a matter of making improvements to the ageing SSK sports car for further use in motorsport: 'According to information from Herr Treviranus the sum of 220,000 RM is already guaranteed,' wrote Nibel in a file note. 'However, he intends to try and get us a total of 110,000 + 180,000.' At Mercedes-Benz they may have been sharing the same delusions as the government with its deflation policy ('Only a hundred metres from the goal'). But only five days later, on 30 May 1932, the second Brüning cabinet collapsed,[10] and transport minister Treviranus was among those who lost their jobs. 'The system is in free fall,' noted Nazi propaganda chief Goebbels with glee. On the very same day Hitler had an audience with Reich President Hindenburg, the ban on the SA was lifted, the Reichstag was dissolved, and new general elections were scheduled for 31 July. The Hitler movement seemed to be close to its goal of taking power in Germany.

However, the aged President Hindenburg, manipulated by a senior army officer, General Kurt Schleicher, had already installed a minority government as a 'cabinet of national concentration' and appointed Franz von Papen as Chancellor. The new minister of transport and postal services was Baron Paul von Eltz-Rübenach. An acknowledged expert on railways and a staunch Catholic, Eltz-Rübenach was also a member of the administration that followed and even remained in office under the Nazis after 30 January 1933. However, he was forced to resign early in 1937 after refusing to accept the 'Golden Party Award' because of the Nazis' assault on churches.

These were turbulent times. Mass unemployment was reaching its height, yet on 20 June 1932 Hans Nibel nevertheless enquired of the new Reich Minister of Transport, Eltz-Rübenach, 'whether it might not be possible for us to receive government support for the design and development of our racing cars, since we are unfortunately unable to undertake the exceptionally costly development of racing cars from our own resources. As far as we know, Italian and French factories that build racing cars are supported by their own governments, since international races have a promotional value beyond that for the marque of car in question, and give a great boost for the industry of that country.'

Four days later Nibel made a personal visit to the ministry and sent two more letters on the subject of financial assistance, before Eltz-Rübenach drafted his final rejection on 30 June: 'To my regret I have to confirm from the outset that the funds necessary for a new design cannot be raised. But even if we restricted ourselves to improvements to the design, which might give a promise of success, this would require a level of funding which is unfortunately not available to the ministry, given the extremely strained financial situation and the severest cuts to our budget. There is the additional factor that even in former times when finances were more favourable, the ministry ran up against severe reservations and objections both from the Government Audit Office and from the Reichstag Budget Committee, regarding the distribution of subsidies intended to promote the German automobile industry through motor racing. In the present situation, such opposition is even more predictable.'

For the moment the political situation following the cabinet change put an end to any hope of government subsidies. To get that kind of money there first had to be a regime that better appreciated the propaganda value of future German racing victories and knew how to exploit them. In this respect, the car-friendly Hitler and the equally keen motorsports enthusiasts among his entourage would come as a blessing for the national racing ambitions of the corporate bosses in Untertürkheim and Zwickau.

But how much would this racing car project actually cost? Precise figures were never mentioned, but on 11 July 1932 Councillor von Opel, speaking at a board meeting of the Reich Automobile Industry Federation, named a ball-park figure for the first time, much to the annoyance of Daimler-Benz boss Wilhelm Kissel: around 1 million RM was the estimate for building a national German racing car. It was indeed an exorbitant sum if we consider that in 1932 Daimler-Benz AG was only just in a position to make investments totalling some 490,000 RM. At the end of a wretched financial year Kissel and his fellow directors in Untertürkheim were presented with a gross loss of 10.9 million RM. At this point, then, one thing was clear: without outside help, without start-up financing, the Mercedes-Benz racing car project would never get into gear.

When, on 17 July 1932, shortly before the Reichstag elections, Rudolf Caracciola, the top German driver, won the German Grand Prix at the Nürburgring in an Italian car – an Alfa Romeo – it gave the chairman of Daimler-Benz's supervisory board, E.G. von Stauss, a pretext to raise the subject of racing car subsidies at the ministry once again, but this time through the Reich Automobile Industry Federation and its chairman, Robert

Allmers. Yet this initiative failed, as did the attempt by the newly founded Auto Union AG in a letter of 12 August 1932 to the Reich Minister of Transport, likewise requesting financial support for racing car construction.

The race for subsidies

So now two German automobile groups were competing for non-existent state funding for the construction of two different German national racing cars, for neither of which were there any serious plans for a design or even a budget. But from Untertürkheim and Zwickau even more strings were being pulled: the Automobile Club of Germany (AvD) and the General German Automobile Club (ADAC) were jointly to set up 'an appeal for funds to build German racing cars'. In all this, the rather more elite AvD seemed to be secretly taking the side of Daimler-Benz AG. A document of 15 September 1932, drafted by an AvD official named Juhasz, stated: 'Every patriotically minded fellow-countryman is able to help if he contributes as much as is in his power to the national fund for German racing cars. Every gift, however small, is welcome. Because of the strong lead that foreign countries have, work must start without delay, and by 1933, when we will be dedicating a memorial to Benz, one of the two German inventors of the motor car, we must have German racing cars once again.'

Juhasz sent the document to von Stauss, and noted in a covering letter: 'The motivation of the necessity of motor racing is something I consider absolutely necessary in order to counter the objection (which will certainly come!) as to whether, in the present time of crisis, collections for racing cars are really a matter of great urgency.'

Von Stauss immediately had a meeting with the top people at the AvD to explain to them the financial requirements for the national racing car with the Mercedes-Benz badge. By now Daimler-Benz chief Kissel had put the costs at 720,000 RM. Von Stauss had tried unsuccessfully to drag further details out of von Brauchitsch. However, the new white hope of German motor racing had written about this to Alfred Neubauer – 'without asking me,' as von Stauss reported. At that time Neubauer, though still racing manager for Daimler-Benz, was being wooed by Auto Union.

The AvD chairman, Consul Fritsch, thought the sum of 720,000 RM was still far too high and argued plausibly enough that 'designers and production workers were there anyway to build racing cars and so no added costs would be incurred by Daimler-Benz'. But von Stauss, ingenious banker that he was, parried attacks of that kind: 'I replied to [Fritsch] that the design and construction of the cars was such a protracted process that it took valuable workers away from their real jobs for long periods and that of course this had to be fully taken into account. What is more, I pointed out to him that Daimler would in any case make its plant and equipment available free of charge, nor would it demand any payment for goodwill. However, the cash outlays really did have to be invoiced. I finally deflected the discussion by indicating that the figures quoted had to be accepted as justified.'

Kissel was presenting his colleague von Stauss with pure gold. The whole racing car project was becoming significantly more expensive; the figure that Councillor von Opel had blurted out was indeed accurate: 'If we are going to do this thing properly, then we can hardly get by with a smaller sum; because it's not just a matter of developing and testing one car, but immediately turning out four or five cars, all of which then have to be properly worked up. We know from experience that specialised cars like this never succeed at the first go, but they have to undergo a number of different modifications and improvements before they can be entered in a race. Based on this experience, we have to think in terms of a sum of

Dr Wilhelm Kissel led the board of directors at Benz in Mannheim. After the Daimler-Benz merger in 1926, he became CEO of the new company at its headquarters in Stuttgart-Untertürkheim. (Daimler AG)

around 1 million RM. I would not recommend giving a detailed breakdown of the figure, since that kind of documentation can very easily get into the hands of third parties and that could cause all sorts of difficulties. I would therefore be grateful if you can continue, as you have done so far, to avoid being pressed to provide such details yourself, or to ask us to provide them, because this could only weaken our position. I would also recommend that you do not discuss details even with our friends such as Messrs von Brauchitsch, Stuck etc. I assume that you share my view and further assume that you are also happy for me to ask Herr Neubauer, for the same reasons, not to reveal anything specific. Our racing drivers are of course aware that the modification of the SSK car from the 1931 to the 1932 model alone cost us more than 150,000 RM – for three vehicles. Thus we can justify our statement that a new design, from which four or five vehicles will have to be built to racing standard, requires an expenditure of around 1 million RM.'

The chief executive of the hard-pressed Daimler-Benz AG needed so much money to build his German national racing car that not only the AvD but also the ADAC had to be involved in the fund-raising operation. If these two competing clubs made common cause it was clear that the revenue collected was only to benefit Daimler-Benz AG. At the same time Kissel was aware that the acceptance of such donations made his company dependent and put it under certain obligations: 'Even if the way we handle the procurement of funds to build racing cars, as is now envisaged, gives cause for concerns about the implications that could arise in the future, there still remains a considerable plus-factor in favour of going ahead with the operation.'

On 29 September 1932 the chairmen of AvD and ADAC had a meeting in Berlin with Kissel and Nibel. By now Neubauer had told his two bosses in Untertürkheim that the design and building of five Grand Prix racing cars together with two reserve cars would cost exactly 1,112,000 RM. The game was getting more expensive all the time. And this was with considerable massaging of the detailed figures by Neubauer. The cost of building one racing car was put in at only 70,000 RM, while the salary of a 'first-class driver' was budgeted at no more than 48,000. In the 1931 racing season Rudolf Caracciola had picked up four times that amount with Mercedes-Benz, thanks to his generous share of starting money and winners' bonuses. The races did indeed offer drivers and companies the opportunity to earn big money – but only if they were successful. However, Kissel and Nibel wanted to finance the rewards of success through government and private subsidies, while taking little or no risk themselves.

Yet despite being assiduously wooed, the top officials of AvD and ADAC failed to sign up, and instead confronted the management of Mercedes-Benz with awkward questions: what happens if the fund-raising only brings in, say, a quarter of a million instead of a million Reichsmarks? Can Daimler-Benz still guarantee to build a national racing car? Baron von Brandenstein (of AvD) made the point on behalf of both clubs that 'they could not at this stage enter into any commitment to any company as to how the money would be applied, and that in this regard both clubs would be completely free, if they saw fit, to give the sum of money to [another car company] Hanomag, for example.' What an affront! To rank Hanomag alongside the prestigious Daimler-Benz AG! Hanomag – a manufacturer of small cars, which so far had made its name from building cheap products that had been tellingly nicknamed '*Kommissbrot*' (meaning roughly 'army ration bread').

At the same time the only competitor for the promotional funds had long been known: the newly founded Auto Union, whose plans were famously being forged by none other than Ferdinand Porsche. For future racing duties the Saxon firm had already hooked Porsche's friend and Mercedes-Benz driver Hans Stuck. Another senior employee from Untertürkheim, Alfred Neubauer, was intending to go over to the opposition, but Kissel just managed to dissuade him with a generous bonus. Instead, at the beginning of 1933, Auto Union signed up Willy Walb, who until then had been number two in the Mercedes-Benz racing organisation.

Another deserter from the executive floor in Untertürkheim was the Chief Press Officer, Dr Richard Voelter, who, as early as 1 October 1932, had joined DKW in Zwickau as Head of Advertising on a salary of 850 RM per month. From then on, Voelter would extract propaganda value from the sporting successes of Auto Union, since their racing division reported directly to the group's advertising department. Voelter, born in 1892, was a qualified lawyer who had served in the First World War as a cavalry captain. Even in peacetime this dashing ex-officer regularly turned up for exercises with the military reserve, and, not least, was a member of the Nazi Party from 1925 onwards – as was his wife Else, who liked to be called 'the First Nazi Lady of Württemberg'. Even before Hitler's men came into power the ambitious couple opened quite a few doors at Daimler-Benz to their Brownshirt party comrades. By 1931 the Voelters had split up, but as we read in an approving assessment by the district military authorities in Chemnitz dated 25 June 1936, 'Dr Voelter has been active for many years on behalf of the National Socialist German Workers' Party.'

Even in 1931, when Richard Voelter got divorced and launched his new professional as well as marital life in Saxony, the abandoned Else remained under the protection of the Mercedes star in Untertürkheim. After the Nazis seized power, the former Frau Voelter, in collaboration with the Stuttgart management, sold production cars on special terms to Nazi bigwigs. From 1938 onwards Else Voelter was additionally involved in the 'Aryanisation' of Jewish-owned businesses. It was the same Else and Richard Voelter who, as early as September 1926, at the trackside of the Solitude race, introduced their party leader, Adolf Hitler, to the Mercedes-Benz team and its then chief designer, Ferdinand Porsche. Hitler was a great car fan, and was a particularly good customer for the powerful

Laurel-bedecked Willy Walb won the sports car class at Solitude in 1926 driving the big Mercedes-Benz K. The car in the foreground is the Grand Prix Mercedes 2-litre 8-cylinder that was driven by Otto Merz to victory in the race car class. It was during this event that Adolf Hitler, at that time a radical but rather insignificant party leader, was introduced to Ferdinand Porsche by Mercedes-Benz press officer Richard Voelter. (Daimler AG)

supercharged automobiles of Daimler-Benz AG. They were supplied by another Nazi of the earliest years, Jakob Werlin, who was also on the Mercedes-Benz payroll. As head of the Munich office he was one of the group's most important and successful car salesmen and at the same time the principal door-opener for, and contact with, the Nazi leadership.

Hitler's car dealer

It was in April 1921 that the young salesman Jakob Werlin took up his post as branch manager in Munich for the firm of Benz & Cie. Born on 10 May 1886 in the Austrian province of Styria, Werlin served his apprenticeship in the Puch car factory in Graz, then worked for a few years as branch manager in Budapest, before volunteering in 1914 for the army where, by the time he was discharged in 1917, he had reached the rank of company sergeant-major. After that he went back to selling cars, this time for the

Ferdinand Porsche shows Adolf Hitler a new toy. Behind his boyishly delighted boss, NSKK-Führer Adolf Hühnlein looks very impressed with the KdF-Wagen model. To the right in the foreground is Jakob Werlin, Hitler's car dealer and personal advisor in questions of motoring business – and a member of the Daimler-Benz board of directors. (Volkswagen AG)

Hansa-Lloyd works in Essen, before moving down to Munich where, in a way he could not have dreamed of, he combined his professional, personal and political interests and made a successful career for himself.

The branch of Benz & Cie and its garages was situated at 39 Schellingstrasse in Munich's fashionably bohemian Schwabing district. The same building housed the printing firm of Adolf Müller. Müller printed for the Nazi Party's publisher, the Franz Eher Verlag, turning out books, pamphlets and the newspaper *Völkischer Beobachter* ('National Observer'). So it was inevitable that Werlin would meet the Nazi leader, three years his junior, and the two got on famously. The fact that they both had Austrian roots and shared an enthusiasm for cars was the clincher. As Werlin wrote decades later, the printer Müller introduced Hitler to him with the words: 'I've brought a new customer for you.' The Nazi leader, who was now famous (or notorious) in Munich, had already owned two cars made by the somewhat less renowned Selve company, and wanted to acquire his first big Benz from Werlin.

Forty years later, in his grandiose apologia, Werlin, the former Nazi jack-of-all-trades, tried to present himself as a highly successful yet totally non-political lobbyist on behalf of the motor industry: 'I had never made any secret of my acquaintance with Hitler or my role as his advisor, which embraced everything under the heading of motorisation. I was now actually prepared to stick my neck out. It is true, I helped, with all the resources available to me, to do things like promote the construction of autobahns and push through Hitler's plans for the "People's Car" [*Volkswagen*]. I was the co-founder of the VW factory; and where I could, I promoted motor racing, which in the 1930s brought victory and fame to Germany's Silver Arrows and worldwide sales success for the manufacturers.'

That sounds boastful, but is an absolutely accurate statement. Werlin was soon a member of Hitler's closest entourage in Munich, and thenceforth acted as 'personal confidant of the *Führer*' in all matters concerning motor vehicles. In 1932 he joined the SS and in the following year the one-time car salesman made a career leap to join the Management Board of Daimler-Benz AG.

From January 1942 onwards he functioned as the *Führer*'s Inspector-General for the Motor Industry and in this capacity paid frequent visits to the Polish and Russian territories conquered by Hitler's troops. At the same time as being a member of the Management Board of Daimler-Benz AG, he was also an *Obersturmführer* in the SS, on Himmler's personal staff.

Whether or not Werlin was aware of German war crimes and the genocide of the European Jews has never been subject to official scrutiny. Instead, at a Denazification tribunal on 29 January 1947, a 'declaration of honour' was made on his behalf by his former colleague, Wilhelm Haspel, who had by then been reinstated as Chief Executive of Daimler-Benz. Haspel went as far as to praise Werlin's 'outstanding services' to the corporation. From 1942 Haspel himself, as the immediate successor to Wilhelm Kissel at the head of Daimler-Benz, was responsible for, among other things, the employment of forced labour in the company. After the war ended he was forced to resign temporarily from the business, but was later allowed to return to the top seat. As it happened, Haspel had never been a member of the Nazi Party and – thanks in part to Werlin's influence with Hitler – was made group CEO at Untertürkheim, even though his wife was, according to Nazi criteria, classed as a 'semi-Jewess'.

At the end of the war in May 1945, Werlin was immediately put into an internment camp by the US Army. Since he was party member no. 3208977 and by then an SS *Oberführer* (equivalent to a colonel), the Denazification tribunal classified him as a *Hauptschuldiger* or principal offender. The '*Führer*'s car dealer' remained in prison until 9 November 1949, which, significantly, was the 26th anniversary of Hitler's Munich *putsch*. Later Werlin returned to his familiar trade and was soon selling Untertürkheim's cars again, with the blessing of top management. In

Jakob Werlin made a profit out of his personal relationship with Adolf Hitler, and most of the time the liaison was also of benefit to the three-pointed star of Untertürkheim. (Daimler AG)

1950 he set up the firm of Jakob Werlin & Söhne (Sons), with the official Mercedes-Benz dealerships in the Upper Bavarian towns of Rosenheim and Traunstein.

A loyal customer of Daimler-Benz

Hitler placed a lot of value on appearances. That included running large motor cars – symbols of force, strength, power and superiority. Right back in the early 1920s the party had presented its '*Führer*' with an official car and chauffeur. Even in his early years Hitler's car-fetishism distinguished him, with his extremism and self-aggrandisement, from other actors on the political stage of the Weimar Republic. The fact that the car-proud German society of the 1950s, '60s and '70s ultimately had its roots deep in the age of Nazi dictatorship is due not least to Hitler's mission to motorise.

In the early years of the post-war Federal Republic there was a saying that the 'first Mercedes' was the sign of the buyer's personal success. We can imagine what a powerful symbol that must have been at a time when any kind of car was still really an unattainable luxury. At all events, in the late summer of 1923, a brand new Benz, 'a Model 10, 30 h.p., open, with black paintwork and black leather' was offered to a Councillor Geo. Semler of Munich. He did not take it up, so Jakob Werlin sold it to 'Herr Adolf H.' That year, hyperinflation was rampant, yet Hitler had generous patrons and was able to make a down-payment of 10,000 Swiss francs, to which he added $100 US, which meant that '$101.45 must now be paid, in order to reach the sum set out in the order form of $2,000 payable immediately in cash.'

A short time later, on 30 October, Werlin sold his Austrian compatriot a second, even larger Benz, a 16/50hp 'open-top'. The selling price shown on the receipt to the NSDAP was 135,000,000,000,000 (135 thousand billion) marks 'paid in cash'. However, the fact is that the sum was paid over in Dutch guilders at a substantially more favourable exchange rate, and not in cash but as a cheque for Fl. 5,000. The balance of Fl. 1,000 was to be paid within 14 days. In this way Hitler and his Nazi Party avoided paying the luxury tax. That was billed separately, in the fictitious sum of 19,200,000,000,000 marks, to the supposed purchaser, the firm of Franz Eher (Successors). The manoeuvre did, however, catch the eye of the Mannheim Tax Office, a fact that was pointed out by Benz head office to their assiduous salesman, Werlin, in a letter dated 18 February 1924.

For the time being, however, the car-mad Hitler had to do without his newly acquired Benz, as he was imprisoned for questioning in the ancient castle of Landsberg. After the bloody debacle of his failed *putsch* of 9 November 1923[11] both the official Nazi Party cars had been parked in the garage of Werlin's Benz showroom in Munich, before being confiscated there by the Bavarian authorities. On 1 April 1924 Hitler was sentenced to five years' imprisonment.[12] But the Nazi leader, while sitting out his term in ridiculously lenient conditions, was already thinking about acquiring another new Benz. He summoned Werlin to an audience at the prison on 12 September 1924 and discussed the latest range. The following day he wrote to the conscientious Munich showroom manager: 'Might I now ask you, as soon as a reply has been received from Mannheim [the headquarters of Benz & Cie], to very kindly inform me at what price I could have the 11/40 or the 16/15, and also whether the 11/50 could be delivered immediately. In any case, however, I would ask you to reserve for me the grey car, which you currently have in Munich, until such time as my future fate has been clarified [*ie* when he was told the date of his release].'

Hitler's upper-class patrons supplied the imprisoned Nazi leader with cash while he worked on *Mein Kampf* in what he called his 'Landsberg University'. As well as writing *Mein Kampf*, he is even said to have had enough time on his hands to draw aerodynamic profiles for future vehicles, which after his release he placed at the disposal of the company – though the Daimler-Benz company historian tends to consign this story to the realm of legend. On the other hand there is solid evidence that, when Hitler was released on 20 December 1924, Werlin provided a large Benz limousine from the Munich showroom to collect his party chairman. However, the story that Werlin personally took the wheel, accompanied by the printer Müller and Hitler's personal photographer Heinrich Hoffmann, was disputed more than four decades later by Werlin's sons Hans and Otto.

Be that as it may, this intimate business relationship and a shared passion for Mercedes-Benz automobiles were the foundation of a lifelong bond between the two men. Werlin was one of the chosen few who had access to Hitler at any time. And he would make copious use of the fact. In following the unwholesome trail of those early successes, I quote from Werlin's correspondence with his client – a man given to making constant special requests but pretty impatient with any delay in delivery.

From the year 1925 we read the following: '*Sehr geehrter Herr Hitler!* Having returned from Untertürkheim I would like to give you a brief report on the status and extent of the work being done on your car. Your letter did not fail to make an impression in Unterturkheim and you may rest assured that the Daimler-Motoren-Gesellschaft is making every effort to complete the work with all possible speed. Herr Direktor Gross will be writing to you personally on the matter, if he has not already done so. All the improvements that were required have been carried out on the car. You will receive a car which, with regard to performance and handling, you will not recognise.'

Of course, all this would take a little time, but Werlin assured Hitler: 'If we were unable to satisfy you with regard to delivery-date, then I definitely hope that you will enjoy the same boyish delight in the car, as you did in looking forward to its arrival.'

Even after the merger of Benz and Daimler, Werlin remained on the case in Munich, as did the Voelters and others of like mind at the company's headquarters in Stuttgart. One such was the General Manager, Carl Werner, who was already making company cars available free of charge for election campaigns and Nazi party events. Indeed, the Chief Executive, Wilhelm Kissel, considered that sort of thing obligatory.

The fact that by the end of 1933 three of the then seven-strong Management Board of Daimler-Benz AG belonged to the NSDAP speaks volumes. The fourth to join the Party was Kissel himself, who, despite a general veto on membership having been imposed since 1 May 1934 because so many people wanted to join the Nazis, was allowed to join its ranks with retrospective effect from 1 March 1934. True, he was a member of the SS anyway.[13]

Thus it was no coincidence that, long before the Nazi coup of 1933, many a small favour was done. Göring, Goebbels and Strasser[14] were among those to receive special discounts when buying new cars, and when the 'boyish delight' of the Nazi leader threatened to wane, Daimler-Benz dispatched their most prominent employee, Rudolf Caracciola himself, down to Munich to sort things out.

Hitler at home to racing drivers

The car in question was the latest Mercedes-Benz model, the 770, a 7.7-litre straight-eight and the company's biggest and most expensive private car, which, as the 'big Mercedes', was intended to compete with the eye-catching and, at the time, far more exclusive 12-cylinder Maybach 'Zeppelin'. In 1931, when the Mercedes-Benz 770 first went into production, precisely 42 units were manufactured. One of the purchasers was Adolf Hitler, and to finance the hefty price of 38,000 RM Daimler-Benz was given advertising space in the *Völkischer Beobachter* free of charge. But the limo was not delivered on time, apparently due to a number of special requests made by the prominent client, and the irritated customer had to be mollified. Thus, on the instructions of Director Kissel, Rudolf Caracciola personally drove Hitler's new 770 over to Munich – which was why the famous racing driver chauffeured the by now equally prominent Hitler and his niece Angela ('Geli') Raubal[15] around Munich and its environs.

Caracciola was apparently more struck by Fräulein Raubal's beauty than by the political prestige of the Nazi leader. Admittedly, Caracciola would wait until 1945 before voicing this opinion, by which time he found himself in good company. And he no doubt found himself in equally good company in writing the short dedication at the end of his motor racing memoirs ('as told to' Oskar Weller), which had already sold more than 80,000 copies by 1943: 'In motor racing we see one of the most magnificent affirmations of life that there can be. And in the new Germany, motoring and especially motorsport, has returned to its place of honour, for which we have Adolf Hitler to thank. It was granted to me to become the world's most successful racing driver, with over two hundred victories. When the victory of arms is won, the *Führer* will again give the order for the racing cars to join battle as well. Then we will once more step forward and show our gratitude – through deeds…!'[16]

However, neither Caracciola nor any other racing drivers drafted as temporary chauffeurs chose to answer the popular but corny joke that questioned whether the *Führer* (leader) did in fact possess a *Führerschein* (driving licence). After the collapse of the Nazi dictatorship Manfred von Brauchitsch claimed that, during a display of motor vehicles, Hitler had insisted on being driven no faster than 60kph (37mph). This was a speed at which he could still stand upright and acknowledge the cheers of his so-called *Volksgenossen* or fellow-Germans.

During the Third Reich, the Führer's face always adorned the race programme for the German Grand Prix, signalling clearly who was responsible for the success of the Silver Arrows. (Reuss)

DER NÜRBURGRING

HERAUSGEBER:
NÜRBURGRING GESELLSCHAFT MIT BESCHRÄNKTER HAFTUNG, ADENAU
FERNSPRECHER 131

Adolf Hitler
der Förderer der deutschen Kraftfahrt

As a motoring enthusiast Hitler was certainly a member of the ADAC. In the Bavarian State Archive he can be found listed as member no. 56180 of ADAC, Section 1, District X b, for the years 1926 to 1931. A club membership card was issued to 'Adolf Hitler, author', to whom 'assistance in the event of death due to an accident in his own vehicle' was to be afforded.

With or without his own driving licence, there is no doubt about Hitler's preference for Mercedes-Benz automobiles. To the end he remained a loyal customer, and the most prominent one, of the Untertürkheim corporation, which even devoted an exhibition to him where people could gaze in awe at the official cars from his 'campaigning days'. 'In his battle for Germany up to the seizure of power the *Führer* covered over a million kilometres. This is equivalent to 23 times the circumference of the earth.' So wrote Werlin on 18 February to Hitler's adjutant, Fritz Wiedemann.[17]

As might be expected, Hitler enjoyed motorsport, something that rubbed off on other top Nazis, who were to benefit greatly from the grandiose staging of his racetrack battles. Long before he knew Caracciola and von Brauchitsch, in fact almost a decade before coming to power, Hitler met another future motor racing idol when he was the guest of Hans Stuck at Sterz, Stuck's country estate in Upper Bavaria. An ex-army officer who then studied agriculture, Stuck was born in 1900 into a notable industry-owning family in Baden. On his mother's side he was descended from a line of barons of the Holy Roman Empire named von Villiez, also a Baden family. In his memoirs, published in the early 1970s, Stuck describes the meeting with Hitler as quite fortuitous. In Munich Stuck had met Hitler's chauffeur, Julius Schreck, and struck up a friendship, not knowing of course who his 'boss' was. Since Schreck was passionate about field sports, Stuck apparently invited him to Sterz for some shooting. And on that occasion, 'some time in May 1925', to his complete surprise Hitler came along as well. Stuck says he led his guest into the drawing room, pushed some newspapers and magazines into his hands and said he could do whatever he felt like. Then Stuck changed and went out hunting with Schreck. Hitler was left alone until late that evening.[18]

But did it all happen in such a random way? Stuck moved in the best circles, and was friends with Crown Prince Wilhelm and the flying ace Ernst Udet. Would a man with such connections really invite a very ordinary chauffeur to come shooting? Still less a character like Julius Schreck, who signed up as 'SS man No. 1' in 1925, and was a brutal thug and anti-Semite. Back in 1919 he had been in the *Freikorps Epp* and taken part in the bloody suppression of the Munich soviet.[19] After that he was actively involved in raids and assassinations for the Nazis, and was convicted for damage to property, theft and wilful injury. Would a man like Julius Schreck have been friends with the aristocratic Hans Stuck? And would he have brought Hitler with him on a visit, quite by chance and without prior arrangement?

It is a fact that Hans Stuck would profit constantly and to an astonishing degree from his acquaintance with Adolf Hitler, though he gave a less than full account of this in his memoirs. When all else failed, there was always the *Führer*. And Hitler had a soft spot for racing drivers, especially for Hans Stuck who, between 1927 and 1930, won victory after victory for Austro-Daimler in mountain climbs all over Europe – and then in the wake of the world slump never got another racing assignment. According to his own account, Stuck met Julius Schreck by chance in Munich, and Schreck arranged a meeting for him with Hitler.

'I told him that Austro-Daimler had closed its factory in Vienna,' wrote Stuck of that meeting, 'and that Mercedes-Benz was no longer entering cars in races. There was still Alfa Romeo in Italy and Bugatti in France. Abroad, of course. Foreign cars. Hitler listened pensively, with furrowed brow. "I have money," he said. "But I need every *pfennig*. Our campaign is swallowing up everything. But we *will* come to power." He looked at me with a compelling but strangely vacant gaze. "You're a good driver. You're an excellent driver, Herr Stuck. When I get into power…" He turned and looked at a portrait of Frederick the Great hanging on the wall. Then he abruptly turned to face me again. "I cannot arrange a racing car for you, Herr Stuck. Not yet. But I can promise you one thing: as long as you don't drive any foreign cars for foreign firms, then you'll get a car from me – as soon as we're in power. Then the Reich will provide you with a racing car, Herr Stuck."'

Stuck writes that at the time he simply smiled inwardly: 'I swear I thought it was a joke, the sort of thing only a fantasist says with a straight face. I mean – a Reich racing car!' The fact is, however, that Stuck went on racing as a private driver but – for whatever reason – only in German-built machines. From Austro-Daimler he switched to Mercedes-Benz sports cars. Two influential people – Crown Prince Wilhelm and Ina Merck, wife of the owner of the Merck pharmaceutical company – persuaded Daimler-

Benz AG to let Stuck have an SSK, so that he could keep up his reputation as 'King of the Mountains'. By now he had at his side Paula von Reznicek, *née* Heimann. She was considered Germany's best female tennis player, and was still married to the journalist Burkhard von Reznicek. She herself wrote for leading newspapers and society magazines and knew everybody who was anybody. The fashionable racing driver and the tennis-playing journalist became an item and were married at the end of 1932 in the town hall of Berlin's Charlottenburg district. The couple proved to be brilliant self-promoters, and Paula acted as Hans's manager. However, after 1933 the successful relationship came under political pressure when the 'Reich Chamber of Culture' wished to establish whether, under the terms of National Socialist racial ideology, Frau Stuck should be classed as 'non-Aryan', 'semi-Jewess' or 'Jewess'.

By now, her husband, together with Ferdinand Porsche and Auto Union, was pursuing the 'Reich Racing car' project that he claimed previously to have privately mocked – and did not hesitate to make use of his contact with Hitler. Initially the aim was to obtain state subsidies, but as the grip of Nazi dictatorship tightened, ultimately he became concerned about his wife and his future career as a racing driver.

Left: The woman behind Hans Stuck. With her journalistic talent and connections, Paula von Reznicek helped to promote the career of her second husband, but having Jewish blood meant that her life in Nazi Germany was overshadowed by constant threat. (Audi AG)

Opposite: Manfred von Brauchitsch after his victory at the AVUS Race in 1932, accompanied by his mechanic, Willy Zimmer, and Alfred Neubauer, the head of the Mercedes-Benz race department. (Daimler AG)

On the final straight

In the critical year of 1932 Daimler-Benz also activated its contacts with the Nazis. The NSDAP had been gaining more and more votes and supporters, and it seemed likely that in a government reshuffle Hitler's party would soon be given a position of responsibility from which it would have a modest say in the formulation of national policy. How fortunate for the Untertürkheim company to have a man like Jakob Werlin around. On 14 May Werlin reported to CEO Kissel on a conversation with Hitler: 'Naturally, I did not fail to mention that we have always shown the greatest goodwill towards the Party, and I gave some examples.' Other companies could probably not make such a claim, 'whereas for many years we had cherished and nurtured our links with the NSDAP in recognition of its future prospects and always from devotion to the cause.' And on 18 May Kissel wrote back to Werlin: 'We certainly have no reason to pay any less attention than hitherto to Herr Hitler and his friends; in fact, he will […] be able to rely on us just as much as he has done in the past.'

For the sake of the company, there were no reservations, nor any shrinking from contact. When Manfred von Brauchitsch won his sensational victory

over the renegade Rudolf Caracciola and his Alfa Romeo in the AVUS Race on 22 May, Daimler-Benz AG finally had a big-name German driver once again, whom they could march down to Munich[20] in support of their national racing car project. So it was no doubt through Werlin's mediation that young von Brauchitsch – whose uncle was to be promoted by Hitler to commander-in-chief of the army in 1938 – was allowed for the first time to put his case in complete privacy to the leader of the Nazi party in the Bavarian capital:

'In the briefest terms possible, I presented my ideas and explained to him that, to develop and build a modern racing car, my company needed about two million marks. I expressed the hope that, with his opportunities, he could procure this sum in the interest of national sport. He listened very carefully to all this. Then he stood up, stuck both hands in his trouser pockets and paced up and down a few times. Finally he began his reply. He promised me he would ensure that the German motor industry would be put in a position to be internationally competitive once more. Suddenly he whipped his hands from his pockets and accompanied his words with wild gesticulation. He forgot the racing car and talked with zeal and great fanaticism, as if to a large audience, about his massive plans for creating a nation of Greater Germany. I listened to this with some astonishment. I thought him no more than a fantasist, who would never achieve these goals, but I was somehow inspired and could sense the hypnotic power in that man's eyes. It occurred to me that many of his ideas were the sort of thing we discussed around the family dinner table, long before we knew anything about him. In those days one still talked about His Majesty the Kaiser. And now here was a man who spoke of himself just as my relatives had spoken of the Kaiser, whose name they still only mentioned in a whisper. At the end of his political exposé about the role of the German nation under his leadership, the *Führer* did not forget to mention racing cars.'

On the subject of promoting racing car construction, Hitler would get in touch with Werlin in due course. But because von Brauchitsch heard no more about it, he himself, as he tells us, made his way to the Obersalzberg, Hitler's alpine retreat, some six months later – in other words shortly before the Nazis seized power. He claims he turned up at the Berghof 'spontaneously' and 'unannounced', whereupon the hard-pressed master of the house immediately gave up half an hour to discuss nothing but racing cars with him. What is more, von Brauchitsch was introduced to the Nazi leader's closest associates:[21] Göring, Goebbels, Streicher, Röhm, Hess, Himmler and everyone who mattered in the Party. Not to mention Heinrich Hoffmann, the 'court photographer', and SS-*Sturmführer* Schaub, Hitler's major-domo and dog-handler. Von Brauchitsch had come on behalf of Daimler-Benz AG, and the good tidings from Hitler were: 'Your company will get the money the moment I am in power.'

Curiously, in saying this the Nazi leader had given his word on the financing of a national racing car to two drivers simultaneously – von Brauchitsch and Stuck – and thus unwittingly to two German automobile companies. For by now Hans Stuck had changed sides and was no longer lobbying for Mercedes-Benz but for the combined interests of Auto Union.

Notes

1 Fritz Kortner (1892–1970) was born in Vienna as a Jew (real name Nathan Kohn) and became a celebrated actor and film and theatre director. He began his career in Berlin in 1919 with leading parts in Expressionist productions of German classical drama. After the Nazis came to power he fled with his family to New York, returning to Europe in 1947. He ran major theatre companies in Germany and Austria until his death.

2 Max Schmeling (1905–2005) was Germany's greatest boxer and one of the greatest in the world. In 1924, after becoming German light-heavyweight vice-champion, he turned professional. In 1926 he won the German light-heavyweight championship, starred in a film and made friends in show business and literary circles. European champion in 1927, he moved up to heavyweight and was German champion in 1928. In the same year he had his first fights in the USA, and in 1930 became World Heavyweight Champion in New York. He married a film actress, Anny Ondra, in 1933 and the following year beat Walter Neusel in Hamburg in front of a crowd of 100,000. In 1936, in the greatest surprise in boxing history, he knocked out the unbeaten American Joe Louis, a victory that the Nazis seized on as proof of 'Aryan superiority'. However, in 1938 Louis knocked him out in just over 2 minutes, and Schmeling fought his last pre-war match in 1939. In the *Reichskristallnacht* pogrom (see Chapter 4, Note 1) of November 1938 he hid two Jewish youths in his Berlin apartment. In the war he was drafted into the Wehrmacht but was invalided out in 1943. After the war he returned to boxing, first as a fighter, then as a referee. In 1952 he went into business with a Coca-Cola franchise. In his final years honours were heaped upon him.

3 The Weimar Republic was the new democratic German state established in 1919, following the country's defeat in the First World War and the Kaiser's abdication. It was named after the town where the constitution was signed, but the seat of government remained in Berlin. It had an executive president elected for a seven-year term, but under him the complexion of the Reichstag (parliament) could change and frequently did. The republic faced huge problems from the outset, both economic and political, with the hyperinflation of 1923, the inexorable rise of Nazism (despite being outlawed for a time) and the Depression of 1929–32. In January 1933 Hitler was appointed Chancellor (prime minister) by President Hindenburg, ostensibly under the Weimar constitution, but Hitler immediately Nazified all the organs of state and when Hindenburg died in 1934 the presidency lapsed with him and Hitler had absolute power. Confusingly, even during the republic the state was referred to as a 'Reich',

as in Reichsmark, Reich Ministry etc. This did not change until 1949, when the new federal republic was given the name *Bund*, as in *Bundesrepublik*, *Bundeswehr* etc.

4 The initials AVUS stood for *Automobil-Verkehrs- und Übungs-Strasse* (motor traffic and practice road). Construction of the urban motorway, for occasional racing use, was started in 1907 but not completed until 1921.

5 Alfred Hugenberg (1865–1951) was a right-wing media magnate who also owned the famous UFA film studios in Berlin. He was a deputy in the Reichstag for the DNVP (nationalist party) from 1920 to 1933 and party chairman from 1928. He was Hitler's first Minister of Economics in 1933. In 1943 the Nazis bought out his press empire for a large sum. Hugenberg was not indicted as a war criminal after the Second World War and was allowed to keep his fortune.

6 The brown-uniformed SA or *Sturmabteilung* (most often translated as 'Stormtroopers' but actually meaning 'Assault unit') constituted the paramilitary wing of the NSDAP.

7 Ernst Udet (1896–1941) was a dashing First World War fighter pilot who served with Göring in the Richthofen squadron. After years as a stunt flyer and test-pilot he joined the newly formed Luftwaffe in 1935 and rose to become Director of Armaments. He was never a convinced Nazi but succumbed to drink and women, fell out of favour with Göring and shot himself in November 1941. Crown Prince Wilhelm (1882–1951) was the eldest son of the deposed Kaiser. In the Weimar republic he had no official status, but was something of a playboy. In 1932 he supported Hitler in his failed bid to replace Hindenburg as president, but was probably not a committed Nazi.

8 See Manfred von Brauchitsch, *Ohne Kampf kein Sieg* ('No Victory Without Struggle'), East Berlin 1964, p.67.

9 In 1950, when Rosenberger brought an action for reimbursement against Porsche before the Stuttgart District Court, even the lawyers for the opposing side granted the truth of this claim. The ex-racing driver, who had emigrated to the USA, considered that he had been deprived of his rightful share of the business due to his Jewish faith.

10 Heinrich Brüning (1885–1970) was one of the last Chancellors of Weimar Germany. His support came only from the political centre. He was under constant attack from the Nationalist and Nazi parties, who held a huge rally in Harzburg on 11 October 1931, at which they vowed to oust the Brüning cabinet, since it was seen as too weak to withstand the advance of Bolshevism. Brüning was struggling with the impact of the world Depression, and introduced a deflationary package of price and wage cuts to keep the German economy moving. He also proposed splitting up some of the great landed estates of East Prussia. This was too much for President Hindenburg, who asked for his resignation on 29 May 1932. Brüning was replaced by the wealthy, aristocratic diplomat Franz von Papen. The following year, when the Nazis seized power, Brüning escaped to Holland and from there went to the USA, where he lectured at Harvard. He returned to Germany in 1947.

11 In November 1923 Hitler mistakenly believed he had enough support to seize the reins of government in the semi-autonomous state of Bavaria. On the night of 8 November a force of armed Nazis surrounded the Bürgerbrau beer-cellar, where the Bavarian prime minister, Kahr, was holding a public meeting. With the backing of General Ludendorff, a First World War hero, Hitler briefly captured Kahr and others and forced them to sign over their powers to the Nazis. But as soon as Kahr was released he went back on his word. The next day, around noon, Hitler, Ludendorff, Göring and others led a march through the city to the Feldherrnhalle military memorial. Before they reached it the police opened fire on them. Hitler and Göring were injured (Göring seriously) and a total of 16 Nazi supporters and three police were killed. Hitler was arrested and put on trial for high treason.

12 Although sentenced to five years imprisonment, Hitler was released after only seven months. During that time he was allowed to wear his own clothes, had his own rooms and a special diet, and could associate freely with the 40 other Nazi prisoners, as well as receive frequent guests. During his spell in Landsberg, Hitler, aided by Rudolf Hess, wrote most of the first volume of his political manifesto, *Mein Kampf* ('My Struggle').

13 In 1930 the SS was separated from the SA. In order to emphasis the superiority of the SS, a large number of 'honorary' members were recruited from the aristocracy and senior business circles. By 1938 Himmler could boast that nearly one in five SS *Obergruppenführers* (a rank equivalent to general) came from titled families. Honorary members had no duties or powers but were entitled to wear the SS uniform. After the war most were classified merely as *Mitfahrer*, or fellow-travellers, rather than as war criminals.

14 Gregor Strasser (1892–1934) joined the Nazi Party in 1920 and later did much to expand its organisation in the industrial Rhineland. Unlike Hitler he was a genuine socialist, and was neither strongly anti-Semitic nor anti-Bolshevist. When he challenged Hitler from his northern power-base, Hitler had him murdered in the 'Night of the Long Knives' of June 1934.

15 'Geli' Raubal (1908–31) was the daughter of Hitler's half-sister Angela. Hitler was obsessed by her, and in 1929, when she was 21 and Hitler 40, she came to Munich to study. He took her under his roof, escorted her to restaurants and the opera and jealously watched her every move. Eventually, after a violent quarrel, she apparently shot herself, though her death raised many suspicions. Whatever the truth, Hitler was distraught and from then on kept her photograph and belongings in a locked room, as a shrine.

16 Quoted from Rudolf Caracciola/Oskar Weller *Rennen – Sieg – Rekorde!* ('Races – Victories – Records!'), Stuttgart 1943.

17 Fritz Wiedemann (1891–1970) served in the German army in the First World War and became Hitler's personal adjutant in 1935. He had a lengthy affair with a half-Jewish socialite, Princess Stephanie von Hohenlohe, under whose influence he tried, without Hitler's permission, to keep communications with the British government open in the months leading up to the war. When Hitler learned of his relationship Wiedemann was dismissed and sent as German Consul-General to San Francisco, where he engaged in espionage. He was then posted as consul in Tientsin, China, were he spent the rest of the war. He gave evidence at the Nuremberg war crime tribunal and was released in 1948.

18 Quoted from Hans Stuck, *Zweimal Hans Stuck, Ein Rennfahrer-Tagebuch* ('Hans Stuck Twice Over, Diary of a Racing Driver'), Stuttgart 1972.

19 At the end of the First World War many extreme German nationalists from the disbanded army formed illegal militias known as *Freikorps*, of which the one led by General von Epp was the most notorious. Some operated in East Prussia, others in Berlin and Munich. In 1919, taking their cue from the Russian Revolution, a group of Socialists established a short-lived *Räterepublik*, or soviet, in Munich, which was crushed with much bloodshed by von Epp and his men.

20 The Nazi Party always had its headquarters in Munich, from 1931 in the lavishly appointed 'Brown House' in Briennerstrasse. Even after the Nazis seized power and the regime operated from Berlin, the party organisation remained in Munich.

21 At this time, around December 1932, Göring was President, or Speaker, of the Reichstag; Goebbels was a Deputy in the Reichstag as well as Hitler's campaign manager; Julius Streicher was a *Gauleiter* (NSDAP regional party leader) and editor of the violently anti-Semitic weekly *Der Stürmer*; Ernst Röhm was chief-of-staff of the SA (Hitler had him murdered in 1934); Rudolf Hess was Hitler's secretary and chairman of the central policy committee of the Nazi Party (appointed deputy *Führer* in 1933); Himmler was *Reichsführer*–SS and also, from 1933, in charge of the police, secret services and concentration camps.

CHAPTER THREE

RACING IN THE SERVICE
OF THE REGIME

With the appointment of Hitler as Reich Chancellor on 30 January 1933 and the new Reichstag elections immediately set for 5 March, the SA brownshirts and the Nazi party were masters of the streets. Hitler exploited his power as head of government to expand and secure his dictatorship. He sent out the propaganda message that this was necessary in order for him to carry forward his vision for the German people without hindrance.

And rather a lot of people were willing to make common cause with the Nazis – either from total conviction or because there was a certain overlapping of interests. Some were overwhelmed by the '*Führer* myth', others seduced by the calculation that they might secure advantages or a share of power – no matter whether they were from the affluent middle class, the aristocracy or the military elite, whether bureaucrats, white-collar staff, manual workers or unemployed. Step by step, day by day, a little more was required from them in terms of collaboration and opportunism, of playing along and averting their eyes – for which they were rewarded with small perks or greater privileges.

It was high season for careerists, for the despised *Märzgefallene*,[1] the hangers-on and profiteers of the Nazi regime. It was the start of the seduction and enticement, the allure of a restoration of national greatness, which made Nazism palatable to almost everyone. And motorsport in those years became a microcosm of the nation as a whole, in which not

Meet your sponsor. Dr Hans Nibel presenting the new W25 to Führer and Reich Chancellor Adolf Hitler on 4 January 1934 at the Mercedes-Benz showroom in Munich. They are accompanied by Jakob Werlin and Dr Joseph Goebbels. (Daimler AG)

only racing drivers but many others managed to weave their way adroitly around the circuits and through the chicanes of the dictatorship. But the drivers were the pampered idols of a system that was both mendacious and criminal. The Nazi leadership set great store by overblown theatricality and public affirmation, in return for which they allowed relative freedom of action and dispensed undreamed-of benefits.

Thus the professional racing driver under the Third Reich became the paradigm of the age, a man ostensibly quite uninterested in politics, who for precisely that reason mutated into a profiteer from Nazi policies. The recovery in both economic and national fortunes – which Hitler had promised the German people – was to occur for a time, and under a policy of massive rearmament gave the German motor industry cause to be grateful, since with the help of government contracts it set new production records. And the works drivers for Mercedes-Benz and Auto Union would, with victories in their Silver Arrows, contribute to the respect and recognition paid to the Nazi regime and at the same time lend it an outward glamour.

The car-friendly dictatorship

The key date in the relationship between the Nazi regime and the German motor industry was 11 February 1933. That was the day when Hitler opened the International Car and Motorcycle Exhibition in Berlin – the first German Chancellor to grace this show with his presence – and used it as a platform to announce his programme of 'national motorisation': abolition of the vehicle tax, reduction of corporation tax and government support for road-building and motorsport were clear signals that in Hitler's state cars and car manufacturers would play a key role. From this, Nazi propaganda would successfully mythologise the *Führer* as the original 'creator of the autobahns', even though Munich highways engineer and Nazi Party member Fritz Todt had included in his job-creation programme the so-called *Ha-Fra-Ba* plans, which had existed since the 1920s and envisaged a motorway linking the Hanseatic cities of the north (Hamburg, Bremen and Lübeck) with Frankfurt in central Germany and Basel just across the southern border with Switzerland.

But such connections counted for little; the only thing that mattered was that the new Reich Chancellor was a friend of motorisation, and for that reason the National Federation of the German Motor Industry soon launched a '*Führer* Fund' of 300,000 RM. A year after seizing power Hitler would finally start promoting the 'People's Car', the affordable automobile for everyone. Even this had its predecessors, but only Germany's first dictator had the will to put wheels on what had so far been a dream of national mobility. And he did so in the face of initial resistance from a less than enthusiastic industry and its umbrella-organisation.

The man who would design this *Volkswagen* had already curried favour with Hitler. Immediately after his speech on 11 February 1933, Ferdinand Porsche personally thanked the new Reich Chancellor in a telegram: 'As the creator of many notable designs in the sphere of German and Austrian motor transport and aviation and one who has shared your struggle for more than 30 years to achieve today's success, I congratulate Your Excellency on your profound speech at the opening of the German Automobile Exhibition. I hope it will be granted to me and my staff, in future and to an increased extent, to place our skill and determination at the disposal of the German people.'

Anyone sending a message as ingratiating as that could be sure of being given an audience: three months later, on 10 May 1933, Porsche and Hitler met in the Reich Chancellery.

Jockeying for position

Hans Stuck, the designated works driver for Auto Union and a personal friend of Porsche, gives an account in his memoirs of a telephone call he claims to have received a month after Hitler took power on 30 January 1933: 'Adolf Hitler here. You remember the time, Herr Stuck, when I told you the Reich would help you to build a racing car once I came to power? Well, I've finally got here. I've seen how you have remained loyal to Germany. You've had some fine successes for Germany in a German car. In Brazil and Argentina. Please draft the necessary proposals for me. When you are ready, come and see me!'

If this call actually took place it poses the question whether Hitler knew that Stuck had switched from Mercedes-Benz to Auto Union. For according to all available sources, the new Reich Chancellor intended to channel state subsidies exclusively to Untertürkheim. It is far more likely that Stuck himself had exploited his acquaintance with Hitler for the benefit of Porsche and Auto Union, and in his own interest as designated lead driver of the new racing stable.

On 11 February 1933 Hitler made the definitive announcement that there would be government funds for the building of a German national racing car. Only now did both Daimler-Benz and Auto Union show their determination to launch their own racing car projects. On 27 February Porsche and the board of Auto Union agreed in principle on a contract. On 7 March a working conference was held in Zwickau, since the new racing car was to be built there, at the Horch factory. By now the political omens looked more favourable than ever, for after the Reichstag elections on 5 March the Nazis were more firmly in the seat of power. Now it was a matter of exploiting the Reich Chancellor's passion for motor cars.

On 10 March Daimler-Benz boss Wilhelm Kissel got a call from Consul Fritsch, the vice-president of AvD, who had received a letter from the Reich Ministry of Transport about the Automobile Club's fund-raising appeal for a national racing car. At the end of the budgetary year there was a small surplus of 100,000 RM in the ministry's budget, which, when added to the 50,000 already earmarked from state funds and a further 90,000 raised by private donations, meant there was a bottom line of nearly a quarter of a million Reichsmarks! Fritsch informed Kissel that he intended to request further assistance from the transport ministry's 1933 budget, amounting to 300,000 RM. Hans Stuck had apparently already got his word in first with Fritsch, but the latter assured Kissel that he would 'not be bankrolling any other company.'

This put Mercedes-Benz on maximum alert – Auto Union was trying to get its hands on state subsidies through the AvD's warmed-up appeal for donations! For this reason Kissel sent a ten-page letter of warning to the Governors of the Automobile Club of Germany, to the effect that Daimler-Benz AG had the sole right to pocket these subsidies. And Porsche got short shrift as well: unlike the new boys at Auto Union there was no need for Daimler-Benz to show proof of their capabilities by advertising the fact they had a supposedly brilliant designer. The next day the head of Mercedes-Benz wrote in similarly sharp terms to the person responsible for racing car subsidies at the transport ministry: 'We are the one German company which, in the harshest post-war period, when it was necessary to restore the name of Germany, not only very successfully deployed its own strength and resources in defending the reputation of the German automobile industry, but also returned it to its position in the world. It would therefore be contrary to the German sense of justice if the funds collected by public donation, and those which the Reich is prepared to give, were to be shared out.' And for that reason Kissel requested speedy notification 'as to whether and to what ultimate extent we can expect support from the Reich with regard to this project. It will be no surprise to you to learn that we cannot spend our own financial resources, since these are fully taken up by current commitments.' And to avoid any possible doubt, Daimler-Benz AG raised the undisguised threat of Hitler's intentions: 'We think we know the views of the Herr Reich Chancellor and believe we ought to put our plan into effect as quickly as possible.'

As a matter of honour, on 15 March, Kissel also wrote to the '*hochverehrter* (highly esteemed) Herr Reich Chancellor Adolf Hitler'. It would cost about a million Reichsmarks to raise respect for Germany through the construction, initially, of some five Mercedes-Benz racing cars. With an eye to the competition, Kissel asked Hitler for direct state subsidy without routing it through the racing car appeal of the AvD and ADAC – the automobile clubs which had at that time not yet been Nazified: 'We would not need the financing all at once, but in stages over the course of this year. Since, in the course of the company's history, our marque has contributed frequently and significantly to the respect paid to Germany at sporting events, we would dedicate all our skill and knowledge to this and would deem it an honour if we were enabled to represent the German flag in the sport of the future.'

It is true that, thanks to Jakob Werlin, Mercedes-Benz had a better line to the Reich Chancellor, yet Auto Union seems to have been equally sure of its influence with the Reich Ministry of Transport and on 17 March signed a contract with Ferdinand Porsche's Hochleistungs-Fahrzeugbau GmbH ('High-Performance Vehicle Construction Co'), which was to run until the planned expiry of the new 750kg racing formula at the end of 1936. Porsche received 75,000 RM for planning and following through the design of a racing car that had to fulfil the following criteria: '1) The engine must develop 250 b.h.p. at 4,500 r.p.m. 2) The weight of the complete vehicle, without tyres or fuel, has to be below 800 kg in 1933, and in 1934 must, in accordance with international regulation, be less than 750 kg. […] 3) The complete car must prove itself by doing 10 uninterrupted laps of the AVUS circuit in Berlin, and on each of the straights reach a maximum speed of 250 k.p.h. (150 m.p.h.).'

In its contract, Auto Union had to bow to the sensitivities – or vanity – of the commissioned designer: 'The car must be entered and raced under the designation chosen by Auto Union, with the additional words *Typ Porsche*.' However, Auto Union later omitted to do this – much to Porsche's annoyance. Nonetheless, the inventive technician benefited greatly from another provision, right up to the year 1936: 'Should any subsidies be provided by government, the automobile clubs or any third parties, these monies shall accrue solely to Auto Union up to a total of 100,000 Reichsmarks. Any sum in excess of this figure received from an above-mentioned source shall be divided equally between Auto Union and Dr Porsche GmbH.'

Indeed, by June 1936 Auto Union would have to pay over a total of 592,428.50 RM to Porsche from these state funds, so a considerable portion of the subsidies from the Nazi regime did not end up with the Auto Union automobile group at all, but in Porsche's pocket! After three years had elapsed this was also noticed by the Reich Ministry of Transport. A civil servant named Brandenburg wrote to Auto Union on 16 May 1936, warning them that 'this arrangement, which apparently dates back to the time before the seizure of power, is one which I cannot say is acceptable. I can only approve future funding for your company on the condition that you separate your contract with Dr Porsche from the question of financial assistance from the Reich.'

This gave Auto Union the leverage they needed to part company with their expensive designer. But that did not prevent him from attending the group's most important races and record runs – even without payment – right up to the 1937 season, the life of the 750kg formula having been extended by a year. Financially, Porsche did not have to go short; by that time he had landed some very different but lucrative orders. Despite all the resistance from the boards of virtually every motor group, as well as from the Reich Federation of the German Automobile Industry, Porsche was allowed to turn Hitler's pipe dream into reality and build the *Volkswagen*. As a sideline the *Führer*'s favourite designer would work once more for Daimler-Benz on a fee basis, building a special car that was to pursue the world absolute land speed record. This was a 'national project', which will be looked at in detail elsewhere. In the meantime we turn our attention to the spring of 1933 and follow the duel for state aid for the building of Germany's national racing cars.

Corporate indignation

Daimler-Benz chief executive Wilhelm Kissel had always asked the authorities in Berlin to take on the full cost of Untertürkheim's national racing car and for this he had named a total figure of at least 1 million RM. But on 4 May 1933 Brandenburg, at the Ministry of Transport, announced that at most only 300,000 to 400,000 RM could be provided. It seems that a decision had already been made at the ministry that Auto Union was also to be subsidised from the state's coffers.

On 6 April Kissel sent a letter to Brandenburg by express delivery asking for 'adequate funds' which could be drawn from 'not at once, but in successive stages through the year' – and at the same time took a sideswipe at the competition and Porsche's plans: 'To build racing cars that are intended to represent not only our marque but the whole German nation in major races, does not only require designers; it demands the whole spirit and orientation of a firm that has the appropriate experience.'

The following day the chief designer of Mercedes-Benz, Hans Nibel, approached the Reich Transport Minister, Baron von Eltz-Rübenach, with the request that he 'ensure that the monies be distributed in the way that is imperative in the interest of achieving the goal of creating a good German racing car.' With an eye on Auto Union, but without once mentioning the name of that unwelcome competitor, he offered the criticism that 'another firm has applied, which clearly wishes to take up racing car building for reasons of prestige, particularly since this gives it the opportunity to use state funds to gain experience in an area hitherto completely new to it. We would consider it a great injustice to our company if that firm, which so far has left it to us to represent the German industry in major races at home and abroad, should now, since the Reich Ministry of Transport has generously decided to promote German motorsport in the national interest, be treated in the same way as us, who have already from our own resources successfully carried the German colours in motorsport at home and abroad.'

On 7 April Kissel gave a hint that 'all our forces will be mobilised to create a racing car model that has the best prospects of success'. This martial pronouncement was directed at Carl Eduard, Duke of Saxe-Coburg-Gotha,[2] who had by now been appointed by Eltz-Rübenach as 'motoring activities officer'. The influential duke was a *Gruppenführer* (equivalent to lieutenant-general) in the SA and would later be honorary head of the

NSKK, the National Socialist Corps of Motorists. Even before the Nazis came to power he had made a name for himself as the co-founder and chairman of the 'German Motor Vehicle Users Association', and was determined to educate the German public to give unreserved preference to German products. This industrious official and token aristocrat in the Nazi party proved to be a friend to Auto Union, and on the subject of racing car subsidies recommended to Kissel on 11 April, 'with a German salute': 'Since a similar application has already been received from Auto Union, it would no doubt be more appropriate if the two interested companies were to reach a mutual understanding.' However, it was a suggestion that the Daimler-Benz chief ruled out in his reply dated 20 April: 'We are the oldest car manufacturer in the world,' Kissel began his indignant riposte, and went on to inveigh against the Saxon competitor: 'It would therefore, in our view, violate the sense of justice of every German, if the funds which the Reich is willing to provide were to be allocated to a company that has not so far been engaged in building racing cars.'

To his friends and supervisory board members from Deutsche Bank, Alfred Blinzig and von Stauss, he expressed his outrage over the AvD's Consul Fritsch and 'several other influential gentlemen in that club' who,

The official poster for the AVUS Race in 1933, the first important international race meeting in Hitler's new Germany. The Nazi swastika is combined with the flag of the former republic and a 'national' racing car in the shape of a Mercedes-Benz SSK. (Daimler AG)

he claimed, had urged Auto Union to build racing cars: 'That wretched AvD, which should have been pickled in oil and vinegar long ago, has nothing better to do than work against the firm, our company, which it has in fact almost exclusively lived off since the end of the war.'

Kissel wrote in fury and was contemplating revenge: 'Once our new racing cars are ready and running in big races, I very much hope that the Porsche car is entered too and that we then see it off. Since Herr Stuck has gone over to Auto Union, we have come up with something pretty clever – that is, to persuade Herr Caracciola to enter the AVUS Race on 21 May this year, driving our SSK car. We are using Stuck's car, which we bought back yesterday for 16,000 RM. The money owed us by Herr Stuck and his wife – around 14,000 RM – was deducted and the remainder paid to Stuck in cash. Since midday today, the Stuck car has been here at the factory. We will be able to get the car ready in time for the AVUS Race, so that to the surprise of many, Herr Caracciola will be driving the SSK, which Stuck should have driven if he had not broken his word. Perhaps good fortune will see to it that Herr Caracciola takes first prize in this race. Then we will be able to make a lot out of it. A certain club, whose name I will not mention here, is so keen to see this matter through that it has expressed the willingness to contribute at least 5,000 RM and probably as much as 8,000 RM to buying the Stuck car.'

Misfortune for a top driver

In fact the great Caracciola drove in the 1933 season as a freelance. Together with his Monegasque colleague Louis Chiron, the German driver had sponsored a private racing stable, which was an advantage in the negotiations over starting money for the entry of their two Alfa Romeo P3s. A year before the 750kg formula came into force, the starting fields in Grand Prix races had shrunk further. So Caracciola's guest appearance for his long-standing employer in front of a home crowd would be an absolute sensation, particularly since the SSK – actually hopelessly outmoded but benefiting from streamlined bodywork – would have a chance of victory on the fast AVUS circuit against competition from Alfa Romeo, Bugatti and Maserati, exactly as Manfred von Brauchitsch had done the year before against Caracciola himself.

But it was to turn out quite differently. And somehow it is not without a certain piquancy that, on Hitler's birthday of all days, 20 April 1933,

Germany's best racing driver had a serious accident while practising for the Monaco Grand Prix. Caracciola skidded into a kerb in his Alfa Romeo P3 and sustained very grave injuries. His right femur was smashed, the ball of the joint shattered, and the surgical techniques of the day were stretched to their limit. The operation resulted in his right leg being two inches shorter than his left, and for the rest of his life he could only walk with a limp and in great pain. It was highly doubtful whether 'Caratsch' would ever race again. So not only did Daimler-Benz lose Germany's best driver for the 1933 AVUS Race, but it was also probable that he would not be available to drive the future national racing car.

Auto Union calls at the Reich Chancellery

A lot of government money had been put into the restructured and re-formed Saxon motor group, and for a long time government officials and regional party notables had been involving themselves in the business. Chief among them was *Gauleiter* Martin Mutschmann, the archetypal arrogant and corrupt Nazi satrap, who on 5 May 1933 was appointed by the *Führer* as *Reichstatthalter* or Governor in the former kingdom of Saxony. In February 1934 Mutschmann's personal adjutant, SS-*Standartenführer* Loos, would join the thoroughly pro-Nazi supervisory board of Auto Union and act as direct liaison man with the Nazi leadership. Thus it was in the interest of Saxony's top Nazis that Auto Union should also cash in on subsidies for its racing car project. But because Hitler favoured Mercedes-Benz the situation had to be cleared up in a personal meeting. How did the Auto Union team secure an appointment with the Reich Chancellor?

It was all thanks to Hans Stuck, of course. Or so the racing driver claimed in his memoirs four decades after the meeting in the Reich Chancellery. Nor, it seems, was he a mere go-between on that occasion. Before the audience with Hitler, Porsche turned up at Stuck's flat in Charlottenburg and presented him with the design drawings, and then the two put their case to the *Führer* jointly: 'Hitler asked the sort of questions a motor professional would, like someone who did nothing but work with cars day in day out.'

The Reich Chancellor seemed very excited by the plans for the racing car. 'The car *will* be built, Professor Porsche! And you will drive it, Herr Stuck. [...] Go ahead with everything. [...] There'll be no lack of money.'

However, it probably did not happen like that. Stuck fails to mention that a member of the Auto Union management board, Baron Klaus Detlof von Oertzen, was also present at that audience. The former general manager of the Wanderer factory – one of the constituent firms of Auto Union – was a member of the NSDAP and was there to ask his party leader and Reich Chancellor for financial assistance. Unfortunately, von Oertzen's long-standing clubland friend and former guiding spirit of the racing car project, Adolf Rosenberger, being Jewish, no longer had a chance to sit at the conference table, not even with his business partner Porsche. From his own experience von Oertzen knew only too well how things stood, since he was himself married to a 'non-Aryan'.

In 1987, at the advanced age of 94, he recalled the meeting with Hitler. Von Oertzen is quoted in the official company history of Auto Union, authorised by Audi AG:[3] 'Before that, we had already asked various senior Nazis for support in building the racing car. We knew that Hitler was in the process of handing out money to Daimler-Benz. [...] So I went to see his

Ferdinand Porsche (left), Hans Stuck and Klaus Detlof von Oertzen celebrate their victory at the German Grand Prix in 1934. A year earlier they had asked Hitler for financial support for the Auto Union race car project. (Kirchberg)

deputy, Rudolf Hess.[4] He and I had been pilots together in the First World War. I asked Hess to arrange an appointment for me with Hitler.'

And this did in fact happen, though von Oertzen erroneously dates it in his memoirs to early March 1933, and not 10 May: 'I took with me to that meeting Dr Porsche and the racing driver Hans Stuck, who knew Hitler personally, while I did not. He was to be our intermediary. So three of us arrived. Hitler only had with him his secretary, who wrote down everything that was said between us. [...] In the course of the discussion Hitler turned down my request for capital backing for the Auto Union racing car and at the end of his explanation he said: "Don't bother with it any more!" Then I took my courage in both hands and said to him: "You know, Herr Reich Chancellor" – I never called him *mein Führer* – "it's not so terribly long ago that you were collected in a Mercedes from your imprisonment in Landsberg. You said you wanted to start your party work again. But the press said to you: *Don't bother, Herr Hitler. We'll never listen to you again. It's all over for you.* [...] Now you're saying the same thing to me, that I shouldn't bother with the racing car, I should give up. But I'm not going to do that. I *am* going to bother. It is the duty I owe to ten thousand workers." Hitler did not like me talking like that. He looked at me twice very hard, then ignored my impertinence and turned to Dr Porsche. [...] He asked him how he intended to build the racing car. There was a long discussion and Hitler was interested in all the technicalities. He had all sorts of knowledge that one would not have expected him to have. Then he brought the meeting to an end and said: "You'll be hearing from me." After only three days we were given permission to build the racing car. [...] Hitler had backed the building of our racing car. But he didn't do it for my sake, it was a favour to Porsche.'[5]

Even after the audience with Messrs von Oertzen, Porsche and Stuck, the Reich Chancellor and Nazi leader was tending more towards channelling state funds to Daimler-Benz AG alone. On 11 May 1933, the day after the Auto Union delegation had been received at the Reich Chancellery, Hitler's *chef de cabinet*, Hans Lammers, drafted minutes of the meeting in which he quoted Hitler's decision that, in international races, 'where entry would only be in order to achieve world status for Germany, in the long run only one company can represent the country. The funds available must be concentrated on that one company.'

However, within the Reich Ministry of Transport some rather different decisions had been taken long ago. As early as 28 April 1933 Minister von Eltz-Rübenach had informed Lammers that 'the struggle to regain the world reputation of German motor vehicles is in the interest of the entire German motor industry, so that all promising projects […] ought to be promoted.'

In the end a remarkable compromise was reached between the budgetary responsibility of the ministry and the powerful word of the Reich Chancellor, and it would be upheld year after year. Both Daimler-Benz and Auto Union received financial assistance for building racing cars, though the works team from Untertürkheim generally received more than the one from Zwickau.

What did the Silver Arrows really cost?

The fact that in Hitler's new Germany tax revenue would flow into motor racing was definitely a done deal. In an internal memo dated 29 April 1933 and headed 'Re: Racing car', Chief Executive Kissel informed his staff in

A sort of private/state partnership. From left: Jakob Werlin, Joseph Goebbels, Hans Nibel, Adolf Hitler and Alfred Neubauer. (Daimler AG)

the racing division: 'We will shortly receive a substantial Reich subsidy for the building of a new racing car model. A separate account will be set up for these funds, to which all expenses incurred in the development of the new design are to be charged. Expenditure on personnel, materials and machinery is to be accounted for in the same way as we are already doing with the – likewise state-sponsored – "development of marine and aero engines", *ie* with a "government surcharge", that is to say a kind of user fee for the use of available plant and labour.'

With both Mercedes-Benz and Auto Union this surcharge came to a handsome 250 per cent, a rate that was customary at the time for that kind of 'authorised business' and was justified on the basis of the higher costs involved in developments carried out to order.

However, this had the result that both companies claimed correspondingly higher extra costs for building their national racing cars and putting them on to the track. Was this a matter of falsifying invoices in order to get the highest possible sums from the government? The machines and manpower were available in any case. And expenditure on racing activities could be set against tax as an advertising cost. Or else the expenses could simply be passed on in the sale price of their own range of cars and trucks. That is exactly what Daimler-Benz AG did explicitly in its racing plans for 1940, the first full year of the war. The Army High Command promptly raised a complaint about this and was only prepared to pay 50 per cent of the 'government surcharge', eliciting a protest from Daimler-Benz. So the millions of Reichsmarks that Mercedes-Benz and Auto Union invoiced, season after season from 1933/4, for the building and running of their racing cars – and, in the case of the Saxon group, for their DKW racing motorcycles – have to be treated with caution, even if they do not represent a wholly fictitious cost structure.

Without the incentive of a massive financial boost from the Nazi regime in 1933 neither Daimler-Benz AG nor Auto Union AG would have been willing or able to put their ambitious racing car plans into effect with such speed. True, in the long run the economic recovery of the German motor industry, actively aided by the fiscal benevolence and propaganda of the Nazi regime, would have made it possible to finance the design, construction and racing of the Silver Arrows from internal resources. Yet the fact that, season after season, the National Socialist state paid fat

Final assembly of the first Auto Union P-Wagen at the Horch factory by chief mechanic Ludwig Sebastian (left) and colleagues. In mid-background are Ferdinand Porsche and Robert Eberan von Eberhorst. (Sebastian)

premiums and subsidies soon came to be regarded by the corporate bosses as a rightful state gift that was requested politely but firmly every year, always accompanied by the routine complaint that expenditure on motor racing had risen hugely and that competing for Germany in motorsport was scarcely affordable without the help of the Reich.

For all that, the financial aspect of motor racing activities in Untertürkheim and Zwickau appears to have been perfectly manageable. The expenditure by Auto Union on its racing division accounted for only 0.7 per cent of total sales in 1937/8, and never exceeded 0.92 per cent (1936/7). Even at the beginning of participation in Grand Prix racing the corresponding figure for the financial year 1933/4 was no more than 0.85 per cent. However, since Auto Union's turnover rose strongly year by year until 1938 – not least thanks to massive defence contracts and a lucrative business in official cars – the budget for the Zwickau racing division was able to grow in step, along with its expenditure on engineering. In the course of the 1934 Grand Prix season Auto Union had five cars ready to race, and in 1935 no fewer than seven. By 1936 Zwickau had lined up a full dozen of these 16-cylinder monsters. In 1934 Mercedes-Benz could call upon six W25 racing cars and in the following year a total of eight were in Grand Prix trim.

Similar to the situation at Auto Union, the men in Untertürkheim had a budget that fluctuated around 1 per cent of annual group sales. However, after 1935 their figure was considerably higher in absolute terms, because business activity was growing significantly faster and was profiting far more from Hitler's massive rearmament than was the case with their competitor in Saxony. In 1933, with a turnover of 100.9 million RM, Daimler-Benz AG was still lagging behind Auto Union AG, which chalked up sales of 116 million RM for the financial year 1933/4. In 1936 Untertürkheim's sales were 295.1 million RM, against 235 million for Zwickau in the financial year 1936/7. In 1937 Daimler-Benz pushed its sales up to 399.1 million RM, while those of Auto Union AG were only 276.4 million for the financial year 1937/8. It was no coincidence that from the 1938 racing season onwards Zwickau had great difficulty in matching the financial and technical outlay of the Mercedes-Benz racing division.

Thanks to the quota system for raw materials imposed by the Nazis as part of their preparations for war, the motor groups only experienced significant growth in production outside their rearmament contracts if there were export opportunities for their own range of vehicles. To that extent German racing victories around the world all too quickly became the proven method of promoting sales of German cars abroad. Yet every victory for the Silver Arrows simultaneously heralded the success of the new Nazi Germany – a fact that did not make export trade any easier. However, their *political* advertising for National Socialism earned the gentlemen of Daimler-Benz AG and Auto Union good money year after year until well after the war had started.

The direct subsidies were accompanied by additional bonuses based on their racing success. In the case of Auto Union the bottom-line figure from 1933 to the start of the war totalled more than 2.75 million RM. As a proportion of Zwickau's racing budget each year, the generous government contribution ranged from 19.5 per cent to 28.4 per cent. True, Mercedes-Benz had similar benefits, but in 1933/4 the percentage contribution was significantly higher. In absolute terms, too, Untertürkheim pocketed substantially more – up to 1941 a total of over 4 million RM. That was not just on account of greater success on the racing circuit, but also because of preferential treatment.

Looking at the absolute financial outlay of the two racing divisions in the period from 1933 to 1941, motor historian Peter Kirchberg calculates that Auto Union spent a total of around 15 million RM, while the Mercedes-Benz figure was about 50 per cent higher. Another historian, Wilfried Feldenkirchen, comes up with a very precise figure for Daimler-Benz's racing costs of 18,246,000 RM, though that only covers the period from 1935 to 1940. This omits not only the racing budget for the year 1933/4 but also the final 'state assistance for motorsport' of 350,000 RM, dating from February 1941.

We do know, in fact, what it cost Daimler-Benz AG to get into the 750kg racing formula, from a letter which CEO Kissel wrote on 1 March 1935 to Adolf Hühnlein,[6] the head of the NSKK, asking for support to the tune of about RM 1 million for that season. Kissel also mentions the total expenditure for the 1933/4 period: 'Up to the end of last year the costs amounted to some 2.2 million RM. This is made up of the design, construction and trials of racing cars, entering them in races, the application of knowledge gained in races and the adaptation of the racing cars, as well as expenditure on the drivers themselves and auxiliary staff, and any general costs arising from our participation in motorsport.' This means that we can put a figure of more than 20.5 million RM on Daimler-Benz's total expenditure in the cause of motor racing from 1933 to 1941. That is a good five million more than Auto Union spent on its racing endeavours over the same period.

It is no less interesting to note what Kissel has to say, in the same letter to Hühnlein, about the subsidies paid to Daimler-Benz AG for racing in 1933/4: 'As you may be aware, the Reich granted us assistance totalling some 907,000 RM. Remuneration received from private companies, especially those with an interest in racing, and from clubs, amounted to 310,000 RM, so that for the racing season up to the end of 1934 we had a total inflow of about 1,217,000 RM.' That means quite simply that in the early stages of the new 750kg formula almost 60 per cent of the Mercedes-Benz racing budget was externally financed. For the year 1933/4, the Silver Arrows' debut season, the Nazi regime alone paid more than 40

RUDOLF CARACCIOLA

der erfolgreichste Rennfahrer der Welt

deutscher Meister und Europameister 1935 und 1937

auf

MERCEDES - BENZ

Not quite as it seems. This photograph (above) of Rudolf Caracciola celebrating his victory at the German Grand Prix in 1937 was doctored by Mercedes-Benz marketing staff into a revised version (left) that was much more suitable for those brown-tinged days. (Daimler AG)

per cent of the Untertürkheim racing division's total costs of 2.2 million RM. Incidentally, Kissel fails to mention the additional income in the form of starting money and winners' bonuses from the race organisers. Here, the appearances outside Germany were particularly lucrative because they brought in foreign currency. This was money with which the two competing companies could pay their star foreign drivers and at the same time circumvent the rigid currency restrictions imposed by the Nazi regime. However, as a source of finance it began to dry up gradually in the late 1930s, since, faced with the overwhelming superiority of the Silver Arrows, fewer and fewer foreign clubs and organisers were willing to stage races under the Grand Prix formula of the time, merely to provide a propaganda platform and financial rewards for German motorsport.

As to the level of Nazi subsidies, both companies were in fact in a position to make common cause and to keep each other informed about their requirements. At all events, on 1 March 1935, after reaching agreement by telephone, Kissel sent von Oertzen a copy of his letter to Hühnlein. Three days later von Oertzen sent Kissel a copy of his own begging letter, 'for the same confidential treatment', which he had sent to the NSKK leader the same day: 'Up to the end of 1934 we have spent the massive sum of 2,219, 428 RM on our racing cars.' Interestingly enough, this sum matches pretty closely the 2.2 million RM that Kissel claimed as expenditure by Daimler-Benz AG. However, up to the end of 1934 Auto Union had received significantly less than the Untertürkheimers, namely 692,857 RM. To this we can add a further 260,000 RM from unspecified accessory suppliers and event organisers, 'so that we received 954,857 RM from outside sources, while in the year 1933/4 we spent 1,273,571 RM from our own pocket.' Von Oertzen told Hühnlein that the expenditure for the coming 1935 season would be around 1.95 million RM, and Kissel had named a figure of 2.1 million RM.

There was an equally similar ring to the doleful justifications by the directors for the assistance that was so urgently needed: 'You, my esteemed *Korpsführer*, know what tasks our company has been set, by you and other ministers, which we have to carry out in addition to our normal business and the manufacture of our regular range of models. You also know that Auto Union, as a core German enterprise, is particularly required to resist the pressure exercised by the power of American capital (Opel) and we have to defend our position as the purely German contender in the small-car class.' Von Oertzen, as a man with a Jewish wife, writes with an awareness of what was expected at that time.

Kissel strikes a similarly plaintive note of a suffering national company committed to motor racing – at a time when Daimler-Benz AG had just rounded off the financial year 1934 with the best results in the company's history: 'If it is in fact right in principle that we shoulder some of the

Adolf Hitler arriving at the NSKK's 1935 Führer rally in Coburg, accompanied by Adolf Hühnlein. (Reuss)

burden ourselves, we ask you nevertheless to understand that, in view of our other loss-making assignments, we can only do so to a limited degree. We take the liberty of pointing out that, first and foremost, our branch of industry and our company are rightly being asked to increase our exports extraordinarily steeply, though this causes us considerable and rising losses. The business situation in our industry can be described as reasonably good, thanks to the encouragement received from the Reich government, but in particular from our *Führer* and Chancellor, Adolf Hitler. However, the fact cannot be ignored that we have to set our prices so keenly that they only permit a very minimal profit, and a series of other considerable cost factors which strongly influence the profit-and-loss account are unavoidable.'

The fact that right into the first phase of the war the two groups brazenly asked for and received subsidies and bonuses from the Nazi state was deliberate, and was built into their calculations. As the Romans used to say: *Do ut des!* ('I give that you may give!'). Or to put it more crudely, you scratch my back and I'll scratch yours. No one hands out subsidies without getting something in return. Both sides profit. From government contracts as much as from government subsidies, from German racing successes as much as from nationalist propaganda. The deals were mutually beneficial.

The lure of big money

In the spring of 1933 quite a few top managers in motorsport were still hesitating about which company offered the better prospects. Daimler-Benz's chief executive Wilhelm Kissel sensed danger from their Saxon competitor and set up a cost-heading for prominent personnel in the account recently created for government subventions: 'As is well known, Herr Neubauer was to be engaged by Auto Union. In view of our intention to participate in major races we had to retain Herr Neubauer at all costs, which was only possible if we promised him a correspondingly higher salary and other benefits. The difference between what Herr Neubauer was previously earning, and what he now receives from us, is also to be entered in the racing car account as an exceptional expenditure. The same also applies to Herr Walb.' Yet a month earlier, on 27 March 1933, the same Willy Walb, number two after Alfred Neubauer in the Untertürkheim racing division, had in the utmost secrecy signed a contract with Auto Union. The ex-racing driver, then 43 years old, could look forward to a monthly salary

Three men once employed in the cause of the three-pointed star. From left, Ferdinand Porsche,
Willy Walb and Hans Stuck enjoy their Auto Union victory at the German Grand Prix in
1934. (Audi AG)

of 750 RM plus expenses of 100 RM, and in addition a lucrative promise
that he could collect 5 per cent of all starting money, winners' bonuses and
suppliers' bonuses.

Yet the very next day doubts were assailing Auto Union's recently
widowed race manager-in-waiting. After all, first Benz and then Daimler-
Benz had been his livelihood for the past 20 years: 'Not least due to the
pangs of conscience I feel towards [...] my company, I have suffered a
nervous breakdown which makes it impossible for me to take on the
proposed assignment,' Walb told Auto Union in a letter dated 28 March
1933. A day later he sent in a doctor's certificate and in an accompanying
letter asked the company 'no longer to count on my joining. My physical
and mental condition makes it impossible for me in future to perform
the activities of the kind you have planned for me.' Even so, Auto Union
managed to put the widower's mind at rest. However, due to his notice-
period with Daimler-Benz Walb said he was unable to move to Zwickau in
any case before 1 July. So on 2 May, the day when the Nazis broke up the

labour unions and staff associations, a dramatic scene may well have been played out in the Daimler-Benz chief executive's office in Untertürkheim. For hardly had Kissel sent a memo round establishing that for racing expenses Messrs Neubauer and Walb 'are to be entered under the same code-number 9210010', than the latter handed in his notice.

Before anyone talks of treason or the unfortunate Walb's Thirty Pieces of Silver, it should not be forgotten that even as early as 1933 motor racing was not just about victory and honour but chiefly about power, and still more about large sums of money. For the second half of 1933 and the first half of 1934 the newly appointed racing manager received a pay-packet of 20,581 RM, of which 10,200 RM, or rather less than half, was his salary and the remainder was made up of bonuses! But Walb's opposite number at Daimler-Benz was at least his equal in business acumen: on 29 July 1937 and again on 14 September that year, Alfred Neubauer demanded more money. On 20 October Kissel turned him down, reminding Neubauer of the miserable 1936 season, when Mercedes-Benz was so uncompetitive that for a time it pulled out of racing altogether: 'Despite the unfavourable outcome of the races in the past year your income still came to nearly 25,000 RM – a remuneration which, measured against that received by other men who have made an outstanding contribution to the development of our racing cars, must be described as extremely generous. You must not forget that in the past year, due to the poor results, our drivers have had lower incomes. Thanks to the profit-sharing extended to you, you will specifically gain from the successes. The racing division performed well this year, which means that you will achieve the maximum income promised to you – 30,000 RM. However, this year we cannot also pay you, in addition to that, the sums you earned last year.'

In drawing an interim conclusion, we should not forget the exorbitantly higher earnings of the top drivers – three to five times what a racing manager like Neubauer earned – and we can see that even in the spring of 1933 lavish rewards and bonuses were being handed out. This was not least in expectation of the financial boons that the Nazi regime was planning to dispense very soon. To that extent the racing divisions of both corporations seem to have been a faithful reflection of the new Germany, which was demanding protection by the new men in power to such an extent that, in order to fend off the opportunists, Hitler and his henchmen placed an embargo on new membership of the Nazi Party from 1 May 1933. At that point in time it had some 2.5 million members, of whom about 1.6 million had only joined since 30 January that year.

The first fatality of a new era

Whereas in the spring of 1933 Auto Union could only present Porsche's plans, Mercedes-Benz had a tangible opportunity to demonstrate to the leaders of the new state, as well as to the upstarts from Saxony, the meaning of decades of racing experience. Two Mercedes-Benz SSKs with streamlined bodywork were to compete for the prize in the international AVUS Race on 21 May. Manfred von Brauchitsch was driving the same car as last year, whose cladding gleamed in the same silver as in that victorious race. However, after Rudolf Caracciola's serious accident in Monte Carlo a new man had to be put behind the wheel of the second, white-painted SSK. For this role, Neubauer brought the 44-year-old Otto Merz out of retirement. True, this old hand from Swabia had not raced for nearly two years, but there was no one else

Manfred von Brauchitsch (left), Alfred Neubauer and Otto Merz with the silver-coloured Mercedes-Benz SSK streamliner at the AVUS in 1933. This is one of the last photographs of the Swabian bear, Merz, before he crashed fatally during practice. (Daimler AG)

available. This was a worrying symptom, for it meant that too few qualified home-grown candidates would be found to drive Germany's future national racing cars. There was a delay in getting Merz's car ready and in mid-May the valiant veteran had to drive it from the Untertürkheim works to Berlin on its own wheels. The next day, in the first practice run for the AVUS Race, this long-serving Daimler-Benz works driver was fatally injured when his SSK skidded in the wet and turned over.

Merz's tragic death cast a shadow over the race, but was not a reason for Untertürkheim to withdraw its other car from the starting grid. There was too much at stake, for on the Sunday of the race the elite of the new regime had gathered in the VIP stand. Hitler was not actually present himself, so the honours were taken by Goebbels as Reich Minister of Propaganda, Göring, then Prime Minister of Prussia, and the Hohenzollern Prince August Wilhelm. Known as 'Auwi', the fourth son of the exiled Kaiser wore the smart brown uniform of an *Oberführer* or general in the SA.[7] The three men raised their right arms in unison and joined in singing the Horst Wessel Song as the swastika flag was hoisted. In future the flag business and the parade of the NSKK troops would be even more impeccable, as would the enthusiastic response of the spectators. But the international guests at the race were already receiving a foretaste of how the Nazis would make propaganda capital in the supposedly non-political and fraternal arena of sport in Germany. Even Ernst Udet flew in as though taking part in one of Arnold Fanck's mountain adventure movies. It only needed Leni Reifenstahl to appear for the illusion to be complete.[8]

The first big racing spectacle under the swastika got under way, yet embarrassingly Mercedes-Benz was unable to keep up the pace. After several tyre-bursts von Brauchitsch's silver SSK was beaten into sixth place, while for the first time in its history the AVUS Race was won by a foreign driver in a foreign-built car. The Italian Achille Varzi triumphed in a Bugatti at a record average speed of 206.9kph (128.6mph). What a disgrace for Untertürkheim! Yet what a blessing that only three days after the AVUS fiasco the glad and long-awaited tidings reached the board of Daimler-Benz AG from the Ministry of Transport at 80 Wilhelmstrasse, in Berlin. On 24 May Minister von Eltz-Rübenach approved 'a grant of 500,000 RM to support the building of new German racing car models.' In view of the difficult financial situation this sum could initially only be drawn 'in instalments, according to progress in building the cars'. These arrangements admittedly applied to Auto Union as well, but the Saxon motor group only pocketed 300,000 RM.

For the General Manager of Auto Union, Dr Richard Bruhn, this was no reason for annoyance, as he wrote on 29 May to Ferdinand Porsche: 'this means that we have received final confirmation of the success principally of our concerted approach to the Reich Chancellor, and we gladly take the opportunity once more to express to you our satisfaction at the success of our combined efforts, and at the fact that now, as far as the government is concerned, we have been *gleichgeschaltet* [Nazi jargon meaning 'co-ordinated along Nazi lines'] with our principal competitor with regard to the material support in the building of new German racing car models. Let us now strive with all our strength towards achieving with total success the goal that has been set, in which of course in a very special degree we are dependent on your unceasing and effective cooperation.' In his reply of 2 June Porsche also noted 'with great satisfaction' the *Gleichschaltung* with the competition.

On 30 May Daimler-Benz CEO Kissel immediately fired off several thank you letters to the government benefactors, signing off the one to the Reich Chancellor 'yours with the highest respect', and on the same day also informed Alfred Blinzig, who represented Deutsche Bank on the supervisory board of Daimler-Benz AG, in a confidential letter: 'Even if this message does not fully match our request [...] the decision nevertheless represents extraordinarily welcome support. We have thanked both the Reich Transport Minister and the Reich Chancellor for their decision; in addition, for the sake of courtesy, we have expressed our thanks to permanent secretary at the ministry, Dr Brandenburg, and to His Highness the Duke of Mecklenburg, President of the AvD, although we know both took the side of Auto Union.' And as for further financing, Kissel made it abundantly clear: 'We will endeavour to get as far as we can with the sum allotted to us, but will keep in mind the possibility of submitting a further request at the appropriate time, if further support proves necessary for the manufacture of the five vehicles we have in mind for future races.'

The wolf in sheep's clothing

As early as 28 May 1933, four days after Hitler's new government had dispatched its approval for financial aid, the elite of Germany's motorcycle

A perfect propaganda platform: Hermann Göring and his henchmen attending the Eifel Race in 1933. (Reuss)

riders and motor racing drivers took the track against international competition at the Nürburgring. The race became a stage for Nazi propaganda, even if the planned national racing cars were not even on the starting grid: 'This 11th Eifel Race was, however, more than a sporting event of the normal kind. The visit of Prussian Minister-President Göring turned it into a great day in sporting memory,' gushed writer Hans Bretz in the June 1933 issue of *Der Nürburgring*. 'It was the most glittering manifestation of the new Germany, which not only gave its guests a worthy reception, but at the same time offered them an opportunity to measure their strength against Germany's drivers and machines at an internationally famous venue, as proof of the fact that we are ready to live in peaceful competition with all nations and to vie for a better world order. And so, for the first time on this day, many thousands of new officials were seen. Everything was prepared to make this great day into one that was organisationally in the first rank! ADAC, Nürburgring administration, police, SA, SS and Stahlhelm had joined hands and in intelligent cooperation had done everything to celebrate the day in a worthy fashion. The fact that everything ran with such perfection, that it was possible to keep a hundred thousand spectators in a state of the greatest excitement for a whole day, and that it was possible to handle the arrival and departure of these great crowds without a hitch, is the best proof of the spirit of co-operation in all quarters, and once again a sign of the new Germany!'

And reporter Franz Guthausen, writing in the same ostensibly non-political magazine, described the final stages of the 1933 Eifel Race in these unambiguous terms: 'The mass of people crowding into the stands, on to the promenade and the terrace seats is still growing. It is five in the afternoon. Between the finishing line and the spare-parts stores that conceal the eager back-up teams, an SS *Sturm* has been standing as a guard of honour since this morning, without relief and with remarkable stamina, together with the band of the 28th SA *Standarte*. The interest of the spectators is half focused on the race itself but also on *the* event announced in the programme. A clear pointer to the way things have changed had already been given with the hoisting of the black, white and red swastika flag in the morning, by the one-minute silence in honour of Albert Leo Schlageter,[9] who died for Germany, and by the large number of brown shirts to be seen everywhere.'

No, right from the start motorsport in Nazi Germany was far from being non-political. With Schlageter, the 'Martyr of the Ruhr struggle' – who ten years earlier, almost to the day, had been executed by French occupation forces for sabotage and espionage, to public outrage in Germany – a bridge was being thrown across the gap between the 'Second Reich' of the Kaiser and the new 'Third Reich'. And thus, in front of more than 100,000 spectators at the Nürburgring, in the former Prussian province, the 'Day of Potsdam' was once more being re-enacted; the old elites of pre-1914 society and the new brown-shirted hordes were putting on a show of making common cause on the nation's behalf.[10] Only this time, in the Eifel mountains, it was Duke Carl Eduard of Saxe-Coburg-Gotha who appeared (in place of President Hindenburg), together with Consul Fritsch, sports chairman of the AvD, Major D. Döhmer (retired), general manager of Nürburgring GmbH, and the top echelons of German motorsport officialdom. They were there to stand shoulder to shoulder, not with the Reich Chancellor himself but the regime's number two, Hermann Göring, who at that time combined in his corpulent person the offices of Minister-President of Prussia, Reich Minister of Aviation and Reich Master of Hunting. He rolled up from Neuenahr in a Mercedes-Benz SS and headed for the starting and finishing line while the race was already in progress.

Göring was surrounded by an entourage of senior Nazi officials, quite a few of whom would be heard of again in the rearmament of Germany and the unleashing of the Second World War. There was the ambitious, industrious and intelligent Erhard Milch,[11] who, thanks to his experience as a fighter pilot and his links with industry, was appointed Deputy Reich Commissioner for Aviation as soon as the Nazis came to power. Since May 1933 he had been Permanent Secretary in the ministry and a paid-up member of the NSDAP. Göring was also accompanied by Colonel Walter von Reichenau,[12] a senior official in the Army Ministry. In 1941, as a Field Marshal in Russia, he described the slaughter of the Jews of Kiev by the SS, as well as the bloody crimes of his own troops, as 'the necessity of a harsh but just penalty paid by the subhuman Jews.'

Who knows the names and functions of all those top civilians and military brass who attended the 11th International Eifel Race with Göring on that day in May 1933? They were the cream of German society, as well as provincial heads of government and assemblymen, regional prefects, senior civil servants, burgomasters, and numerous former fighter pilots – in short, the old elites who had made common cause with the new wielders of power.

After the race Göring mounted the podium at the finishing line and addressed the spectators: 'You must have recognised how the new Germany is more intense and passionate about sport, and especially motorsport,' he boomed, while his words were being simultaneously transmitted on national radio. 'This event is valuable to the new Germany because we have been able to show that the things people are saying about us are not true. It can be seen that those Germans who slander us from beyond our borders have no right to speak in the name of Germany. Our guests will have become aware that ours is a Germany in which every individual looks again into a more peaceful future, that the country is experiencing an internal springtime. The people of Germany desire peaceful competition.'

The example of Fascism

There was a reason why Göring might have been happy to live with an Italian victory in the Eifel Race. Tazio Nuvolari won in an Alfa Romeo, which had been entered by the Italian state motor corporation under the guise of the private company Scuderia Ferrari. Its owner, Enzo Ferrari, was to join the Fascist party the following year, 1934, and collect the honorific title of *Commendatore*.

It was no coincidence that Mussolini's Fascists had been quick to integrate motorsport successes into their own political propaganda. In the *Duce*'s Italy, over 300 miles of new trunk roads had been built by the early 1930s, including the first four-lane motorways – and that at a time when there were scarcely 170,000 private cars in the whole of the country. In 1930, to protect the tightly controlled Italian motor industry, import tariffs were doubled. And Mussolini made money available to the sports car maker Alfa Romeo, to enter cars in Grand Prix races. Thanks

Motor racing Mussolini-style. Tazio Nuvolari, winner of the 1938 Italian Grand Prix at Monza, is accompanied by Signore Furmanik and other smartly uniformed fascists. No, Nuvolari wasn't under arrest… (Sebastian)

to the Fascists motorsport would soon be a national mission in Italy, and in 1927 Mussolini himself had been godfather to the Mille Miglia. The 'Thousand Miles' across the length and breadth of Italy on public roads, starting and finishing at Brescia, was rapidly becoming the most spectacular and important long-distance race in the world. Year after year, the government of the *Duce* made 25,000 troops available to police the big event. Mussolini's son-in-law, Count Ciano, sponsored and presented a cup at another racing spectacle staged at Montenero, near Livorno. The flying ace Italo Balbo, formerly one of the strategists of Mussolini's 'March on Rome', had subsequently fallen from favour with the *Duce*, and was dispatched in 1934 to be governor of Libya, then an Italian colony. Once there he set about organising a new motor race, the Gran Premio di Tripoli, long remembered by his countrymen back home.

Achille Varzi and, particularly, Tazio Nuvolari were national idols in an Italy that was turning both hero-worship and the cult of technology, much in the style of the Futurists, into instruments of Fascist domination. The celebrated Italian poet Gabriele D'Annunzio personified the macho posing of the Fascist dictatorship. Born in 1863, he was the bard of heroic nihilism in the mould of Friedrich Nietzsche, and at the same time an aesthete whose sophistication was only matched by his militancy. At Mussolini's side, he agitated for a Fascist coup in Rome, for which the *Duce* later expressed his gratitude in the form of cash, decorations and the title of 'prince'. So it was only logical that Nuvolari, Italy's most heroic racing driver, would sometimes be invited to national 'summit' meetings in the poet's villa, 'Il Vittoriale', on the shores of Lake Garda. In any case, before and after his races D'Annunzio regularly sent Nuvolari telegrams of encouragement and congratulation couched in floridly poetic language. At the encounters on Lake Garda this degenerated into a kind of initiation-ritual when, for example, on 28 April 1932 Nuvolari received D'Annunzio's personal command to go and win the Targa Florio race in Sicily. This was accompanied by a photo of the poet with a personal dedication to Nuvolari, 'the Mantuan of good stock'.

Needless to say, he won the 1932 Targa Florio and for the rest of his life, whenever he raced, would wear as a talisman a brooch in the shape of a tortoise. It was a miniature reproduction of a personal good luck charm which the poet had bequeathed to him as a kind of testimony of honour from one hero to another. It was engraved with the words: 'The slowest creature for the fastest racing driver'. Nuvolari loyally kept and cherished the golden tortoise, and even had replicas made, which he handed out to close friends.

Nuvolari and D'Annunzio were two poets of very different, though not entirely dissimilar, professions. Both worked in the service of the nation, and thus of the Fascists – such as when, for propaganda purposes, the Duce was allowed to pose for press photographers sitting in Nuvolari's victorious Alfa Romeo. Being Italian, the Fascists placed a lot of importance on *bella figura*, always anxious to make a grandiose impression. But in this, as in everything else, they would fail in just as spectacular a fashion as their later, far more brutal, counterparts in Hitler's Reich. Yet it was precisely these grossly exaggerated gestures of power that made Italian Fascism the model for the aesthetically far more amateurish Nazis. The NSDAP chieftains also honoured battle and victory, paid tribute to futuristic technology, and yet at heart were sworn enemies of the modern – which, ironically, they attempted to suppress with the methods of contemporary culture, that is to say, with highly sophisticated techniques of mass-manipulation. It was a strange brew, whose intoxicating effect clouded any sober assessment of the actual circumstances. By worshipping and taking ownership of German racing heroes and German engineering skills, motorsport offered the Nazis the ideal platform from which to present themselves, at moments of glory, as successful and progressive shapers of the new Germany and, alongside the triumphant German drivers and their unbeatable racing cars, to parade as victors on the stage of history.

But for the moment that point had not been reached. Germany's four-wheeled miracle weapons were still just pipe dreams, drawings and blueprints in Stuttgart and Zwickau. The international scene was still dominated by the Italians; which was why, for lack of victorious new German national racing cars, the German Grand prix scheduled for July 1933 was cancelled at short notice. Another reason was that its organising body, the AvD, had been Nazified. Henceforth, the new 'Supreme National Sports Authority' (*Oberste Nationale Sportbehörde* or ONS) acted as the organiser of all motor races in Germany.

The ideology of the street fighters

The man who from the outset acted as president of the state-run ONS was the head of the NSKK, Adolf Hühnlein, who, logically, gave himself the title of 'Leader of German Motor Sport'. In 1933 Hühnlein centred the nation's motorsport activities totally on the spectacular '2,000 Kilometres Through Germany' rally. This was a kind of German Mille Miglia, only on a larger and more extravagant scale, starting on 22 July in the – by German standards – highly sophisticated spa and casino resort of Baden-Baden. Within extremely tight time limits, the race was run at a breakneck pace along public roads across the length and breadth of the Reich. Depending on the class of car or motorcycle, average speeds in the range of 80–100kph (50–62mph) were required continuously over 20 to 34 hours, through the checkpoints in Stuttgart, Ulm, Augsburg, Munich, Nuremberg, Bayreuth, Hof, Chemnitz, Dresden, Berlin, Magdeburg, Braunschweig (Brunswick), Hamelin, Cologne, Nürburgring, Kaiserslautern, Mannheim and back to Baden-Baden. It was a gruelling race that ended in disaster for many: only 103 out of 176 cars, 81 out of 212 motorcycles and just four out of 35 sidecar teams reached the finish under qualifying conditions. *Korpsführer* Hühnlein praised the spirit of the '2,000 Kilometres' racers: 'These men have achieved something superhuman. The true spirit of the Motor SA was alive, the spirit that fights selflessly for the sake of honour. We need

Hühnlein expecting great things to happen during practice for the AVUS Race in 1934. (Perckhammer)

these tough, eager young sportsmen, who submit themselves and their machines to the most severe and rigorous tests when it is a matter of revealing Germany's strength and workmanship to the world.'

Anyone with eyes and ears in motorsport could tell what was brewing in this new Germany. In the past week, since the 'Law against the formation of new parties', the German Reich had become a one-party state. The NSDAP had a monopoly – and the mood of the bulk of the population was on its side. At the '2,000 Kilometres' the top echelons of the German motor industry were represented alongside the enthusiastic Nazi officials, and all of them sent works teams on this lunatic race which, due to the expense of organising it and the high accident rate, would in the end only be held twice. And naturally enough those racing drivers turned up who would later compete in the Silver Arrows, and in so doing some would sacrifice their lives for company and country.

One of these was the seasoned Ernst Henne, born in 1904, who broke the world absolute land speed record for the first time in 1929, and then again in 1930, 1932, 1936 and 1937. Driving a BMW he first reached 216.75kph (134.71mph) and finally touched 279.5kph (173.71mph) – a record that would stand until 1951. In the absence of experienced German racing stars, Daimler-Benz signed up Henne for the 1934 season as an additional candidate for Untertürkheim's new national racing car. Auto Union entered the '2,000 Kilometres' with August Momberger (b.1905), Prince Hermann zu Leiningen (b.1901) and Ernst Günther Burgaller (b.1896), and would enter this trio, along with Hans Stuck, in its first Grand Prix, while the next generation of works drivers in the Saxon racing stable was already appearing in the qualifiers' list: Ernst von Delius (b.1912), Rudolf Hasse (b.1906), Uli Bigalke (b.1910) and Georg Meier (b.1910).

Auto Union's chief executive and Party member von Oertzen himself took the wheel of a Horch and reached the finish, as did the little DKW driven by the future head of the Saxon brigade of the NSKK, *Sturmbannführer* Paul Lein. This 34-year-old amateur driver and Nazi official had the job of organising the German Motorcycle Grand Prix at the Sachsenring circuit near Hohenstein-Ernstthal. And in order that German racing cars could, as soon as possible, run their home Grand Prix in Saxony, Lein successfully made a case for constructing the Grossdeutschlandring or 'Greater Germany Circuit' near Dresden. The Silver Arrows were meant to be there on the starting grid, for the first time, in July 1940. However, this was prevented by the outbreak of the Second World War, and Lein, who by then had been promoted to NSKK *Obergruppenführer*, was killed in the first days of the invasion of Poland, serving as an *Oberleutnant* in a panzer regiment.

A further Auto Union works car, a Wanderer, was driven under NSKK colours by Ferdinand Porsche's son Ferry (b.1909), who reached the finish inside the qualifying time. Another highly gifted young engineer named Rudolf Uhlenhaut (b.1906) was also known to be a talented racing driver and took the wheel of a Daimler-Benz works car licensed by the AvD; needless to say the company also placed works cars at the disposal of official NSKK units.

Someone else who obtained a company drive from Untertürkheim was that dashing sportsman SS-*Hauptsturmführer* Viktor Brack. A personal

Below left: BMW motorcycle ace Ernst Henne played a vivid, but short and accident-prone, part in the early period of the Mercedes-Benz Silver Arrows. (Daimler AG)

Below right: Porsche, father and son. Nazi Government subsidies to Auto Union secured the existence of Porsche's construction bureau at Stuttgart. Moreover, Hitler's benevolence and funding offered Porsche the freedom to do as he pleased – including, in the end, producing V2 rockets with slave labour. (Porsche AG)

friend and occasional chauffeur of Heinrich Himmler, Brack was soon to be promoted to 'Chief of Staff in the *Führer*'s Office' and in 1940 took over responsibility for the establishments where euthanasia was carried out on the mentally and physically handicapped. It was also under his auspices that the lethal gas, Zyklon B, was first used for the mass extermination of human beings. Brack had gathered the relevant experience from deploying mobile 'gas-vans', which was then put to use in the building of extermination camps in the east.[13] Following the trial of Nazi doctors at Nuremberg after the war, Brack was condemned to death by a US military tribunal and hanged on 2 June 1948 at the same Landsberg gaol where, 24 years previously, his equally car-mad *Führer* had taken advice from Jakob Werlin on the purchase of a new Benz car.

Thus the list of winners of the 1933 '2,000 Kilometres Through Germany' produces more than mere names and results; it awakens associations, points to connections, and can be read as a remarkable essence of the history of motorsport in Germany. On the roll of honour the future company chief is next to the up-and-coming Nazi criminal, along with men of distinction and those who kept their distance, collaborators and fellow-travellers, opportunists and those who acted from conviction. Certainly, not all these individuals can be tarred with the same brush, but they did have one thing in common – enthusiasm for motorsport. And for a few years this raging passion, this thrill, this masculinity ritual, brought together people who, in terms of birth and background, action and thought, were in many cases perhaps rather incongruous. In an age of great motorsporting success and long-awaited national renaissance after the shame of Versailles, it was difficult even for the contemporary public to tell what was mere play-acting and what was genuine conviction. The brown gravy of Nazi propaganda was being poured over all motorsporting activities. And now, when there were finally victories to be won, they all wanted to be there. As did almost everyone in a country where so many were so willing to believe that everything was going to get better.

The leader of the NSKK marches ahead

In June 1933, on Hitler's orders, SA *Obergruppenführer* Adolf Hühnlein separated the NSKK, which had existed since 1931, from the 'Motor Stormtroopers' and made it an independent Nazi organisation outside

No-one messed around with Adolf Hühnlein. Auto Union race director Dr Karl Feuereissen side by side with the Korpsführer at the German Grand Prix in 1936. Behind, Bernd Rosemeyer and Hans Stuck show delight at their first and second places for Auto Union, but after the race the track belonged to Hühnlein and his NSKK crew. (Kirchberg)

the SA. He immediately Nazified all the German drivers' associations and automobile clubs, with the eager ADAC at the head of the queue, and grouped them in a single *Deutsche Automobil-Club* (DDAC). In this way Hühnlein became the top man in the German motor world.

A former professional soldier, Hühnlein was born in 1881 in the town of Neustädtlein, Upper Franconia. In 1925 he joined the senior ranks of the SA, as a not-very-bright Party member but all the more loyal for that. With little gift for rhetoric, Hühnlein was known as a man of action, a quality that earned him the highest honours – from the 'Order of Blood' up to the Gold Medal of the Party. By the beginning of the war his NSKK numbered some 500,000 and was principally responsible for the motorised transport of war supplies and troop reinforcements to the front line.

Any member of the corps could obtain a driving licence free of charge. To provide the necessary instruction for 'male youth' Hühnlein set up the

NSKK's own driving schools with generous financial backing from the German motor industry. There, young men were instructed in the technology, use and repair of motorcycles and vehicles. Naturally, this had nothing to do with motor racing but was a paramilitary preparation for the war that would surely come. The *Motor-SA-Schule Nürburgring* was created in the Eifel

As a Jew, German motorcycle racer Leo Steinweg was obliged to abandon racing, and in 1945 he was murdered in a German concentration camp. (Reuss)

mountains as early as June 1933, as a model for more than a hundred other schools that would ultimately be run under NSKK auspices.

As president of the 'Supreme National Sports Authority for German Motoring', Adolf Hühnlein additionally controlled and directed all motor-sport throughout the German Reich, and represented a *de facto* state organisation among the world federations theoretically reserved for national associations engaged in motor car and motorcycle sports. Motor racing in Hitler's Reich was politicised and Hühnlein proved himself a capable Nazi. At a very early stage he introduced the 'Aryan Certificate', when, in the summer of 1933, the ONS sent out new application forms: in future no racing licences would be issued to 'Jews and other non-Aryans'.

Forced off the track and put to death

That meant the end of a sporting career for many drivers, among them Leo Steinweg from Münster, for this successful racer of DKW motorcycles was Jewish. It was on 1 April 1933 that he was forced to hang a sign in the window of his motorcycle shop, which read: 'Germans, don't buy from Jews!' In May of that year he won both the 175cc and 250cc classes at a race meeting in Elberfeld, but on the winners' podium he could not bring himself to raise his right arm in the Hitler salute. At first this refusal had no consequences; Steinweg continued to race, as his wife Emmy recalled, 'until July 1933, when he received the "Licence form for the practice of racing for the year 1934". It included the enquiry as to whether he was Aryan, and further questions. But that one question devastated him. He turned pale and passed the paper to me with trembling hands. I just saw the word *Arier*, and knew for certain that it meant he had to give up the profession he loved – and that was dreadful for him. He tore up the form and disappeared on his motorbike.'[14] It was the start of a long, agonising odyssey of flight and persecution, which led the Jewish motorcyclist into the maw of the Nazi extermination machine. Shortly before the end of the war Leo Steinweg was shot in the Flossenbürg concentration camp.

With an eye to the international laws of sport and foreign press reporting, the Nazi motorsport officials did not, in fact, impose their veto when 'non-German non-Aryans' were entered for the big international races at the Nürburgring or the AVUS. That is why, even as late as 23 July 1939, at the first and last Grand Prix of Greater Germany,[15] Frenchman René Dreyfus

Adolf Rosenberger, Porsche's Jewish financier, was arrested in 1935 and imprisoned at Kislau concentration camp, where this photograph was taken. (Reuss)

was able to drive his Delahaye to fourth place. And other prominent racing drivers of Jewish extraction, such as Guy Moll and Laszlo Hartmann, were allowed without objection to compete against the Silver Arrows. At the same time, however, Adolf Rosenberger, the one-time works driver for Mercedes-Benz and financier of Ferdinand Porsche, was forced to abandon once and for all his temporarily interrupted racing career.

A dispute over compensation

That is why, after the war, Rosenberger sued the German Federal republic for compensation – in the end without success. It made absolutely no difference that he could call on witnesses from the former Auto Union racing stable, who could prove that Hans Stuck was not the only driver to take his turn round the Nürburgring in the first test-drives of the new Grand Prix racing car, in November 1933. Alfred Rosenberger claimed that he had driven as well. And, what is more, only two seconds slower than the great Stuck! Supposing he had qualified? As a works driver, Rosenberger asserted, he could have earned over 100,000 RM. But Hühnlein's 'Aryan clause' and Nazi racial policy made it impossible for a German Jew to race in a Silver Arrow. Instead, Rosenberg was arrested on 5 September 1935 on a charge of 'racial disgrace', and from a police cell in Pforzheim was sent, on 23 September, direct to Kislau concentration camp. Four days later he was released and had to pay 53.40 RM in costs for this 'protective custody'.

Ferdinand Porsche and his son Ferry later insisted that they had made sure their former colleague was quickly released. Adolf Rosenberger disputes this: the only person to help him, he says, was Hans von Veyder-Malberg. He was the man who, after the Nazis seized power, took over Rosenberg's shares in the Porsche company when the Porsches forced their Jewish general manager out of the business. Rosenberger claims, with evidence, that at the time Veyder-Malberg was only acting as a frontman. According to Veyder-Malberg, Rosenberg did in fact cede his share of the business to Ferry Porsche by notarised contract on 30 July 1935. It would be more accurate to say that, because of his Jewish parentage, he was *forced* to sign over the shares.

On 30 November 1949 Adolf Rosenberger pursued an action before the Stuttgart District Court for the restitution of his shares. During the Nazi dictatorship the ex-racing driver had operated in London, Paris and elsewhere as the foreign representative of the Porsche company – with no commercial success, or so the lawyers for Ferdinand and Ferry Porsche claimed. Rosenberger riposted that this was due to the great inventor's defective designs and absence of patent rights.

As a Jew in the Nazi Germany of the mid-1930s he no longer had any legal leverage with which to protect himself against state-decreed injustice. The cinema that he owned in Pforzheim, as well as a house and some land, were 'Aryanised', and even assignments from Porsche dried up in the end. Was this because Rosenberger wasn't doing any business and was just costing money? That was, at all events, the case put by lawyers for the Porsche family, though they did admit that the Nazi authorities had put pressure on Porsche to part company with his Jewish employees. Was that in fact the case? Or had Porsche fired these staff members through over-eagerness to obey or even on his own initiative?

That is the claim made by Alan Arthur Robert, formerly Adolf Rosenberger. A few years after the end of the Second World War he returned to Germany and sought out the Porsches in Stuttgart. What did he want? Ferry Porsche claims that Rosenberger 'demanded that we should make a settlement for DM 200,000; and he wanted half of this sum to be paid back *under the counter*. He argued that the whole DM 200,000 could be set against tax, since it was a compensation payment. However, we found this proposal unacceptable, since it could make our company guilty of tax evasion. We agreed on a compromise. We gave him a new Volkswagen free of charge, and several thousand marks.' In the late 1970s, when Ferry Porsche published this version of events in a book, there was no one to contradict it. Alan Arthur Robert, a.k.a. Adolf Rosenberger, had already died in Los Angeles on 6 December 1967 at the age of 67.

We need to go back to the year 1949, when the Porsche/Piëch clan were once again riding high. Their exclusive little sports car based on the VW was selling extremely well in certain social circles. Scarcely two years had passed since Ferdinand Porsche had been released on bail from imprisonment in France. The Volkswagen, originally commissioned from him by Hitler, was now being mass-produced in Wolfsburg, in the former Fallersleben KdF factory.[16]

The KdF car, transformed into the VW 'Beetle', emerged as a bestseller – and brought in handsome royalties for the designer and his relatives. As at 21

The war is over but Dr Porsche's Volkswagen keeps on going. Even Adolf Rosenberger would get one, although in the end he lost his shares in the Porsche company. (Porsche AG)

June 1948, the trustees of the Allied Property Control organisation valued the Stuttgart-based Porsche company at DM 1,178,000. Yet, for the moment, the Porsche and Piëch families were not allowed to run the business themselves, since Adolf Rosenberger had resurfaced and instituted a legal action for compensation against the clan. He demanded 15 per cent of the company's shares, the proportion he had held before the Nazis took power.

For almost a year documents were exchanged, dates for a hearing set and then postponed. Rosenberger was living in the USA and the lawyers for the other side knew how to play for time. Medical files produced at the trial for the restitution of Rosenberger's 'Aryanised' property in Pforzheim show that for years the general manager of Porsche had been in ill-health. Alan Arthur Robert had cardiac problems. They resulted from a stroke, the cause of which his American doctor attributed to maltreatment in the Kislau concentration camp. However, in 1961 a German state prosecutor ruled this out with the help of 'expert evidence *in absentia*', provided by a medical specialist in Heidelberg on the basis of the available documents, without ever having seen the patient, let alone examined him.

So in 1949 Rosenberger may well have wondered how much time was left to him to enjoy the compensation proceeds that could only be obtained, if at all, after wearisome litigation in distant Germany. He had no heirs. His wife-to-be was, like him, 49 years old and childless. Her name was Anne, and she also hailed from Pforzheim. They had met in Porsche's Stuttgart drawing office, where she worked as a secretary. She too emigrated to the USA with her then husband, Berthold Metzger, who died in 1946. Four years later the widowed Anne Metzger married Adolf Rosenberger, now Alan Robert.

The couple do not appear to have had much money, or assets of any kind in the USA. He did odd jobs in a garage; his tax record shows a modest income year after year. When the compensation proceedings against Porsche finally got under way and the case was listed for 29 September 1950, before the Compensation Tribunal of the Stuttgart Provincial Court, the two parties agreed the same day to a settlement proposed by the court. Adolf Rosenberger received from Porsche the sum of DM 50,000 and a car; he could choose between a VW with luxury trim for immediate delivery, priced at DM 5,450, or, not later than 1 July 1951, a Porsche sports-car worth DM 9,850. With that, all Rosenberger's claims against the firm of Porsche were discharged.

Notes

1 The term *Märzgefallene* ('Casualties of March') was originally applied to the democratic revolutionaries of March 1848 who died in street fighting against the Prussian army. However, in 1933 it was the contemptuous name given by Nazi 'old campaigners' to the hordes of opportunistic new members who joined the Nazi Party once it was in power, following a massive rally held in Potsdam in March of that year. The rush to sign up as Nazis was so great that a temporary ban on new membership was imposed on 19 April.

2 Carl Eduard (a.k.a. Charles Edward), Duke of Saxe-Coburg-Gotha (1884–1954) was a grandson of Queen Victoria, being the only son of her eighth child, Leopold. Though born and educated in England, he was sent to Germany in 1900 to take up the vacant dukedom of Saxe-Coburg-Gotha (Prince Albert's family title). He served in the Imperial German Army in the First World War, and in 1917 was stripped of his title of Duke of Albany under the British Titles of Enemy Princes Act. In 1918 he was also deprived of his German dukedom, and joined the extreme right wing nationalists. He supported Ehrhardt (q.v.) and was an early National Socialist sympathiser, having met Hitler in 1922. In 1932 he backed Hitler's bid for the presidency, and in May 1933 joined the Nazi Party and the SA, in which, by 1936, he had reached the rank of *Obergruppenführer*, and held the same rank in the NSKK. Other posts he held included NSDAP Deputy in the Reichstag and President of the German Red Cross, which, under Nazism, carried out euthanasia. In 1946 he was arrested and imprisoned. At a Denazification Tribunal in 1950 he was classified as a fellow-traveller and fined 5,000 DM. He died of cancer in 1954, aged 70.

3 Audi AG: One of the constituent companies of Auto Union was Horch, which as well as being a surname is also the imperative form of the German verb *horchen*, meaning 'hark' or 'listen'. The equivalent verb in Latin, *audire*, has the imperative singular form *audi* – hence the name of the successful post-war German car company, which still sports the linked-circle badge of Auto Union.

4 Rudolf Hess (1894–1987) joined the German army in 1914 and was commissioned as a lieutenant in 1917, fighting on the Romanian front. In the spring of 1918 he transferred to the army's Flying Corps and trained as a fighter pilot. Though he saw very little action in the air he retained his flying skills, which explains how, in May 1941, he was able to take an aircraft without authorisation and fly all the way to Scotland, where he landed by parachute, supposedly with a peace plan to deliver to Churchill. This was shortly before Hitler's fateful invasion of Russia. It has never been established whether Hess acted entirely on his own initiative, though Hitler subsequently denounced him as a traitor. In 1946 Hess was condemned as a war-criminal to life imprisonment and he spent the rest of his days in Spandau prison, Berlin, where, at the age of 93, he apparently hanged himself.

5 The author has this to say about von Oertzen's testimony: 'Von Oertzen's statements in old age do not always appear strictly accurate. They are sometimes contradictory. For example, Hitler seems not to have remembered Porsche, whereas his son, Ferry Porsche, assures us that it was Hitler himself who mentioned a meeting with Ferdinand Porsche at the Solitude race in 1926 – a meeting that Porsche Sen. had apparently long since forgotten. In 1935 von Oertzen took over the Auto Union concession in South Africa. This was probably not just because of his 'non-Aryan' wife, but also because of a possible involvement in a bribery scandal in connection with the removal of the Danish founder of DKW, Rasmussen.'

6 Adolf Hühnlein (1881–1942) was a Bavarian career officer who commanded a company and later served on the Army General Staff in the First World War. After the war he joined the *Freikorps Epp* (see Chapter 2, Note 19) and participated in the crushing of the Munich Soviet and of communist groups in the Ruhr. He took part in Hitler's 1923 *putsch*, and from 1925 to 1930 was in charge of motor transport for the SA. In 1933 he was appointed head of the newly created NSKK, which he developed into a paramilitary organisation supporting the *Wehrmacht*. On his death he received a state funeral and was posthumously awarded the *Deutscher Orden*, the highest decoration of the Third Reich.

7 Prince August Wilhelm of Prussia (1887–1949) – not to be confused with his elder brother, Crown Prince Wilhelm – had to abandon his royal position in 1919 after the abdication and exile of his father

the Kaiser. He went into banking. From 1927 he was a member of the *Stahlhelm*, a right-wing army veterans' association. He joined the NSDAP in 1930 and the SA in 1932. In the years up to Hitler's seizure of power, the prince was instrumental in gathering support for him in conservative and royalist circles. He received the Gold Medal of the Nazi Party but played no part in the war. He was interned in May 1945 and was condemned in 1948 to 30 months in a labour camp.

8 Ernst Udet (see Chapter 2, Note 6) found employment in the early 1930s as a stunt pilot in a series of popular mountain adventure films by Arnold Fanck, with titles like *Storm over Mont Blanc*, in which he usually rescued a pretty girl, invariably played by Leni Riefenstahl – before she switched to a more successful career behind the camera.

9 Albert Schlageter was a saboteur active in the industrial Ruhr district, which French and Belgian troops occupied in 1923 when Germany fell behind with its post-war reparation payments. In May 1923 Schlageter was arrested, summarily tried and executed by the French authorities. At first it was the Communists who opportunistically hailed him as a martyr, but later the Nazis adopted him as an icon of German nationalism.

10 In 1815, as part of the settlement at the end of the Napoleonic Wars, Prussia – then still a small but militarily sophisticated kingdom in north-eastern Germany – acquired the Rhineland territory, which soon became the heartland of German industry. In 1871, having defeated France in a brief but devastating war, the King of Prussia proclaimed himself emperor (*Kaiser*) of the whole of Germany, and the Second Reich was created which lasted until 1918. After the abdication of Kaiser Wilhelm II that year the other, lesser, monarchies in Germany (Saxony, Bavaria, Baden, Württemberg) also disappeared, though the individual states continued to enjoy considerable independence. This is why, in the 1930s, Prussia still had its own government, finances, police force etc.

11 Erhard Milch (1892–1972) had a Jewish father but was 'Aryanised' through a statement from his mother that another man was his natural father. After flying in the First World War he went to work for the aircraft firm of Junkers. In 1929 he became chief executive of Lufthansa and in 1935 was appointed Inspector General of the new Luftwaffe. During the Spanish Civil War he controlled the notorious Condor Legion, and in the Battle of Britain commanded an Air Fleet based in Scandinavia. He succeeded Ernst Udet as the Luftwaffe's Director of Armaments, but later Göring saw him as a rival and sidelined him. At Nuremberg he was sentenced to life imprisonment, but was released in 1954.

12 Walter von Reichenau (1884–1942) was an ambitious army officer who, unlike many of his colleagues, was always strongly pro-Nazi. He commanded the 10th Army in the invasion of Poland, and the 6th Army in the invasion of Belgium and France, being promoted to Field Marshal in 1940. In the 1941 Russian campaign he issued orders for the mass killing of Jews that would almost certainly have earned him a death-sentence at Nuremberg, had he not been killed in an air crash in 1942.

13 The author is stretching a point here. The gas-trucks organised by Brack used carbon monoxide piped straight from the engine into the sealed rear compartment of the vehicle. This proved too slow and too small-scale a method of killing, which was why the lethal substance Zyklon B was introduced as a more effective means of committing mass-murder.

14 Quoted from Emmy Herzog, *Leben mit Leo: Ein Schicksal im Nationalsozialismus* ('Life with Leo: A Destiny under Nazism'), Münster, 2000.

15 'Greater Germany' (*Grossdeutschland*) was the name given to German Reich territory from 1938 onwards, which by then included Austria and the ethnic German Sudetenland region of Czechoslovakia.

16 KdF stood for *Kraft durch Freude* ('Strength Through Joy'). It was a scheme which used funds seized by the Nazis from labour unions to finance holiday-camps, cruises, sport and entertainment for factory workers. It soon became a major commercial enterprise that, among other things, subsidised the development of the Volkswagen.

CHAPTER FOUR

FOLLOWING
THE LEADER

After 1933, any German who wanted to participate internationally in motorsport had to belong to either the NSKK or another National Socialist organisation. The only exemptions were for those serving in the police or the Wehrmacht. For a personality like Georg 'Schorsch' Meier, the outstanding BMW motorcycle racer and part-time works driver for Auto Union, this requirement was of no small significance at the time: 'I was already a successful cross-country rider when I transferred from the police to the Wehrmacht, and then when I started winning road races they all said "come and join the Party or the NSKK", but I always said no and was happy to stay in the Wehrmacht – as a plain ordinary sergeant who was given leave to race with BMW and Auto Union. True, right through the war they never promoted me, so by 1945 I must have been the most senior sergeant in the whole Wehrmacht. But I think I did the right thing.'

With the exception of Meier, all the top German racing drivers joined a National Socialist organisation. Bernd Rosemeyer, the best and most popular driver of that era, was a member of the SS, as were the successful freelance drivers Bobby Kohlrausch and Huschke von Hanstein. The majority of the other motorsport idols joined the NSKK. In retrospect the National Socialist Corps of Drivers has often been represented as a 'fairly non-political association of motorsports enthusiasts'. Not a few have claimed ironically that the initials NSKK stood for *'Nur Säufer, keine Kämpfer'* ('Just Boozers, Not Fighters'), and in doing so try to take the edge off the Nazi ideology of Hühnlein and his henchmen.

Rudolf Caracciola meeting Hitler in 1938 at the annual parade of German racing drivers and their machines in front of the Reich Chancellery in Berlin. (Reuss)

During the Nazi era, none of the courageous but opportunistic German racing drivers dared to say anything openly critical of NSKK-Führer Hühnlein and his henchmen, but after the war they admitted that he was a ridiculous character. (Reuss)

This interpretation left its mark, especially after 1945, in the correspondingly lenient sentences of the Denazification Tribunals, to the extent that a senior rank in the NSKK was always taken to be the sign of a fellow-traveller rather than something more sinister; and the later a case was heard – or in some cases the longer it lasted – the more likely NSKK membership was to lead to an acquittal. The Nuremberg war crimes trials had unwittingly reinforced this approach in Denazification hearings by not classing the NSKK – nor, incidentally, the SA or the mounted SS – as criminal organisations. This assessment by the International Court may have been made principally for procedural reasons, since the main task of the tribunal was, of course, to investigate and indict the leading war criminals. Nonetheless, it led to the judgement that the NSKK was pretty much a playground for harmless car and motorbike buffs. Only in recent years has this viewpoint been substantially corrected.

The NSKK played a prominent part in the crimes committed against the Jewish population in what became notorious as the *Reichskristallnacht*.[1]

During the war it was responsible not only for the logistics of transport and supply but also, in conjunction with police battalions, handled the 'pacification of the hinterland in the east'. This deceptively mild formulation conceals among other things the operations of NSKK units that, under the guise of 'auxiliary police', took part in the deportation and execution of Jews, first in Poland and later in Russia and the Ukraine. Documents held in the Central Office for Administration of Provincial Justice in Ludwigsburg prove that Adolf Hühnlein, in his preface to the NSKK souvenir book *Wir waren mit in Polen* ('We did our bit in Poland'), was anticipating Nazi war crimes as early as the spring of 1940: 'It has never been our style in the NSKK to sit on our hands and do nothing until an assignment falls like a ripe fruit into our lap. When we have to get stuck into the fray, the Corps is there with the old fighting spirit. So it was only natural that the NSKK did its bit in Poland like the rest, and in the liberated provinces and the *Generalgouvernement*[2] we showed our mettle in carrying out our assignments.'

Fellow travellers and profiteers

After 1945 the racetrack heroes, even if not involved in such crimes, would conscientiously play down the role of the NSKK and its leader Hühnlein, to say nothing of their own conduct. Yet almost without exception they had been members of the NSKK – as had been the man who would later become Federal Chancellor, Kurt Georg Kiesinger, the defence minister from Bavaria, Franz-Josef Strauss, the magazine publisher Franz Burda, the classical historian Alfred Heuss, the political theorist Theodor Eschenburg and many other highly respected Germans. Is this because the NSKK was so 'harmless'? Or was it not because cars and motorcycles, motorsport and male bonding attracted the most adventurous sons of the upper and lower-middle class to follow the NSKK banner? Anti-Semites and Nazis, dignitaries and nonentities, young and old were united in their fascination for technology and German motor racing victories. It is even possible that such shared enthusiasms and overlapping interests may have undermined the 'moral resistance' which the supposedly 'better circles' swore to uphold, though even that claim was often an empty one.

The heroes of German motorsport thus found themselves in the best of company. And those who wanted to compete in races probably did not have many reservations about Nazism. The important thing was to be one of the

The same procedure occurred every year: the podium at the German Grand Prix in 1939, Caracciola and Hühnlein saluting their Sieg Heil!, the grand finale of the Nazi opera at the Nürburgring. The silver racing cars and the uniformed Nazi troopers were part of the same show. (Daimler AG)

winners. More than six decades after his races during the Nazi dictatorship, Paul Pietsch admitted: 'I was just another member of the NSKK. It was only later that I said to myself: You're doing yourself no good, my lad. Then I went off to Italy and did a lot of driving there for Maserati.'

True, Pietsch was not in the first rank of German Silver Arrow drivers. In the 1935 racing season he was in fact a works driver for Auto Union, but was then – due to his lack of success – forced to drive privately again before making a spectacular appearance for Maserati in the first German Grand prix at the Nürburgring in 1939, and once again attracting the attention of Mercedes-Benz and Auto Union. But in this way Pietsch was spared from the regular promotions within the NSKK that were linked to success on the circuit.

The Nazi-controlled German press, however, was obliged to take these NSKK ranks very seriously and always to mention them when reporting on motorsport, so as to indicate clearly for *whose* fame and honour the drivers were racing from success to success. Where today a particular sponsor might be mentioned, the last pre-war race in the European Championship, the Swiss Grand Prix on 20 August 1939, was, for example, won by NSKK-*Hauptsturmführer* Lang, ahead of NSKK-*Staffelführer* Caracciola, NSKK-*Sturmführer* von Brauchitsch and NSKK-*Truppführer* Müller.

One man who at that time adhered to, or was forced to adhere to, this contemporary nomenclature was the influential Berlin journalist Siegfried Doerschlag, who as early as June 1932 founded his 'DDD' (*Der Doerschlag Dienst*), a news and PR service for transport and the world of motoring that continued to flourish right through the Nazi period. On 27 October 1946 Doerschlag wrote, in a letter of mitigation for von Brauchitsch's Denazification tribunal: 'If Manfred von Brauchitsch is said to have been a Nazi from 1933 onwards, then by the same token all the great racing drivers, Caracciola, Rosemeyer, Stuck, Lang, Hasse, von Delius etc were more or less *compulsorily* forced to join the NSKK, and then after each victory were ceremoniously *promoted* by *Korpsführer* Hühnlein in front of thousands of spectators at the finishing-line. [...] What they were thinking to themselves was a very different matter.' In Doerschlag's opinion the politically flexible conduct of the racing drivers could be explained by the 'the psychosis of

A hero's welcome at Untertürkheim: Manfred von Brauchitsch arrives at the Daimler-Benz factory after his victory in the Eifel Race of 1934. (Daimler AG)

the Hühnlein era and the boom in motor racing.' By way of straightforward exoneration, he told von Brauchitsch: 'Of course there was a dictatorship in sport too, and a top driver like you had to howl with the wolves.'

All the same, some may have howled rather louder than others. And they may have even done so not just as a consciously calculated ploy, but even for a while, perhaps, out of an inner conviction. From all appearances, Manfred von Brauchitsch was one of the latter. Descended from minor nobility in northern Germany, he had joined the 'Ehrhardt Brigade' as a pioneer in 1923, long before the start of his racing career. In 1920 this semi-legal militia unit took part in the counter-revolutionary coup against the fledgling Weimar Republic, as well helping to crush Communist uprisings. The brigade was named after its leader, *Korvettenkapitän* (Lieutenant-Commander) Hermann Ehrhardt, who went on to found the extreme right-wing secret league 'Organisation Consul', responsible for the assassinations of the leading centrist politician Matthias Erzberger and the Foreign Minister Walther Rathenau.

Von Brauchitsch owed it to a motorcycling accident that he did not opt for the career of an army officer like his uncle Walther von Brauchitsch, who, under Hitler, rose to the rank of Field Marshal and commander-in-chief of the army. Walther von Brauchitsch's career may have been helped by the fact that Hitler persuaded his first wife to divorce him, and even paid the costs of the court proceedings. This left the top army man free to make an honest woman of his mistress, an enthusiastic Nazi named Charlotte Rüpper. Thanks to his uncle's close connections with the Nazi regime, Manfred von Brauchitsch, by now a professional racing driver, enjoyed quasi-military privileges – even after 1933 he was allowed *not* to join the NSDAP – and could thus remain completely 'non-political'. The racing driver did, however, join the NSKK so that he could continue to indulge his passion for speed.

Just a year older than von Brauchitsch, Robert 'Bobby' Kohlrausch, from a wealthy middle-class family, also joined a *Freikorps*, but in contrast to Brauchitsch young Robert admitted to having been there when his unit went into action against the 'political enemy': 'In the Communist troubles of 1919–22 I was a part-time volunteer in Eisenach, and during the Spartacist revolt I belonged to the Marburg students' *Freikorps*, which liberated Thuringia from the Spartacists.' Shortly afterwards,

Though very much a journeyman racer, former Freikorps fighter Robert 'Bobby' Kohlrausch described himself as 'the most successful SS driver in German motorsport', overlooking the fact that Bernd Rosemeyer had joined the SS in 1932. Kohlrausch managed to survive the Second World War and, post-war, continued to drive racing cars in East Germany. (Reuss)

Kohlrausch continued his professional education in technical colleges and universities, working between times as a motorcycle test engineer at the Wanderer factory in Chemnitz, where he immediately discovered a new hobby which, like his *Freikorps* missions, demanded everything of a chap: 'During my student years I was very successful in motorsport and took part in motorcycle competitions in 1923–1929. From 1929 to the present I have been driving cars in races, cross-country and endurance events and have managed to win about 90 first prizes in national and international competitions.' From December 1923 Kohlrausch was NSDAP member no. 209008 and in his CV, dated 12 February 1936, he made the claim: 'This makes me the most successful SS driver in German motorsport.'

A very special case
In saying this, SS-*Untersturmführer* Kohlrausch, as he then was, carefully failed to mention the fact that Bernd Rosemeyer, five years younger but equal in rank, was already driving in Grand Prix races for Auto Union, and at the end of the 1935 season, on 29 September in Brno, actually came first in the Czech Grand Prix. Rosemeyer was soaring to the position of being the greatest sporting idol of German youth. With his cool, devil-may-care style, 'blond Bernd' captured the hearts of the Germans. It is true that the

Bernd Rosemeyer does his duty as one of the most prominent sportsmen in Nazi Germany.
(Kirchberg)

boxing idol Max Schmeling achieved a similar rating at the time, but Bernd Rosemeyer was unique. And he belonged to the organisation that, by the twisted criteria of the Nazi state, brought together Germany's elite.

On his own admission, Rosemeyer joined the SS as early as 1932, having joined the SA 'two months previously'. Before marrying the well-known aviatrix Elly Beinhorn, on 13 July 1936, the SS *Obersturmführer* had to fill in a 'questionnaire on application for engagement and marriage': 'I, Bernd Rosemeyer, was born on 14 October 1909, in Lingen an der Ems, the son of the manufacturer Wilhelm Rosemeyer and his wife Louise, *née* Funke. From the age of six I attended the eight-year elementary school in that town. I then began an apprenticeship in my father's firm, to learn the trade of mechanic, and passed with distinction. During the apprenticeship I attended a technical college. At the age of 16 I gained my driving licence for vehicles in classes 1, 2 and 3b. I then worked as a volunteer in various positions. When I was 21 I devoted myself to motorcycle racing, which I practised successfully until 1934. I then joined the racing stable of Auto Union in order to represent Germany at home and abroad, and am still with that company. Last autumn I also learned to fly, in

Johannisthal.' None of this indicates any particular political commitment to Nazism on the part of the 26-year-old, and in the questionnaire Rosemeyer clearly answered the question about his religious faith with the word 'Catholic'.

The young racing driver does not seem to have given much thought to politics, but his sense of status as one of the nation's star sportsmen must have been very sure. As a member of the SS, documents show that he was assigned to the personal staff of Heinrich Himmler. In the conditions prevailing in the Nazi regime, this type of SS membership must have ensured Rosemeyer immense advantages in the form of protection and privileges, freedom of action, and freedom in his private life. And he did

Wearing an SA uniform, Bernd Rosemeyer is the main attraction at the first motorcycle race in his home town of Lingen. The event was organised by the local SA and took place on 6 August 1933. (Remling)

Von der SA Motorsportveranstaltung.
Bernd Rosemeyer vor dem Start.

not even have to pay ostensible lip-service to his political masters. His sometime fellow-driver with Auto Union, Paul Pietsch, made this sober comment six decades later: 'Well, all right, Rosemeyer *was* in the SS in those days. Every time he won they promoted him, and he ended up a *Hauptsturmführer* no less [equivalent to army captain]. But what was he supposed to do? If the regime offered them that sort of thing, were they meant to say no? If they *had* done they'd have been dropped, of course!'

But is that why Rosemeyer joined the SS? On his own admission he signed up *before* the Nazis seized power, as witnessed by his SS and SA membership numbers, even though his SS card shows him as an 'SS candidate' only after November 1933. Professor Bernd Rosemeyer Jr, who never knew his father personally, writes: 'As far as my father is concerned, I only know from my mother's stories that it was through the Lingen Sports Club, for which he once rode motorcycles, that he joined the SS, without his opinion really being asked at all. Apart from that, it was at a time when certainly no

During the entire Nazi period no German motorcycle racer was forced to wear a swastika armband during a race, yet Bernd Rosemeyer, unlike his colleagues within the NSU factory team, did so at the Hockenheim circuit on 27 August 1933. Was his motive to further his racing ambitions, or did he wear this armband because he was a Nazi supporter? (Herz)

The successful Auto Union team – Rosemeyer, Stuck, von Delius – and fur-coated Elly Beinhorn-Rosemeyer at their official reception in Zwickau in 1936. They were not interested in the political situation, but lived with it. And lived very well. (Kirchberg)

sportsman could foresee how the regime would develop in the future. So I can understand how he may have been a bit careless. [...] My mother never concerned herself very seriously with these questions and at the ripe old age of 96 she cannot remember much any more.' The racing driver's son, a well-known and successful sports doctor in Munich, went on to emphasise: 'Both my father and my mother were interested in their sport, but not in politics.'

In times of such great political upheaval as the years of Nazi dictatorship, that sort of indifference must have required a very skilful balancing act. After all, the logic of a totalitarian system like National Socialism implies that everything is interpreted and seen as 'political'. That also includes inaction, toleration and keeping silent. 'You help to construct a facade of a nice, ordinary Germany, which other countries can get along with, but which of course in reality doesn't actually exist.' So wrote Sebastian Haffner in a review of his own life before he emigrated to Britain to protect his 'non-Aryan' wife and because, as a lawyer and journalist, he wanted no more to do with a state based on injustice. The great and lesser racing events in the Eifel, on the AVUS and elsewhere in the Nazi Reich were grand illusions and self-delusions of Potemkinesque[4] dimensions – magnificent facades concealing a brutal dictatorship.

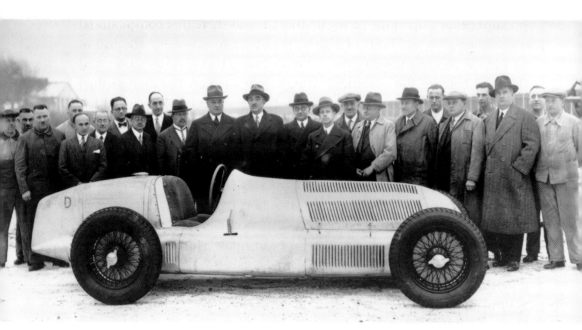

The first Mercedes-Benz W25. Among the mechanics and other employees are Dr Hans Nibel (12th from left), Fritz Nallinger (14th from left) and Alfred Neubauer (third from right). (Daimler AG)

Rearming for the racetrack

In May 1933, when the elite of Italy's drivers demonstrated their dazzling superiority and that of their French Bugattis and Italian Alfa Romeos on the AVUS and at the Nürburgring, the engineers, foremen and technicians got down to work in the test departments in Zwickau and Untertürkheim. While the Saxon newcomers to Grand Prix racing were largely dependent, for cost reasons, on the technical benefits of series production at Horch, and in the use of machines and materials had to rely very much on available capacity in the factory, their competitors in the Stuttgart racing team were largely self-sufficient and, above all, had larger budgets to work with.

Both works stables drew on a select band of skilled mechanics, on fitters and turners who with a watchmaker's precision produced nothing less than works of engineering art. As an example of the minute exactitude of their handiwork, the gearwheels in the drive for the vanes of the superchargers could not have a play of more than a 100th of a millimetre. Thus it was virtually inevitable that the cream of the company's craftsmen and specialists ended up in the racing division. It was there that conspiratorial associations grew up, units of highly specialised technicians, who had to react in the shortest possible time to innovations by the competition, and who thus became the spearhead of new technologies. The endless duel between the two companies accentuated their efforts and ensured that ever better solutions would be found ever faster. Thanks to this, the Silver Arrows reached a pitch of performance that rapidly put them ahead of foreign competitors, and this would remain the case for years to come.

Yet behind all this technical miracle-working stood human beings with all their strengths and frailties. The ambition of drivers, engineers and mechanics, coupled with the prospect of success, nourished with idealism, a passion for technology, pride and a need to prove themselves – not to mention a belief in Germany's superiority – set processes of group dynamics in motion and put the technology-mad stars under added pressure, which in turn promoted the inner cohesion of these motor racing specialists. To this extent the Grand Prix races, as the most demanding category of international motorsport, are very similar to the conditions produced by modern industrialised warfare in the development and production of new weapon systems – constant pressure of time and performance and the

It was an honour and a pleasure to work within the racing department at Auto Union, and only the best workers and craftsmen were selected. (Kirchberg)

Left: Dr Fritz Nallinger was a highly talented engineer who designed and built the most powerful racing cars of the time. Later, during the Second World War, this technical genius turned his efforts to military activity and he designed a long-range bomber capable of attacking New York. (Daimler AG)

Opposite: Hans Stuck tests a long-tailed version of the Auto Union P-Wagen at the AVUS in 1934. The novel appearance of this car impressed contemporary reporters. (Audi AG)

completely unrestricted exploitation of technical and financial resources. This was planning, testing and deployment for the 'ultimate victory', whether on the racetrack or the battlefront. The boundaries became blurred because the technical thought-processes of the engineers always remained the same. When the Silver Arrows appeared, Hitler was on the warpath.

It was no coincidence that from 1939 onwards the bulk of all those highly qualified experts switched seamlessly over to the armaments divisions of their companies and went on working. The Chief Technologist at Daimler-Benz, Fritz Nallinger, together with his engineers, then developed new aircraft armaments instead of Silver Arrows, and in the final phase of the war that was already lost they even designed an 'America-bomber' for German reprisal raids on New York. Even the German racing pros brought with them their motorsport experience: for a time Manfred von Brauchitsch acted as a test-driver of tanks, while his stablemate Hermann Lang drove test-runs in a converted Silver Arrow intended to serve as a high-speed launch-ramp for rockets and jet fighters.

All this had its origins in 1933: the new 750kg racing formula forced the designers of both the German national racing cars to make extravagant use of costly light alloys. That needed a lot of money and more knowledge than was generally available in motor racing at the time. Right from the start it turned into a huge adventure, since thanks to consistent lightweight design and highly developed supercharger technology, massive engines of

up 6 litres and more than 600bhp could be transplanted into the single-seat racing cars. These were mighty power-units with superchargers and special fuel, tuned for sheer performance, and contemporary chassis technology could scarcely keep pace with them. Wheel suspension, spring-struts, oscillation-dampers and, most of all, tyres, were basically incapable of transmitting the brute power of the new engines to the track without a loss of performance. Both drivers and engineers were in absolutely unknown territory and to cope with it they did not operate systematically so much as by a process of trial and error. Auto Union's Chief Engineer, Robert Eberan gave a glimpse of the truth at a conference of the Society of German Engineers in 1939: 'People have to realise that the state of development of today's racing cars is not the product of research but the result of a careful exploration of the performance boundaries of man, machine and material. The rapid flow of developments in racing car construction compels us to move on, from one success to the next, to new development challenges, before there has even been time to create the basis of research and testing that is simply absent in the frontier areas.'

Despite all the common ground in technical strategy – high horsepower, low weight – the two rival concerns worked on entirely different concepts with regard to chassis design. From the beginning of the Silver Arrow era to its end, Auto Union remained true to the mid-engine layout, which was unorthodox in those days but favoured by Porsche – probably inspired by the Benz 'teardrop' car. Mercedes-Benz, on the other hand, relied on the rather conservative front engine until war brought an enforced end to motor racing, remaining loyal to it even under the regime of Hans Nibel and Fritz Nallinger, both of whom, interestingly, had designed the above-mentioned Benz 'teardrop' in 1923!

It is necessary here to explain the technical consequences of this to the non-mechanically-minded layman: top-class drivers could get the hang of the controls in a Mercedes-Benz racing car with no trouble, but it was rather more difficult in an Auto Union Silver Arrow. With its notorious understeer the rear end of the Saxon racing model tended to go into a spin straight away and the car would skid off the track. However, if the driver successfully adapted to the unfamiliar handling of the mid-engined car – as Bernd Rosemeyer did – this more than made up for the usually superior engine performance of the Silver Arrows from Stuttgart.

However, their sophisticated supercharger technology catapulted both German cars into hitherto undreamed of heights of horsepower. As his power unit, Porsche chose a V16 engine, initially of 4.4-litre capacity, and a Roots supercharger. The cylinder blocks thus became smaller, which in theory – thanks to a favourable surface-to-volume ratio – meant fewer problems of overheating and therefore greater opportunities for utilising capacity. On paper the engineers worked on the basis of 280bhp at 4,500rpm. This was a considerable advance on the roughly 215bhp of the then dominant Alfa Romeo eight-cylinder engine. Early in 1938 – and thus almost at the end of its development – this engine, conceived for Auto Union, was enlarged to 6.5 litres and generated 560bhp at an astonishingly low 5,000rpm. At that time these were quantum leaps in technology, which largely help to explain the fascination sparked by these silver racing cars wherever in the world they took to the track.

To complete the figure-work: at Mercedes-Benz Nibel and his colleagues relied on a series-production eight-cylinder engine, initially of 3.4 litres, which when fitted with a supercharger delivered 325bhp at 5,500rpm. After a good five years of development the eight-cylinder unit from Untertürkheim reached a capacity of 5.7 litres and could deliver 650bhp at 5,500rpm. All of this was achieved by the engineers in both Zwickau and Untertürkheim through the use of superchargers that worked at higher pressures, and with the aid of sophisticated fuel mixtures based on benzol

A Silver Arrow from the start: even the official Mercedes-Benz press release of March 1934 stated that the new W25 Grand Prix car was silver. (Daimler AG)

and alcohol compounds. However, it was not least due to the support and opportunities provided by the big automobile groups and their suppliers. There were fully floating axles, hydraulic brakes, special racing tyre compounds and other technical innovations. In the long run the Italian, French and British racing car manufacturers would have nothing to put up against the state-backed outlay on the German side. To borrow a term from boxing: the Silver Arrows won by a technical knockout.

On the road to domination

The first of Auto Union's racing cars – to the chagrin of the Saxon company known to the press as the 'P-Wagen' after its designer, Porsche – comprised 1,622 components. It took more than six months for them all to be cast, finished and assembled. The 60-strong racing division worked in three shifts, 24 hours a day, until the first prototype was rolled out in October 1933.

The first test runs began on public roads around the Horch company site. The eye-catching racing shell made from duraluminium weighed in at just 45kg and gave the car a very unusual silhouette. On 13 November the silver-coloured 'P-Wagen' was unloaded from a trailer under the

strictest secrecy and completed its first trial run on the southern loop of
the Nürburgring. The previous day the Nazi regime had confirmed its hold
on power through a 'Reichstag Election' in which all the candidates were
from the Nazi Party and the whole electorate was obliged to vote. With a
turnout of 95.2 per cent, a remarkable 92.2 per cent of the votes cast were
for Hitler's party, the remaining 7.8 per cent being invalid. The course for
the future was set, and this was also true of Auto Union, where racing
manager Walb personally drove the prototype on its first test runs.

Despite being new to the Grand Prix game, the Saxons and their national
racing car got into gear rather faster than their more experienced rivals in
Untertürkheim, for it was not until 18 November that the new Mercedes-
Benz W25 completed its maiden circuits of the factory perimeter. When it
was first presented to the public its stylish unpainted aluminium bodywork
shimmered like silver. The competition may have got on to the track earlier,
but the Untertürkheimers presented the W25 to their most important
sponsor even before serious trials got under way. Hitler was attending

*Alfred Neubauer, Joseph Goebbels, Hans Nibel, Adolf Hitler and Jakob Werlin examine the
new national racing car at the Mercedes-Benz showroom in Munich on 4 January 1934.
(Daimler AG)*

important sessions of his party at the 'Brown House' in Munich, which is why the racing monster was shipped to the Bavarian capital immediately after New Year, and made a big impression there. Goebbels noted in his diary for 4 January 1934: 'Went out for coffee with Hitler. He is touchingly nice to me. Inspected the new racing car at Mercedes. A fantastic job. First class!'

Auto Union countered with the first official test-run on the AVUS on 12 January. This ensured not only headlines for Porsche's design but also support from prominent party members, such as Hitler's chief adjutant Wilhelm Brückner, the head of the NSKK Adolf Hühnlein, *Reichssportführer* Hans von Tschammer und Osten, and several people from the Reich Ministry of Propaganda. With top speeds of well over 250kph (155mph), Hans Stuck easily exceeded the requirements for the new racing car agreed in the contract between Porsche and Auto Union. The press went wild about the 'fuselage on wheels'. The driver's seat placed right forward and very low, and the elegance of the long, tailfin-like rear end, represented a break with all normal concepts of racing car construction to date. This silver arrow on wheels nourished the nation's hopes of great racetrack victories.

Ferdinand Porsche seized his moment and on 17 January sent a paper to the Reich Ministry of Transport in which he again proposed the building of a 'People's Car'. Just as in 1933 radio had been brought to the masses with the *Volksempfänger*, or People's Receiver, so the motorcar was to be made affordable to a broad stratum of society. The selling price he estimated for his design, with its 26bhp rear-mounted flat-twin engine, was 1,500 RM. Scarcely three months later Porsche was having a meeting with Hitler. And Jakob Werlin, the 'fixer', was there too. True, Porsche was designing a racing car for Auto Union to compete in, yet as a member of the board of Daimler-Benz AG he was as interested as his company was in the small car project.

In this new Germany, so receptive to motor transport, to the building of motorways and not least to motorsport, the way seemed to have been smoothed for technical advances. They were marvellous times for what the press and government propaganda lauded as 'German engineering skills and workmanship'. They were radiant times, when the metallic silver of the new national racing cars would replace Germany's traditional racing white in Grand Prix events.

In early 1934 it was on the political stage, rather than the racetrack, that bonus points were being collected. Mercedes-Benz was anxious about its number one driver: Rudolf Caracciola had still not recovered from the effects of his racing accident in Monte Carlo. The limping champion was in severe pain and had so far not completed any test-drives. As if that was not bad enough, the convalescent suffered a terrible personal blow when, on 4 February, his wife Charlotte was killed in an avalanche while skiing in Arosa. For the foreseeable future Caracciola would be out of circulation, and this presented Daimler-Benz AG with a serious problem.

On 18 January of that year their only available works driver, Manfred von Brauchitsch, had already embarked on the first serious test-drives of the W25 in Italy: 'During the winter months the engineers and mechanics had worked tirelessly to assemble a miraculous single-seater. I was selected to do the first test-runs of this dazzling silver machine on the *autostrada* from Milan to Varese.' So the W25 was definitely *not* painted white, as von Brauchitsch noted in his very first book of memoirs, published in East Germany in 1953, scarcely two decades after the event. We should make a careful note of this, in view of the legends that arose later.

The first direct encounter between the two German racing stables took place a few days later on the Grand Prix circuit in Monza, where on 21 January 1934 the rivals from Auto Union also arrived to carry out an extensive programme of trials, with Willy Walb, Hans Stuck and Prince Hermann zu Leiningen, which ended on 2 February. Mercedes-Benz, on the other hand, soon had to give up after von Brauchitsch flew off the track, probably due to a damaged tyre. The driver got out very shaken, though unhurt, but the only available W25 was so badly damaged that it could not be repaired on site.

In distant Berlin the holders of the state purse-strings pricked up their ears. The man from the transport ministry, Brandenburg, wrote a letter on 25 January to Daimler-Benz's Chief Executive, Kissel, enquiring how far the construction of the racing cars had progressed, and, most importantly, who was to drive them. On 30 January, exactly one year after the Nazis took power, Kissel's reply was signed neither 'with a German salute' nor 'Heil Hitler', but simply 'yours faithfully'. Significantly Kissel said nothing about the Monza accident: 'The car is back in our workshops and, after some minor modifications have been carried out, will be shipped back to northern Italy in about 14 days to undertake further test-drives.' The Herr Direktor attempted to reassure official circles: 'The results of our test-drives were thoroughly satisfactory. We have been able to satisfy ourselves that the car's roadholding is excellent.' He also skilfully skirted round the tricky subject of racing drivers' contracts: 'The driver question has not yet been finally settled; as soon as it has been, we will be sure to inform you.'

Up to that point Daimler-Benz had received nearly half a million Reichsmarks from the Nazi government, but the second W25 model, which in fact had been completed by mid-February, could nevertheless not yet be inspected by the Reich Ministry of Transport. In a second letter dated 22 March Kissel maintained 'that the second racing car will not be ready until tomorrow'. And because the precious machine had to be sent off immediately to northern Italy for further test-drives the overdue inspection could not take place until after Easter. However, having said this, Kissel did not forget to request – politely and purely by the way – the next subvention of 50,000 RM. Incidentally, this letter *was* signed 'with a German salute'. The next request for a further handout from the state coffers would follow on 14 April.

Kissel very wisely kept quiet about the fact that at recent test-drives on the Nürburgring there had been another accident. The victim this time

Many accidents hampered Mercedes-Benz test sessions – this is Ernst Henne's wrecked W25 after his Nürburgring crash in April 1934. (Daimler AG)

On 6 March 1934 the new P-Wagen fulfilled the agreement between Auto Union and Porsche. Hans Stuck reached speeds of over 265kph (165mph) and even managed to set three class world records. (Audi AG)

was Ernst Henne, the world-record-holding motorcycle rider recently hired from BMW, whose W25 ran off the track in the *Bergwerk* (Coalmine) section. Henne was flung from the silver car and landed unconscious head first in a nearby stream. A farmer's wife saved the helpless driver from drowning. It is possible that when he accelerated he was taken by surprise by the sudden kicking-in of the supercharger; other racing drivers mentioned that it took quite a time to get used to this violent surge of power. Yet the designer, Nibel, wrote a letter on 12 April to the *eminence grise* of the Supervisory Board of Daimler-Benz, State Councillor von Stauss, informing him of Henne's accident at over 100mph and ending with the laconic comment: 'Cause: over-eagerness.'

Things went far better for the competitors from Saxony. On 6 March Hans Stuck set up three straight world records on the AVUS: an average speed of 217.11kph (134.93mph) over a timed hour run, 217.018kph (134.877mph) over 200km, and 216.875kph (134.788mph) over 100 miles. On the long straight of this urban motorway circuit Stuck had reached top speeds of over 265kph (165mph). A few days before the opening of the International Car and Motorcycle Exhibition in Berlin it was the Zwickau team that seized the headlines, giving scant pleasure to their wrong-footed rivals, who, due to growing uncertainty about their stricken star Caracciola, had serious worries about whether they could succeed with the remnants of their 'purely German racing stable', and without further ado signed up the 36-year-old Luigi Fagioli as a works driver. The seasoned warhorse certainly lacked the driving finesse of his compatriots Varzi and Nuvolari, but they had committed themselves elsewhere long ago. In any case, those two national heroes of Fascist Italy saw no reason to yield to the advances of German racing stables, which had neither enough foreign currency to pay them nor any experience of the successful deployment of genuine, single-seater Grand Prix racing cars.

Constant demands for and acceptance of financial donations from the budget of the Reich Ministry of Transport placed particular pressure on the gentlemen in Untertürkheim just as much as on their opposite numbers in Zwickau. For he who pays the piper calls the tune. This was true not only of the ministry bureaucrats but also of the Nazi party functionaries, chief among them Hühnlein, the head of the NSKK. On 19 April 1934 the men from Daimler-Benz and Auto Union met at the ONS in Berlin to agree on a racing programme for the year. Both German stables would enter for the Grand Prix races in France (1 July), Germany (15 July), Switzerland (26 August), Italy (9 September), Spain (23 September), Brno in Czechoslovakia (30 September), and the Gran Premio di Roma (scheduled for 14 October, but later cancelled); in addition they were to take part in circuit racing in Italy for the Coppa Acerbo (15 August), in the mountain-climbs on the Kesselberg in Austria (17 June) and the Klausen Pass in Switzerland (5 August), and in the German mountain Grand Prix at Freiburg im Breisgau (19 August). The dates were two weeks or sometimes only one week apart, and required enormous logistical skill which, with German thoroughness and precision, both Auto Union and Mercedes-Benz gradually learned to master. Furthermore, depending on the international rating of the race, government bonuses beckoned, courtesy of the Reich Ministry of Transport: in 'Group I' events, that is to say Grand Prix races, the sums of 10,000 and 5,000 RM were offered as rewards for first and second place respectively, while in Group II these placings earned 7,000 and 3,000 RM. In any case, racing abroad was lucrative because of the foreign currency earnings.

So it was that Auto Union and Mercedes-Benz were quite often on the road across Europe simultaneously, each with three different convoys of trucks, in order to get their silver racing machines to the track on time, or else to get them back to the factory for necessary refits. This exemplary perfectionism was still only emerging during the Silver Arrows' first season, but later was largely the result of sheer force of numbers: in their best years both stables could each call on at least 12 race-ready cars, an immense supply, which was to push foreign competitors ever further back in the running.

However, for the 1934 season the two German rivals would have the use of only three or four driveable Silver Arrows each, at best. This sometimes resulted in technical and organisational bottlenecks, which meant, for instance, that both stables had to abandon their planned participation in the Belgian Grand Prix on 29 July. The picture was different for the hill-climbs, which could be covered with significantly less effort and expense. Thus Hans Stuck, celebrated as the 'mountain king', pulled off the trick of entering and winning two extra hill-climbs, contrary to what had been agreed with the ONS, while his competitors from Untertürkheim were conspicuous by their absence.

When all these dates were being agreed on 19 April in Berlin, it was of course impossible to ignore the fact that both Auto Union and Mercedes-Benz were making a relatively late entry into motor racing. The Monaco Grand Prix had already been run on 2 April without German participation and had been won by Guy Moll in an Alfa Romeo ahead of his team-mate Louis Chiron. Equally, there was no question of a German excursion to North Africa for the next important Grand Prix, which would take place in Tripoli on 6 May. That race would also end in a magnificent triumph for Alfa Romeo, with Varzi, Moll and Chiron taking the first three places.

It was perfectly clear to the NSKK's Hühnlein, the ONS and the Reich Ministry of Transport that the début of the new German racing cars had to take place in Germany. With an eye to the propaganda impact and the 'home advantage', the start of the first AVUS Race was fixed for 27 May in Berlin. Just a week later the Eifel Race would have to be run on the Nürburgring. The first thing was to catch up on the foreign manufacturers. In Hühnlein's ringing words at a press conference before the AVUS Race: 'Come one, come all! – May fortune smile on us or not! – What does it matter? – German drivers are once more joining battle in German machines!' But Mercedes-Benz works driver and NSKK member Ernst Henne knew the truth: 'We'll have to drive for our lives if we want to outstrip the foreigners.'

However, although this double début was predictable as soon as the international racing calendar was published, and was deliberately planned by the motor racing officials of the Nazi Party, it presented the Mercedes-Benz racing division with very serious problems, as Kissel told the Reich Minister of Transport in a letter dated 26 April. The plain fact was that preparation of the cars was behind schedule, and a hoped-for postponement of the AVUS Race was impossible because the international race dates had been fixed long in advance. For this reason Kissel, under great pressure, indicated 'that our participation is doubtful to say the least, the more so when we were informed that it would not be possible to drive on the AVUS circuit before 20 May, i.e. seven days before the race. However, since it has now been made possible for us to carry out test-drives despite the closure of one carriageway, we intend to make every effort to prepare for the AVUS Race, and we will carry out tyre tests using both German and foreign makes. Whether we can take part in the AVUS Race depends on the outcome of our trials on the AVUS circuit. As soon as we see how things stand, we will take the liberty of informing you.' Even the selection of drivers remained an open question, 'because the participation of Herr Caracciola is to date still uncertain.'

Wheels must roll

In the meantime the Nazi regime had got itself into a precarious situation. Reports from all corners of the Reich were rattling the nerves of Hitler and his cohorts: the Gestapo and its informers were talking about a definite shift of mood; the 'national renewal' had brought no material improvements to the mass of the German people. In the ranks of the roughneck Party army, Ernst Röhm's SA stormtroopers, slogans were openly circulating which called for a 'second revolution', while business and industry had to struggle with chronic raw material shortages. On 11 May propaganda minister Josef Goebbels launched a week-long nationwide press campaign against 'whingers, nit-pickers and agitators'. Internationally the Nazi regime was becoming increasingly isolated. Germany's export figures were in decline, while, despite a lack of foreign currency, imports were rising. The value of the Reichsmark was heading south, and instead of the promised boom a slump was looming. Conservative forces around ex-chancellor Franz von Papen, the very people who had placed the levers of power in Hitler's hands and who were then swiftly sidelined by the new brown-shirted masters of the nation, were once again scenting potential victory, particularly as senior officers in the regular army, the Reichswehr, were confronting the threat from a 'People's Army' in the shape of the SA.

A power-vacuum suddenly seemed to be opening up, for the venerable President Hindenburg was terminally ill and had withdrawn to his country estate in East Prussia. In April 1934 his imminent demise was made public. Something had to happen. More than a year after seizing power Hitler began to reorganise his hold on Germany. Positive distractions for the doubting *Volksgenossen* ('racial comrades') would benefit the Nazi regime; more than ever, national successes were needed. Thus, in its way, the first outing of the new German racing cars formed a small but glittering piece in the mosaic image of the supposedly magnificent achievements of Hitler's state cobbled together by its propagandists.

Among the German public, however, expectations of the gleaming silver wonder-cars were pitched high before the race, precisely because the racing divisions in Zwickau and Untertürkheim had maintained a cloak of silence

The Auto Union team during practice at the AVUS Race in 1934, heavily secured by ambitious NSKK troopers. (Perckhammer)

and even the Nazi-dominated press could scarcely elicit any information from them. The Berlin edition of the politically innocent *Allgemeine Automobile-Zeitung* ('General Motor News') described in its report on the AVUS Race how openly and willingly foreign drivers and technicians gave out information about their new racing car designs, while the two German firms put up the shutters completely: 'But during the practice sessions, why were Auto Union and Mercedes-Benz constantly roped off and surrounded by a cordon of SA soldiers? Doesn't this encourage rumour-mongering? All the other companies told us the capacity of their engines; only the Germans kept it secret.'

However, until the end of the Third Reich both Daimler-Benz and Auto Union continued to cultivate an obsessive secrecy about their racing cars. By deliberately circulating false information Alfred Neubauer became adept at creating smokescreens, while behind the popular Chief Engineer's broad back very different things were going on; but not until long after 1945 did he talk about them, and then only in salty anecdotes – the truth of which could never be guaranteed. 'At the beginning everything was frightfully secret,' Rudolf Caracciola recalled in the middle of the war, when discussing this kind of PR spin. 'No one was allowed to know anything very precise about the new racing cars. Cubic capacity, engine revs and output, the layout of steering, suspension, transmission – nothing could be spoken or written about any of those things.'

On the morning of 24 May, a Thursday, the practice runs for the AVUS Race began. And, at a stroke, the noise and speed of the new silver racing cars altered the public's perception. From then on the Nazi strategy of sheer overwhelming power found its motor-racing counterpart in the appearance of the new national racing cars: the futuristic-looking Auto Union, whose V16 power unit had such an immensely deep, hollow roar because the supercharger was fitted between the carburettors and the engine; and the front-engined Mercedes-Benz, which was different not only visually but acoustically too, its eight cylinders producing a shrill and distinctive shriek because the Roots supercharger pumped air directly into the carburettor and thence into the engine. The result was a concentrated assault on all the senses, comprising a roaring din, breakneck speed, gleaming metal and an acrid smell reminiscent of burnt almonds, which came from the rhizinus oil added to the fuel. These silver projectiles electrified not just the spectators

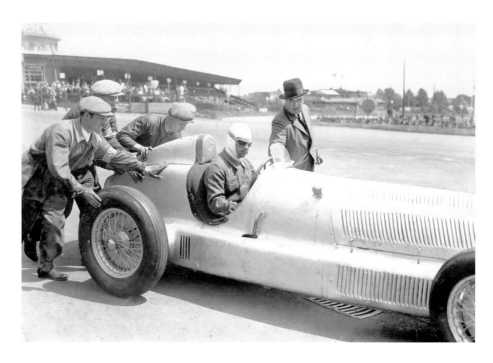

Nearly a year after his terrible crash at Monte Carlo, Rudolf Caracciola embarks on his first practice with the silver Mercedes-Benz W25 at the AVUS in 1934. (Daimler AG)

lining the track, but also the volubly droning radio commentators. In the first live broadcast from the AVUS on Friday morning the voices of Walther Beumelburg, Eduard Roderich Dietze, Christian Pfeil and Hugo Morero interrupted each other as they tried in vain to be heard above the noise and then, despite all their loquacious enthusiasm, were reduced to complete silence when once again, at the end of the two long straights, Rudolf Caracciola sped towards them through the Grunewald woods on the south or north bend. Yes, Caracciola was racing again for the first time since his accident more than a year earlier – still suffering from his injuries, but quickly becoming attuned to his new silver weapon.

Indeed, for the great 'Caratsch' this was a novel experience: 'It was a beautiful, mild spring day. The silver fish was being pushed on to the track,' Caracciola recounted in his ghosted memoirs. 'I had expected the car to be fast. That's what it was built for. But the fact that it was quite so fast, far quicker than any racing car I had ever driven in my life, was a real delight. But what really struck me was the fantastic acceleration. I'd never experienced anything like it. If I pressed the throttle pedal a bit too hard, the thing took me flying several hundred meters through the countryside. Incredible forces were lurking in that car. And the performance was matched by a really good sound: the howl of the supercharger – shrill, exciting, penetrating – could be heard for miles. It was a sound that would soon be heard on every racing circuit in Europe and would stay in the memory for a long time.'

And that shrieking wail from his silver racing car was very similar to the shrill klaxon fitted to Stuka dive-bombers, whose noise, scarcely six years later, would herald very different victories in the German newsreels. There is no question about it: this overwhelming and deafening Grand Prix sport would be the perfect stage for National Socialism to present in spectacular fashion the supposed superiority of Germany. It was a martial prelude, albeit with some accompanying discords.

The age of silver

Auto Union and Mercedes-Benz were represented by three cars each in the AVUS Race, driven by Stuck, Momberger and von Leiningen for Auto Union and by Caracciola, Fagioli and von Brauchitsch for their rival. In Friday's practice, Stuck clocked up an average of 245kph (152mph), a new unofficial lap record, while the day before Caracciola was the fastest of the Daimler-Benz threesome, with an average of 230kph (143mph). The star drivers were to some extent bluffing, since their starting positions had been allocated by a lottery, but their times certainly gave an indication of the relative power of their machines. 'However, the impression is gaining more and more ground that the German cars have a chance of winning, if they can just hold on,' reported an enthusiastic paper, the *Berliner Illustrierte Nachtausgabe*. The story appeared on the front page of its second edition on Saturday 26 May 1934, under the headline: 'The last practice laps before the great battle on the AVUS', along with a photograph of the three silver Auto Union cars.

In view of the legend of the Silver Arrows that spread later, we have to be quite precise at this point and look at other black-and-white photographs published at that time. For these also lead one to conclude that, at the AVUS Race, not only the Saxon machines but also the W25s were in gleaming silver livery. Built from bare aluminium polished to a high shine, or possibly coated with clear varnish or even with silver paint, the new generation of racing cars from Untertürkheim gleamed resplendently, even if in the case of the W25 driven by von Brauchitsch the two rear wire-spoked wheel-rims appeared to be painted white, whereas those on Fagioli's car can be clearly identified as silver.

It is possible that von Brauchitsch's wheel-rims were the last white-painted relics from an earlier developmental stage of the new design. But it was no later than at the first emergence of the rival product from Saxony that the Daimler-Benz technicians must have figured out for themselves that the duraluminium cladding developed for Auto Union by Porsche's colleague Erwin Kommenda, even when left in its bare metallic colour, fitted the basic concept of the new 750kg racing formula. A consistently pursued reduction in weight would be the key to racing victory. The striking silver gleam of the Auto Unions' aluminium skin was the result of thorough polishing and made it possible to largely dispense with costly painting, as well as saving the 2 or 3kg in weight that the many coats of lacquer would have added. It is no surprise, therefore, that the new W25s

Mechanics push-start Hermann Prinz zu Leiningen's Auto Union for a practice lap during the AVUS Race weekend in 1934. (Perckhammer)

In May 1934 Mercedes-Benz presented its new W25 'Silver Arrows' at the AVUS practice session, but the day before the race all three cars were withdrawn due to problems with the fuel supply – an embarrassing start. (Perckhammer)

also completed their practice runs in gleaming metallic silver. Two months earlier, on 1 March 1934, Daimler-Benz had even published a press release in which they officially described the W25 as a 'silvery arrow'.

The customary colour for German racing cars, as prescribed at the time by international regulations, was white, but neither at the AVUS, nor at the next race at the Nürburgring, nor even at the very first foreign start, in the French Grand Prix at Montlhéry, was the silver livery a topic that the national and international press found worthy of mention. Foreign observers were more interested in the fact that the silver bullet-cars from Zwickau bore the traditional German flag of red, white and black (as opposed to the red, black and gold of the Weimar Republic), together with a swastika flag painted on the long streamlined tail. Apart from this, it was seen as quite normal and perfectly understandable that the German cars should take the track in silver livery. Had not silver been described as 'heraldic white' in medieval times? And had not Manfred von Brauchitsch entered the AVUS Race in a silver streamlined SSK in 1932 and 1933? So who was going to enforce some petty regulation against these committed patriots who set out to reverse Germany's situation not only in politics but in motorsport?

In this new Germany the same men who determined what was white and what was not also ultimately decided who was and was not an enemy of the state, and in German motorsport it was the ONS, run by Nazi functionaries, that had the final say. This comprised representatives – nominated by Hühnlein – of the Reich Ministries of Transport, the Interior and Propaganda, the Reich Foreign Ministry, the regular army and the Automobile Industry Federation. This party-dominated and politically motivated authority also promoted Germany's interests in the world motor racing body, the AIACR. Though actually quite non-political this union of the world's 19 most important national automobile clubs had bowed to the realities of Hitler's power and, through an amendment to its constitution, agreed to accept within its ranks for the first time a governmental authority, in the shape of the ONS.

So at this point, in order to distance myself from the legend of the Silver Arrows created much later, in the 1950s, I have to say: no, the apparently 'new' German racing colour of silver was *not* new and had in fact become a familiar sight to the press and public since the very first test-drives of the new national racing cars. Consequently it was not considered worthy of special mention.

An embarrassing debut

However, something that really caught people's attention – and, indeed, caused consternation and outrage before the AVUS Race – was the surprising and abrupt decision by Daimler-Benz to pull out, which spectators only heard about on Sunday morning. There was talk of problems with the fuel pipe, but none of those lining the track really knew. Only one thing was certain: the withdrawal was a great embarrassment for the company. As late as 25 May, that is to say the Friday before the race, a civil servant named König, writing on behalf of Reich Transport Minister von Eltz-Rübenach, sent a brief note to the directors in Untertürkheim: 'Having last year made available to you a sizeable one-time subsidy for the design of a modern racing car, I have set aside funds this year as well, for the promotion of racing car construction. However, I would like to withhold

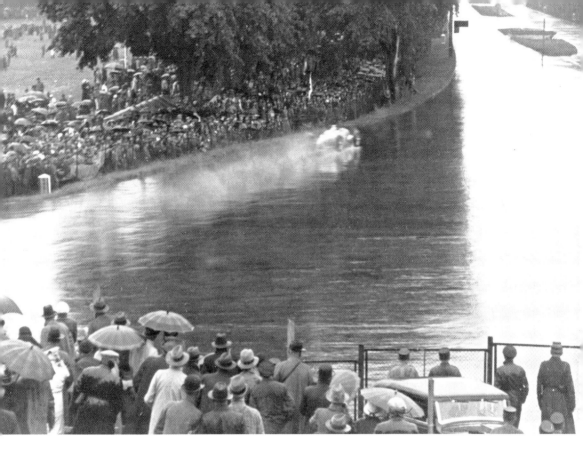

Hans Stuck hurries away from the field in his Auto Union during the early stages of the rain-soaked AVUS Race in 1934. (Audi AG)

approval for committing these funds until after the AVUS Race on 27th inst. Following this race I will ask the Supreme National Sports authority for German motoring to take soundings in the automobile industry and then make some proposals to me for the allocation of subsidies.' And now Daimler-Benz AG was not even going to provide the first required proof of performance by entering for the AVUS!

On the very Sunday of the race, Nibel, the Chief Designer, was attempting to pour oil on troubled waters in a conversation with Chief Secretary Brandenburg of the Ministry on the fringes of the event. On Monday he again phoned Brandenburg before finally, on Wednesday 30 May, Chief Executive Kissel personally handed a letter to the Minister, signed with a 'Heil Hitler!' and countersigned by Nibel. In this the two men mounted a wordy and convoluted attempt at damage limitation. The letter also sheds revealing light on the technical conditions under which top-class motor racing was run in those days. For this reason I would like to quote extensively from it:

'In submitting the report we had already pointed out that our participation in the race was doubtful, since our trials on the AVUS circuit had not been completed. Then, in the course of the month of May, working day and night, the cars were made ready for the AVUS Race, and thanks to our efforts we were able to bring three racing cars to the track for the final practice in time for the race. After our preliminary trials and the practice runs on the first practice day, Thursday 24 May, had produced satisfactory results, we found in the trials that took place on Friday that in all the cars there was a drop-off in performance at high speed, and thus a loss of speed, which at first could not be explained. Since the cause of the fault was traced to fuel-starvation, we first carried out other tests such as changing the jets and spark plugs and then we examined the fuel-pump supplied by Junkers, in the presence of a specialist engineer from that company, and we discovered that dirt had got into the pump's pressure regulating valve, preventing the valve from closing. Examination of the foreign bodies found in the valve-seating revealed that they were parts of the interior coating of the Aviotub hose used for the fuel line. Thus, it appears we have identified the cause of the fuel starvation, and it was pointed out by the Junkers engineer that in his experience, when using an Aviotub hose a careful fine-gauge filtering of the fuel is necessary immediately before it reaches the pump, since fibres can become detached from the inside of the hose.

'At this point, the fuel-pumps were removed from all the cars and dismantled under the supervision of the Junkers engineer, then examined, cleaned and during the night of Friday to Saturday fitted with suction-pipe connections and petrol-filters, which have already proved their effectiveness in the building of aero engines. We were justified in hoping that these measures will now guarantee a secure flow of fuel. Nevertheless, during the practice on Saturday we found that the cars could not even be brought up to the speeds achieved in earlier test-runs and in the practice on Thursday. What is more, the malfunctions that occurred were even more extensive than on the previous day. Again and again there were clear indications of fuel-starvation, and even of the fuel supply cutting out as soon as the car was driven off. Neither enlarging the jets, nor widening the float-needle aperture, nor switching spark plugs, had any success, so that the only remaining explanation for the lack of fuel was, once again, the irregular functioning of the fuel supply.

'We would like to point out here that there are certain difficulties connected with the fuel feed, because it has to function perfectly both with and without pressure from the supercharger. The fact that the malfunctioning of the fuel feed only occurred on the penultimate day of practice, and was not noticed earlier, is due to it not being previously possible for us to drive the cars in their racing condition at high speeds for lengthy periods, because although we had already carried out quite extensive stationary tests of the Aviotub hose, with satisfactory results, the conditions when the car is moving are very different due to the violent shaking from the road surface. In the course of the practice on Saturday afternoon, it also turned out that at high revs the fuel-starvation led to overheating of the plugs due to weakness of the mixture, so that further malfunctions such as pistons seizing up and burn-out were feared if the cars were to be driven for several laps with significant fuel-starvation. Thus, on the Saturday evening shortly before the cars were taken away from us, we were faced with the fact that our cars were saddled with a defect that could not be cured.

'If we had entered the race with this defect, not only would we have been unable to drive at high speeds, but we would also have had the prospect that our cars might drop out after a few laps. In these circumstances we took the very hard and regrettable decision to withdraw our cars from the race. As soon as the cars were back at our factory we started work on rectifying the known defects and we hope to make such rapid progress that at least we will be able to take part in the Eifel on the following Sunday with a prospect of winning.'

The public humiliation for Daimler-Benz AG was enormous, the more so since Auto Union checked in on the grid with its three promised P-Wagens. However, the Untertürkheimers were lucky in that on the Sunday of the race the competitors from Saxony committed typical beginners' errors, which robbed them of a victory that was within their grasp. At all events, following the Reich press conference on 28 May 1934 the newspaper editors – no doubt under personal orders from Goebbels – treated Germany's disgrace with caution: 'The wish has been expressed in *the very highest and most influential quarters* that the AVUS Race must not be given prominence in the layout of the Monday editions. In its place, major coverage should be given to the Dresden Theatre Week, especially the speech by the Minister of Propaganda.'

However, over the next days and weeks the specialist journals of the time voiced implicit criticism of Willy Walb, Auto Union's racing manager. The *Allgemeine Automobil-Zeitung* had this to say about Walb's tactics in the 15-lap race: 'The battle orders from Auto Union's race management were apparently these: Stuck is to drive as fast as the wet surface will allow, while Leiningen and Momberger will only occupy themselves with chasing the Alfa Romeos. We know our cars are faster. For reasons of safety there will be no overtaking until the last lap. Further order: after the 10th lap, stop and change tyres! Refuel if necessary.' But in wet weather the wear on tyres is far slighter – how slight, no one at Continental or Auto Union was able to estimate. What is more, the Alfa Romeos were driving on Belgian Englebert tyres, which seemed to demonstrate certain advantages over German tyre design.

Nonetheless, to begin with Auto Union's strategy seemed to pay off. As the *AAZ*'s correspondent noted: 'Despite the torrential rain, Stuck is driving like a madman and after two laps is lying a full minute ahead of the Alfa Romeos,

Sole survivor. August Momberger managed to keep his Auto Union in the race and finished in a distant third place, whereas team-mates Hans Stuck and Hermann Prinz zu Leiningen had to retire. (Perckhammer)

which are bunched fairly close together. However, Prince zu Leiningen's car was losing cooling water and pulled out after the sixth lap, while his team-mate Momberger pushed past the two Alfas of Chiron and Varzi to take third place behind Guy Moll and the leader, Stuck. Everything seemed to be going in the Saxons' favour. The drama was reaching its climax! Stuck and Momberger *had* to stop and change their rear tyres although neither needed to. It took so long that Moll passed Stuck, and Varzi passed Momberger. And now the chase was on. Both Stuck and Momberger were still in good shape as they were pushed back on to the track, but both returned from the next lap with their tails between their legs. In Stuck's case one could hear from a long way off that his clutch was slipping. According to unreliable eyewitnesses he engaged it too harshly when accelerating out of the South Curve, just 400 yards behind Moll, whom he had to and could catch up with. It was all over. To begin with nothing was heard from Momberger. The car still seemed to be hale and hearty. Nevertheless, he stopped again at the end of the 11th round and had a *conversation* lasting a few seconds. It later emerged that he told the pit crew that his gearshift had suffered in the breakneck chases round the bends. Since he was the only one left in the race he was ordered to go right through the bend in fourth gear without changing down. This he did with such *élan*, despite the lack of acceleration out of the bends, that he got closer and closer to the two Alfas that were now in the lead. He had almost pipped Varzi, whose right rear tyre had lost its tread in the last lap.'

So August Momberger, in the last remaining P-Wagen, ended up in third place, 18 seconds behind Achille Varzi and 1 minute 45.3 seconds behind the winner, Guy Moll. 'But the Auto Union cars were definitely faster,' the *AAZ* reassured its readers, 'and they would have taken the first two places if they had not been forced to change tyres in the cold weather, while all the other cars carried on. If, if, if…!!! – Up to the tenth lap, in pouring rain, Stuck achieved an average speed of 210.3kph [130.7mph] and, as the AVUS circuit gradually dried out, Momberger did the fastest lap of the day at 225.8kph [140.3mph], while the Alfas never got higher than an average of 207kph [128.6mph]. The honours of the day went to the young Guy Moll, the Alfa Romeo cars and the Engelbert tyres, which even without anti-skid protection showed no tendency to slide! Nonetheless, we have every right to be proud of our Auto Union cars. They have fulfilled their promise, and their manager Willy Walb has certainly taken on board a great deal, which will stand them in good stead in the next races.'

Auto-mobilisation

The Nazi officials at the AVUS Race had long ago learned how to stage such motorsport events as impeccably organised propaganda spectacles. Prior to the Nazi era motorsport was no more than a thrilling entertainment for the masses, at which a handful of well-paid specialists placed their driving skills at the service of commercial interests and offered a sensation-seeking public some excitement in their leisure hours. But now the parades of the Nazis and their covert 'sponsorship' of the German works teams turned the excitement of the race into a national event of the first rank. The racetrack became a battlefield for the nation's honour; more than ever before, each German driver was racing for his country. And if one of these popular horsepower heroes were to lose his life in the process, there was the comfort that he had died for his country.

This cheap emotionalism combined with generous funding of technical innovation could be seen to be having the desired effect, and not only among the crowds strung out along the Nürburgring or the AVUS. It also flattered the old elite of the racing circuit who either took part in motorsport or else promoted it from the boardrooms of companies and motorsport associations. And in particular it sent a signal to the up-and-coming works technicians and engineers, telling them that their constant efforts to produce promising inventions would be suitably rewarded by the Nazi regime. The corporate automobile enthusiasts, ostensibly non-political and interested only in technical advances and sporting success, became the greatest profiteers from the Hitler state. A big impression was also made on the youngsters growing up in that era, who would model themselves on the daredevil heroes of the circuit, whether they saw them in real life, relived the experience through newsreels, or listened at home to commentary on the radio. It was a profound change in perception – the one-time spectacle and leisure pursuit had become a matter of national devotion and edification. Before the advent of the Nazis it had been very different.

In the summer of 1932, when the young Manfred von Brauchitsch, intending to add further lustre to his surprise AVUS win, played the lead role in the motor racing film *Kampf* ('Battle') for Majestic-Film GmbH, something terrible happened. For when the movie was shown in cinemas in December 1932 the official censor gave it an 'Adults Only' certificate – which drastically reduced box-office takings. Although Majestic made several cuts and edits, *Kampf* failed, even at the fourth attempt, to secure the coveted 'U' rating.

The reason given by the Censor's office in Berlin on 10 January 1933, only days before Hitler seized power, casts a revealing light on the way motor racing was viewed in official circles. It was not the love scenes, by now considerably toned down, that were considered a threat to youth, but the fact that 'through the nerve-racking effect of the race scenes the film is likely to exercise the minds of young audiences to such an extent as to constitute the offence of inflaming the imagination'. The Censor went on to make a subtly different point: 'Even if it is conceded that automobile racing is accessible to young people, both on and around the track, the fact cannot be ignored that the impressions from personal experience of such a race are far less strong than those created by a film aimed at sensation, where the action and events are compressed into a short space of time, and are thus much more intense than under normal conditions. The proliferation of accidents seen in the film, as well as the lengthy life-and-death struggle of the drivers in constant mortal danger, which inspires a new fear and terror at every bend, produces in young audiences an excessive stimulation of the imagination, which the drafters of the Cinematograph Act, in § 3 section 2, wished to obviate.'

But what the film censors objected too in January 1933 as harmful to youth was now, little more than a year later, considered to be in the best interests of the state. At the 1934 AVUS Race, the elites of old and new Germany had assembled almost in their entirety on the VIP stand: the Reich Minister of Transport Baron Paul von Eltz-Rübenach, Army Minister Werner Blomberg, Labour Minister Franz Seldte, Minister for Science, Education and Schools Bernhard Rust, Commander-in-Chief of the Army Baron Werner von Fritsch, and a minister without portfolio named Hanns Kerrl. In addition there were half a dozen permanent secretaries and more Nazi bigwigs, such as Robert Ley, head of the DAF (German Labour Front), the Reich Youth Leader Baldur von Schirach, and State Counsellor and SA-*Obergruppenführer* Viktor Lutze, who would soon afterwards deliver his commanding officer, Ernst Röhm,[5] to execution and would himself become the new leader of the SA. Finally there was Hitler's deputy, Rudolf

Hess. There were an awful lot of brown shirts beside the racetrack; only the Reich Chancellor was conspicuous by his absence.

In fact Hitler was never to attend a race at either the AVUS or the Nürburgring, even though he was concerned for the success of the silver racing cars, co-financed them, and always kept himself informed about them. But political affairs were much more important to him, quite apart from the fact that in the early summer he always made a pilgrimage to Bayreuth to attend the annual Wagner Festival in the company of a woman he deeply admired, the composer's daughter-in-law Winifred Wagner.[6] The clash of dates would have made a visit to the German Grand Prix difficult. That is why in 1937, after the double Grand Prix victory of the Mercedes-Benz works drivers Caracciola and von Brauchitsch, Hitler had them flown at short notice down to Bayreuth for a private reception.

On the other hand the *Führer* may have shrunk from the slight, but possible, risk that on the very day of his official visit to a circuit he might have to witness a defeat of the German drivers. There had been a precedent for this at the 1936 Berlin Olympics (when, incidentally, the Bayreuth Festival had been split into two, in order to avoid the diary clash). In the quarter-final of the football tournament, the German national team was beaten 2–0 by Norway – under the very eyes of Hitler! From then on he refused to attend any more internationals, so as not to be obliged to put on a brave face after another German defeat. And needless to say, the football team's national trainer on that occasion, Otto Nerz, was swiftly replaced by his assistant, Sepp Herberger.

So it was unthinkable that Hitler would have watched the 1934 AVUS Race together with his retinue on the VIP stand, for the winner, the young Guy Moll, was not only a Frenchman, born in colonial Algeria in 1911, but came from a Jewish family. It was only at the start of the season that Scuderia Ferrari, the official works stable of Alfa Romeo, had signed up the talented 23-year-old, who immediately returned the favour by winning the Monaco Grand Prix and then the Berlin event as well. He rose to become France's sporting idol, but speculation remained about what further success this racing star with Jewish roots could achieve in the era of the Silver Arrows. No one ever found out. On 15 August 1934 he was killed in his Alfa Romeo when, competing for the Coppa Acerbo, he made a vain attempt to overtake the Mercedes-Benz of Ernst Henne.

After his unexpected victory in the 1934 AVUS Race driving an Alfa Romeo streamliner, Guy Moll seemed on the brink of a brilliant career – but later that year he was to crash fatally in the Coppa Acerbo. (Perckhammer)

In those spring days of 1934 Hitler needed successes more than ever. Motor racing provided a bit of distraction and edification for the nation, but more particularly it was a showcase for the efficiency of National Socialism. The analogy with ancient chariot racing comes to mind, yet the Roman saying about 'bread and circuses' is modest in comparison with the bombast of National Socialism. The propaganda circus deployed by the Nazis far exceeded anything ever seen before. Every race held on home soil resembled a small Nazi Party rally. Even at that 1934 AVUS Race it seemed both odd and significant that the SA Stormtroopers, despite being justifiably reviled in the better circles of society as crass and brutal, were putting on a show of discipline and order beside the track. The parading and deployment of thousands of Brownshirts impressed even the reporter from the financial paper *Berliner Börsenzeitung*: 'The AVUS has probably never been so hermetically sealed off and so impeccably secured as it was that day. *Obergruppenführer* Hühnlein has deployed the entire Berlin Motor-SA and the NSKK in order to guarantee the utmost security for visitors. Even behind every cheeky cameraman there stood an SA man, whose job was to prevent any excessively reckless stunts. Thus the race went off without the slightest mishap, something the Motor-SA [...] may be very proud of.'

Just a week later all these efforts would pay off. At the Eifel Race on the Nürburgring circuit, surrounded by his fellow-marchers, Adolf Hühnlein was able for the first time to celebrate a German victory for a German driver in a German car, by posing as erect as a ramrod and giving the straight-armed 'Hitler salute'. And Hühnlein, the highest-ranking motorsport official in the Nazi state, closed the day, 3 June 1934, with a ritual that in future he would perform with pride and joy almost every weekend: he sent a telegram to his *Führer* proclaiming a triumph for the German racing cars: 'With a superior victory over the best foreign drivers and machines today at the Nürburgring, von Brauchitsch, coming first in his class in a Mercedes-Benz, and Stuck, second in an Auto Union, have been able to give the first visible expression

The German way of winning. For the first victory, at the Eifel Race in 1934, Manfred von Brauchitsch and Adolf Hühnlein honour the Führer with a Nazi salute. (Daimler AG)

The Mercedes-Benz team at the Nürburgring on the Wednesday before the 1934 Eifel Race. For their debut the three W25s were silver, not white. This contradicts the long-standing, Neubauer-originated myth that these new racing cars only became 'Silver Arrows' after their white paint was scraped off on the eve of the race, in order to save 2kg and reach a 750kg weight limit. (Reichle)

of our gratitude for the active support that, through you, *mein Führer*, the German motor industry has received. In the motorcycle class NSU and DKW also succeeded in gaining first and second place respectively. *Heil meinem Führer*! Signed Hühnlein, *Obergruppenführer*.'

Silver-plated legends

The outcome of the AVUS Race turned the actual power relationships in Grand Prix racing under the new 750kg formula on their head. Both the Auto Union racing cars and their still non-functioning counterparts from Mercedes-Benz were already way ahead of Alfa Romeo, Bugatti and Maserati with regard to performance, chassis and aerodynamics. And it was on Sunday 3 June at the Nürburgring – extremely challenging to both man and machine – that this superiority could be fully exploited for the first time. Auto Union again entered three cars, while Mercedes-Benz put only two on the starting grid, because Caracciola still did not feel fit enough for the demands of the Nürburgring. Photographs from the time show that even in the practice laps the two Mercedes machines boasted the same silver gleam as the racing cars from Auto Union.

Shortly after the start of the race Austrian driver Emil Frankl, driving a Bugatti, lost his life in an accident. Yet the Eifel Race went on, and Luigi Fagioli in his W25 took the lead ahead of his stablemate von Brauchitsch.

But racing manager Neubauer immediately gave orders to switch places. Fagioli obeyed; from the second lap onward von Brauchitsch was ahead of the Italian, but in a planned pit-stop to change tyres the latter had a violent row with Neubauer. True, Fagioli did resume the race, but he pulled out shortly before the finish. It was ostensibly due to 'a trivial defect', as Chief Executive Kissel told an inquisitive journalist on 9 June. However, von Brauchitsch won in the second W25 and gave 'the German salute' to NSKK-*Führer* Hühnlein. The fastest Auto Union car, driven by Stuck, came in second, over one minute behind von Brauchitsch's silver Mercedes-Benz, which thus took the honours on its first outing. In the home factory in Untertürkheim a celebration party would be given for the entire workforce. The first victory for one of the new national racing cars was suitably lauded in the Nazi-controlled press, and indeed marks the beginning of German domination of international Grand Prix racing that would last until the Second World War.

In 1958 the gifted – and not a little conceited – Alfred Neubauer told the story, with the help of co-author Harvey T. Rowe, of how the very first start by the Mercedes-Benz cars in that 1934 Eifel Race hung by a slender thread. The new machines had to weigh in at a maximum of 750kg, but the day before the race the W25s were 2kg too heavy, and so would not have been allowed to start. As von Brauchitsch is reported to have complained in despair that evening: 'We had to think of something, otherwise we would have been stuffed!' The German idiom he actually used was *lackiert*, meaning 'lacquered' or 'painted', and apparently it was his use of this word that suddenly gave Neubauer the idea of sandpapering off the white paint overnight, thereby immediately removing the two kilos of excess weight – the birth of the Silver Arrows. That is the anecdote that appeared in the first edition of Neubauer's memoirs, and the same story is still being put about by Daimler AG. Interestingly, in 1951 Neubauer had published a small book entitled *Heute Lacht Man Darüber* ('Nowadays We Laugh About It') in which a chapter dealt with the problems caused by weight formulas. Though he wrote about his own experiences during the 750kg formula era, he made no mention at all of weight problems during the 1934 Eifel Race; but he did cite an article published in the French magazine *L'Auto* in 1906 which told of an unnamed driver who had to scratch the paint off his racing car in order to save 1 or 2kg. Quite a remarkable coincidence, isn't it?

The Daimler company archives have, since the 1980s, referred to a discovery made by Karl Ludvigsen – a motor-racing expert with close links to the house of Mercedes-Benz – when examining the documents in the works archive. The note he found mentions various modifications to the W25 carried out immediately before the cars were entered in the Eifel Race. These technical alterations, so the theory goes, were the reason why the vehicles registered more than 750kg on the official scales. Plausible as this may seem, not a single contemporary account mentions a nocturnal colour change from white to the silver of bare aluminium. And – as already stressed – contemporary photographs taken during the practice laps do not show any white-painted Mercedes-Benz bodies. Moreover, Daimler company archivists had to admit during their '1934 Paint-Job Symposium' in 2007 that they could not provide any historical photographs showing an indisputably white Mercedes-Benz W25.

Professor Peter Kirchberg, a great expert on Auto Union's racing history, gives little credence to the story of rubbing off the white paint on the eve of the race: 'Even if the two cars of Fagioli and Brauchitsch *had* tipped the scales at more than 750kg, quite different tricks could have been used to get a quick reduction in weight.' Kirchberg has actually been able to discuss this subject with former Auto Union race mechanics and refers in this connection to the memoirs, also published in 1958, of race mechanic Rudolf Friedrich, who stated: 'Usually it was only the cars from Scuderia Ferrari that were the correct weight. Their Alfa Romeos were often 10–15kg under weight. With the German cars it was always such a close thing that before the weigh-in we removed a few heavy components from the car. The way we did it – and Mercedes-Benz did pretty much the same – was this: a mechanic climbed under the car with a big tin basin. While he disconnected the oil-hose from the sump and let the oil run into the tin basin [because the cars were weighed without fuel], he unscrewed the shock-absorber nuts located behind the sump – they had already been loosened with a spanner, unnoticed – and let them drop into the oil along with the heavy shock-absorber washers made of steel and extruded material.' If it was that easy to fool people in the days of the Silver Arrows, why bother with the awkward and time-consuming business of sandpapering paint off?

Manfred von Brauchitsch himself, expressly named by Neubauer as the originator of the idea, and who, before the Neubauer memoirs were published, had fled from the Federal Republic to the Communist GDR (East Germany) because of worries about an impending trial for treason, made no mention in his own 1953 biography of a colour change during the night before the Eifel Race. However, it is interesting that the GDR's new trophy sportsman, on *rewriting* his own recollections six years after the publication of Neubauer's memoirs, presented himself as a convert to anti-Nazi resistance, and claimed to have personally contributed the idea of rubbing off the white paint. Perhaps this confirmation of the paint story was a little thank-you to old friends, sent across the frontier of a divided Germany. So many unanswered questions: yet the legend of the first Silver Arrows spread around the world and continued to be nurtured after Neubauer's death in 1980 – and even after the collapse of the GDR it was preserved for the company archives in an interview with von Brauchitsch. It was a matter of honour that, after the Wall came down, von Brauchitsch should be a welcome guest of the Daimler-Benz company, and he was much in demand at official motor racing occasions as an eyewitness of those days. In a private capacity he continued, as ever, to race Mercedes-Benz machines.

The man who was for many years Porsche's racing manager and, later, chairman of sport at the AvD, was the one-time SS-*Untersturmführer* Baron

Manfred von Brauchitsch on his way to victory in the Eifel Race on 3 June 1934. The key element of the 'paint-scraping' myth, namely that the W25s were over the regulation weight limit during practice, is false because the Eifel Race was not run to the 750kg formula. (Daimler AG)

Fritz Huschke von Hanstein. In his book *Automobilsport*, published in 1978, he allowed himself a quiet joke by reacting to the Silver Arrow legend with a variant of his own. On page 26 he spins an extravagant yarn in the manner of another German nobleman, the egregious Baron von Münchhausen: 'In 1934, when a new racing formula was introduced which permitted a maximum weight of 750kg, it is said that on the day of the technical weigh-in for the first race the Auto Union cars weighed a mite too much. While everyone was still puzzling as to where weight could be saved, the designer Professor Ferdinand Porsche already had a penknife in his hand and began to scrape off the white racing paint specified for Germany. When the paint had been removed by the mechanics, all of a sudden the weight was exactly correct, and the car appeared in the flashing silver of its metal bodywork. And since white and silver are similar anyway, the meticulous gentlemen of the committee turned a blind eye. From then on the racing cars of Auto Union and Mercedes pursued their victorious progress from 1934 to 1939 as *Silver Arrows*.'

However, not even this ironic trope could shift the stubborn persistence of the Neubauer fairy tale. If a legend sounds better than the workaday truth, it is always the legend that gets printed. Today the Silver Arrows myth seems to have become ineradicable, and will remain so because it is part of the treasure-house of stories that reinforce the identity of a major corporation. That the legend of the scratched-off paintwork could become established the moment its seed was sown is also due to the fact that in 1958 the remnants of the former Auto Union GmbH came under the ownership of Daimler-Benz AG. In the conditions of a divided Germany it was all the easier in the West to suppress the information that the Saxon racing cars were resplendent in silver at the start of their first race on the AVUS – *before* their rivals from Stuttgart. And so, since the 1950s, the idea of the Silver Arrows was consistently and exclusively regarded by public opinion in the Federal Republic as synonymous with Mercedes-Benz racing cars. It sometimes even happened that particularly canny journalists designated the Auto Union racing cars as 'Silver Fish' to distinguish them from the Silver Arrows of Mercedes-Benz.

However, with the founding of the Audi NSU Auto Union AG, the forerunner of today's Audi AG, under the umbrella of the Volkswagen group, the picture has changed for Daimler-Benz since the 1980s. For it was natural that for image and marketing reasons the competitor in Ingolstadt (Audi) would hark back to the tradition of Auto Union's racing history. Curiously, the term 'Silver Arrow' was actually protected in favour of Audi AG under trademark law, until an agreement was reached with Daimler-Benz AG in December 1992. Audi waived any right to market current models under the Silver Arrow name, and in return Mercedes-Benz renounced its claim to the Horch symbol (see Chapter 3, Note 2). At the same time, however, the Audi board made it clear to their opposite numbers in Untertürkheim that 'in presenting the history of our firm we cannot dispense with the designation *Silver Arrow*, since in the 1930s racing cars of both Mercedes and Auto Union were so named in the press. Thus, wherever historical events are publicised by our company, be it in book form, in films or on video, we must be able to make correct historical use of this designation.'

Another attempt to sweep away the legend was made in 1994 by Eugen Reichle, then aged 83. Reichle had in fact been one of Daimler-Benz's race mechanics at the 1934 Eifel event. He is quoted in the trade magazine *Motor Klassik* as saying that the Mercedes-Benz racing cars were already silver then. There was no question of the white paint being sandpapered off on the night before the race. At the time Daimler-Benz made no counter-claim, and Reichle died in 1997 firmly convinced that he was in the right. Yet Alfred Neubauer's myth lived on – more than seven decades after Manfred von Brauchitsch's victory on the Nürburgring – until 2007, when the author of this book had the opportunity to present the German TV company ARD and the quality newspaper *Süddeutsche Zeitung* with details from the official race regulations, preserved in the archives of the ADAC in Munich: the 1934 Eifel Race (as well as the AVUS event the same year) was not run to the 750kg formula at all, but was a free formula competition that divided the cars by engine capacity alone (over or under 1,500cc) and rendered their weight irrelevant. There was simply no need for last-minute paint-scraping the night before the race.

Diversionary tactics

The 'Third Reich' of the Nazis was a dictatorship by consensus, which relied on tacit acceptance by the mass of the population and at the same time endeavoured to compensate for the disenfranchisement of the common people and sidelining of the old elites by offering social benefits and nationalistic posturing. Among these diversionary tactics, the racing

Hail the victor! Homecoming at the Mercedes-Benz headquarters in Stuttgart-Untertürkheim after the début Eifel victory in 1934: admiring employees and officials surround Manfred von Brauchitsch, sitting in his winning W25, along with Alfred Neubauer and other team personnel. The swastika-adorned entrance conveys the sponsor's message… (Daimler AG)

successes of the mighty Silver Arrows were, of course, a grandiose affirmation of German identity. Year after year Hitler and the other top Nazis blustered about 'the restoration of national honour', preached abroad on 'the revision of the Treaty of Versailles' and at the same time proposed 'peace through an equal right to rearm' in order to mollify the long-suffering German people with rearmament and job-creation. There were also a few social benefits, ranging from Winter Aid to 'Strength through Joy', in the hope that these would 'buy' acceptance of political murder, persecution of the Jews and the establishment of a state built on injustice.

But this megalomaniac enterprise would presumably work best where the Nazi regime posed as completely 'non-political'. In the cinema and on the sports field. In concerts and operettas. All these opportunities for leisure distractions were ideally united in motor racing. Whether it was outside on the track with martial music, parades of NSKK troops and the noise and excitement of the race, or at home in the front room, clustered round a 'People's receiver' – where the live radio broadcast was acoustically embedded in an agreeably lulling musical background – on Sunday afternoons Germany was victorious all over the world. It was an unsuspected foretaste of what was to come.

From time to time the politicians offered their thanks to the racing car manufacturers whom they had encouraged both financially and ideologically. On 6 June 1934 Reich Transport Minister von Eltz-Rübenach again sent his written congratulations to the technical management of Daimler-Benz AG 'on the superior victory of your racing car at the Nürburgring', and went on: 'I am glad that the technical defects described by you could be swiftly remedied.' Even the secret opponent of the Untertürkheimers and promoter of Auto Union, Carl Eduard, Duke of Saxe-Coburg-Gotha, sent his congratulations – if belatedly: 'My delight at your successes is all the greater since I was able to contribute to them in a modest way. When I submitted to the Reich Transport Minister the allocation of the sum approved for new racing designs, I was certain of the success of the participating companies. I wish you all the best for the future as well. Heil Hitler!' Kissel replied with another 'Heil Hitler' and thanked the Duke for his 'warm advocacy in the decision on Reich funding for the building of racing cars. We ask Your Royal Highness to accept our assurances that in the future, too, we will do all we can to secure more fine victories. We know that in this way we will best be able to repay our deeply felt debt of gratitude towards the Reich.'

Auto Union was soon to celebrate its first victory as well. True, the rivals from Stuttgart were absent, yet Hans Stuck's victory in the Felsberg Race in the Saar region on 10 June 1934 garnered, among other things, some political bonus-points. A few days after the date of 13 January 1935 had been fixed for the plebiscite over the future of the Saar territory (then under international control[7]), the appearance of Hans Stuck on the track was a symbolic gesture, as if to say 'The Saar stays German!' In hill-climbs, Auto Union's number one driver had no competition to fear. And a week later, on 17 June, in the first encounter between the rival German racing stables since the Eifel Race, Stuck won the Kesselberg Race in Austria, with a clear lead over Nürburgring winner von Brauchitsch.

The previous day Wilhelm Kissel had conferred in Munich with Adolf Hühnlein over the granting of further subventions. It was not only on the track that successes were being organised. This is perhaps why, in the battle for subsidies, the rivals from Saxony were, literally, showing the flag more prominently than ever. For the tensely awaited first foreign Grand Prix the tails of the three Auto Union cars were painted with a swastika as well as the national flag. When the three works cars from Mercedes-Benz appeared at the Grand Prix de l'Automobile Club de France in Montlhéry they lacked these adornments. The race started on 1 July 1934. During the previous night Hitler and the SS had decapitated the SA in a bloodbath (see Note 5). The murder of Röhm and other high-ranking SA officers was part and parcel of a targeted liquidation of declared opponents of Hitler. Among those shot by the SS was Dr Erich Klausener, a leading figure in the 'Catholic Action' organisation, and also, as a permanent secretary in the Reich Ministry of Transport, quite simply *the* man behind the Nürburgring.[8]

The head of the NSKK in danger?

Even a loyal paladin and party warrior like Adolf Hühnlein could be under threat in times like these. He was not only in charge of the NSKK but also held the senior rank of *Obergruppenführer* in the SA. He was also known to be a political ally and friend of Ernst Röhm. For those reasons alone the '*Führer* of German motorsport' and chairman of the ONS ran the risk of getting into dangerous waters surrounding the supposedly imminent 'Röhm *putsch*'. Mercedes-Benz racing manager Alfred Neubauer, in his anecdotal memoirs, circulated the story that Hühnlein was lucky to have been spending that weekend with the German racing teams in Montlhéry for the French Grand Prix: 'A man was sitting with us, whose face was pale and whose lips trembled. It was *Obergruppenführer* and major (retd.) Adolf Hühnlein – boss of the NSKK. Admittedly, this man was a leading Nazi, but at heart he was not a bad type. A coarse clod from Bavaria but decent enough under it all.' With these blustering words in the late 1950s Neubauer put a harmless complexion on Hühnlein's role and function, in order once more to perpetuate the legend that motor racing was completely non-political under the Third Reich.

Would Hühnlein in fact have been in danger of his life had he been in Germany? More than a month later Erwin Kraus, his number two in the NSKK and then its technical consultant, accused SS Region South of having circulated false reports in the wake of the 'Röhm *putsch*', to the effect that he, Kraus, had been arrested and Hühnlein shot. While the unsuspecting NSKK chief was watching the Grand Prix at Montlhéry the SS had indeed searched his house and various NSKK offices during the 'Night of the Long Knives'. Was this a revenge operation? On his return Hühnlein complained to Himmler that it was. This was probably the start of lasting conflict between the two Nazi officials. At all events, the SS leadership would encroach more and more on Hühnlein's turf and use their stronger political muscle against the NSKK.

On the other hand, it is apparent that even after the state-sanctioned murder of the top ranks of the SA, Hühnlein, the party loyalist, remained among Hitler's closest entourage. Particularly so since this family man from Franconia restricted his leadership claims to the fields of motoring and motor racing, and apart from that always remained a loyal Party supporter – a Nazi noted for his conviviality, and a convinced anti-Semite with a dubious talent for public speaking. In 1932 none other than Joseph Goebbels, when attending the annual Nazi commemoration of the miserably unsuccessful Munich *putsch*, noted in his diary: '9 November. Day of the Dead! Big demonstration in front of the banners. Major Hühnlein made a speech. Ghastly.'

Neubauer and Hühnlein – absolutely non-political? (Sebastian)

But 10 years later, on 21 June 1942, at the state funeral for Hühnlein following his death three days earlier after a lengthy illness, it was Goebbels of all people who gave the address: 'The *Führer* and the Party mourn one of their oldest comrades-in-arms, hundreds of thousands of German men of the NSKK [mourn] their beloved and revered corps leader, the old guard of the Party [mourn] a good friend and colleague, and the entire German people [mourn] one of the most prominent personalities of our National Socialist revolution, and the present political and governmental conditions it has created.' Adolf Hühnlein may in retrospect have been caricatured as a ridiculous figure by many of the star drivers, yet in his lifetime the racetrack heroes, mindful of their privileged position, found it convenient always to be on the best of terms with their corps leader.

Hühnlein, who in 1936 was personally promoted by Hitler to the rank of major-general and appointed chairman of the ONS, not only controlled the whole of motorsport but also sat on the board of the company that built the autobahns, and was a member of the Reich Transport Council and the Reich Chamber of Labour. In addition to the 'Order of Blood' and the Party Gold Medal, Hühnlein was allowed, after the 1938 Party Congress, to use the title *Reichsleiter*, one of the highest distinctions in the NSDAP, which he shared with few others. At his state funeral, Hitler awarded him posthumously the Supreme Degree of the German Order, the highest decoration of the Nazi state. In 1942 Hühnlein was only the third German to receive this honour. No, the top men in German motor racing had no choice but to stay in his good books. To their mutual advantage, of course. The fact that from time to time Hühnlein seems to have favoured the directors of Daimler-Benz AG slightly more than their Auto Union competitors would lead again and again to some highly intriguing situations. And in one case – indirectly at least – would even contribute to the death of probably the most popular German racing driver of the time.

It will all be fine

On 1 July 1934, in the French town of Montlhéry, far away from events in the German Reich, the Silver Arrows were heading for their last big defeat of the season. Certainly at the start Stuck, Caracciola and Fagioli got away quicker than the competition. But not a single German car reached the finishing line. The Alfa Romeos of Scuderia Ferrari celebrated a triple victory, with Chiron, Varzi and Moll/Trossi taking the first three places. Four laps behind, Robert Benoist in a Bugatti was fourth and last over the line. Scarcely six years later, the French racetrack hero and First World War aviator was to show his mettle in a very different situation. For after the German occupation of France Benoist moved on to become one of the leading figures in the Resistance – until he fell into the hands of the Gestapo on 7 June 1944 and was murdered by the SS in Buchenwald concentration camp on 14 September that year. His Bugatti stablemate, William Grover-Williams, who lived in France and won the Monaco Grand Prix in 1929, also went underground and operated as a British agent against the German occupiers. He too was arrested by the Gestapo, probably on 14 March 1945, and was shot in a concentration camp. Another driver who joined the Resistance was Jean-Pierre Wimille, the most successful French racing driver of those years; but he succeeded in eluding the unwelcome attentions of the Nazis. On 5 September 1945, in the first race held in Europe after the end of the Second World War, held in the Bois de Boulogne in Paris, he won the large car class in a Bugatti.

None of this could be foreseen, of course, on that hot July Sunday in 1934 at Montlhéry, near Paris. And even as the Nazi dictatorship, with its rearmament, territorial claims and political blackmail, was bringing the Second World War steadily closer, every weekend the top European drivers were living in a strange kind of symbiosis. They seemed like a little international family, untouched by the big political goings-on in Fascist Italy and National Socialist Germany. At least, that is the beautiful myth.

Naturally, they were all pros, sportsmen in great demand who belonged to a small, elite community: Rudolf Caracciola, the German with an Italian surname; his friend Louis Chiron, whose partner 'Baby' Hoffman, the heiress to a fortune, would later marry the widower 'Caratsch'; Tazio Nuvolari and Achille Varzi, the idols and rivals of motor-racing-mad Fascist Italy; their compatriot Luigi Fagioli, who combined motor racing with manufacturing pasta; the Frenchman René Dreyfus, of Jewish extraction, who astonishingly took part in the German Grand Prix at the Nürburgring as late as 1939, because at that time the Nazis were only robbing *German* Jews of their property and possessions, not to mention their lives. All these men drove for their home countries – it was a patriotic age – but first and foremost they drove for themselves. And if things are going well on

Louis Chiron's Alfa Romeo takes the lead at the start of the 1934 French Grand Prix at Montlhéry, followed by Rudolf Caracciola's Mercedes-Benz. The Italian racing cars entered by the Scuderia Ferrari took the first three places, but thereafter the 'Silver Arrows' won all of the season's major Grands Prix. (Reuss)

the racetrack, the pampered German motor-racing elite told themselves, perhaps everything is fine in politics too. After all, they had unbeatably fast cars to drive at last and did not want to miss out on winning. And in a moment of honesty even Manfred von Brauchitsch confirmed this decades later: 'Thinking that everything would be fine under the Nazis, those funny little members of the master race in their ridiculous uniforms – that was one of the many self-delusions we had in those days.'

Government aid as of right

On 13 July 1934, that is to say after the wipe-out in the French Grand Prix and immediately before the most important race of the year for the German stables – the German Grand Prix at the Nürburgring – Daimler-Benz chief executive Kissel sent another written approach to Adolf Hühnlein and requested an early remittance of the 300,000 RM set aside as a subsidy, as well as 'further sums for the subvention of racing car construction'. He wrote that the accumulated costs since the beginning of the racing car project and up to the 1934 year-end would 'far exceed the sum of 1½ million marks'. On the same day a letter on this subject also went to Reich Transport Minister von Eltz-Rübenach, who replied on 25 July, ten days after Hans Stuck had won the German Grand Prix and inflicted an embarrassing defeat on Mercedes-Benz. The Ministry only paid out 100,000 RM; the remainder of the promised sum was broken down into four instalments of 50,000 RM and only remitted in the middle of August, September, October and November. In return for participating in ten selected national and international races, the two corporations could expect further subsidies amounting to 100,000 RM, 'the allocation of which I reserve to myself,' the Reich Minister informed them, and held out the prospect of 'further funds up to a total of 100,000 RM for the payment of success-related bonuses for those German firms which gain first prizes in the aforementioned racing events.'

Stuck's win for Auto Union at the Nürburgring was the start of an unparalleled series of victories. Wherever the Silver Arrows appeared from this time on, the foreign competition always lost out. On 5 August Caracciola, in a Mercedes-Benz, won the Klausen Pass hill-climb, and

on 15 August Fagioli took the Coppa Acerbo. Auto Union and its top driver, Stuck, triumphed again in the Grosser Bergpreis von Deutschland (German Mountain Grand Prix) on 19 August at the Schauinsland circuit near Freiburg, and on 26 August in the Swiss Grand Prix, while on 9 September Mercedes-Benz won the Italian Grand Prix. Fagioli took over the W25 originally driven by Caracciola and steered it to victory at Monza, and also secured first place for the Untertürkheim company in the Spanish Grand Prix. Stuck – in the absence of Mercedes-Benz – won the Mont Ventoux hill-climb on 16 September, and in the last race of the season, Czechoslovakia's Masaryk Prize on 30 September, Auto Union again took the honours, with Stuck beating Fagioli to the chequered flag.

In the space of four months the Silver Arrows had turned the pecking order in international motor racing completely on its head. The German works' racing stables had entered 13 races and won 11 of them. Auto Union had clocked up six wins, and Mercedes-Benz five. The four-wheeled advertising platforms for Germany's reawakened international standing had been undefeated since 15 July.

Meanwhile, Untertürkheim continued to enjoy rather better contacts with the regime. Jakob Werlin informed his board colleagues by telephone on 10 October 1934 about the outcome of a meeting at the Reich Transport

Opposite: The undisputed Auto Union team leader in 1934. Hans Stuck, the winner of three Grands Prix and four mountain climbs that year, is seen on his way to victory in the season's last Grand Prix, at Brno on 30 September. (Audi AG)

Right: At the 1934 Spanish Grand Prix at the Lasarte circuit near San Sebastian, race winner Luigi Fagioli flashes past Alfred Neubauer and a mechanic signalling his position. (Daimler AG)

Ministry: of the 100,000 RM in subsidies, Mercedes-Benz and Auto Union indeed received half each. However, the success bonus of 100,000 RM was divided in a ratio of 4:3 in favour of the Untertürkheimers, who received a sum of 57,145 RM while the balance of 42,855 RM went to Auto Union. The symbolic impact of this decision on both competing companies, and the discretion with which the state subsidies were handled, is shown by the instruction passed on by Werlin: 'The condition was very expressly laid down that the allocation of the performance bonus may not be used for propaganda purposes.'

By now NSKK chief Hühnlein was playing a major part in the distribution of state subsidies. In the light of the German successes, both he and the ministerial bureaucrats were worried by the fact that the international federation of automobile clubs (the AIACR) – the body responsible for drawing up motor racing's regulations – were 'making efforts to alter the rules for the next race season in such way that in future supercharged

Hans Stuck stormed away to victory after the start of the 1934 Swiss Grand Prix at the Bremgarten circuit in Berne. Note the difference between the modern shape of the Auto Union compared with the Alfa Romeo in second place (Achille Varzi) and the number 26 Maserati (Geoffredo Zehender). (Audi AG)

engines will no longer be permitted,' as Werlin reported to Kissel on 10 October. 'This proposal is clearly directed against the German motor industry, and it is urgently necessary that an objection is raised immediately against any plan of this kind, if possible by Schippert [Carl Schippert, another board member] at the Automobile Exhibition in Paris.'

However, the really serious haggling that took place at the autumn conference of the AIACR was not over a possible ban on superchargers, but about the future classification of racing cars. To protect the two car companies, Hühnlein would later make sure that the 750kg formula dominated by the German racing stables would not be phased out at the end of the 1936 season, as planned, but would be renewed for another year. Most importantly, however, he achieved his objective that from 1935 onwards the most successful driver in that class would be awarded the title of 'European Champion'. It was another propaganda coup for the Nazi regime and its heroes in the Silver Arrows; and until the Second World War brought an end to Grand Prix racing, only German drivers were ever crowned European Champion.

Germany's racing successes also meant that Hühnlein's position was strengthened. When it came to motorsport he now had a hand in everything. And here the NSKK leader reflected the particular nature of Nazi dictatorship. In the distributing of favours there were more and more levels of authority and sycophantic courtiers, who could be played off against each other. Hühnlein and his NSKK were in competition with Himmler's SS; the bureaucracy in the Reich Transport Ministry also wanted to be courted; but the most useful thing to have – if it could somehow be found – was a direct line to Hitler's chancellery. If you could in some way invoke 'the *Führer*'s will', you would beat every other argument.

Ultimately all the directors of Daimler-Benz and Auto Union, as well as their drivers, were concerned about one thing: gaining advantages – for the company and for their own advancement. And until Hitler, as the final court of appeal, reached a decision – if he ever did! – everyone tried to weave their way through the Nazi bureaucracy and secure a *fait accompli* which would then receive a retrospective blessing from on high. This system, described by a number of historians as a chaos of overlapping powers and accountabilities, was ideal soil for the string-pullers and motorsport lobbyists to operate in. And in the end the racing drivers themselves, through contacts with the top SS men and other Nazi heavyweights, procured advantages that would ease their path both on the racetrack and in their private lives.

So these were great times for men such as Jakob Werlin, who on 11 October reported to his Chief Executive, Wilhelm Kissel, about a personal chat with the head of the NSKK. Regarding subsidies, Hühnlein recommended that expenses for the 1934 season be drawn up in advance, in case the Ministry of Finance was planning to introduce cuts. But there was no cause for alarm: 'This is one of the points that Herr Hühnlein intends to discuss with the *Führer*.' Admittedly, the Reich Transport Ministry would, in a letter to Kissel of 22 December, point out the financial stringency that made it necessary to postpone further subsidies until the next financial year, commencing 1 April 1935. But Hühnlein took over this matter himself, once and for all. On 19 December 1934 he had called on Hitler and on 19 January 1935 he assured Kissel that he would intervene on behalf of funding: 'In addition, I would ask you in future to route all requests for subvention through me, so that I am in a position from the outset to represent the wishes of the German vehicle industry to the Reich Transport Ministry in accordance with the requirements of the further development of German motorsport.'

In a swift reply, dated 21 January, Kissel was 'pleased' and 'deeply grateful' to note this, and at the same time informed the *Korpsführer* that Daimler-Benz had spent on its racing activities a sum which, after deduction of all subsidies received so far, was considerably in excess of a million Reichsmarks. For this reason he made a request to Hühnlein for 'adequate funds'. Victories by German racing cars were a national matter and should therefore receive full support from the National Socialist state. Considering the subsidies already granted, this was a view not fully shared by a number of Hitler's senior officials. After all, the racing successes did not *just* increase the reputation of the Third Reich, but also the fame of the companies, which, in return for this double honour, were fully expected to divert some of their own funds in that direction.

Peacefully united in milking the system

Mercedes-Benz and Auto Union were and remained rivals, but when it came to efficiently draining off tax-payers' money the two corporate bosses

Up where we belong: Sieg Heil! The celebratory German salute demonstrated during the winner's ceremony at the Belgian Grand Prix in 1935. And the winners were Rudolf Caracciola, Mercedes-Benz – and the Nazi regime. (Daimler AG)

continued to keep each other updated. In a concerted campaign in early March 1935, Hühnlein received urgent letters from both sides almost simultaneously. Needless to say, Kissel and von Oertzen had informed each other about the wording. On 1 March Kissel sent von Oertzen a copy of his draft letter to Hühnlein, and on 4 March von Oertzen returned the favour with a copy of *his* letter, for which Daimler-Benz's CEO immediately thanked him: 'I am glad to see that, in this submission, you have worked from roughly the same figures as us, and have made the matter as urgent as we have. I have asked Herr Werlin to present the matter personally with appropriate emphasis. I hope and wish that we may very soon achieve success!'

How did the corporations justify their begging letters, now that they were in excellent financial shape thanks to government-financed rearmament and a recovery in the automobile market? In the 1934 financial year Daimler-Benz AG had made an operating profit of 27.56 million RM on sales of 146.8 million. Their profit after tax and financial costs was 4.12 million. Kissel was careful to explain that 'the business situation in our industry must certainly be regarded as good, thanks to the support we have received from the Reich government, and especially from our *Führer* and Chancellor Adolf Hitler; nevertheless, it cannot be denied that pricing is extremely keen, allowing us only a very minimal profit. Furthermore, there are a number of considerable cost-factors which have an unavoidable impact on our profit-and-loss account.' For not only must 'racing cars be made ready for the coming season,' but 'manufacturing to meet the spring and summer demand' must be put in hand. As though this information was quite astonishing from the Chief Executive of a motor group, Kissel went on to make this plea to Hühnlein: 'At all events we ask you, *sehr geehrter* [esteemed] *Herr Korpsführer*, to see to it that we receive state aid for the current year, which at least approximately covers our costs, and we particularly request you urgently to ensure that a large transfer of money, if at all possible amounting to about 1 million RM, is made as quickly as possible.'

Von Oertzen, in his 4 March letter to Hühnlein, made this point: 'Up to the end of 1935 we had spent the enormous sum of 2,219,428 RM on our racing cars. After deducting state subsidies as well as revenues from

Sieg Heil...ho hum... At times, especially when abroad, German rituals became a boring routine, even for the Germans themselves. These Auto Union mechanics seem somewhat unenthusiastic during the ceremony before the start of the Hungarian Grand Prix at Budapest in 1936. (Kirchberg)

starts and prizes, and contributions from the accessories industry, Auto Union 'has spent from its own pocket in the years 1933/34 the sum of 1,273,571 RM.' From this he concluded that 'all the relevant government departments, but in particular the *Führer* and Reich Chancellor himself, will be sympathetic if we are obliged to ask you to arrange a considerably higher government subvention than has been the case hitherto.'

Like their Mercedes-Benz competitors, Auto Union also planned to start the 1935 season with new racing cars and new engines. The outlay was getting even higher, since the German works teams would be entering nearly twice as many events, each time with not just two or three cars, as in 1934, but with four to six.

Both von Oertzen and Kissel cast a shroud of secrecy over the precise details of their calculations. However, on 5 March Kissel sent some convincing cost estimates to Werlin, his colleague on the board and in the Party, by airmail and special messenger. He put the cost of race entries in Germany at 35,000 RM and abroad at 50,000 RM per event, but did not provide any other data because 'we want to avoid exposing our plans concerning the racing cars and their engines more than is necessary, so that there won't be too much talk about them and we will prevent the competition from learning anything of our intentions.'

Mercedes-Benz were tooling up massively for the coming races, for which six new, even more powerful 4-litre engines were being built. Depending on the fuel mixture, their output was more than 370bhp. Furthermore, three power units from the previous year were to be updated to a similar standard and held in reserve. Four of the total of six cars from the 1934 season were modified to take the new engine, and two more were built from new, which were to be entered in 'formula-free events' – 4.3-litre engines were built for these, with considerably higher performance and delivering over 400bhp. The costs of these undertakings, as given by Kissel to Werlin, came to 960,000 RM. But that was not enough: 'The results of last year's races have prompted our technicians to move forward in the design principles of the chassis as well. After repeated trials and studies they have come to the conclusion that it is essential to prepare a chassis for the 1935 season, which will not incorporate a floating rear axle, as was previously the norm, but a design which makes use of parallel-sprung wheels. The particular reason for this is, in view of the high speeds, to guarantee the best possible roadholding even in wet weather. That is why you will find, under the heading *Manufacture of 5 new chassis units* – the sum of 400,000 RM.'

Compared with the first year of racing the expenditure had nearly doubled, but each newly-built racing car worked out cheaper for the company than the first generation of Silver Arrows. For now there was a payback from the cost-intensive learning curve of the years 1933–4. 'No half measures' was the watchword. They would now harvest what, with powerful support, they had sown a year ago.

Mercedes-Benz and Auto Union were entering all the Grand Prix races with at least three cars each, and usually with four. For the German Grand Prix, Untertürkheim even entered a fifth W25, which the former race mechanic Hermann Lang was allowed to drive. At the same time Daimler-Benz AG had to cope with the death of its Chief Designer, Hans Nibel, who suffered a stroke on 25 November 1934. Under his successor Max Sailer, the engineer Rudolf Uhlenhaut – equally gifted as a racing driver – carried development forward so dramatically that Mercedes-Benz was able to dominate Grand Prix racing until the late summer of the 1935 season.

Of course, Auto Union remained the keenest competitor, particularly since its team had been strengthened by the young Bernd Rosemeyer, who had already created a stir as a motorcycle racer for the DKW works stable. He swiftly proved to be the discovery of the year, winning his first Grand Prix at the end of the season. Yet compared to Mercedes-Benz the Saxon Silver Arrows would all too often be handicapped by various defects and misfortunes.

Victories to order

A replenishment of the subsidies was no longer really necessary for the sweeping success of the German racing cars. The season had already begun when, on 29 April 1935, the Reich Transport Ministry allocated to each of the companies a grant of 200,000 RM. That was precisely one fifth of the sum that was apparently so urgently needed. On 24 June a supplement of 125,000 RM was paid out. However, Mercedes-Benz and Auto Union were battling for sharply increased success bonuses now totalling 180,000 RM, which would be awarded for 15 circuit races – six Grands Prix and nine big international events. The Nazi government now paid 10,000 RM for a win in an internationally important event, and a second place would henceforth be rewarded with 5,000 RM. The first two positions in less important outings such as the AVUS or the Eifel were still worth 7,000 and 3,000 RM respectively to the Ministry. There was a clear and unambiguous statement from the state sponsors as to why the subsidies should continue to be paid: 'Since the rest of the world is setting out to challenge with all its resources the undoubted predominance that Germany under its National Socialist government has been able to achieve in the field of automobile racing in such a short time, the Reich government intends to encourage the further development of German racing cars through state aid this year as well.'

However, the list of events qualifying for 'government performance bonuses' in 1935 no longer included a single hill-climb. This was a measure that the Mercedes-Benz lobbyists in Hühnlein's ONS had pushed through in the light of Hans Stuck's successes for Auto Union the previous year. And although the Saxon company expressly abandoned its entry for the Monaco Grand Prix on 22 April 1935, a meeting in the Reich Transport Ministry in mid-April nonetheless included it on the list of events qualifying for state success bonuses. Thus when the Italian Fagioli won the first race of the season in Monte Carlo for Mercedes-Benz – in a record time – he presented his racing stable with 10,000 RM from the state coffers. On the other hand the reward for second place was not paid out, because the Silver Arrows of Manfred von Brauchitsch and Rudolf Caracciola both retired.

However, it was significant that the Tunis Grand Prix on 5 May was missing from the bonus list. Daimler-Benz did not even enter this event, whereas Auto Union kept its word to its new star Achille Varzi and placed one of their new V16s at his disposal, in which he promptly won the race. The season's first encounter between the two companies took place two weeks later, at the Tripoli Grand Prix in Libya, which Caracciola settled in favour of Mercedes-Benz. Only five laps before the finish Varzi still looked like being the winner, but then a faulty tyre forced him into second place. Fagioli in another Mercedes-Benz came third, while von Brauchitsch in the third car from Untertürkheim, and Stuck in the second Auto Union, both pulled out. Two weeks later, at the AVUS Race on 26 May, Stuck won the first qualifying heat and Caracciola the second, but the final was won by Fagioli. The Eifel Race on 16 June saw another success for Mercedes-Benz, though the headlines focussed less on the victorious Caracciola and more on newcomer Rosemeyer, who lay second in the Auto Union 16-cylinder until his final lap.

Left: The first Italian at Auto Union: Achille Varzi prepares for an AVUS test run in 1935 with the mighty V16 – the beginning of a sometimes successful but in the end unpleasant relationship. (Audi AG)

Opposite: Winning at any expense: for the high-speed AVUS Race in 1935, Auto Union created special streamliners that had their origins in land speed record-breaking. (Audi AG)

Jubilation in the press was entirely permissible, but even in the ostensibly non-political world of motor racing, research that went a bit too deep was not welcomed by the government. Nonetheless, on 17 June the *Frankfurter Zeitung* – the last daily paper in Germany that could to some extent ignore the strictures of Nazi censorship – came up with this news item: 'The racing-manager of Auto Union, *Oberingenieur* Walb, stated at the end of the Eifel Race, that in the last lap two spark plugs in Rosemeyer's car had failed [it was well known that Auto Union racing cars had 16-cylinder engines], so that he was prevented from reaching full speed on the straights. We can add to our report the fact that in Rosemeyer's car the windscreen shattered in about the fourth lap. This means that in the enormous speeds of this race (on the straights the cars reached speeds of around 220kph) the young driver was exposed to the full pressure of the airflow. This is not merely a great stress on the body, but also an actual handicap, since under these conditions it is no longer possible to hear the engine, and when changing gear one can only be guided by feel and by the rev counter.'

On the very same day there was a reaction from the Nazi censors. At the daily Reich press conference an instruction was issued to all editors: 'The statement by Auto Union about the failure of the driver [Rosemeyer] in yesterday's Nürburg race, which has been printed in this morning's edition

Ferdinand Porsche and Bernd Rosemeyer at the Nürburgring. (Porsche AG)

of the *Frankfurter Zeitung* is not to be picked up [by other newspapers].' So this kind of precise detail on the actual background to the victories and defeats of the German national racing cars was not to be conveyed to a shocked public. German technology does not fail, nor does it in any way bow to the trivial chances and mishaps of the racetrack. What is more, the comments by the Auto Union racing manager were designed to belittle the success of Mercedes-Benz and its champion driver.

Caracciola celebrated a further win at the French Grand Prix on 23 June, and the triumph was completed by von Brauchitsch taking second place. The silver racing cars passed the chequered flag in quick succession, thus taking impressive revenge for the previous year's humiliation at the same Montlhéry circuit. By now the W25 delivered more than 445bhp, and the Auto Union B-type around 400bhp. Compared with this the most powerful Alfa Romeo produced just 330, the best Maserati 290, and the hopelessly outdated Bugatti Type 59 a mere 240bhp. For their Grand Prix, the organisers from the Automobile Club de France had furnished the course with three narrow chicanes, which were intended to rein in the superior speed of the German cars. Indeed, Chiron and Nuvolari, in their Scuderia Ferrari Alfa Romeos, did benefit from this measure for a while, but in the end the Silver

Arrows won through, as they were bound to. But because Fagioli engaged in a bitter duel with Caracciola and in doing so put too much pressure on his team-mate, the Untertürkheimers missed the triple triumph that had been within their grasp – much to Neubauer's annoyance. Auto Union was dogged by engine damage and carburettor problems; Rosemeyer was a good four laps behind and finished in fifth place.

With an eye to the most important race of the year, the German Grand Prix on 28 July, the Silver Arrows from Saxony took a temporary break from racing, in which the technical problems were to be cured. The Mercedes-Benz team were on their own: on 30 June Fagioli won the Penya-Rhin Grand Prix in Barcelona ahead of Caracciola. On 14 July Caracciola came first in the Belgian Grand Prix ahead of the Fagioli/von Brauchitsch duo. This meant that when they went on to the starting grid at the Nürburgring the silver national racing cars had been unbeaten for more than a year.

Unpalatable truths

Was this all 'completely non-political', as the racetrack heroes never tired of telling us after 1945? In neighbouring countries things were regarded very differently at the time. On 22 July 1935 a very percipient article appeared in the Swiss newspaper *Berner Tagwacht*. Under the headline '*Deutschland,*

Nationalist fervour at the 1936 German Grand Prix. (Kirchberg)

Deutschland über alles! A racing car to conquer Europe', its anonymous author wrote:

'The Third Reich – rapidly isolated by the excessively bold sallies of its new men – needs successes […] Sweeping victories require men with brains. From the *intellectual stormtroopers*, marching faithfully in step and making a din with their blaring trumpets, we can expect nothing; the *intellectual soldiery* have been forced to desert the flag. We suddenly recall a category that has stayed behind and who might perhaps be in a position to achieve success: the technicians. For them business is business, whether it be black, red or brown, for war or for peace: it's all work. Only money gets you ahead! […] At a cosy meeting in Berlin – it was in the first spring of the revolution – some people got Adolf Hitler excited about a German People's car. In the same way, a racing car now has to be built, which will give Germany status in the world and bring in much-needed orders for industry. The men were careful to bring the racing car plans with them – the People's Car could wait. Adolf, who is in the advertising business himself, has always had a liking for bluffers – and a good nose for attention-grabbing novelties; once he heard about world status, something he had decided to work for in willing self-sacrifice all his life, he was ready for anything. […] And *HE* declared, as though the idea had been originally his: *We need successes, victories, records! Gentlemen – we'll build the racing car! And would you be good enough to work out plans for the People's Car.* The *Führer* commands – the Reichsbank opens wide its coffers…Since Mercedes-Benz is an international company that bears a famous old name, and since Auto Union possesses in Dr – now Reich Designer – Porsche, a designer of intelligence and genius, both firms will be given the contract.

'Success is on its way. In 1934 the entire world of sport is agog: German cars dominate the international races […] Success has arrived. The promotional idea is working. The world gasps at the miracle of German technology, this brilliant creation of German designers. […] The racing cars cost money: wide open cash-boxes at the Reichsbank, a staff of designers, a staff of highly qualified workers, a staff of ruthless racing drivers – and the fastest racing car comes into being and drives to victory.

'The racing-stables of Mercedes and Auto Union travel far and wide. The elite of European drivers are signed up: Caracciola, Varzi, Fagioli, Brauchitsch, Stuck. Men with courage and nerve, but who cost money. They are equally at home in St Moritz and Davos, in Monte Carlo and Nice. It's a straight bargain: the risk of death, pain and blood in return for money, lots of money…Good publicity is always expensive. […] The flags flutter high in the wind. Victories are celebrated at the factories. *Heil!* Speeches, more flags. *Hoch!* A brisk, up-beat speech by Hühnlein, the head of the Nazi Corps of Drivers: *Be proud, lads! German brains, German workmanship, German energy…* […]

'The workers proudly sing the German national anthem and – carry on working. The other section of the "national community", the directors, race managers and drivers, Herr Hühnlein and his staff, all head off into town. The Town Hall. The Burgomaster. Microphone, speech. Triumphal procession through enthusiastic crowds, who have assembled "spontaneously", of course. The grandest hotel. Gala dinner. Speech: *Heil Deutschland!* Onward to new victories! *Heil!* […] That is what the face of the new Germany is like. The facade: party rallies with fireworks costing millions, weddings for bigwigs with presents costing millions, subsidies amounting to millions for serial bankrupts, for the smoke-and-mirrors merchants. Only one thing has yet to come: a massive crash – but it's already approaching.

Awaiting Adolf Hühnlein: in the middle of this typical Nürburgring scenario Bernd Rosemeyer's trademark Tyrolean hat can be spotted in the foreground. (Kirchberg)

'Behind it all is the reality: soup kitchens and pennies for beggars, collecting-boxes and Winter Aid (for which Mercedes-Benz actually donated 50,000 marks…) a starving nation, a humiliated, bleeding working class. Bread and circuses for the people, but for the bosses profits such as they have not seen for a many a year.

'A Roman circus under the sign of the swastika – it is no different from the history of Rome and its profligate Caesars.'

At the time, then, it was quite possible for outsiders to know and assess what intentions actually lay concealed behind the victories of Germany's Silver Arrows. In the Nazi-controlled press, however, the state subsidies for motor racing were an absolutely taboo subject, and were treated with secrecy both by the companies and by the authorities and Party offices. Nor was it just the Nazi regime that had suitable means of control and censorship. The motor manufacturers reacted to unwelcome reporting by withdrawing their advertising. In the case of Daimler-Benz just one article in the sports section of the mass-circulation *BZ am Mittag* was enough to arouse the displeasure of director Jakob Werlin. As a result the chief sports editor of the Ullstein publishing house wrote to Kissel on 9 December 1933, very humbly and with a German salute: 'I would like to take this opportunity to remind you of the differences, not yet settled, between Herr Direktor Werlin and our company, which arose at the end of the 2,000 Kilometres [Through Germany]. At the time Daimler-Benz AG took the position of blocking all advertisement orders to our company until this matter had been remedied. The last information we had from Herr Direktor Werlin is that he intended to leave the decision to the Reich Ministry for Propaganda and National Enlightenment. However, we have had no communication whatever from that quarter.'

Even supposedly non-political sports reporting was a minefield in the Third Reich. Interestingly, in their reporting of German racing successes the foreign specialist press also ignored – against their better judgement? – the information circulating *sub rosa* about the financial background to Mercedes-Benz's and Auto Union's victories. However, to quite a number of those correspondents the Nazi state subsidies were almost certainly an open secret, though right up to 1945 they were denied by the companies concerned. Even after the war they initially kept quiet about them, then played them down, and finally dismissed them as a triviality.

All the more significant, in regard to those discreet relationships, was the flurry of activity triggered by the Swiss newspaper article quoted above, which was published on 22 July 1935 but, astonishingly, only became known to Nazi motor racing officials in early October. Adolf Hühnlein personally brought in his closest contact on the Daimler-Benz board, Jakob Werlin: 'Since the writer is clearly employed at your factory, I am sending you the article for your confidential information and ask you to return it.'

Clearly the long arm of the Nazi regime reached far enough even to silence disobliging correspondents in Switzerland. In 1935 there was a precedent for this in the case of the émigré anti-Nazi journalist Berthold Jacob, who was abducted from his Swiss exile by a Gestapo commando team and taken back to Germany. Only after massive international pressure was Jacob released by his captors. In April 1936 Hans Wesemann, the principal German operative involved in the kidnap, was put on trial in Switzerland.

This, then, is the international background against which, on 12 November 1935, Werlin made a 'personal and strictly confidential' request to the head of the Mercedes-Benz Automobil AG in Zürich, a man named Muff, to find out who had written the article criticising the Nazi regime. Muff made some enquiries and replied on 4 December: 'It appears that at the time in question a man claiming to be a German emigrant came to our Bern office, introduced himself as a PhD and sports writer and sought financial assistance. Naturally, this was not given. Unfortunately the man's name was not recorded. According to my researches, he was quite tall and had red hair, and the staff there believe his name began with B and was the name of a German town. This made me think of a Herr Bielefeld, formerly on the staff of *Motor-Kritik*, but this is not definite. Needless to say, I got nothing from the *Berner Tagwacht*. I will continue my investigations.'

Werlin did not let go and further letters were exchanged, but all his enquiries drew a blank, so that on 6 April 1936 Muff noted: 'After all the investigations that have been carried out, it has proved impossible, short of some lucky coincidence, to find out who wrote the offending article. Nor has it been possible for me, since our recent conversation in Berlin, to make any progress in this matter. In the opinion of those questioned the author of the article was probably a sports writer living abroad. I am extremely sorry that in this matter, in which naturally I am also very interested, I have been unable to come to a more positive result.'

Bad losers?

The first and only defeat of the vastly superior German racing cars in the 1935 season occurred, believe it or not, at the German Grand Prix on 28 July, which was won – against all expectations but not undeservedly – by Tazio Nuvolari. The 43-year-old veteran pulled the trick off in an Alfa Romeo P3 that was almost three years old and had a thoroughly antiquated fixed axle, yet held its own against the modern German cars with their floating axles and a performance margin of more than 120bhp. The adverse weather conditions in the Eifel highlands particularly suited Nuvolari's driving skills, for the race started in the rain and the Nürburgring's northern loop never fully dried out in the course of the 22 laps. In addition almost everything went wrong for his German competitors. Stuck's engine flooded at the start, and as the team tried to push-start it mechanic Rudolf Friedrich was run over and seriously injured by stablemate Varzi. Suffering from the shock of this accident, Varzi finally asked to be replaced by the substitute driver, Prince zu Leiningen. Due to technical problems Auto Union's white hope, Bernd Rosemeyer, was unable to hang on to his lead in the long run, while their second rookie driver, Paul Pietsch, was thoroughly beaten and ended in ninth place.

Mercedes-Benz had as many as five irons in the fire, but their star driver Caracciola was feeling unwell and only managed to scrape third place. The cause of his indisposition was later diagnosed as a tapeworm. Fagioli was dogged by problems with his shock absorbers, while the team's up-and-coming drivers Hermann Lang and Hanns Geier were just too inexperienced. Consequently the only hope left for a German victory lay with Manfred von Brauchitsch. He did in fact take the lead, and halfway through the race achieved the fastest lap times of the whole weekend, with 10min 33.4sec and 10min 32.0sec. Nuvolari, who had being lying second up till then, only achieved a personal best of 10min 43sec. However, its higher speed cost the leading Mercedes-Benz more tyre rubber than had been calculated.

Racing manager Neubauer played tactical games for too long and, like von Brauchitsch, took the risk of doing without another tyre change. Two laps before the end von Brauchitsch still had a 32-second lead over Nuvolari: another pit stop would lose him at least a minute, and then in the very last lap he would have to catch up at least half a minute on Nuvolari. No, that wouldn't work. Von Brauchitsch had to drive on! In the last lap the 29-year-old German had a lead of as much as 43 seconds over Nuvolari's

Alfa Romeo when, scarcely 10km from the finish, the nearside rear tyre of the Mercedes tore itself to shreds going into the Carousel. Von Brauchitsch managed to keep the yawing car under control, but then the offside rear tyre also burst. Managing a mere 60kph (37mph), Germany's silver hope

The wrong man won! The Italian ace, Tazio Nuvolari, picking up the spoils of victory after the German Grand Prix of 1935. Despite this upset on home ground, for NSKK-Führer Adolf Hühnlein it has to be business as usual and his obligatory post-race speech will follow. (Reuss)

was still limping towards the line on bare rims long after Nuvolari had been flagged in as the winner.

In the August 1935 issue of *German Motoring – the Organ of the National Socialist Corps of Drivers*, journalist Hans Bindert wrote about the 'lucky chance' of Nuvolari's win: 'The German Grand Prix fell to Italy through a fickle twist of fate. Nonetheless, the applause for the tough Italian who trusted his luck was honest and warm. [...] Von Brauchitsch later came in fifth. Seldom if ever has a driver received such an ovation. There was not a single spectator, nor a single radio listener who, after this mighty struggle, would not have given the final victory to von Brauchitsch. If a demonstration of respect can ever compensate him in human terms for having victory snatched from him at the last minute, then this tribute certainly did so. In his closing address *Korpsführer* Hühnlein turned first to von Brauchitsch and thanked him, to another wave of applause from the crowd, for the heroic battle he had waged regardless of his own safety, before he was forced to concede the final victory to Nuvolari. Then he handed the Italian the prize of honour, endowed by the *Führer* and Reich Chancellor.' Bindert then quotes verbatim from Hühnlein's speech: 'Although we have [...] yielded first place to a foreign country, we can

That 'fickle twist of fate'. Manfred von Brauchitsch losing shreds of a rear tyre – and victory – on the last lap of the German Grand Prix in 1935 at the Nürburgring. (Daimler AG)

Hitler greets Caracciola, and following their Führer are Adolf Hühnlein and his NSKK deputy, Erwin Kraus, both having already passed Hermann Lang. Alfred Neubauer appears keen to give the customary German salute at this early-morning parade in front of the Reich Chancellery in Berlin in 1937. (Reuss)

nevertheless look with pride at the result of this race. The next eight places were all taken by German cars. [...] German brains, German workmanship and the exemplary comradeship between designer, worker and driver have once again produced achievements of which we can be proud. Our watchword has always been: carry on working! We don't sit around resting and rusting. Long live our wonderful motorsport and especially motor racing!' And what rounded off both the occasion and the article? 'With a *Sieg-Heil* to the *Führer*, in which the crowd of 300,000 enthusiastically joined, the Grosser Preis von Deutschland came to a worthy conclusion.'

Long after the Second World War, Rudolf Caracciola had this to say about Hühnlein's annual NSKK ritual at the Nürburgring: 'The organisers were uniformed, the club members were uniformed; after the race, sections of the uniformed Drivers' Corps paraded on the track. At the end of a race we were tired and sweaty. Even so we had to stand and listen to a long patriotic speech. If we won, it was a victory for the Fatherland; if we lost... well, of course that just wasn't allowed to happen.'

However, this did not prevent Caracciola – the star German driver resident in Switzerland even before 1933 – from occasionally beating the drum for Adolf Hitler in Nazi Germany. At the elections for the Greater German Reichstag on 10 April 1938, which was simultaneously linked by the Nazis with a referendum on the *Anschluss* or annexation of Austria, the reigning European Champion entered the fray with a clarion-call that appeared in the Nazi party newspaper, the *Völkischer Beobachter* ('National Observer'): 'We racing drivers are fighters for the global reputation of the German automobile industry. Our victories are at the same time triumphs of German engineering skill and workmanship. The *Führer* has given our factories the opportunity once more to build racing cars whose victories have erased the bitter memory of the years 1931–2 when Germany had to stand on the sidelines of motorsport. The unique successes of these new racing cars in the past four years are a victorious symbol of our *Führer*'s achievement in rebuilding the nation. Let us thank him for it on 10 April with a heartfelt *yes*!'

It is worth noting that, despite the strict foreign currency controls in Nazi Germany, Caracciola's salary was, of course, paid in Swiss francs. A fact that, despite his critical remarks, Hühnlein could do nothing to change. During the Second World War the most prominent of Daimler-Benz's works drivers continued to live in his villa in the Italian-speaking Swiss canton of Ticino, drawing a respectable salary from Untertürkheim, until in 1942 the firm's top management yielded to political pressure and ceased the payments.

Notes

1 *Reichskristallnacht* ('national crystal night') was the ironically innocuous name given to a well-orchestrated wave of violence against Jews and Jewish property which took place throughout Germany on 9–10 November 1938. The name refers to the vast amount of broken glass. It was organised by the SS in reprisal for the assassination of a minor German diplomat in Paris, Ernst vom Rath, by a German Jewish refugee. (The intended target had been the German ambassador; ironically, vom Rath himself was totally opposed to Nazism.) Reinhard Heydrich of the SS proudly reported to Hermann Göring that 74 Jews were killed or seriously injured, 20,000 arrested, 815 shops and 171 homes destroyed and 191 synagogues set ablaze. Although US President F.D. Roosevelt made a speech of condemnation a few days later, no international sanctions were imposed on Germany.

2 *Generalgouvernement*. Following the occupation of Poland by German forces in 1939 the country was divided into two administrative parts. In the western region, ethnic Poles were driven from their property which was then handed over to German-speakers brought in from the rest of Poland. This territory, known as the Warthegau, was incorporated into the Reich. The remainder of the country,

given the name *Generalgouvernement*, was treated as a slave state under the ruthless and arbitrary rule of Governor-General Hans Frank, who was hanged as a war criminal at Nuremberg in 1946.

3 The Ehrhardt Brigade had been established as Navy Brigade II by Lieutenant-Commander Hermann Ehrhardt in 1918, and took part in the counter-revolutionary Kapp *putsch* in Berlin in March 1920. In 1922 an offshoot of the by then defunct Ehrhardt Brigade, known as 'Organisation Consul', was responsible for the assassination of Germany's Foreign Minister, Walther Rathenau, in one of the most serious early challenges to the Weimar Republic.

4 Marshal Grigori Potemkin (1739–91) was the chief minister and sometime lover of the Empress Catherine the Great of Russia. One of his ways of giving a false impression of Russia's prosperity to important foreign visitors was to arrange for wooden facades of fine houses to be erected, concealing the hovels behind, and to people these with soldiers dressed as happy peasants.

5 At this time the SA was a serious rival both to the SS and the Reichswehr (the regular army), and there were rumours that Röhm was planning a coup. Whether or not this was true Hitler was determined to rid himself of the threat, and, with the eager collaboration of the SS, he ordered the liquidation of the senior ranks of the SA in the so-called 'Night of the Long Knives', on 30 June 1934. Röhm himself was arrested and imprisoned, and on 1 July Hitler gave orders for his old campaigning colleague to be shot.

6 Winifred Wagner (1897–1980) was born Winifred Williams in Hastings but was orphaned at the age of three and brought up by distant relatives in Berlin. Her guardian, a musician, was a friend of the Wagners, and introduced Winifred to the composer's widow Cosima, who saw the young woman as a suitable bride for her bisexual son Siegfried. The marriage duly took place, and after Siegfried's premature death Winifred took over the management of the Bayreuth Festival. In the early 1920s Winifred met and befriended the young Wagner enthusiast Adolf Hitler. An early supporter of Nazism, she visited Hitler in prison and the friendship blossomed. There were even rumours of a sexual relationship. (Before her widowhood, Winifred was already notoriously promiscuous.) After the war she was given a light sentence as a Nazi fellow-traveller. Right up to her death, she never renounced her admiration and affection for Hitler.

7 The Saar territory covered some 1,000 square miles (2,600 square kilometres) west of the Rhine. Until quite recently it was an important centre of the coal and steel industries. In 1919 the Treaty of Versailles placed the Saar under League of Nations control for 15 years, but France was allowed to exploit its resources. When the mandate expired a plebiscite was held to establish whether the population wished to be part of France or Germany. Ninety per cent voted for Germany, and this was hailed by Hitler as a triumph. Today the Saar, with its capital at Saarbrücken, is a *Land* or state of the Federal Republic.

8 A chilling account of Klausener's murder can be found in *The SS: A Warning from History* by Guido Knopp (Sutton Publishing, 2003): 'Shortly before 1 pm *Hauptsturmführer* Kurt Gildisch parked his car in front of the Reich Ministry of Transport. Gildisch asked for the office of a departmental head, Dr Erich Klausener. [...] As leader of "Catholic Action" [in his free time] Klausener had organised a demonstration of more than 60,000 people the previous week, in Berlin's Hoppegarten. [...] What is more, the civil servant had a background that did not appeal to Göring and Heydrich. Under the Weimar Republic Klausener had worked in the police department of the Prussian Ministry of the Interior. No one knew the criminal records of old Nazis better than he. Klausener was just leaving his office when his murderer confronted him. Gildisch told him he was under arrest. As the official reached for his jacket, the killer fired two shots into his head. An SS guard took up position outside the victim's office. Without looking round, Gildisch left the ministry building. Other assignments awaited him.'

CHAPTER FIVE

WORLD DOMINATION
ON THE RACETRACK

The heroes of Hitler's motor racing battles went along with the Nazi system, doing their bit to keep the big wheel turning. They were cheered and admired as idols of their age, as shining examples for a young generation brought up to be tough, courageous and fearless, and almost all of them managed to survive beyond the end of Germany's dictatorship – unlike so many of their young admirers, who were left dead by Hitler's war of annihilation. It is not a question of apportioning blame, merely one of asking whether men like that should still be the stuff of legend, honoured and glorified as heroic racing drivers just as they used to be. Should they be treated as separate from the times and circumstances under which their successes were achieved?

We should recall Victor Klemperer who, in December 1946, completed the manuscript for his book on the language of the Third Reich. The central notion, which Klemperer examines, dissects and finally attempts to dispose of, is heroism: 'Certainly [...] there were occasionally some real heroes among sportsmen and soldiers, even in Nazi Germany. But in general I remain sceptical about heroism, especially in those two professions. In both cases the heroism was often too obvious, too profitable, too satisfying to vanity, to be genuine. Certainly, those racing drivers were literally cavaliers of industry, their breakneck rides were intended to benefit German manufacturers and thus the Fatherland, and perhaps they were even intended to contribute to the general good, by adding their experience to the perfection of automobile construction. But there was so

The German racing cars even climbed alpine mountains. Manfred von Brauchitsch during practice for the Großglockner race in 1938 with his Mercedes-Benz. (Daimler AG)

much vanity, so much gladiatorial reward at stake! And while the racing drivers were presented with garlands and prizes, the soldiers received medals and promotion. No, I believe that heroism is very rarely genuine, if it is performed in the glare of publicity and if its success is handsomely rewarded. Heroism is purer and more significant the quieter it is, the less of an audience it has, the less profitable it is to the hero himself, and the less *ornamental* he is. What I accuse the Nazi notion of heroism of is precisely that inescapable superficiality, the boastfulness of its demeanour.'

In the slipstream of the system

In his memoir *No Victory Without Struggle*, published in the GDR in 1964, Manfred von Brauchitsch, the former racing driver and by then a highly decorated sports bureaucrat in the Communist government, leaves us in no doubt as to how much he despised Hitler and his ridiculous Nazis – or so he claims. However, what he does not mention is that this did not prevent him, at the 4th International Car and Motorcycle Exhibition in Berlin on 15 February 1936, from giving a wildly applauded speech of welcome to his *Führer*. Strange how perceptions alter over a long life in sport.

It may, then, have been no coincidence that, more than 50 years later, René Dreyfus still held particular memories of von Brauchitsch. In 1940 the champion French driver travelled to the USA to take part in the Indianapolis 500, and, because of his Jewish blood, thought it wiser not to return to his homeland, by then under occupation. Looking back on his former colleagues from Germany, he was pretty certain, to the end of his life, that von Brauchitsch was the only one who had been, in his heart of hearts, a Nazi sympathiser.

But let us listen to the original voice of Manfred von Brauchitsch, speaking in 1936. The speech he made that February day was broadcast on radio: '*Mein Führer*, as the representative of German racing drivers I thank you, *mein Führer*, for everything you have given us. If, in the last few years, I… [he stumbles and starts again] If, in the last few years, German racing cars have sped from victory to victory, if today we in motorsport stand at the head of all nations, then the credit goes not so much to us or to our industry; the achievement is principally yours. Through your measures, you have created the technical prerequisites for our successes, you have steered the interest of the German nation towards motoring and motorsport. Yet that alone would not have enabled us to gain victory; something else was crucial. You have given us back a belief in the future of Germany, a belief in ourselves. And in so doing you have inspired us with the ambition to do honour to our Fatherland. This ambition and faith in victory is also essential for success in our hard manual work. And on… [he starts again] On behalf of my colleagues, I therefore thank you, *mein Führer*. Your example and your work oblige us to dedicate all our skill, indeed our lives, to the people of our Germany. And we pledge to you, this year once more to do all we can to ensure that the proud flag of the Third Reich flies as a sign of victory over the racetracks of Europe.'

Was this lip service, given under duress, or a voluntary statement of gratitude, made out of conviction? Perhaps von Brauchitsch had particular cause to sound this hymn of praise, as a precaution. For a month earlier, in January 1936, the 30-year-old racing driver rashly picked a fight with Baldur von Schirach, the Reich Youth Leader,[1] two years younger than himself. In an attempt to settle the matter he not only involved NSKK-*Führer* Hühnlein and Hitler's chief adjutant, Wilhelm Brückner, but even appealed personally to the dictator himself. It was a small, private

The racing driver as a fearless and stern fighter, even a martial idol who could drive young Germans directly from the German Grand Prix 1936 at the Nürburgring to glory in the Second World War. (Daimler AG)

episode but it throws a revealing light on the racing driver's judgement and political naïvety.

On 1 April 1936 von Schirach wrote to Manfred's uncle, Field-Marshall Walther von Brauchitsch, commander-in-chief of the army: 'Although I do not know exactly, *hochverehrter Herr General*, how you are related to the racing driver Manfred von Brauchitsch, I nevertheless feel it is right to inform you that at 10:15 a.m. this morning, in their apartment, 60 Hohenzollerndamm, Berlin, I treated Manfred von Brauchitsch and his brother to a horse-whipping.' According to the Nazi functionary, the two brothers 'when in a drunken state in the Hotel Post und Jäger, in Urfeld, uttered insulting statements about my wife. One of the brothers said, among other things, that "while the Reich Youth Leader is travelling around the world, his wife has her own ways of amusing herself" (or something similar). A forester and his wife who were present and heard these remarks immediately left the premises. The next morning my wife called on Herr von Brauchitsch at the hotel and demanded an apology from him. When he gave an impertinent reply, standing with his hands in his pockets, she struck him in the face and left the building. When I returned from my election tour on Sunday, my wife reported the incident to me by telephone from Urfeld, where we own a small country house. I immediately tried to establish where Herr von Brauchitsch was staying. He himself has made absolutely no attempt to settle this matter of honour with me.'

Two days later the chastened racing driver demanded 'satisfaction with weapons', but von Schirach declined to oblige. Von Brauchitsch did not, however, give up, as he later wrote: 'The civil and criminal actions which I immediately initiated in the courts, could not be pursued because Herr von Schirach was a Reichstag Deputy and had the protection of immunity. My application for the immunity to be lifted was refused by the President of the German Reichstag.[2] In the meantime the incident has become more widely known about, through no fault of mine. In my opinion a person in a high position, least of all, should be allowed with impunity to belabour other national comrades with a horse-whip.' On 4 September von Brauchitsch wrote to the *Führer* in person to make it clear that he had not insulted Henriette von Schirach, adding furthermore that 'in the legal proceedings initiated not even an investigation by the Central State

Nazis and proud of it. The official celebration at the Mercedes-Benz factory in Untertürkheim after the German Grand Prix in 1937. Nearest to the microphone is Dr Wilhelm Kissel, and behind him (from left) are Neubauer, Lang, von Brauchitsch and Caracciola. (Daimler AG)

Prosecution Service in the Reich Ministry of Justice could find any evidence that any statements to that effect had been made.'

A decade later Manfred von Brauchitsch would make use of this curious incident in order to emerge without a stain from the Denazification Tribunal in the Starnberg District Court. In October 1946, in the course of the judicial examination of his personal conduct during the National Socialist dictatorship, he submitted a lengthy written statement: 'In January 1936 I and my brother Harald were recuperating as we did every year, staying with the Brackenhofer family at the Hotel Post in Urfeld on [lake] Walchensee. The evening before we left for Berlin we were sitting at a large table in the *Bauernstube* [public bar] with the landlord, when a forester I knew, and a woman who was unknown to me, sat down at our table. As far as I recall, the conversation revolved around the usual everyday concerns. Towards 10 p.m. I said goodnight and went to my room. My brother came up a little later. The next morning at breakfast a very irate lady suddenly came up to my table, introduced herself curtly as Frau von Schirach and asked me if I was Manfred von Brauchitsch. No sooner had I responded politely than I received a well-aimed box on the ears, and she screamed at me: "I'll teach you to slander me and my husband and to say that 'while he is travelling round the world, his wife has her own way of amusing herself!'" With that she disappeared.'

Truth and fiction are probably somewhat at odds regarding the question of what actually happened to the von Brauchitsch brothers in their Berlin apartment on 1 April 1936. In the aforementioned letter to the racing driver's uncle, von Schirach describes the events as follows: 'I made my witnesses known to Herr Manfred von Brauchitsch and his brother and told them that in my view they were not honourable men, because they had insulted a respectable German woman. I went on to say that for this reason I could not, as is customary between men of honour, settle the matter with pistols, but was compelled to thrash them with a horsewhip. Having said this, I first thrashed the brother and then Manfred von Brauchitsch himself. Neither man put up any resistance. Manfred von Brauchitsch fled through two rooms as I struck at him. My witnesses did not of course play any part in this altercation.'

Five months later Manfred von Brauchitsch described the incident as follows: 'On 1.4.1936 *Reichsjugendführer* Baldur von Schirach appeared in my private apartment with a large number of members of his staff, locked my aged mother in a bedroom and then, under the protection of the persons he had brought with him, attacked my brother and me with a leather whip. In view of the persons present no form of defence was possible.'

What could a motor-racing hero, humiliated in such a manner, do

Manfred von Brauchitsch – a contradictory opportunist. (Daimler AG)

in such a hopeless situation? He sought the help of a powerful man in whom he trusted, and wrote to Hitler: 'If I approach you directly today, I do so in the conviction that it is the last way remaining open to me to receive satisfaction for the gravest wrong that can be inflicted on a man. Furthermore, I do it because I believe that atonement for this wrong is not my concern alone, but is called for in the interest of the public at large.'

The *Führer* as custodian of justice? Before we let these lines move us to tears over such naïvety, we should bear in mind with whom it was that von Brauchitsch had crossed swords. As early as 1925, at the tender age of 18, Baldur von Schirach had joined the NSDAP as member no. 17251. It was he who, after 1936, turned the Hitler Youth into the official state youth organisation and in doing so trained six million young people to obedience, loyalty, battle and the sacrifice of death. When the *Reichsjugendführer* got married in 1932, Hitler was a witness. And Frau von Schirach, who was supposedly so insulted by Manfred von Brauchitsch, was the daughter of Hitler's long-time personal photographer, Heinrich Hoffmann. Having a father-in-law in that business was useful, and together they published a number of highly popular illustrated books: *The Triumph of the Will: The Struggle and Rise of Adolf Hitler and his Government* (1933), *Young People Around Hitler* (1934) and *Hitler, as No One Knows Him* (1935). What is more, his spouse Henriette was a close friend of Eva Braun.[3] Poor Manfred von Brauchitsch; how simple-minded, what a gross over-estimation of himself that he should count on his relationship with Hitler to demand right and justice!

Von Brauchitsch wrote his letter to Hitler at the end of a completely screwed-up season, a good two weeks after the Swiss Grand Prix on 23 August 1936. For him it was the last race of the year, since Daimler-Benz AG decided, after an unparalleled series of breakdowns, to withdraw from motor racing for the rest of the season to thoroughly overhaul their failure-prone supercharged eight-cylinder cars. The Schirach incident had no effect on his contractual situation with Daimler-Benz AG, and for the whole of the season von Brauchitsch continued to be among the exclusive group of regular Mercedes-Benz drivers.

Less than two weeks after von Schirach and his cohorts had pounced on him, he was among the starters at the first Grand Prix of the year, at Monte Carlo on 13 April. But in the second of a hundred laps he had to pull out after getting involved in a mass pile-up at the Harbour Chicane. In his second 1936 outing he was in one of four works cars entered for the Gran Premio di Tripoli on 10 May, but again had to retire due to problems with the fuel pipe. Only a week later the exigencies of the calendar meant that for logistical reasons only two Mercedes-Benz cars could race in Tunis – those of Caracciola, the established number one, and Chiron. The Monegasque, who had been signed up as a works driver for the 1936 season, not least at Caracciola's insistence, would in the next few months lose his well-heeled partner Alice to his friend Rudi. Chiron's arrival meant that von Brauchitsch suddenly had another driver ahead of him in the pecking order.

In the run-up to the Olympic Games and rebuilding work on Berlin's urban motorway, the AVUS Race did not take place, so that the next circuit event entered by Mercedes-Benz was the Gran Premio de Penya Rhin, run on 7 June on the Montjuich Park road circuit in Barcelona. They again entered only two cars, in which Caracciola came second and Chiron sixth. The winner was Nuvolari in the new Alfa Romeo 12C-36, and the two Auto Union cars driven by von Delius and Rosemeyer took fourth and fifth places respectively.

Why, virtually on the eve of the Spanish Civil War, a total of only four of Germany's Silver Arrows appeared in the future capital of the Republicans is explained by the fact that just a week later, on 14 July, the Eifel Race was scheduled for the Nürburgring – an event that was significantly more important to German interests. For this Auto Union and Mercedes-Benz each lined up five cars, but von Brauchitsch retired with engine damage in the seventh of ten laps. In rain and encroaching fog Rosemeyer triumphed over the great Nuvolari, and in 'blond Bernd' Germany finally found its new sporting idol. Only a few days later, on 19 June, Max Schmeling also boxed his way back into the headlines when he KO'd the supposedly unbeatable Joe Louis at New York's Yankee Stadium in an eliminating bout for the world heavyweight championship (see Chapter 2, Note 2). Great days, great deeds, great names. The German nation was beside itself and proudly and happily closed ranks even more tightly behind the *Führer*.

But things were less rosy even for a racing hero of the calibre of Manfred von Brauchitsch. On 21 June, a week after the Eifel Race, he was on the grid for the Budapest City Race along with Caracciola and Chiron, but after an accident he once more failed to finish. In this outing to Hungary the Silver Arrows would, for the second time in the current season, be defeated by Nuvolari.

After more than a month's break from racing, the German Grand Prix was slated for 26 July. Six days before the opening of the Summer Olympics in Berlin, it was the noisy overture for a continuous series of German sporting successes. Von Brauchitsch led from the start, but the 1936 W25 with its extremely short wheelbase and supercharged 4.7-litre power unit once again proved unreliable. After an extended pit stop von Brauchitsch had no more stomach for the fray. The former race mechanic Hermann Lang was allowed to take over the ailing car and managed to come in seventh despite a painful handicap, having broken the little finger of his right hand in a clumsy gearchange during the race. His team-mate Louis Chiron survived an accident at high speed but was seriously injured and would never race for Mercedes-Benz again, though he did continue his career after 1945. Once more the winner was Rosemeyer. The shy victor, with tears of joy in his eyes, received a kiss from Elly Beinhorn, the young aviatrix to whom he had recently become engaged. It was a moment captured by every picture magazine as well as the German newsreels.

While Auto Union and 'blond Bernd' raced from victory to victory, Mercedes-Benz temporarily bowed out of the racing scene and from 12 to 15 August carried out intensive test drives with overhauled racing cars. Caracciola and von

Racing the German way: the 1936 Grand Prix at the Nürburgring has been started by a cannon volley, smoke from which can be seen lingering above the starting line while Hans Stuck and eventual winner Bernd Rosemeyer lead away the field. (Reuss)

Brauchitsch were at the wheel. Not until 23 August did the Untertürkheimers reappear, with four cars entered in the Swiss Grand Prix in Bern. But after 50 of the 70 laps von Brauchitsch dropped out with an overheated engine, while Caracciola, who had taken an early lead, had to admit defeat even sooner. It seems he hindered the markedly faster Rosemeyer so much that after the race the new Auto Union star took to his bed and, in a chance meeting with his rival in the hotel, loudly gave him a piece of his mind.

It was the closing chapter of a thin season for the Daimler-Benz stable, since top management decided to avoid further humiliation by withdrawing from the remaining races. They wanted some peace and quiet to prepare for the coming year. Neither Caracciola nor von Brauchitsch needed to fear for their places in the team. For the 1937 season the rookie driver Lang was given the chance to move up to third place in the Untertürkheim stable's internal pecking order, as Chiron had already left and Fagioli had to go too. A small portion of the foreign currency thus saved would be used to sign up a young Englishman, Richard 'Dick' Seaman. Previously, Earl Howe, the 'grand old

Ancient and modern at the 1936 German Grand Prix. Raymond Sommer drove his privately entered, outclassed Alfa Romeo to a distant ninth place, while Luigi Fagioli, who had to share his car with Rudolf Caracciola later in the race, ended up the best Mercedes-Benz finisher in fifth place. Note the uniformed NSKK troopers and officers in the crowd. (Reuss)

Glamorous heroine and hero: aviatrix Elly Beinhorn and racing driver husband Bernd Rosemeyer. (Kirchberg)

man' of British motorsport, had consulted his political friends in Whitehall and Westminster and encouraged Seaman to accept the Mercedes-Benz offer. In the period of Britain's appeasement policy such Anglo-German contacts were considered highly desirable. However, at Mercedes-Benz Seaman was probably instructed not to talk too loudly yet about the offer of a contract. After all, enquiries had still to be made at the highest level in the Reich – in other words, probably to Hitler himself – as to whether there were any political reservations about signing up a British driver.

A racing driver faces the Denazification Tribunal

Against this background, it is clear that Manfred von Brauchitsch's position at Mercedes-Benz cannot have been seriously threatened by the incident with von Schirach. But ten years later, how, and from where, was the chairperson of the Starnberg Denazification Tribunal, Johanna Tralow, to find out the details of his career as a racing driver? What did the minor deceptions and possible lies on the CV of a prominent racing driver, sometime NSKK *Sturmführer* and urbane opportunist, amount to compared to the presumed guilt of murderers and war criminals, accessories and accomplices, who would also get away unscathed from the Denazification proceedings?

In any case, there was no question here of Nazi crimes but rather of how skilfully and flexibly one of the great sporting idols of Nazi Germany managed, both on and off the racing circuit, to avoid flying off the track and to steer a course that would serve his own interests.

Von Brauchitsch's Denazification hearing began in Starnberg, near Munich, on 7 November 1946. According to the court record the wretched von Schirach business played a central part in the famous ex-driver's plea in justification: 'No one would look at me any more. In the factory, among former friends, I was an outcast. I refused to drive [in Germany] any more. I wanted to drive for Maserati in Italy, and travelled to Bologna. But Hühnlein banned me from doing this. I negotiated with Auto Union. But my sense of tradition won through and I signed a contract with Daimler-Benz for 1937, which was worse than the one for 1934. The contract carried no guarantee [instead, he was given a W125 car, which was better, as his results show: a win in the Monaco Grand Prix, five second places, in the German and Swiss Grands Prix, the Coppa Acerbo, the Masaryk Race and the British Grand Prix at Castle Donington]. In 1938–9 our cars were so good and so superior that we automatically earned more money.'

Von Brauchitsch clamed that from 1939 onwards he paid no more dues to the NSKK, 'so was not a member,' and furthermore, the former NSKK

Signed by Mercedes-Benz for 1937, Richard Seaman soon played the role of a good Briton within a German team. Perhaps unwillingly and naïvely, he sometimes appeared to show a little too much understanding of and even sympathy for Nazi Germany in public. (Daimler AG)

Sturmführer asserted: 'I put up a lot of passive resistance. But that all sounds a bit mundane.' The tribunal wanted to know how it was that in the Second World War he served as a part-time tank test-driver: 'I was brought in as a professional adviser on things which people believed I really knew something about. I kept myself too much in the background to be given a real service rank.' The record also mentions a ladies' underwear shop 'in Prague, on the right-hand side of Wenceslas Square', an 'Aryanised' business that was said to have been taken over by von Brauchitsch. In the final phase of the war, when things were getting really serious for him and he was ordered to the battlefront, he 'withdrew in September '44 to Professor Zutt's psychiatric sanatorium in Ulanen-Allee, Berlin.' So was the racetrack hero a talented malingerer? 'I didn't take it as far as Article 51,' von Brauchitsch assured the tribunal (this article concerned people not responsible for their actions on grounds of mental incapacity). He also pointed to his low service rank: 'When I was released from the army I was a sergeant.'

The Denazification Tribunal took a long time to arrive at a verdict. What is more, the very busy defendant does not seem to have devoted a significant amount of time to the hearing. For on 5 December the chairperson wrote very courteously to von Brauchitsch: 'Please inform us when you might expect to be in a position to continue with the proceedings.' By 12 March 1947 things had reached such a point that the Tribunal decreed that the defendant need only take an oath. Von Brauchitsch swore: 'I did not serve as a *Sturmführer* in the NSKK.' At which point the hearing was terminated.

However, someone in the purlieus of the Bavarian judiciary must have been less than fully satisfied with this strange ending. At all events, six months later, on 10 September 1947, a resumption of the case was put in hand. The racing driver's income and assets appeared so high to the newly constituted tribunal that they could not rule out the possibility that he had, after all, perhaps profited from his status as a *Sturmführer* in the NSKK. Yet in the hearing on 14 October von Brauchitsch responded: 'I hear what you say about the comparative income in the NSKK. I can only say that we earned money because we were just quicker round the bends. We didn't trouble ourselves about the matter.' It appears that the former racing driver put a convincing case; at least, in his closing words von Brauchitsch was both relaxed and self-confident: 'I can only add that basically I did not expect anything else, because as 100 per cent sportsmen

The great pretender. Seen after finishing second in the 1935 Belgian Grand Prix, Manfred von Brauchitsch claimed during his Denazification hearing in 1946–47 to have been a victim of Nazi politics – and, astonishingly, he was believed. (Daimler AG)

we never concerned ourselves with anything political. We were employed internationally. It didn't matter to us who was running the government. Originally I was very bitter and puzzled about having to defend myself merely for the fact that I was promoted by reason of my successes. I make this statement with an absolutely clear conscience.'

The chairman of the tribunal seems to have shared the viewpoint of the former racing driver and on 14 November 1947 handed down his decision: 'Under the Law on Liberation from National Socialism and Militarism, Manfred von Brauchitsch is declared to have no case to answer.'

He who howls with the wolves

They were gifted with the art of survival, the racing drivers of that era – as streamlined as their silver cars, capable of making progress even when the wind was blowing full in their faces, and never losing sight of their own interests. If this was true of Manfred von Brauchitsch, it applied even more so to Hans Stuck. Stuck's son Hans-Joachim – the offspring of his third marriage, to Christa Thielmann – may be familiar to the public today thanks to his spectacular successes and constant media presence, yet the career and triumphs of the patriarch of his family, who lived through the Nazi dictatorship and died in 1978, are far more dramatic.

Officially, Hans Stuck always insisted that he first saw the light of day in 1900. A birth date in 1896 or even 1895 is probably nearer the truth. As a close student of the racing scene, Richard von Frankenberg, put it in 1956: 'It is sometimes claimed that the people running motorsport in those days made Stuck out to be younger than he really was to avoid any accusations of accepting men who were too old to drive Grand Prix cars.' Frankenberg has established that 'in the First World War Hans Stuck was old enough to serve as an officer in the 76th Field Artillery Regiment, from which anyone with the slightest knowledge of arithmetic can deduce that he must have been born well before the turn of the century.'

This can only mean that in 1934 Hans Stuck was probably nearly 40 when political developments placed German racing drivers in a position where they dominated Grand Prix events in technically superior machines. It was his one big chance, as it was for all the other national heroes in their Silver Arrows. But here Stuck had the advantage that he had got to know Hitler personally long before 1933, and, what is more, was far more skilful than the much younger von Brauchitsch in exploiting the whole gamut of his contacts with the *Führer* and other top Nazis.

Adding a sheen to the regime: Hans Stuck and Bernd Rosemeyer with the Führer during a reception in Berlin. (Kirchberg)

On 15 July 1934 Stuck won the German Grand Prix at the Nürburgring – the first Grand Prix win by one of the new national racing cars. And this victory fell not to Mercedes-Benz but to the much younger Auto Union company. It was Stuck who, with designer Porsche and managing director von Oertzen, had asked Hitler for support in 1933. And a full year later, after nearly five energy-draining hours of racing round the Nürburgring circuit, the same Hans Stuck still had time to pose for the newsreel cameras in his victorious silver machine and to proclaim with a radiant smile for the millions of cinemagoers: 'Well, I'm extremely pleased that we have been able to gain a victory in the German Grand Prix with a German driver in a German vehicle. It was done with the great work and support of our *Führer*, for which I now thank him. *Heil unserem Führer!*' And from a thousand throats came back an enthusiastic roar of *'Heil!'*

But in that glorious era it was Auto Union's star driver, of all people, who had a genuine problem: Stuck's second wife Paula, *née* Heimann and previously

Hans Stuck at the Freiburg mountain climb in 1937: three years earlier Nazi supporters had painted the track with graffiti declaring the Auto Union works driver a 'Jewboy' because of his marriage to Paula von Reznicek, who had Jewish antecedents. (Kirchberg)

married to a man named Reznicek, was a well-known tennis player and a successful journalist, but had Jewish antecedents. Before the practice for the 1934 German Grand Prix, scarcely five weeks after Stuck's magnificent victory at the Nürburgring, some words had been crudely painted on the track by an unknown hand: 'Hans Stuck's a Jewboy – send him packing!' His colleagues refused to start the race until the graffiti had been removed, as Stuck recalled many years after the war. Apparently it was not a problem for NSKK-*Führer* Hühnlein, because the racist slogan was erased, the race at Freiburg's Schauinsland circuit went ahead, and Stuck won once again. But elsewhere, even in the Auto Union factory, anti-Semitic slogans attacking Stuck and his wife kept on appearing. What was to be done?

Stuck depended on his successes, his fame – and his Nazi contacts. Since his victory in the German Grand Prix he was a welcome guest at the homes of many Party grandees. 'I get congratulations by the bucket-load, am requested to visit Hitler. Göring, Goebbels and many senior Party members want to talk to me. I deal with one thing after the other and can hardly fend off the honours. I have to drive the racing car in a triumphal procession from Berlin to Zwickau, with SA men sealing off the streets. All work has stopped, the schools are closed, everyone is standing on the kerbside and waving. I would never have dreamed that a sportsman could be so honoured and fêted. Tears of joy cloud my racing-goggles. At the Horch factory the entire workforce have formed up in a rectangle, and I have to drive through the middle. Speeches are given, telegrams read out, and among the workers, racing drivers and government officials there is nothing but enthusiasm. I am introduced to Himmler and his adjutant, [Karl] Wolff, at a victory celebration afterwards in the Chemnitzer Hof [hotel]. (It was Wolff who, along with Göring, would later hold a protective hand over me and my wife, in the difficulties that arose because she was only half-Aryan.) Göring will forever be remembered for saying '*I decide who is Aryan*.' And my wife Paula benefited from that. True, she was removed from all her jobs with the press, but she was allowed to accompany me. Only she was never again able to appear in public. No easy matter for a girl with her temperament!'

The Stucks' bitterest opponents watched them carefully. The man was not supposed to get too many headlines. On 4 July 1935 – in other words a good three weeks before the German Grand Prix – Goebbels issued clearly targeted instructions at the Reich press conference: 'The Ministry of Propaganda asks that in future no lengthy articles be published about the racing driver Stuck's practice drives, but rather such tributes must be reserved for reports on the actual races, provided his performance is worthy of praise.'

World records as an aim in life
Hans and Paula Stuck were adept at marketing themselves. And with a sure touch Stuck also exploited his amicable relationships with senior figures in the Nazi government for completely different though no less self-seeking reasons – when, for example, Auto Union did not offer to renew his contract at the end of 1937. There was a need to build a car that would break world records, and there is a certain piquancy in the fact that the prominent racing driver now wanted to realise this national prestige project with the help of Daimler-Benz AG. Under the strictest secrecy this company had been commissioned by the Reich Ministry of Aviation to develop an aero engine designated Type DB 601. Even in the early stages of its development the V12 power-unit with a cubic capacity of 33.9 litres was delivering about 1,300hp, and was thus considered the most powerful engine hitherto produced for the rearmament programme, which was now in full swing. If one, or better still two, of these units were to be built into an aerodynamically perfected car, then the absolute land speed record could be broken. This record was held by Britain's Malcolm Campbell in his famous *Bluebird*, powered by a 2,300hp Rolls-Royce aero engine, which on 3 September 1935 had covered a measured mile at an average speed of 484.619kph (301.192mph).

To win the absolute land speed record for the greater glory of Germany – this was the almost obsessive aim that preoccupied Stuck more and more intensely during the 1936 season. From 1935 on it became customary to make these attempts on the Bonneville Salt Flats in Utah, USA, which was the only place in the world that offered reasonably suitable terrain for such crazy explorations of the frontiers of land speed. But by now the new German *Autobahnen* provided terrain over which German racing cars in Class B (5- to 8-litre engines) at least could establish world records over different distances. The AVUS was too narrow and too short for speeds in excess of 300kph (185mph), and the record-breaking runs carried out in 1934 and 1935 on high-speed roads in Italy and Hungary had far less propaganda impact than the pursuit of the world record now envisaged on the 'Führer's Highway'. Hitler had turned the motorway's first spadeful of earth in Frankfurt on 23 September 1933, and on 19 May 1935 he opened the initial Frankfurt–Darmstadt–Mannheim section. By the beginning of 1936 the motorway was to be extended as far as Heidelberg.

Thanks to Stuck's input, the racing car department of Auto Union reacted more swiftly and astutely than their rivals in Untertürkheim. And no less importantly, the head of racing at Auto Union, Dr Karl Feuereissen, wanted to make his name with some spectacular successes. As early as the end of 1935 an approach was made to the Head Construction Office of the Reich Autobahnen in Frankfurt, a list was obtained of all the bends and straight stretches, and on 21 December site visits were made to those sections of the Frankfurt–Heidelberg motorway that might be suitable for speed-record runs. Most of it was dead straight, and even the long, elegantly sweeping curves allowed maximum speeds of well above 300kph (185mph). But in his attempt to beat the record Stuck would have to negotiate a relatively tight bend near Mannheim, and turn off towards Heidelberg. At the end of the motorway, just before entering the old university city, drivers would

In 1936 Auto Union was the first of the two German teams to use the newly built autobahn between Frankfurt and Heidelberg for world record runs – a superb propaganda exercise. Hans Stuck and Ferdinand Porsche look on while a mechanic changes plugs. (Porsche AG)

have to brake almost to a stop, then make a 180-degree turn, before racing at full throttle back to Frankfurt. But it all seemed feasible, and tyre manufacturer Continental also gave the green light.

On 16 January 1936 Auto Union applied 'in strictest secrecy' for 'permission to attempt speed records on the Frankfurt–Heidelberg *autobahn* in our racing car, with Stuck as driver. We intend to challenge the following world records: 1 km standing start, 1 mile standing start, 10 miles flying start, 50 km standing, 50 miles standing, 100 km standing, 100 miles standing, 200 km standing.' It should be noted that Stuck wanted to aim for *absolute* world records in these long-distance attempts. To be on the safe side, Auto Union applied to try for the '5 km flying start, 5 miles flying start and 10 km standing start', which were only Class B world record attempts. However, in every case they would be carried out in exactly the same car, Auto Union's upgraded and further improved Grand Prix model, whose 16-cylinder engine had been enlarged to a capacity of 6 litres and, with a supercharger, now delivered 520bhp. This meant that the Silver Arrow from Zwickau was the most powerful formula racing car in the world, compared to which the W25, also modified during the racing season, showed a deficit of 50 to 70bhp.

This was one of the reasons why, in 1936, shares in Daimler-Benz AG were hardly a recommended buy. It was their competitor Auto Union that, making use for the first time of the '*Führer*'s Highway', was going out to break world records. For two days the Frankfurt–Heidelberg autobahn was completely closed to traffic. Secret orders were sent out, which created a great stir even in the preparatory stages, particularly since the provincial police forces were excluded and, on instructions from Hühnlein's ONS, handed over responsibility for closing the road, setting up telephone-posts and timing the runs to the NSKK or SA detachments. The German press, of course, paraded in force, while Ferdinand Porsche stood by with a slide-rule, ready to take the interim timings reported by telephone and use them to predict new record speeds. A week and a half before the test-runs Auto Union had undertaken to bear the costs for the necessary additional road surfacing at the turn-round point in Heidelberg.

Hans Stuck began his record attempts on the morning of Monday 23 March 1936 and initially only covered the 5km stretch. Not until the second attempt did he succeed in breaking the international record in Class B. The

Spot the difference. At the turn-round in Heidelberg during an autobahn run (above), the tyres of Hans Stuck's Auto Union are observed by an engineer from the Continental tyre company to make sure they are safe for the driver to make his return run. As released for publication, however, the photo was doctored (below) to remove the engineer and look more exciting. (Blum)

old record had been held since the autumn of 1935 by Caracciola, driving a
Mercedes-Benz at an average speed of 311.985kph (193.899mph) near the
Hungarian town of Györ. At a speed of 312.423kph (194.172mph), Stuck
was only marginally faster, but admittedly 'no longer had full performance
on the return run; it turned out that the output of the petrol-pump was too
low for such long stretches, which meant the engine got so hot that two
pistons seized up.'

It was repaired overnight, but on Tuesday morning rain prevented
further record attempts. However, because the closure of the autobahn
could not be prolonged by another day, on Wednesday Stuck nonetheless
went out on the wet road, and amid intermittent showers actually set up
five absolute world records. The impact on his contemporaries must have
been immense; even the *Frankfurter Zeitung*, the most serious newspaper
in the generally pro-Nazi German press, and then still totally averse to
open Nazi propaganda, published a striking tribute to the new records
the following day: 'Over various distances, he achieved average speeds of
between 262 and 286kph, in other words speeds that even today would not
disgrace an aircraft. Figures do not usually mean much to readers unless
they are already familiar with the subject matter. Perhaps we can give a
more tangible idea of the great triumph that these record runs represent
by pointing out that the Frankfurt–Darmstadt stretch was covered in about
five minutes, and Frankfurt–Heidelberg in roughly 17 minutes. This is all
the more remarkable, since the new records were set up in a car that was
less powerful than the specially-designed vehicle *Speed of the Wind*, in which
the Briton George Eyston achieved the previous world top speed [at this
distance]. What is more, things were made harder for Stuck by the rain
which fell over an area of about 15 kilometres and somewhat impaired his
best performance in the last run. But in themselves the records are not what
is most significant about these successful test-runs. Far more important is
the fact that they were established in Germany, and thus supply unique and
convincing evidence of the quality of the Reich autobahns.'

Stuck, Porsche, Feuereissen and the men from Continental Tyres preferred
to keep to themselves the fact that the rain and damp road surface on the
return run near Viernheim were probably an advantage and contributed to the
fact that, after 160km (100 miles), the almost completely worn-down tyres
could cool off and be conserved. Nevertheless, the Nazi paper *Angriff* crowed:

'Now we see for the first time how unsurpassed are German products and German driving skill,' and NSKK boss Hühnlein sent a personal telegram to Stuck: 'The successful assault on five world records and international class records by a German driver in a German car with German tyres, is a masterly achievement in which the factory and the driver share equal honours.'

Hans Stuck seemed to have found his true *métier*. The physically strenuous record runs were more suited to a man who specialised in short, fast hill-climbs than were the long Grand Prix drives with continuous stress over many hours. This realisation was underlined by the fact that in the 1936 season the much younger Rosemeyer completely outclassed the still fast and seasoned Stuck in the big circuit races, and finally rose to the number one position within Auto Union. Stuck's personnel file at the factory includes a comment by Feuereissen regarding the relationship between his drivers: 'In the middle of 1935 endless gripes by Stuck against Rosemeyer, who he senses as competitor.' So it was high time for Stuck to take another new direction in his long career in motorsport.

The pursuit of speed records exceeded in its megalomania even the

While Hans Stuck (with camera) gradually became outclassed by Bernd Rosemeyer (left) in circuit races for Auto Union, he was a superb exponent of record-breaking and his ambitions turned in that direction. In 1936 he initiated a plan to take Ferdinand Porsche (centre) back to Mercedes-Benz to build a contender for the outright land speed record. (Kirchberg)

headline-grabbing series of victories by the Silver Arrows. The record runs in modified Grand Prix racing cars on the Frankfurt–Heidelberg autobahn were national prestige events of the first rank, in which, needless to say, Mercedes-Benz and Auto Union sent their top drivers Caracciola and Rosemeyer into battle, but no longer Stuck.

It was when a pure exhibition of German greatness and German performance was staged on 28 January 1938 that national idol Rosemeyer gave his life for *Führer, Volk und Vaterland*, in the technically and competitively questionable and frantic pursuit of speeds in the frontier zone of 450kph (280mph). The structure of world records at that time related to engine-capacity classes in which heavily modified power units from the Grand Prix world could be entered, yet even such specially built vehicles fell far short of the speeds necessary if one wanted to attack the absolute world speed record with any chance of success. For this it was necessary to reach not 450kph, but at least 650kph (400mph).

Making common cause with the Professor

It is no wonder, then, that Hans Stuck secured for his own project the support of a designer accustomed to thinking on a similarly megalomaniac scale and who, furthermore, like Stuck himself, enjoyed the goodwill of Hitler and was willing to exploit it fully for his own ends. Professor Ferdinand Porsche immediately took up with enthusiasm the idea of attacking the world record in collaboration with his old motor-racing friend. In any case, Porsche's contract with Auto Union was about to run out. Even though he would continue to appear regularly at races and record runs, his expensive services were no longer required in Chemnitz and Zwickau. The Grand Prix racing car for the new formula coming into effect in 1938 was being designed by in-house staff headed by development chief Eberan von Eberhorst.

This was a matter of no great regret to Porsche, because since 1934 his own company had been working on the People's Car. The Volkswagen was a very different and even more gigantic project for Hitler and the car-obsessed nation, but most of all for himself. By birth and background alone Porsche stood no chance of joining the ranks of the founding fathers of automobile manufacture, but in the sixth decade of his life he sensed the undreamed-of opportunity of becoming the managing director of his own state-of-the-art car factory.

Looking for reliable test-drivers, he placed an order with Himmler for 60 SS men who for six months, working in two shifts, would be allowed to drive the cars to the limit through hedge and ditch. Despite the high – for the time – daily pay of 12 RM the turnover was also high, and more than 100 men were involved in the test-driving. There were serious accidents and the drivers became notorious for pub brawls, damage to property and theft. However, none of this prevented Porsche from employing the men in black uniforms as security men and drivers in the future Volkswagen factory. After 1938 a special unit, the SS-*Sturm Volkswagenwerk*, was even set up.

As historian Hans Mommsen writes in his standard work on the Volkswagen plant in the Third Reich: 'Ferdinand Porsche did not trouble himself with the political implications of putting the task of factory security into the hands of the SS. This measure reflected the strong affinity between the professional technocrats and the SS, who posed as a highly efficient elite.' At the same time, Mommsen takes a somewhat benevolent view of this particular automobile technocrat: 'With the sureness of a sleepwalker Porsche succeeded to a great extent in staying aloof from the chronic power struggles between the satraps of National Socialism, and, admittedly backed by the unarguable respect he enjoyed from Adolf Hitler, he was able to maintain a largely independent stance. His unorthodox manner, his relaxed and never subservient way of dealing with the Party notables, and his international renown as a motor car designer, as well as his spectacular successes in racing car construction, gave him an exceptional position within the regime, which in some respects allowed him to break ranks from time to time.'

It could be put another way: Porsche's direct line to Hitler gave him ample opportunity to pursue his own advantage with a ruthless consistency. The central files of the NSDAP record Ferdinand Porsche as member no. 5643287. Having applied for admission on 8 October 1937, he was accepted with retrospective effect from 1 May of that year. And in the final phase of the Second World War, Porsche, aged nearly 70, was to be found in the ranks of the SS. On 3 April 1944 the central personnel office of the SS in Berlin received a returned and completed 'questionnaire for senior SS officers' in the name of SS-*Oberführer* Prof. Dr. Ing. h.c. Ferdinand Porsche. His son Ferry had already joined the staff of the SS Danube Division as early as 1 August 1941, as no. 346167.

Jakob Werlin, a Party member, SS-*Oberführer*, and member of the

Daimler-Benz board, pulled the strings for the Volkswagen project as Hitler's amanuensis in matters of motor car policy, although nearly 40 years later Porsche's nephew and personal secretary Ghislaine Kaes told how unbearable and repugnant Werlin was to his uncle. Werlin was nonetheless an effective operator on Porsche's behalf, opening doors both in the Reich Chancellery and at Daimler-Benz AG. Up till then the entire German motor industry had, probably rightly, regarded as completely unrealistic all plans to produce and market a four-seater car below the magic 1,000 RM price barrier set by Hitler. But suddenly, in the summer of 1936, chief executive and SS member Wilhelm Kissel succeeded in getting Daimler-Benz to let him build 30 prototypes, which under prolonged testing would demonstrate the viability of a mass-produced 'Volks-Porsche'.

On the one hand this was applauded by the Nazi regime, but on the other it annoyed the bosses of Opel and Auto Union, who up to that point were selling the country's only 'cheap' cars, priced at around 1,500 RM, but were now, thanks to Hitler and Porsche, faced with competition from the state-sponsored Volkswagen. For, at the sensible suggestion of Franz Josef Popp, chief executive of BMW and a friend of Kissel, the production and marketing of Porsche's vehicle was taken over by *Kraft durch Freude*, the quasi-leisure organisation of the German Labour Front, or DAF. Following the forcible dissolution of the unions, the DAF had pillaged their assets and was now functioning as a conveyor belt between the workers and the Nazi regime. A German *Volksgenosse* (which roughly translates as 'national partner' or even 'co-racialist') could now not only enjoy holiday cruises in KdF ships but also save up conscientiously for the new KdF car. From August 1938 until early 1945 no less than 336,638 Volkswagen savers did just that, and handed over a total of 280 million RM – without getting a single car in return. As late as October 1944 a further 5,010 savers signed up for the KdF car, before the collapse of the Nazi regime finally put an end to this fraud.

However, Kissel's activities on behalf of the Volkswagen were chiefly a clear signal to Porsche himself. The *Führer*'s favourite designer was once again to be bound contractually to Daimler-Benz AG, contrary to the sentiment of its own board but with active support from the Nazi string-pullers Werlin and von Stauss. Not least of the reasons for this was to get Porsche away from the clutches of the competition in Saxony.

In view of these new circumstances the bold plans of Auto Union

From Volkswagen to Kampfwagen: the military derivative of the 'People's Car'. (Porsche AG)

works driver Hans Stuck to build, together with Ferdinand Porsche, a world-record-beating car at Daimler-Benz AG suddenly gained a special attraction and had excellent chances of success – particularly since Porsche was also meant to provide ideas for a new racing car model, which had to be designed for the class that would replace the 750kg formula.

Intoxicated by records

With backing from his old Luftwaffe chum Ernst Udet, Stuck made sure he could use the top-secret DB 601 aero engine, which Daimler-Benz had built under government contract and at the taxpayers' expense. Stuck also knew the Reich Minister of Aviation, Hermann Göring, personally. It was under Göring's protective wing that Udet, the popular flying ace and stunt-pilot, had achieved swift promotion and, since 10 June 1936, had held the post of Head of the Technical Division of the Luftwaffe. All the plans for new developments in military aircraft construction went across Udet's desk, including Project DB 601. The assault on the absolute speed record on land and water – which Stuck also intended to challenge, with the aid of a record-breaking boat from Untertürkheim – was a matter of national importance.

On 22 October 1936 Ernst Henne gained the absolute world motorcycle

Left: Record-breaking on the Führer's highway: Rudolf Caracciola embarks on a run in his streamlined Mercedes-Benz on the Frankfurt–Darmstadt autobahn in 1936. (Daimler AG)

Opposite: Caracciola, Neubauer and the Mercedes-Benz crew rejoice after setting a new class world record of 366.9kph (228mph) for the 'flying mile' in October 1936. During such official and important events on the autobahn, Mercedes-Benz and Auto Union were obliged by the ONS and Adolf Hühnlein to run their record cars with swastika emblems. (Daimler AG)

speed record on his supercharged BMW machine, reaching a speed of 272kph (169mph) on the Frankfurt–Heidelberg autobahn; and a few days later Rudolf Caracciola set up three class world records, one of which was the 'flying mile' at a speed of 366.9kph (228mph). All of this inspired the top men in government, the Party and the companies involved to further deeds in the service of Germany's motor-sporting greatness.

Admittedly, in June the American Automobile Association had lodged a protest against Stuck's Auto Union records, on the grounds that the Reich autobahn did not meet the prescribed conditions for record runs, but that was of only marginal importance in the light of the racing driver's great goal. By early 1937 all the preparations had been made and all the strings pulled in order to obtain the highest political blessing of all: 'Now I only need the certainty that my plans will be welcomed and approved in government quarters too. From long experience I know I have to go to the organ-grinder, not the monkey. So I request an audience with Adolf Hitler. When, after a relatively short time, I am summoned to the Reich Chancellery, I pack all my plans and contracts into a briefcase and take them with me as supporting documentation. But my heart is really thumping.' But he had nothing to fear; Hitler was delighted. 'Absolute world records on land and water – that fits our propaganda. You will have every support;

I am authorising my *Reichsleiter*, Bouhler,[4] to assist you. He is to help you to
realise your plans. For anything connected with this matter, you should go
to him. And good luck, Herr Stuck. I will keep myself fully posted.'

By now, however, Porsche and Stuck, as well as their future partners
in Untertürkheim, knew that the Frankfurt–Heidelberg autobahn was
unsuitable for the targeted speeds of over 600kph (370mph). Therefore the
attempt on the world record would have to take place on the Bonneville
Salt Flats in Utah. This was a serious snag for such a nationally significant
project, so it was necessary to keep a low profile for the moment. The first
thing Stuck had to do was to bring the construction of the world record car
under the roof of Daimler-Benz AG, if only because that was where the DB
601 aero engine originated.

A corporation in dire straits

In the summer of 1936 the Untertürkheim company was under constant
pressure. After two victories by Caracciola driving the new W125 in Monte
Carlo and Tunis, Mercedes-Benz suddenly came up against competition
from Auto Union, and could see no light at the end of the tunnel.
Indeed, they did not win another race that year. The short wheelbase of
the Mercedes-Benz machine gave it very tricky handling characteristics,

which, to make matters worse, were accompanied by a series of engine failures. The German Grand Prix on 26 July ended in a double victory for their rival. Rosemeyer and Stuck, first and second, were followed by an Alfa Romeo and, in fourth place, another Auto Union, driven by the rookie Rudolf Hasse. The best Mercedes-Benz – driven by Fagioli and then taken over by Caracciola, who piloted it to the finish – came in fifth, only just ahead of another Auto Union with von Delius at the wheel. It was a motor-racing fiasco for Untertürkheim, particularly as Adolf Hühnlein and the men from the transport ministry now demanded a swift explanation. After all, on 8 July a further 400,000 RM had been remitted to the company as 'aid for the perfection of German racing cars'.

On 31 July Daimler-Benz boss Kissel attempted, in a five-page letter, to plead shortage of money, bad luck and technical breakdowns to justify the fact that shortly before the race at the Nürburgring they had carried out substantial improvements because of complaints by the drivers. He gave a long-winded description of the unfortunate way the German Grand Prix had turned out for his stable of five cars, and then, right at the end, rather timidly revealed the bitter truth: 'However, in order to be able to thoroughly overhaul the cars, it is necessary to pause for breath, since the improvements first have to be carried out, and then tested.' Although, in view of the subsidies from the Nazi regime, entering for big international events was obligatory, Mercedes-Benz did not take part in the next three races in Italy.

The Mercedes-Benz crisis summer of 1936 could not, then, have been a better time for Stuck to approach the cash-strapped Kissel, first by telephone and then in writing. On 17 August, only a few days after his serious accident in practice for the Coppa Acerbo, Stuck reported from Zürich's prestigious Hotel Baur au Lac that 'an application to the Ministry of Aviation is definitely on,' and, urging the strictest secrecy, asked for a quick reply: 'For years I have been planning the realisation of my life's dream – the absolute world record, which has been held by [Malcolm] Campbell for years, with support from the British government. Recently I have begun to put my plans into action, having carried out the preliminary studies and trained myself for record runs. Quite some time ago I spoke to Dr Porsche, who said that if the car were built by you, he would be willing to take on the design work. Heinkel has offered to provide the bodywork and streamlining free of charge. The Ministry of Aviation has charged

Udet with examining the matter, and Udet has said he is willing, with your agreement, to consult Dr Porsche and to place two of the appropriate engines at his disposal. As for the cost of building the car, that will be met by me, that is to say, by a friend of mine in conjunction with myself. He is the Baron de Blonay, a Swiss from Geneva, who is founder and chairman of DAS. We are convinced that as well as Heinkel, other German firms will supply materials very cheaply or for nothing.'

However, among other members of the Daimler-Benz board the subject of Stuck was a hot potato, on which they did not wish to burn their fingers. Now of all times, after a series of devastating mishaps, was surely not the moment to sign up a top driver from the competition? Would the public not get the impression that it was necessary to lure a man like Stuck away from the successful Auto Union in order to become competitive again? In any case, the racing division was just being restructured, and the young Rudolf Uhlenhaut was finally taking charge. In difficult times like these, should they even be thinking about building a world record car? Designed by Porsche? Driven by Stuck? And did not the attempt to sign up Stuck at the end of the 1934 season fail miserably? Not only Auto Union but also the top men in the Nazi Party prevented it.

Rosemeyer and Stuck are welcomed home in Zwickau, where the Auto Union race department was based within the Horch factory. At this time, at the end of 1936, Stuck had already made discreet contact with Mercedes-Benz to offer his world record project. (Kirchberg)

It seems that even Stuck's immediate rival, Caracciola, in league with racing manager Neubauer, had worked against such a switch. And in any case, Stuck's 'non-Aryan wife' was hardly an ideal adjunct to a contractual relationship. On 30 September 1936 Wilhelm Kissel was told by Wolfgang von Hentig (who, like Karl C. Müller and Jakob Werlin, was one of the most died-in-the-wool Nazis on the Daimler-Benz board) about a letter written to him by Stuck: 'According to the account by Herr Stuck, which I am certain did not come from him but from his wife, what emerges is that he intends to operate as a private driver for the coming year, in order, as I suspect, to have the opportunity to drive our racing cars. However, this must of course be ruled out for the reasons that have been frequently discussed and agreed.' Clearly Hentig did not need to spell out these reasons. Yet Kissel kept open his option to bring the world record project to fruition. More letters were written on the subject and more phone calls made.

On 13 October Stuck informed Kissel 'in strict confidence' about a new, 'very good' contractual offer from Auto Union, and at the same time tried to offer his services as a 'team driver' ('guaranteed sum for race-starts at the same level as for the star drivers with Mercedes and Auto Union, approximately 100,000 marks') or 'private driver' (about 50,000 RM less). Self-importantly, he reported on 21 December 1936 on a piquant proviso in Auto Union's offer: 'Should we discover through the press or hearsay during your activities in 1937 that you intend in the foreseeable future to undertake any record attempts in another car, we reserve the right to terminate the contract immediately.' Stuck said that he was unable to accept this condition from Auto Union, but did not wish to 'expose myself to the risk of being put out of action in mid-season.' And because nothing went on in German motor racing without the knowledge and approval of the top Nazis, he had already made the necessary dispositions in the appropriate quarters: 'Once *Herr Korpsführer* Hühnlein and *Herr Reichsleiter* Bouhler have been informed in principle of your and my plans and both gentlemen have raised no objections to a change of company under such circumstances, it would perhaps be tempting providence to remain with the Union in that situation.' To achieve his 'great plan of a lifetime', Stuck would therefore leave Auto Union and join Mercedes-Benz 'even before the start of the season': 'You too will understand this, *sehr verehrter Herr*

Direktor! It makes no difference to me whether you use me as a private driver or a team driver. You will have the support of the authorities either way. If Caracciola is against my being a team driver, I propose myself as a private driver. The cost to you is some 50,000 marks less, since I will use my start money to pay my expenses.' And to make really certain that the changeover would take place, Stuck concluded his letter with an attestation that is both remarkable and shocking: 'For the sake of good order, and to counter a rumour, I would like to mention that my wife is not a Jewess, but is of mixed parentage as recognised by Reich law and is going to be naturalised as German. The *Führer* has been informed of this.'

Kissel replied swiftly, the day before Christmas: 'Herr Caracciola and the other drivers will certainly have no objection if you are entrusted with carrying out the record runs. I have already given you my promise, that the management and supervisory boards have approved your employment on terms still to be agreed.' This seems to have crowned Stuck's dreams of world records, even though Kissel turned down an immediate transfer: 'I am entirely sympathetic with your position. With regard to all the circumstances which I have to take into account in dealing with my management colleagues, with the supervisory board and others, I would ask you very kindly to consider the matter again and to sign on again with Auto Union for the next racing season.' The clause in Stuck's new contract did not throw up any problems for Kissel: 'The preparation of the [speed record] car will go on until the autumn or even winter of next year. I have found out that assembling it is out of the question before September 1937.' A transfer in the very last year of the current racing formula would 'cause an upset at too early a stage,' Kissel believed, but added as consolation: 'We will certainly not lose touch with each other.' The head of Daimler-Benz AG ended his letter with an attempt to combine private life with politics: 'I was very pleased with the venison you sent me from Silesia. My warmest thanks to you for it. I have known for quite some time that your lady wife is not Jewish. There'll be absolutely no trouble on that account.'

Hans Stuck returned his thanks promptly, but in his letter, dated 25 December, he asked Kissel 'to confirm the written negotiations over this project. This world record car has been my goal in life for as long as I can remember, and I would like to commit myself to it, because I have a financial involvement in it. I am at your disposal at all times – and if you cannot speak to me personally, a written statement from you would fully suffice. I will then immediately inform the senior authorities, *Korpsführer* Hühnlein and *Reichsleiter* Bouhler, that the project will be carried out on my side, even without changing companies, since earlier, on their advice, I obtained permission to do so.'

The decision rested with Kissel, for clearly he did not require a board decision before confirming to Stuck in a letter dated 13 January 1937 and marked 'strictly confidential': 'My firm is basically in agreement that you should carry out the record runs in a car that has yet to be manufactured. As you know, we ourselves will handle the building of the car, at out own expense, including the cost of the design by Dr Porsche GmbH' – even though that company was tied to Auto Union under a contract that still had nearly a year to run. It is true that Kissel made it a condition for present and future generations that the patent rights in the world record car project would not lie with Hans Stuck as a racing driver and private citizen; no, the idea of 'building such a vehicle using our aircraft engines already existed within our company at the time when our late lamented Dr Nibel was still alive. We never dropped the idea. In the summer of last year you for your part also picked up the idea and revived it with us. I spoke to Colonel Udet at the time. He welcomed it warmly when I told him we were going to put the idea of building a world record car into effect, and gave me his verbal consent to the use of two aero engines designed by us, although certain concerns had to be discussed and cleared out of the way.'

This means that Stuck's political and personal contacts had certainly played a part. But so, of course, did the wishes of *Führer* and Fatherland: 'Since the national interest as well as that of our company, and of yourself as driver, will be paramount in the carrying out of record runs, it is necessary, through quiet and inconspicuous surveys and studies, to obtain clarity about how the whole thing is to be managed and financed – that is to say, with the closest attention paid not only to your interests, but to those of the nation and our company. It would therefore be exceptionally helpful if you could tell me, after appropriate consideration and review, how you envisage the execution and financing of the record runs. If I am broaching this question once again today, it is because it may very well be possible that, in conjunction with approval by my company for your carrying out the record runs, certain wishes and conditions on the part of senior persons in the Reich may also be imposed, which will then have to be fulfilled both by you and by ourselves.'

Dependence and precaution

It should be noted that Chief Executive of Daimler-Benz AG and future 'Director of Defence Economy' Dr Wilhelm Kissel was, in early 1937, dependent on the wishes of the Nazi regime when making his entrepreneurial decisions. His main concern was with the doubtful location of the attempt on the world record. Was it permissible to launch it in the USA, on the Bonneville Salt Flats? This question was not merely political. In an era of rigorous government quotas for foreign currency the matter of financing had to be settled. Was Stuck himself allowed to bring in money from foreign financiers in this 'matter of the highest national interest'? Not least, there remained the residual risk of whether Stuck was in fact allowed to attempt the world record in a Mercedes-Benz car. Would his wife, being of 'recognised mixed parentage', be seen as a hindrance by 'senior persons in the Reich'? What is more, the Stucks were now living in Switzerland. Would the Auto Union directors make representations to the Party against their renegade driver's project?

These were the many unanswered questions that Kissel put to Stuck in extremely convoluted language, 'so that at the very next opportunity we can firstly get in touch with the office which we principally need to pay attention to. You will understand, therefore, that if we do this, it appears absolutely essential to know your plans and intentions regarding the execution and financing of the record attempts, so that, among other things, we can establish whether these are to be accepted and approved, and whether and to what extent complications may arise at the highest Reich level regarding the manning or execution of the runs. [...] I look forward to hearing from you and send my best wishes to your esteemed wife. Heil Hitler! Sincerely, Kissel.'

On 20 January Stuck replied that, despite Kissel's reservations, he saw himself 'as the recognised driver and financial partner' and pointed out his political connections: 'I do not believe that any contrary wish has been expressed in the top echelons. They were already expecting me to switch companies, as I did of course give an indication of this in December to *Herr Reichsleiter* Bouhler, who seemed delighted with our plan and its execution, and who will certainly, when the time comes, speak with the *Führer* along these lines. *Reichsleiter* Bouhler knows that I have been occupied with this project for a long time and have invested my savings in it. We had already talked last year in Tripoli about the possibility of doing it.'

That was on the occasion of the 1936 Tripoli Race at which, because of political sensitivities in the Berlin-Rome axis, he was obliged to hand the victory to his Italian team-mate at Auto Union, Achille Varzi. This incident, which will be examined in more detail later, proves how much mutual back-scratching was involved in the relationship between the top Nazis and the heroes of motorsport. Stuck's highly-developed feel for this kind of personal diplomacy was still bearing fruit: '*Korpsführer* Hühnlein is also in the picture,' the racing driver wrote on 20 January, 'and I believe Minister-President Göring[5] has been made aware of your plans and mine.'

Stuck wanted to be 'materially' (*ie* financially) responsible for 'effecting the record runs, provided I get the foreign currency permit'. Should he fail to obtain this, two Swiss friends, Baron de Blonay and a certain Max Klingler, 'still say they are ready to meet the relevant costs. On the basis of what we have found out so far, we estimate these at around 100–150,000 marks.' It was a naïve assumption that Swiss financiers, of all people, would pick up the tab for a *German* world record, which furthermore would be attempted in the USA – particularly as Stuck's estimate did not even include the expenses for '4–5 mechanics, the engineer, the manager, my wife and myself'. Also left out of account was the cost of transporting the record car 'from the ship to the starting area and back again', as well as for 'closing off and sweeping the lake-bed, payment for the timekeepers and necessary officials'. However, for Hans Stuck, ever adept at marketing himself, one thing was clear at all events: 'All these costs can be screwed down a long way by appropriate exploitation of foreign press and film rights. At our last conversation you said this exploitation would be left in my hands. Simply by using my name alone I would be able to strike all sorts of deals. But if we bring in the names of Mercedes and Porsche as well, then with clever handling a great deal of money can be extracted from the business.'

However, after the propaganda battle at the 1936 Berlin Olympics the mood abroad was unlikely to be at all favourable to media coverage of further German triumphs. As early as 19 June, shortly after the opening of the 'Nazi Olympiad' in the capital of the Reich, the Americans were given a sharp

lesson in how cleverly Hitler's state could turn such sporting successes to their advantage when Max Schmeling defeated Joe Louis. That was why, when the German heroes took their Silver Arrows on to the grid for the Vanderbilt Cup in New York during the summer of 1937, they got a taste of how little the free world relished more German victories and propaganda. It was with good reason that in 1936 Belgium and France decided not to open their Grands Prix to racing cars but held them as sports cars events instead. The modicum of success left open by Germany's national racing cars fell to the little Alfa Romeo works team headed by Enzo Ferrari – and as the sporting representative of Italian Fascism that team was no longer welcome, in France at least, since the French had broken off both diplomatic relations and sporting contacts with Italy following the bloody and brutal occupation of Abyssinia by Mussolini's troops. For the time being the Scuderia Ferrari was no longer represented on French racetracks for the same reason. And the Spanish Grand Prix, which was won in Barcelona on 7 June 1936 by Nuvolari ahead of Caracciola, would in future be cancelled completely once General Franco had plunged his country into civil war. With massive support from Hitler and Mussolini he would soon embark on a bloodstained dictatorship.

The luck of the Devil

On 20 February 1937, at the annual reception for German racing drivers before the opening of the International Car and Motorcycle Exhibition, Hans Stuck seized his opportunity to bring Hitler up to date personally on his plans for the world record. And he did it in such a way that the *Führer*'s entire entourage as well as other racing idols must have been able to hear every word. In his memoirs, published in 1972, Stuck shifts this opportunistic sally two years forward to 1939. It would then have been politically much more awkward, since the racing driver claims in his book that he was chiefly concerned with obtaining protection for his wife Paula.

In fact on that day in 1937 Stuck probably approached Hitler solely to put the case for the world record car planned by himself and Porsche. On 14 March, a few days before the crafty driver signed his new works contract with Auto Union, he wrote in plain terms to Kissel: 'In view of the fact that, as a result of my conversation outside the Reich Chancellery the *Führer* is aware that I am the driver for the planned project and even wished me *"Hals and Beinbruch"* [a German expression equivalent to 'Break

Silver Arrow drivers and motorcycle riders in military order saluting Hitler, Hühnlein and other Nazi bosses in front of the Reich Chancellery in Berlin. It was at this reception early in 1937 that Hans Stuck presented his world record plans to Hitler and promptly received the Führer's approval. (Kirchberg)

a leg'], I believe all the reservations about this have now been removed and I can be handed something positive by you.'

Just ten days later, on 24 March, Kissel replied: 'Dear Herr Stuck, on behalf of the Management Board and Supervisory Board of Daimler-Benz AG, I can confirm that we have examined and accepted your proposal to build a car to attempt the absolute world speed record.' And as Stuck had wanted, the letter ended with the statement: 'We further confirm herewith that, by virtue of your preliminary work and financial participation, you will be the sole driver of this car.'

Stuck seemed to have achieved the goal of his dreams and desires. He was indeed a *Hans im Glück* (roughly 'a lucky devil') since, almost simultaneously, Auto Union concluded a new contract with him on 19 March, even though they were aware of his ambition to join their competitor. No other driver of that era had been handed such a mouth-watering deal: Hans Stuck would remain as works driver for Auto Union, although he had reached agreement with Mercedes-Benz about an assault on the world record. That sort of thing does not come about without helpful political string-pulling. And in the future too, Stuck would be able to count on his friends and cleverly exploit these contacts for his own ends. He would need to, since for him the end of the 1937 season with Auto Union was anything but happy.

True, at Mercedes-Benz there were still forces at work against him, among them racing manager Alfred Neubauer. On 23 March Neubauer drafted a memorandum for the top management, pointing to world speed record projects in Britain and the USA which were significantly further advanced, and on balance advising against embarking on the building of a car to challenge the record themselves. He went on to hint that Rudolf Caracciola, the top Untertürkheim driver, was by no means indifferent about Stuck driving the record car. What is more, according to Neubauer the Nazi sports authorities were already having second thoughts about the whole project.

Clearly, however, Neubauer did not get his views across to his superiors to the extent that he had hoped. At all events, on 6 April, in answer to a direct enquiry from Kissel, he submitted a five-page dossier 'Re: world record car – Hans Stuck', which attempted with painstaking precision to pull apart Stuck's plans as well as the first design drawings by Porsche GmbH. He raised the question: 'If Herr Stuck drives the car, then the whole world of sport and the trade press will certainly ask why Mercedes-Benz did not select one of its proven drivers, but instead a driver from an outside stable. All the more so as in 1934 and 1936 Caracciola set up world records for us, which he still holds.' In any case, Neubauer questioned Stuck's copyright on the idea for a world record car, because, he said, as early as 1924 the same idea came up in the Untertürkheim factory and at that time 'Herr Dr Porsche' had developed the plan for achieving a 'world best performance' with one or two of the 6-litre engines. Furthermore, in late 1935 a visit had been paid to Untertürkheim 'on world record matters' by none other than 'Mr Pillsbury, whom the American Automobile Association, with regard to sports affairs' had selected to head up the preparations for Malcolm Campbell's attempt at the land speed record. What need was there for Hans Stuck, whose cost calculations were wrong in any case? The 'expedition on to American soil' would, according to Stuck, 'not exceed 50,000 RM – or at most 80,000 RM', from which Neubauer concluded: 'These costs are very small in relation to the total expenditure, so that cannot be the only reason why no one but Herr Stuck has been considered.' In any case the racing manager doubted 'whether Herr Stuck can actually come up with the guarantee for the sums of money.'

As if that were not enough, Neubauer warned that, because of the world record project, it would be necessary to accept Stuck in the company's own 'racing fraternity' from 1938 at the latest. 'The question is whether that is intended and desired, and here I point out our earlier employment intentions regarding Herr Stuck.' At the time, Neubauer claimed, Stuck had simply used Untertürkheim's approaches as a clever way of substantially improving his contract with Auto Union. And if, in addition, Stuck offered 'to set up the press deals and write the articles' then that would not work to the benefit of Daimler-Benz AG either: 'In his typical way, he will tell stories of fatalities and suchlike, in order to steer the interest towards his performance; at the same time we will actually come out of it in a negative way, because the vehicle is described as *dangerous*. In this connection I should add that Herr Caracciola said about his record attempts that you

Rudolf Caracciola and Alfred Neubauer tried in vain to oppose Hans Stuck's plan to build and drive a land speed world record car designed by Porsche and financed by Mercedes-Benz. (Molter)

simply do not feel the car gliding over the ground and so there is really no skill in driving a car like that. This also raises the question of how much coverage Herr Dr Porsche will get in these articles, since the press will once again, of course, only give a secondary mention to Mercedes-Benz but will present the design as a miracle worked by Dr Porsche.' Neubauer had seen the initial drawings from the Porsche office and immediately suggested a fundamental modification: 'It would seem more suitable from every point of view to fit the car with two engines, in order to gain a massive lead, but with the present design that is quite out of the question.'

And in order perhaps to overturn the entire project after all, he referred at the very beginning of his paper to the national interest, for neither Daimler-Benz AG nor the Nazi government could afford to be let down by the world record car. And because 'Britain and America also have plans for world record cars' it would be 'necessary first of all to find out, with great caution of course (industrial espionage), how much of these plans is fact.'

No, German motorsport was anything but non-political in those days, even though in his Denazification tribunal after the war the same Alfred Neubauer claimed vehemently but naïvely that it was. And because it *was* political, he wrote to his chief executive on 6 April 1937: 'It is necessary to test the attitude of *Herr Korpsführer* Hühnlein, as boss of motoring in Germany, without whose approval, as we have learnt from experience, there is no chance of getting any foreign currency for sports purposes.'

The chosen location for the world record runs would prove a further stumbling block. Utah's Bonneville Salt Flats flood in the spring. Not until the autumn, when the bed of the lake had dried out and the salty surface was rock hard, could a flat track be prepared. Thus Stuck and Porsche could not put their plans into effect in America until autumn 1938 at the earliest. The nightmare of only being able to go for a world record in the USA would certainly occupy the minds of those with political responsibilities and lead them to consider whether perhaps a stretch of autobahn could be developed into a track suitable for world records.

These thoughts gained even greater currency when the presence of the Mercedes-Benz and Auto Union cars at the lavishly sponsored Vanderbilt Cup in New York on 5 July 1937 provoked massive anti-German demonstrations. After that, could the USA still be regarded as a suitable setting for the great assault on the Anglo-American speed records? It is no surprise that the top men in the Nazi regime and Mercedes-Benz were seeking alternatives. On 19 July Kissel reported, in a letter to the office of Emil Georg von Stauss, that: 'From a discussion I had with the Inspector-General of German Highways, Herr Dr. Ing. Todt,[6] I know that he has a project under way in the context of his autobahns, which would make it possible in future to attempt the major world speed records in Germany. Herr Todt believes that his planned facility will be finished in the course of next year. If this means that we are no longer obliged to go to America but are able to attempt the records in Germany, then the circumstances that led us to negotiate with Herr Stuck largely cease to apply anyway.'

Two American views of the German visit to New York for the Vanderbilt Cup race in July 1937, from the New York Daily News of 7 July 1937 (above) and the New York Times of 5 July 1937.

So despite all Kissel's earlier assurances Stuck's contract with Mercedes-Benz was now being called into question. And it transpired that Porsche's record car would not be ready by the end of 1937 as planned either. But most important of all, Stuck's performance at the wheel in the current season was giving cause for criticism. He was no longer bringing in results that matched his financial rewards or the potential of his car and technical support. Except for wins in the hill-climbs at Schauinsland in the Black Forest and La Turbie near Nice the veteran's score was modest. In Grand Prix races he was now not merely overshadowed by the outstanding Rosemeyer; gradually even the second rank of the Auto Union works team were threatening to challenge his accustomed status. In the absence of the top drivers from both German stables, who were racing in the Vanderbilt Cup, the Belgian Grand Prix was won by Auto Union rookie Rudi Hasse with a clear lead over Stuck, who even had difficulty holding his own against the young Hermann Lang in the best Mercedes-Benz. To make matters worse the Saxon team's season was clouded by the death in the German Grand Prix at the Nürburgring on 25 July of Ernst von Delius, another promising talent.

The fact that Hans Stuck made frequent complaints about alleged defects in his car scarcely improved the aging driver's position. His verbose explanations for his lack of success in circuit races were increasingly regarded as special pleading. Added to this, the well-paid veteran had probably revealed the financial details of his lucrative contract to Rosemeyer. Young Bernd, despite competition from Caracciola and Nuvolari, by now enjoyed an undisputed reputation as the world's fastest driver, but appeared to be earning less with Auto Union than Stuck was, so he angrily demanded a substantial raise. This did no harm either to the darling of the German fans or to Auto Union but created more trouble for Stuck, because by passing on contractual details he was in breach of rules laid down in law.

The confused situation finally reached a climax on 12 September at the Gran Premio d'Italia, which Stuck had managed to win at Monza the previous season but was this year held at Livorno. Matters came to a head because the frustrated Stuck, after a less than enthralling drive, simply shot past the pits and parked his allegedly faulty car beside the track, so that his crew had absolutely no chance to check the real or imagined defect and possibly remedy it. The immediate consequence was that Auto Union fired its long-serving driver.

Nor did the board of Daimler-Benz AG fail to notice that Stuck's 1937 performance at the wheel left a lot to be desired. But the man who had been prematurely sacked by their Saxon competitors was now knocking all the more loudly on Untertürkheim's door, insisting that he be hired to drive the world record car and wishing to discuss further contractual possibilities. On 5 November Stuck and his wife Paula called on Kissel and Max Sailer. The next day Kissel drafted a three-page note for the file about the course of the discussion. The building of the record car could not begin before May 1938, which meant the attempt at the world record would be postponed until the autumn of 1939. 'To Herr Stuck's enquiry whether he could still bank on carrying out the record runs, I replied that the Board would abide by their promise, although the conditions differed from those at the time when we envisaged making the record runs in America, as did the financing, which Herr Stuck wanted to handle himself.' And Kissel enquired whether under these circumstances Stuck would still be financially involved in building the record car. The racing driver replied that he would and that for this he envisaged a sum 'initially in the region of 50,000 RM'. Kissel clearly thought this was too little and asked in addition 'that he should not make any approaches to the authorities, because we for our part had taken the necessary steps.'

Thus at the beginning of the 1938 season Hans Stuck had his back to the wall, with no prospect of any drives with either Auto Union or Mercedes-Benz. But because a new system based on engine capacity had replaced the previous 750kg formula he asked Kissel and Sailer whether it might not be possible to let him compete as a private driver of redundant racing cars in 'a series of races abroad [...] in South America, Finland etc.' Stuck, faced with imminent discharge from service, even asked if he could have 'on loan' a power unit for a special boat for record attempts, to be constructed at the Lürsen shipyard near Bremen. But on this matter, too, Kissel and Sailer did not want to commit themselves without knowing more precise details.

At all events, Stuck now knew that the hour had struck. Just two days later he presented himself at the 'Brown House' in Munich: 'After consultation with the highest authorities I am told that since I am financially involved in the two big projects I have for Germany, it is undesirable for me to drive for foreign countries. The view is held that this would not be permissible.'

And in order to make his employment as a 'private driver' for Daimler-Benz AG still more digestible, Stuck put forward no less than *fifteen* international racing fixtures of rather second- or even third-class status, which he could enter and win in 1938 in one of last year's cars. Entering the old cars would cost at the most 25,000 RM, he said, a snip for 'a series of big sports victories'. The only condition was that Stuck would receive, in addition to all starting and prize money, a guaranteed sum of about 25–30,000 RM, which he proposed to extract from the accessory suppliers with the backing of the Daimler-Benz board. And of course Untertürkheim would also take responsibility for paying all his insurance premiums for accident cover on and off the track. Stuck signed his letter to Kissel with a fulsome greeting. The latter swiftly replied on 13 November, with equally fulsome good wishes, a 'Heil Hitler', and a flat refusal.

However, Kissel assured Stuck that, should his plan to build a boat for the water speed record – in other words the second 'national project' – actually come to fruition, Daimler-Benz AG would make available a suitable engine on a loan basis, 'provided the concerns [of the board] have been dealt with'. For Stuck this was poor consolation, since it meant that his two vague world record projects would not, for the moment, earn him a single pfennig. Without a contract for the 1938 season he would no longer have any income worth mentioning – a sorry predicament for a hitherto highly-paid national motor racing hero.

Among good friends
But Stuck had other possibilities in the form of his influential friends in the SS. On 2 May 1938 they invited Auto Union's chief press officer and long-serving Party member Dr Richard Voelter to a special meeting concerning Stuck's future. It should be noted that this was scarcely a month after the opening fixture of the season, at Pau in south-west France, and only two weeks before the second Grand Prix of the year, in Tripoli. It is true that in both races Mercedes-Benz was represented by the new 3-litre supercharged model, but Auto Union did not enter. The Zwickau racing division was under great pressure following the accident that killed Bernd Rosemeyer, and preparations for the new racing formula had become bogged down. There was even uncertainty about the allocation of drivers, particularly as the Nazi leadership wanted to have their say and to help the controversial

Stuck in securing a contract. So Voelter felt compelled to pay a call on SS-*Gruppenführer* Wolff[7] in order 'to find out, ahead of the latest negotiations with Stuck, the precise attitude of the *Reichsführung* SS [Himmler's office] and the reasons why it is backing Stuck so strongly.'

The meeting lasted nearly an hour and a half, during which Voelter briefly met Himmler without being able to 'broach the Stuck question' with him. The following day Voelter, who himself boasted the Golden Party Award of the NSDAP, made a note of the gist of the conversation. This states that he spoke unambiguously to Wolff: 'I told him we were not altogether happy about the *Reichsführung* SS making such a strong case for Stuck, who after all was suspect due to having a non-Aryan wife. *Gruppenführer* Wolff then explained to me that two or three years ago, when the public harassment of Stuck because of his wife's Jewish antecedents had intensified, Stuck had applied to the *Führer*'s office for protection and a decision on his case, and that the *Reichsführung* SS or the Gestapo had been brought in. On the basis of an investigation at the time, the *Führer* decided personally that attacks against Stuck because of his wife should be forbidden and a line drawn under the Stuck business, which meant that Stuck had been rehabilitated and that in future his wife's non-Aryan background should have no influence on his sporting activities. However, since this had led to a personal relationship between Stuck and *Reichsleiter* Bouhler [head of Hitler's office] and, given his difficulty in finding a new engagement, Stuck now had to turn again to the *Reichsführung* SS and *Reichsleiter* Bouhler for help and influence.'

Naturally Wolff, speaking for the *Reichsführung* SS, said he 'did not want to exert any unilateral pressure in favour of Stuck'; however, Voelter should not 'get too upset about personal differences that have arisen between Stuck and the Auto Union board, or the people handling his case in the sports department and racing management.' It was 'regrettable that a driver of Stuck's reputation can no longer be accepted in a German team and that he may be compelled to sign contracts with foreign firms.' Wolff added that 'Stuck has without doubt behaved very ineptly and has managed to fall spectacularly between two stools.'

Voelter endeavoured to argue the contrary and announced that the differences with Stuck lay 'substantially deeper'. On the one hand the racing driver had long ceased to be a star, on the other he was 'as experience shows, a danger to any team through his often unfriendly attitude and frequent squabbles with his team-mates, for which his wife was admittedly to blame; and for us to re-engage Stuck would mean having more problems in the team, whereas now that Stuck is no longer with us, we have impeccable discipline and comradeship. Thirdly, all the bad feeling and differences of the last few years which […] had twice led

No mountain was high enough to stop Hans Stuck. Having been sacked by Auto Union in September 1937, he used the influence of high-ranking SS allies to regain his lost seat in the team in June 1938. As a result his racing career continued and he managed to win the Grossglockner mountain climb on 28 August 1938. (Sebastian)

to a premature termination of the contract between Stuck and Auto Union and had already resulted in the Stuck file being ten times larger than the personnel files of our other drivers, had undermined the necessary trust between works and drivers without which there can be no successful collaboration, and in such a way that I did not believe that trust could be restored, even with the greatest goodwill on both sides.'

Wolff took all this on board but did not think that as a racing driver Hans Stuck was 'finally on a downhill slide'. So he asked Auto Union, with an eye to publicity and to a driver who still enjoyed a great reputation, to consider once more 'whether in spite of all that had happened Stuck could not be given one last chance.'

Auto Union did not dare to go against the will of the SS any longer, and Stuck was given a new racing contract. It should be noted that Auto Union no longer negotiated directly with Stuck, but with Wolff and Himmler, who acted as managers for their racing protégé. This was something that, understandably, they did not want to shout from the rooftops. On 28 May 1938 Auto Union sent their offer to Stuck but immediately ran into more trouble with Himmler and his henchmen, because what they proposed was that Stuck would not take part in formula races as an official member

Opposite: The Auto Union team for 1938 – without Hans Stuck. The driver line-up comprised (from left) Tazio Nuvolari, Hermann Paul Müller, Georg 'Schorsch' Meier, Ulrich Bigalke and Rudolf Hasse. (Audi AG)

Right: After the rift, Hans Stuck was back with Auto Union for the 1938 German Grand Prix. Backed by the SS at a high level, Stuck was able to achieve an implausible combination: simultaneously driving in races for Auto Union and working with Mercedes-Benz on a streamlined contender for the land speed world record. (Audi AG)

of the works team, but would only be entered for a number of non-formula events – especially hill-climbs such as the *Grosser Bergpreis von Deutschland* – as a private driver in one of last year's cars. What is more the salary they offered was extremely modest.

That is why the chief executive in Chemnitz, Dr Bruhn, immediately received a phone call from the Gestapo: on the line was SS-*Gruppenführer* Wolff, speaking on behalf of Himmler. According to Bruhn's note of the call on 25 June, none other than Himmler himself was 'surprised and very disconcerted' because Auto Union's offer to Stuck was 'unsatisfactory' and lacked the 'generosity' asked for by the SS. Again in Himmler's name, Wolff blatantly threatened Bruhn that 'if Auto Union persists in its attitude then he would see to it that the entire SS and the entire police would never order another car from Auto Union.' Bruhn finally reacted to the telephoned threat. 'In the circumstances we will raise our offer to Stuck; you will then pass this on to Stuck, as that seems to be the way negotiations now have to be conducted.'

The same day the Auto Union board sent a telegram to Wolff stating that they were prepared to 'double all the financial elements' of the contractual offer. This meant that Stuck's contractual terms would be identical to those Auto Union had agreed with its new star driver and designated successor to

Rosemeyer, Tazio Nuvolari. The new offer to Stuck was exorbitantly high, so it is no surprise that Wolff immediately telegraphed back: '*Reichsführer-SS* conveys warmest thanks for your co-operation. Accepts your offer of 26 June. *Reichsführer*-SS confident Stuck will justify your decision through total commitment and exemplary comradeship.'

Due in part to a very thinned-down international Grand Prix calendar, in 1938 Auto Union only entered for six circuit races. Stuck was absent at the first appearance of the Silver Arrows from Saxony in Reims on 3 July, but he did take part in the German Grand Prix (3rd place), the Swiss (4th) and the Italian (retired). This earned him just 9,000 RM in starting money. On the other hand he swept the board in hill-climbs, with five starts and five wins, and picked up further income of 45,000 RM in starting and prize money. Here the uncrowned 'mountain king' made his usual crafty calculation and cleaned up easily in his last three wins of the 1938 season, because at the Maiola Pass in Switzerland and in two hill-climbs in Romania he faced no noteworthy competition.

On the way to the world speed record

Protected and cared for by his SS patrons – a fact that was crucial to the survival of his wife Paula – and on the payroll of Auto Union, Stuck was already focusing on the coming 1939 season, which would see the launch of the assault on the world speed record for land vehicles, as agreed with Daimler-Benz and its chief executive.

The speed that had now to be beaten dated from 19 November 1937, when the record held for so long by Malcolm Campbell was finally taken by another Briton, George Eyston, who drove across the Bonneville Salt Flats at an average speed of 312mph (502kph). Theoretically this was still within the realms of possibility for the 1,650bhp DB 601 power unit. But on 27 August 1938 Porsche's staff, housed in a section of their own at Untertürkheim, were thrown into confusion when Eyston achieved a new world record of 345.20mph (555.42kph) in *Thunderbolt*, powered by two 2,300bhp aero engines. Then on 15 September the Anglo-American John Cobb surpassed this in his twin-engined *Railton Special* at a speed of 350.06mph (563.24kph), which the very next day he pushed up to 357.33mph (574.94kph).

To beat this, the Porsche engineers now had to shoot for 600kph (370mph), which meant that their T80 record car – not designed for twin engines – needed a far more powerful engine capable of delivering over 3,000bhp. Though Daimler-Benz's 44.5-litre V12 test engine, designated DB 603, should be capable of this it was still only at the trial stage. The engineers were therefore running out of time, and to make matters worse the record runs by Cobb and Eyston rendered completely obsolete the stretch of the Berlin–Leipzig–Halle autobahn that had been earmarked as the 'German world record track'. Only just completed in autumn 1938, this 10km section near Dessau was dead straight, level and up to 29m (about 32yd) wide, with no central reservation or barrier; but to reach a speed of 600kph the world record car needed a run-up of at least 6km, leaving only 4km in which to decelerate and stop. World records over the 'flying kilometre' or 'flying mile' were quite possible in theory, but there was the risk that the deceleration stretch would be insufficient for careful braking and bringing the car to a safe halt.

The new autobahn near Dessau was the scene of Rudolf Caracciola's class world record of 399.56kph (248mph) in February 1939 with a new Mercedes-Benz streamliner powered by a 3-litre engine based on the Grand Prix version. However, even the 10km Dessau straight was not sufficiently long or wide for an attempt on the outright land speed world record with the Mercedes-Benz T80 project. (Daimler AG)

For normal speed records for specific classes, using highly tuned and streamlined racing cars at speeds around 400kph (250mph), the Dessau 'track' may have been more suitable than the Frankfurt–Darmstadt autobahn, but to use it for an attempt on the absolute world record would have been sheer suicide. So on Christmas Eve 1938 Wilhelm Kissel sent a strictly confidential message to Hühnlein, the NSKK chief: 'During your last visit to our factory we told you that in the battle to raise Germany's international status we were involved in building a world record car. The work has progressed to the extent that we expect to have the car ready by May of next year. It is impossible to carry out the world record attempt in Germany, because even on the new record track near Dessau the run-up and run-down are too short. This forces us for better or worse to move the record attempt to America. […] According to information obtained from America, the best time for mounting record attempts, when the floor of the Salt Lake has to be dry, is from 15 August to 15 September.'

From 1 September 1939 the 'battle to raise Germany's international status' would, of course, be waged on another front. Kissel was not to know that, but in view of the massive rearmament contracts being worked on at Daimler-Benz and elsewhere, the possibility could not have been completely unforeseen. Yet on what proved, unexpectedly, to be the

Megalomania from Mercedes-Benz. Hans Stuck's dream project, the T80 land speed record car with a 44.5-litre engine, was built but never ran. (Daimler AG)

33142

An aeroplane with six wheels. The T80's streamlined bodywork illustrates how an engineer's experience with high-speed cars can carry over into wartime. (Daimler AG)

last Christmas of peacetime, Kissel made some very special requests to Hühnlein. The dollar equivalent of around 250,000 RM was needed for the German world record in the USA, and it was needed not later than mid-July 1939: 'Germany's plan to attempt the world record stands or falls on the granting of this sum, which for this company means the same as continuing or ceasing to build this car.'

Stupidly, Hühnlein had already, with reference to the 1938 season, warned Kissel against using up too much foreign currency, and the sum now being requested far exceeded the quotas normally granted hitherto. This was why he continued to bank on carrying out the world record runs on the Dessau section of the autobahn. Mercedes-Benz was therefore obliged to tone down its demands somewhat, and on 18 February 1939 Kissel asked Hühnlein 'should the Dessau track prove unsuitable for record runs, to obtain the *Führer*'s permission to carry out these runs on the Great Salt Lake in America, for which foreign currency to the value of 100,000 RM to 150,000 RM will be needed.' The answer came back on 21 March that Hühnlein had not had an opportunity 'to speak with our *Führer*'. So finally, on 3 June, Neubauer summed up the situation for Kissel: 'The world record car is far enough advanced today that, according to Dr Schmidt of the aircraft test-engine construction department, a type DB 603 running-in engine for the car can be delivered towards the end of June. Accordingly the world record car should be ready for running-in purposes by the end of July. So far only trial tyres and wheels have been supplied, which permit a speed of 400kph. In the opinion of the aircraft test-engine department, the final engine cannot be delivered earlier than the end of August.' And even when this was written, in June 1939, no decision had yet been made as to where the world record attempts were to take place.

Neubauer's conclusion was sobering: 'There is therefore no question of us being able to set up a world record before the end of 1939. In the case of America we must also bear in mind that, should there be an accident, there is a risk that the vehicle will be confiscated by the authorities, and possibly the engine dismantled and examined. (Secrecy of Type 603).' But because Cobb, the rival of the record-breaking Eyston, would probably make another attempt in August or September 1939 in a greatly improved vehicle, the 600kph mark was likely to be exceeded, which meant, in Neubauer's words, that 'the record car prepared by us with only one engine will be superseded. Herr Dr Porsche, who I have just spoken to about this, is also of the view that our car will be outperformed this year. [...] The next thing to do would be to design and build a new record car, in which two such engines are used.'

While Europe was being dragged inexorably towards war by Hitler's Germany, the strategists in Untertürkheim remained undaunted in their plans to achieve German world records. Neubauer, however, remained strongly opposed to allowing Stuck to take the wheel of the record car: 'It is doubtful whether either our *Führer* or Herr *Korpsführer* Hühnlein feel that Stuck is acceptable for this world performance. On the other hand, I would not, for our part, use any of our drivers, because the whole thing is too dubious.'

In the danger zone

In saying this, Neubauer was not alluding only to the rivalry between Hühnlein, the head of the NSKK, and SS *Reichsführer* Heinrich Himmler, Stuck's personal patron. In June 1939 there was another reason why Stuck might be becoming unsuitable as a world record driver in the eyes of many top Nazis.

By that time robbing German Jews of their civil rights had already taken on a terrible new dimension, and it was becoming increasingly risky for even a thoroughly popular racing driver to be married to a 'non-Aryan' woman. An old Nazi campaigner named Hans Hinkel,[8] who had joined the NSDAP as member no. 287 and since 1935 had 'special responsibilities' in Goebbels' propaganda ministry, now began to take a very close interest in the 'Paula Stuck case'. Hinkel was responsible for listing of all those engaged in 'cultural' activities, and assessing them politically. In Nazi jargon this entailed systematically 'de-Judifying' all fields that had an impact on the public. In this respect Hinkel was so zealous and successful that at the outbreak of war he was also responsible for matters concerning the deportation of Jews.

On 30 December 1938 he wrote to SS-*Gruppenführer* Wolff: 'The wife of the well-known racing driver Stuck is, as far as has been so far established, half-Jewish. However, there have been repeated claims that this woman is fully Jewish. Frau Stuck is a professional writer and in autumn 1937 had her novel *Viermal Liebe* ['Four Times Love'] published by a Swiss publisher and is currently publishing a children's book with another Swiss firm. When I looked into her antecedents, I received from the President of the Reich Chamber of Literature, among other things, the following information: "Frau Stuck points out that Herr *Gruppenführer* Wolff

Hans Stuck was the master of adaptation – a flexible friend to Nazi leaders who managed to survive his machinations. (Kirchberg)

(Gestapo) is in the picture about the detail of these events. I got in touch with him, and through his office in the person of Herr *Hauptsturmführer* Schallemeyer, was told that Herr Stuck had handed a gift to *Gruppenführer* Wolff to pass on to the *Führer*, which he did. On that occasion the *Führer* said something to the effect that the unpleasant remarks about Stuck and his not-pure-Aryan wife must cease. It has to be recognised that a man like Stuck drives great races for Germany. I am told that *Obergruppenführer* Brückner[9] was present at this conversation." Since I have acquired this information, may I ask you to send me a brief report on the matter. It would be particularly important for me to find out whether there is a wish that Frau Stuck be allowed to continue her activity unhindered, since otherwise, under the prevailing regulations, her admission to the Reich Chamber of Culture would have to be refused on account of her being, as far as can be established to date, at least half Jewish.'

On 19 February 1939 Hinkel once again 'reminded' Wolff of the 'statement requested' and asked him to 'deal with this matter'. But Stuck enjoyed the protection of the SS *Reichsführer* and his staff. Himmler and Wolff were playing for time; they pointed to an 'appraisal of the wife of the racing driver Stuck' issued on 28 July 1938. On 29 June 1939 Hinkel complained that the document in question could not be found in the Ministry of Propaganda, and requested a copy. On 11 August and again on 1 September – that is to say, the day Germany invaded Poland – Hinkel again reminded Wolff about the overdue copy of the 'appraisal'.

By contrast, where it concerned the interests of the racing driver entrusted to their care the senior ranks of the SS were able to speed things up considerably. Following Stuck's recent complaints against his employer Auto Union for having placed him at a disadvantage vis-à-vis his stablemates, the name of Feuereissen, the racing manager, was reported to Himmler. On 12 July Feuereissen wrote a note about the interview, which he described as 'more unpleasant than can be imagined'. True, Himmler hinted that he 'had no personal interest whatever in the matter, and anyway Stuck was not an SS man, and therefore his success would not be credited to the SS.' However, he made it very plain to the helpless Feuereissen that Germany was not really so richly endowed with racing drivers that it could do without a man like Stuck, particularly since for the moment up-and-coming drivers were in very limited supply, and, indeed,

Near the danger zone: Paula Stuck (left) as timekeeper during the weekend of the Tripoli Grand Prix in 1937 together with Elly Beinhorn (second left), Italo Balbo (in uniform) and Bernd Rosemeyer (right). (Kirchberg)

there was always the possibility that the number of racing drivers might be reduced through fatal accidents.

Where Paula Stuck was concerned the SS top brass took their time in replying to Hinkel and Goebbels. Wolff did not raise this matter again until 21 September ('currently at the *Führer*'s headquarters'), when he wrote: 'The proportion of Frau Stuck's Jewish blood is not known to me personally, and I have not gone into the question in depth, since in the office here no enquiry relating to it is to hand, nor is any such procedure available. I only know the fundamental decision of the *Führer*, which is set out in the account I submitted to the President of the Reich Chamber of Literature. I am not able to judge whether this statement by the *Führer* is sufficient for a decision to be reached on the matter of Frau Stuck, whereby she is entitled to write books that are sold in Germany as well as other countries. I will leave it to you to obtain a definitive decision from the *Führer* when the time comes. It would be appropriate to do this through SA-*Obergruppenführer* Brückner, with reference to the *Führer*'s earlier remarks – particularly since I am convinced that in the event of a negative outcome to her application [for admission to the Reich Chamber of Literature] she would complain to the *Führer* about the decision. I would further point out that – as far as I am informed – Frau Stuck, as Germany's top woman tennis player, has been and will continue to be selected by *Reichssportführer* von Tschammer und Osten to carry the German colours in international tournaments.'

At a moment when the German war machine was operating at full power against Poland, and Warsaw was already being forced into unconditional surrender, Hinkel at the Reich Ministry of Propaganda was not letting go. On 28 September he made a direct approach to Brückner, Hitler's chief adjutant: 'Since you are said to have been present at the meeting [between Hitler and Himmler], may I ask you in due course to send me a brief report on this matter or else get the *Führer* to make a definite decision as to whether it his wish that Frau Stuck should not be prevented from pursuing her activities.'

It is clear that Brückner was unable to produce the desired clarification. On Stuck's index card held by the Reich Chamber of Culture, describing him as a 'racing driver and engineer' who was engaged in writing, we find a typewritten entry that reads 'Of German blood. Wife half-Jewish', with a later handwritten comment: 'Antecedents not yet fully clarified. (poss. Full Jewish).' This is stamped and signed by an SS *Oberscharführer* from the information department of the Central Office of Reich Security (*Reichssicherheitshauptamt*), which was not set up until 27 September: 'No unfavourable citations have been received.' A further stamp on this index card confirms: 'No concerns about using him to address the troops.' Hans Stuck, therefore, could give lectures to servicemen and earn fees for this activity. The racing driver was never drafted himself, because Professor Ferdinand Sauerbruch, having by now reached the position of Senior Medical Officer to the Wehrmacht, had issued Stuck with the necessary certificate in person.

His own chances of surviving the Second World War unharmed were therefore theoretically good – whereas for the Nazis, the case of Paula Stuck had not yet been shelved. It was at the height of the 'Battle of Britain' that the 'final solution of the Jewish question' was placed urgently on the Nazis' political agenda. On 5 September 1940 the film *Jud Süss* ('The Jew Süss') received its world premiere at the Venice Film Festival, and just three weeks later it was being shown in German cinemas. On 22 and 23 October, German Jews from the states of Baden and the Palatinate were deported by train in a 'night and fog' operation to the Gurs concentration camp in southern France. It was a logistical prelude to organised mass-murder.

It was obvious to those concerned that the Paula Stuck affair also required finalisation, and on 10 September 1940 the Reich Office for *Sippenforschung* (research into family relationships) informed Himmler's personal staff that 'Frau Paula Emilie Valeska Maria Stuck is half-Jewish'. Consequently, under the perverted criteria of Nazi racism, the wife of the prominent racing driver was not for the moment under threat of deportation, especially as her husband continued to enjoy the personal protection of the SS grandees; and, what is more, was apparently being useful to these gentlemen in their foreign transactions.

The art of survival

At the outbreak of war Stuck was, on his own admission, staying in Switzerland, waiting to see how things turned out. It was certainly unusual even for a racing driver to be allowed to remain in neutral Switzerland unmolested. At all events he promised he would handle some transactions for his SS friends. On 13 October 1939 he wrote 'at present from Bern' to Himmler and Wolff about these intentions: '*Sehr geehrter Herr Reichsführer! Sehr geehrter Herr Gruppenführer!* […] The interest abroad in the German *Kübelwagen* [literally 'Bucket Car', the name given to the VW in its military and utility truck version] and the Volkswagen private car, is extraordinary and a sure source of foreign currency. I would just need a bit of backing while I find out about prices and obtain a permit to introduce this type of car into Switzerland, Holland and Romania. In this respect, foreign countries are leaving nothing untried and are offering their cars at bargain prices.'

He enclosed an initial 'activity report for the period 26 September to 6 October 1939', in which he listed his contacts for the purpose of exporting Volkswagens, including names and addresses of people in the USA, South America, Holland, Bulgaria, Yugoslavia, Romania, Italy and Japan, as well as indirect enquiries from 'Swiss confidants' in Greece and Spain. His potential partners ranged from his Jewish brother-in-law – who had emigrated to Brazil – up to HRH Prince Bernhard of the Netherlands, to whom he had shown an Auto Union racing car at Zandvoort in the pre-war years. According to Stuck a Swiss colonel named Fierz had expressed the view to him personally 'that the Swiss authorities' would acquire 'quite a large number ' of Volkswagens.

An 'old German Party member' in Bucharest, a car salesman named Ernst Habermann, told Stuck 'that the Romanian army intended to obtain cars cheaply for officers and state bureaucrats. [...] Habermann assumes that this would be around 4–5,000 *Kübelwagen* and about 1,000 Volkswagen saloons.' And just as soon as a showroom car could be supplied, Stuck saw himself in a position, thanks to King Carol of Romania and Prince Bernhard, of being able to demonstrate 'the Volkswagen to the appropriate military authorities' in Bucharest and Amsterdam.

The industrious racing driver was also anxious to circumvent the foreign embargoes against Germany, and in the same activity report he informed the SS leadership that a company called Montan Export AG of Amsterdam wished to ship 5,000 tonnes of steel through Switzerland. Despite the embargoes he had 'found ways and means [...] of bringing the goods into Germany after all.' From Sofia, Bulgaria, Stuck proposed to procure 80,000kg of pig fat, while Yugoslavia would be the source of large quantities of pumpkin-seed oil and olive oil, and a New York import-export firm even promised to deliver via Italy 'any amount of rubber, copper, steel, iron and whatever else might be needed.' All that this zealous accomplice required was the authority to make binding undertakings that the German authorities were in fact able to pay, whether in currency or barter goods. 'I now run the risk of being booted out, because other countries are muscling in,' Stuck complained in his second activity report for 7 to 14 October 1939.

It is clear that attractive deals were beckoning. SS-*Gruppenführer* Wolff reacted swiftly and had a special account opened in the name of Hans Stuck von Villiez at the Berlin private bank of Hardy & Co, to which he immediately credited a cheque for expenses amounting to 13,893 RM. The signatories to this account were Hans Stuck, Paula Stuck – and Wolff himself. However, the record is silent as to whether any transactions relating to any deals went through this account at all. It is possible that Stuck's endeavours were an illusion from the outset, as they were in the case of Volkswagen exports; perhaps his attempts to obtain raw materials for the Reich were motivated by self-importance, to make himself valuable and at the same time to protect himself and his wife Paula. At all events Stuck's efforts and contacts must have been sufficiently important for the SS to open the special bank account.

The record shows that Stuck and his wife continued to be used in troop

Moving on from the past. Hans Stuck with his tiny, newly built Cisitalia racing car at the Hockenheimring in 1947 for Germany's first significant post-war race – which he won against only two other entrants. (Herz)

entertainment activities well into 1942. On Stuck's index card at the Reich Chamber of Culture there is a final entry dated 12 January 1943: 'With effect from 10.11.42 the Wehrmacht High Command requests that the racing driver Hans Stuck and his wife Paula (see card) withdraw from troop entertainment at the earliest possible date and refrain from any further duties.' As to the reason for this ban from frontline deployment we can only surmise, but this suspension coincides exactly with the decisive turning point of the Second World War: General Paulus, who had been commanding the 6th Army on the Eastern Front since November 1942, was trapped in Stalingrad with 250,000 men. At the same time the Nazis were putting into effect the 'final solution of the Jewish question'. Deportations and mass-murder were being carried out at top speed. At the end of November orders were issued that even 'Jews engaged in important war work' should be 'evacuated'. Plans for compulsory legal divorce in 'racially mixed marriages' were already known about.

The Stucks saw out the end of the war in the Austrian ski resort of St Anton, where they did indeed eventually divorce – because Stuck was having an affair with his future third wife Christa. But even after the war had ended, Paula seems to have remained entirely loyal to her former spouse. She acted with the authority of a victim of Nazi persecution, proven by her 'racially persecuted' identity card no. 177.

In contrast to many other prominent racing drivers from Germany, Stuck needed to have no worries about his Denazification tribunal, even though among the motorsport fraternity his connection with the SS must have been an open secret. What is more he had the advantage that since 1928 he had held Austrian citizenship. After the war ended the country that had joined the Reich in the *Anschluss* of 1938 as the *Ostmark* was immediately transformed into the very first innocent victim of National Socialism, which is why Stuck, with his Austrian licence, was allowed to drive in races all over Europe. The other top German drivers could only watch in amazement and occasional irritation as the one-time 'mountain king' appeared in a spanking new, compact Cisitalia racing car, in which he entered and easily won the first big post-war race at Hockenheim in 1947. Stuck once again had Ferdinand Porsche to thank for his outings with Piero Dusio's stable. Porsche's design office in Stuttgart had just produced a mid-engined Grand Prix racing car for the Italian industrialist and head of Cisitalia, and unsurprisingly it closely resembled the proven pre-war Silver Arrows from Zwickau. For that reason alone, Stuck, the old Porsche hand, would prove useful in future development work.

Though nothing came of the revolutionary Porsche four-wheel drive design, because Dusio ran out of money, this did not worry Hans Stuck. Undeterred by past or future, he indulged his passion for racing and cleverly cultivated the retrospective fame of his successes from the age of the Silver Arrows. In 1960 he even became the German hill-climb champion once again, driving a little BMW 700.

Notes

1 Baldur von Schirach (1907–74) was an unlikely recruit to the upper ranks of Nazism. Well-to-do and artistic, he had American blood on both sides of the family. His mother was born in New York and his paternal grandmother in Baltimore. One of his ancestors was Sir Francis Drake. The suicide of his brother in 1918 may have led to his morbid romanticism. At all events, while at Munich University he approached Hitler, promising to assemble a large student audience if Hitler would agree to address them. Schirach delivered and Hitler was impressed. Schirach rapidly rose through the nascent Nazi

youth movement, helping to stifle all rival organisations until the Hitler Youth was compulsory for all boys aged between eight and eighteen, with Schirach at its head. In 1932 he was elected as the youngest deputy in the Reichstag. He married Henriette Hoffmann, daughter of Hitler's personal photographer. She was not his social equal and seems to have been something of an embarrassment to him. Despite falling somewhat from Hitler's favour in the war years, he remained in his post and was later appointed *Gauleiter* of Vienna. At Nuremberg he was sentenced to 20 years imprisonment in Spandau, which he served in full. (See *Hitler's Hitmen* by Guido Knopp, Sutton Publishing, 2000.)

2 At this time the post of President of the Reichstag, roughly equivalent to Speaker, was one of many held by Hermann Göring, who had been appointed in 1932.

3 Eva Braun was working as an assistant in Hoffmann's photographic shop in Munich in 1929 when Hitler came in one evening and saw her. She was on a step-ladder at the time and recalled 'a gentleman of a certain age with a funny moustache […] holding a big felt hat […] I look from the corner of my eye […] and notice that he's staring at my legs.' (See *Hitler's Women* by Guido Knopp, Sutton Publishing, 2001.)

4 Philipp Bouhler (1899–1945) was the son of a Bavarian army officer, and joined the Nazi Party as an early member in 1922. He was appointed head of Hitler's Chancellery or personal office in 1934, where his main task was to deal with complaints and pleas for clemency. Ironically, his office also dealt with cases of euthanasia, where techniques were developed that foreshadowed the Holocaust. During the war, being effectively ousted by Martin Bormann, his influence waned. He committed suicide in May 1945.

5 As the first of his many government posts, in 1933 Hermann Göring was appointed Minister-President (chief minister) of the then semi-autonomous state of Prussia. He was also its Minister of the Interior and head of the Gestapo. Göring was not promoted to *Generalfeldmarschall* until 1938, then in 1940 he became *Reichsmarschall* of the Greater German Reich, for which he had an operetta-like uniform created.

6 Fritz Todt (1891–1942) was a civil engineer and a member of the Nazi Party from 1922. From December 1938 he headed the 'Organisation Todt', which harnessed the labour of 350,000 Germans and later 800,000 foreign workers. One of their main tasks was to build the massive defences of the Westwall and the Atlantic Wall. As a technocrat Todt steered clear of internal power-plotting and expressed open criticism of Hitler, which is why suspicions were aroused when he was killed in an air crash after a meeting at Hitler's military HQ in East Prussia.

7 Karl Wolff (1900–84) was one of the most successful careerists in the SS. From a well-to-do family, he served in the First World War and received numerous decorations. After a brief business career he joined both the Nazi Party and the SS in 1931 and swift promotion followed. In 1933 he became Himmler's personal adjutant, and in 1936 his chief-of-staff. In 1943 he was posted to Italy and in 1945, on his own initiative, negotiated an early surrender to the Allies of German troops there on 2 May, a week before the official surrender in northern Europe. For this reason, and because he was a prosecution witness at Nuremberg, he only received a four-year sentence for war crimes.

8 Hans Hinkel (1901–60) was a professional journalist who became a leading Nazi ideologue. In May 1935 he was appointed Director of the Reich Chamber of Culture, and soon afterwards began working for Goebbels as well. During the Second World War his brief extended to radio entertainment and film production. In 1944 he was in charge of the notorious filming of the brutal execution of the men accused of plotting to assassinate Hitler.

9 Wilhelm Brückner (1884–1954) was appointed Hitler's SA Adjutant in 1930, and later promoted to Chief Adjutant. In earlier life he had been a sports teacher and salesman for a sports goods firm. In 1940 he was dismissed following internal wrangles among Hitler's adjutants, and served in the Wehrmacht for the rest of the war.

CHAPTER SIX

CRONYISM, BRIBERY
AND STRING-PULLING

The many and varied forms of symbiosis between Germany's racing stars and top Nazis ultimately reflect what historians tellingly refer to as 'dictatorship by consensus'. A mutual give-and-take based on a common cause. In the years from 1933 to 1945 that cause was simply Germany. What the Nazis did was intended to restore honour and respect to Germany – or so the majority of Germans seemed to believe, whether tacitly or bawling at the top of their voices. And if the contradictions between what the Nazis proclaimed and what they did became too great, there was always the verbal safety-valve: 'If the *Führer* only knew about that...!' Deep down, people were proud that Germany seemed to be rising at such a pace. But afterwards, of course, everyone claimed to have been somewhere else. Or else they regrettably had to go along with it because there was just no alternative.

The astute journalist Siegfried Doerschlag (see page 115), who had by then been promoted to 'Commissioner for Refugees', wrote on 9 March 1947: 'I am today more convinced than ever that our famous racing drivers such as Caracciola, von Brauchitsch, Hermann Lang, Hans Stuck etc were all left no choice but to subordinate themselves to the NSKK and accept the honours bestowed on them after a victory, in front of the VIP stand and a crowd of ten thousand. At international events it would have been a terrible gaffe and a blow to the national ideal if the German winner of one of those races had turned round at the finishing-line and had simply

Accompanied by an NSKK motorcycle brigade, Bernd Rosemeyer leads the Auto Union team to the Horch factory in Zwickau after its victory at the German Grand Prix in 1936. (Kirchberg)

left that whole gang standing there – the Gauleiters etc who had become so important. Anyone who saw one of those German victories at the Nürburgring, on the AVUS or even abroad would have shared this point of view, even if they had been 100 per cent anti-Hitler.'

Lining up with their hands held out

Not to have taken part would have required a strong character, a bit of political nous and either religious faith or a firm belief in humanity, not to mention a resolute decision never to drive in any more races. But those who went along with Nazism were sooner or later presented with a bill, which they had to pay off with favours of one kind or another. It began at the very top, especially in motor racing. Take, for example, Wilhelm Kissel, the chief executive of Daimler-Benz. Though a very busy man he took a close personal interest in the international deployment of the company's racing machines. What is more, he made sure that on reliability runs an adequate number of cars from Untertürkheim could be crewed by Party members. Unfortunately, there were soon so many enquiries from Party circles that NSKK chief Hühnlein intervened and issued a circular banning the entire German motor industry from handing out vehicles for sports purposes directly to members of the motor formations of the NSDAP.

For this reason, on 15 March 1934 Kissel wrote a consoling letter to a Party member named Weixler, 'General Representative in Bavaria of the Prussian State Mortgage Credit Bank': 'In the same circular [from Hühnlein] companies were asked to list those vehicles which they intend to place at the disposal of members of the motor formations of the NSDAP. We immediately made a number of vehicles available to Herr *Obergruppenführer* Hühnlein, who is dealing with the allocation himself.' For another Party member, Hohmann, and the Munich SS-*Standarte* a works Mercedes-Benz had been earmarked 'to be loaned' for the second – and as it happened, the last – occasion of the '2,000 Kilometres Through Germany' rally. For 'practice purposes' and for 'participation in various competitions', SS-*Sturmhauptführer* Viktor Brack, the future 'chief of staff in the *Führer*'s office' wanted to sneak an SSKL through the back door for Baron von Michel-Tüssling. But Kissel had to refuse him, as he did the Herr Baron's co-driver, a man named Hain, for whom Brack had likewise requested an SSKL for 'practice purposes'. However, 'the 2-litre cars which you and the colleagues

Young bloods and old warhorses in military preparation. German motoring trials were used by the NSKK to train soldiers, who were provided with free driving licences. (Reuss)

in your *Sturm* drove in the 3-Day Harz Mountain Rally, are being prepared for the 2,000-kilometre event. Following approval by Herr *Obergruppenführer* Hühnlein, they will again be at your disposal for participation in this run,' wrote Kissel on 30 May 1934, adding with genuine regret that he had 'no more favourable news for Herr Brack', but nonetheless asking the latter on this occasion 'to return as soon as possible the test-car still in your possession, since its present state calls for a thorough overhaul.'

On 28 June Kissel had better news for a talented driver like Party-member Wolfgang Assenheimer from Heilbronn, who from 17 to 23 June was prevented from taking part in motorsport due to 'participation in an NSDAP political education course'. He had been 'selected from a group of works drivers, i.e. within a factory team, to drive our 1.3 litre car. […] We hope you will be pleased with this assignment.' For – guess what – despite Hühnlein's circular there were opportunities to use one's own discretion in placing motor-sport hopefuls from Party organisations directly into a works car. One of these was SS-*Sturmmann* Herbert Lauenstein, whom Kissel gave the chance 'to drive a 5-litre car from my company in the 2,000-Kilometres Through Germany rally.' On top of that, the boss of Daimler-Benz had obtained from Lauenstein's superior officer some strictly confidential information that was pretty positive. 'His possible employment as a racing driver now depends on his development,' Kissel wrote on 6 July to the SS *Standartenführer* in Mainz.

This brisk business in loaning works cars was to some extent the underpinning of motorsport in the Third Reich. It was a way of cultivating contacts with important Party figures and opened quite a few doors. The two or three annual guest-appearances of Mercedes-Benz's and Auto Union's Grand Prix monsters on the Nürburgring and the AVUS were only the tip of the national motorisation campaign, the shining silver signpost for the car drivers and motorcyclists who, day and night, week after week, took part in second-rank cross-country and orienteering runs – in effect, rehearsals for a very different kind of action a few years later in Paris, Tobruk and Stalingrad.

All supposedly non-political motorsport on German soil was firmly in the hands of Nazi officials, and the borderline between camaraderie and cronyism, between adventure and ideology, was fluid; it provided the stuff of passion and enthusiasm, of masculinity rituals and braggadocio; it was as thick and glutinous as the lubricant in the gearboxes of German racing cars. They all glorified the best experiences of their lives and at the same time fell for the Nazis' line, that motorsport and car ownership, once so elitist and exclusive, were now close to the heart of every red-blooded German. Indeed, in the 1934 announcement of the greatest spectacle of this young motoring nation we read: 'In the 2,000 Kilometres Through Germany there are no winners and runners-up as in speed-racing; instead the prize goes to anyone who reaches Baden-Baden within the prescribed time, regardless of what class he belongs to.' Even if this concept of a 'classless society' actually referred only to cubic cylinder capacity, the Nazis seamlessly transposed it to the protagonists of motor racing. They deliberately chose the sophisticated millionaires' resort of Baden-Baden as the backdrop for the start and finish of the frantic chase across the Third Reich. And ironically it was the giants of the racetrack – highly paid and moving in remote and elevated social circles – who, with their victories in the Silver Arrows, were suddenly transmuted into idols of the nation, into genuinely popular heroes.

The Nazi government did not merely grant subsidies and success bonuses to racing car builders. They also tempted them with arms contracts and bulk purchases of vehicles for civil service and Party departments. In 1938 the NSKK alone handed out more than 2 million RM for the procurement of new official vehicles. First in line for these orders was Daimler-Benz AG with contracts worth 510,408 RM, closely followed by Auto Union with total NSKK orders of 486,615 RM. Now Hühnlein's organisation was certainly a major customer, but – it might be argued – in 1939 all the orders from the NSDAP and its departments only amounted to about 3.9 per cent of the gross turnover of Daimler-Benz AG. At the same time, however, the share of sales accounted for by all government authorities was 12.6 per cent, and by the Wehrmacht a massive 35.9 per cent, while sales to private customers were 36.3 per cent and exports only 11.5 per cent of the total.

In the National Socialist state as a whole it was hard to distinguish between the spheres of influence of government departments and the Party. In view of the constant turf-wars and confusion over accountability, Hühnlein and his henchmen were, of course, much in demand as door-openers in the battle for contracts and raw-material quotas. So it was that at Daimler-Benz and Auto Union the transition between marketing and

Heil Hitler! The Horch factory in Zwickau – home of the Auto Union racing team – had its own NSKK works detachment, like all German car manufacturers. (Kirchberg)

In 1937 Ernst Henne achieved a new outright land speed world record of 279.505kph (173.713mph) with his streamlined BMW motorcycle. (BMW AG)

corruption – or, to put it more elegantly, between advertising and bribery – was a very easy one. NSKK *Werksstürme* or plant detachments were set up in the factories, company cars were provided free of charge, generous discounts granted, contributions made, and the technical or financial sponsorship of NSKK motor-sport schools taken on.

This friendship could also be maintained through small personal favours. Even hotel expenses amounting to 1,317 lire incurred at the 1934 Italian Grand Prix were paid by Auto Union on behalf of 'Fräulein Hühnlein', one of the NSKK chief's two daughters. Applying the prevailing exchange rate, this was equivalent to some 300 RM, or two weeks' salary for a senior editor in the Auto Union press department. And at least one of Hühnlein's daughters was allowed a 'civil service discount' on the purchase of a new BMW.

The Nazi officials were lining up with their hands held out, and the motorised branch of the NSDAP was right in there hustling. On 5 May 1938 Hühnlein's deputy and subsequent successor, NSKK-*Obergruppenführer* Erwin Kraus, even threatened BMW's top management with a cessation of orders for all vehicles – except the 328 sports car that the NSKK was itself planning to enter for races – because the directors of the Bayerische Motorenwerke were refusing to allow NSKK orders to be handled exclusively by one Ernst Henne. Since 1928 Henne had been BMW's contract negotiator, and in the 1934 season was employed to drive Mercedes-Benz racing cars in Grand Prix events. He was one of the NSKK's most prominent members and from 28 November 1937 held the world absolute speed record for motorcycles – 279.505kph (173.713mph) – which he achieved on a supercharged BMW. Why shouldn't this splendid chap also make a profit from NSKK orders?

Just as Auto Union and Mercedes-Benz dominated the racing car scene, in sports car racing it was the BMW 328 that now led the field. Here the NSKK entered its own teams in both national and international events, its 328 sports cars belonging to the Corps but being serviced by the factory. From June 1937 Hühnlein himself promoted a new long-distance race for sports cars and motorcycles, but this non-stop run from Berlin to Rome had to be postponed several times for political reasons – to be precise, the Abyssinian War unleashed by Mussolini. The start of this spectacular race on public roads was finally scheduled for September 1939, before the Hitler regime's own warlike ambitions scuppered this date in turn.

Germany's racing drivers, like the car factories behind them, were ambassadors for Hitler's Reich, and as such they were repeatedly subject to its influence in a specific direction. However, they could also attempt to turn these interventions to their own advantage wherever possible. At an early stage, in one case at least, even the outcome of an important race might be manipulated in the interests of higher German diplomacy.

Over-eager obedience

On 10 May 1936 the Gran Premio di Tripoli took place on the Mehalla circuit in Libya, then an Italian colony. It was a high-speed desert spectacle that lasted more than two and a half hours, was torture for drivers and cars alike – some 525km (325 miles) in roasting heat at average lap speeds of over 200kph (125mph) – and spawned arguments that began soon afterwards and continue to this day. However, the greatest expert on Auto Union racing history, Professor Peter Kirchberg, has little doubt that the victor was allowed to win for political reasons.

On the previous day, 9 May, Italy's *Gran Consiglio del Fascismo*, nominally the highest body in Mussolini's state, held a meeting. This highly important Grand Fascist Council would not convene again until the late summer of 1943, and then it was for the purpose of removing the Dictator and making a separate peace with the Allies. Yet in May 1936 it seemed that *Il Duce* was about to achieve the greatest success of his political career; some 15 centuries after the fall of the Roman Empire, a new fascist *imperium* was proclaimed. Mussolini's dreams of Great Power status were celebrated in the Italian capital, while Marshal Italo Balbo, the Governor of the Libyan colony and race director of the Gran Premio di Tripoli, was flying to North Africa accompanied by a high-ranking state visitor from Germany. This was Philipp Bouhler, Hitler's Head of Chancellery and a big wheel in the Nazi power machine.

The Gran Premio was the most generously funded race of the season. But at the same time events in Rome made the sporting event an important political demonstration. That is why on 2 May 1936 Leo von Bayer-Ehrenberg, a *Sturmführer* in the NSKK and chief of staff of the ONS, sent a rather belated letter to Auto Union's racing manager, Karl Feuereissen. He explained that Adolf Hühnlein was unable to come to Tripoli 'as he has to take part in the East Prussia Run. Given the importance of the race and the sporting friendship that Germany enjoys with Italy, *Korpsführer* Hühnlein is most anxious that the ONS is properly represented. [...] *Reichsleiter* Bouhler will take off from Berlin in a special aircraft for Rome, and from there, with the assistance of the Italian government, will take a specially arranged flight to Tripoli. *Reichsleiter* Bouhler will be accompanied by his wife and his adjutant, *Amtsleiter* [Martin] Bormann, and is expected to arrive in Tripoli on Saturday 9 May at about 14:00. We would ask you, as already requested by telegram, to reserve one double room with bath and one single room with bath in the best hotel, and also to have three entrance tickets for the race ready at the Automobile Club.'

As guest of honour Bouhler was to be given an armband, but not one with a swastika. The armband of the race organiser was a rather better passport to the pit area – exclusive even in those days – as well as to the starting and finishing line and the rest of the track. Feuereissen was to handle everything and, what is more, to marshal a welcoming committee at the airport for Bouhler and Bormann, comprising 'the senior political figures of the German community' in Tripoli, as well as official representatives of Auto Union and Mercedes-Benz and a representative of the Italian Automobile Club. It should be noted that Berlin's wishes were conveyed to distant Tripoli a mere week before the start of the race. Yet there was no question but that Feuereissen would carry out his orders in every particular.

On the Sunday of the race some astonishing things happened: despite a severe crash during practice, Nuvolari was on the starting grid – to the delight of his compatriots; caked in dust and in great pain, he drove the reserve car, a new 12-cylinder Alfa Romeo, but ended up in eighth place. Rosemeyer, in his Auto Union, was admittedly the fastest but had to abandon the race at an early stage when his car caught fire. Chiron, the fastest of the Mercedes-Benz team during practice, encountered problems with his brakes and fuel supply and was not among the leaders for long.
It was Stuck who set the pace, putting himself well ahead of his stablemate, the Italian Varzi, while the best-placed Mercedes-Benzes, driven by Fagioli and Caracciola, were trailing several minutes behind in third and fourth positions. In the eyes of reporters Stuck looked like the certain winner, particularly since Feuereissen showed him the green flag, which in the sign-language of the Saxon racing stable meant 'drive slower'. Stuck followed his instructions, only to realise, four or five laps from the finish,

that Varzi was clearly ignoring the house-rules and, after a completely unexpected burst of speed, was challenging for the lead. However, Italian accounts of the final laps claim that the lead changed hands several times before the pit managers ordered *both* Auto Union drivers to reduce speed. Varzi obeyed, they insist, but Stuck *did not*, which is why the furious Italian finally put in the fastest lap and managed to force Stuck into second place, thus winning the Gran Premio for the third time.

If we are to believe the time-keeping records of the event, in the final lap Varzi must have been as much as six-tenths of a second *faster* than Rosemeyer's outstanding best time in the practice runs. According to the German version, put about by Alfred Neubauer, Stuck had been caught unawares by Varzi's unexpected challenge. However, one thing remains absolutely certain: after 40 laps of the race, Varzi flashed past the finishing line ahead of Stuck. Contemporary estimates of his lead vary between 4.2 and 4.4 seconds, or in one case as much as 4.8 seconds. Either way, by the chronometric standards of the day it was a pretty close result.

Forced to lose in Libya, where political manoeuvres lay behind the result: race leader Hans Stuck was passed by Auto Union team-mate Achille Varzi on the last lap of the 1936 Tripoli Grand Prix. On the day that Mussolini proclaimed his new fascist imperium in Rome, the German authorities managed to produce an Italian victor in this Italian colony. (Audi AG)

In Neubauer's highly imaginative memoirs, the gap was only 0.2 of a second, and he also records the first reactions of the Auto Union team after the chequered flag had dropped: 'Hans Stuck taxied slowly into the pits. He was white with rage. His eyes glinted. His lips were a tight, narrow slit. "What a filthy trick!" he hissed, as his old mechanic, Fritzel Mathaey, helped him out of the car. "That devious bloody Italian broke all our agreements; he downright stole the victory from me!"

'"No, Herr Stuck," said Mathaey. "Varzi couldn't help it."

'"How d'you mean? He overtook me, didn't he? Even though Feuereissen had ordered us to slow down!"

'"It was just a little mistake," said Fritzel. "I saw exactly what happed: Dr Feuereissen did show you the green flag. But he showed Varzi the *red!*"

'An embarrassed Feuereissen avoided Hans Stuck's eye, when moments later Stuck tried to speak to him. He groped awkwardly for a cigarette before answering.

'"Stuck, old man. It's just one of those things. I find the whole thing extremely disagreeable. But I had strict instructions…"

'"Who from? From *Korpsführer* Hühnlein, I suppose."

'"Good God, no. He had nothing to do with it."

'Feuereissen looked round cautiously. There was no one about.

'"Nope. Orders right from the top. Ribbentrop and Co. D'you understand?"

'"No I bloody don't!" Stuck shouted. "You needn't make such a mystery out of it. I just want to know who robbed me of that win!"

'"Shh! Not so loud!"

'The race director took Stuck by the arm and drew him a little way beyond the pits, where he could be sure they would not be overheard.

'"Now, just listen to me. It's the wish of certain people in Germany and Italy that, in races in Italy, an Italian should win if possible – even if a German car is in the lead."

'Stuck, still holding the steering wheel in his hand, flung it to the ground.

'"I see. Greasing the Rome-Berlin *Achse!* [The German word means both 'axle' and 'axis']. Well, to hell with that."'

In his own memoirs, Stuck avoids any mention either of the actual events of the race or of the conversation so minutely described by Neubauer, and restricts himself to the following observation: 'On the evening after the race, which was narrowly won by Varzi, the presentation of the prize took place in the residence in Tripoli of Governor Balbo of Libya.' However, the one-time Auto Union driver does go on to mention in his memoirs the fact that at Marshal Balbo's banquet in honour of the successful drivers there was a sensational flare-up over the remarkable outcome of the race. And he does so in terms very similar to those that Neubauer used 15 years previously: 'My wife was seated on Balbo's immediate right. I was on his left, and next to his wife. This surprised me since I assumed the place of honour would go to Varzi as winner. After the hors-d'oeuvres Balbo tapped the table, stood up and raised his glass to me with the words:

'"A toast to the victor of the day!"

'I was really astonished and said to him that I wasn't the winner at all. It was his fellow-countryman Varzi, to which he replied:

'"You can't fool me, Herr Stuck. I saw very clearly how you were pulled back so that Varzi could go into the lead. I don't like little deals like that. Don't like 'em at all. Politics should be kept out of sport, and I emphasise once again that I consider you the true winner of this Grand Prix."

'I looked across to Varzi, who was standing opposite me, staring at the floor in embarrassment. It must have hit him hard. From then on he was no longer top man.'

Neubauer goes further and claims it was on that evening that Varzi took drugs for the first time and so began the ruin of his pre-war racing career. Neubauer got his ghost-writer to invent a macabre dialogue between Achille Varzi and Ilse (*alias* 'Lil'), the ex-wife of Varzi's racing colleague Paul Pietsch. It is a fact that Varzi was having an affair with the lady and both were known to be morphine users. His ever more extravagant escapades and the resulting lack of success in his races were to cost Varzi his contract with Auto Union in the course of 1936.

And what of the Tripoli result, deliberately fixed for political reasons? Was there really an instruction from Herr von Ribbentrop? It is necessary to curb Neubauer's imagination once again, because in May 1936 Joachim von Ribbentrop was Germany's special envoy in London, and not yet Reich Foreign Minister. But Bouhler, who then outranked him in the Nazi hierarchy, *was* on the spot in Tripoli. Did he perhaps put pressure on Feuereissen? And then there was Balbo's indignation about the apparent

Does he sense manipulation? Marshal Italo Balbo appears less than delighted by the way his Italian compatriot Achille Varzi won the Gran Premio di Tripoli. Legend suggests this was the beginning of Varzi's decline: that evening he took his first shot of heroin, became drug-addicted, and ruined his racing career. (Audi AG)

distortion of the race for political reasons. Both Stuck and Neubauer agree in their accounts of this.

We can also refer to the official Auto Union report. In a typewritten document dated 11 May 1936, that is to say the day after the race, and with a handwritten annotation 'incomplete', we read: 'For most of the race Varzi drove in 4th gear, since soon after the start his 2nd and 3rd gears developed faults, and he did not use 5th gear either, in order to avoid gear-changes altogether. Stuck's car had no mechanical problems at any time during the race. Governor Balbo, who was present throughout the race, accompanied by *Reichsleiter* Bouhler, warmly congratulated our drivers. The reaction of the public was excellent.' This sober summary also reveals that Stuck's two routine pit stops were completed more quickly than Varzi's two stops for refuelling and tyre changes. So to sum up, Stuck's racing car remained intact and trouble-free from start to finish, whereas Varzi had to get by without the use of his highest gear, so eminently necessary on a high-speed track like the Mellaha circuit. In spite of being unable to drive his 16-cylinder Auto Union flat out, the Italian ended up the winner. Scarcely credible, is it?

On 12 May 1936 Feuereissen sent a telegram to his board of directors: 'Delighted to report convincing Auto Union victory in new record time by Varzi. Rosemeyer car burnt out. Rosemeyer unhurt. Recommend specially nice telegram to Stuck, since Stuck held big lead up to 38th lap, then drove gently as per instructions.'

The rest is silence. Only a week after the Tripoli race the Grand Prix de Tunis was scheduled, after which Feuereissen returned from Africa and wrote to the ONS in Berlin. The Auto Union AG archives contain a letter of reply from NSKK *Stürmführer* Leo von Bayer-Ehrenberg, dated 28 May 1936: 'Thank you for your kind letter of 22 inst. and for the trouble you took to welcome and accommodate *Reichsleiter* Bouhler at the Grand Prix of Tripoli. I am sure he was very pleased. It was very kind of you to take personal charge of this.

Best regards and *Heil Hitler*!'

On the art of ducking and weaving

Was not such over-eager obedience in dealing with the Nazi bigwigs the exception rather than the rule? In his own Denazification tribunal early in 1948, Alfred Neubauer even boasted that on a similar occasion he had refrained from exercising any politically motivated influence on his team: 'A particular example of my loyal and fair sporting attitude is surely shown by the fact that in 1938, the year of political crisis, the British driver Richard Seaman won the German Grand Prix in a Mercedes-Benz, and was awarded the *Führer*'s Prize. Had I had a National Socialist attitude, a single directive would have been enough for me to rob Seaman of first place, and let his place be taken by the Caracciola/Lang team, who were just behind.'

The only problem with this argument is that Seaman had a lead of more than four minutes, and had Neubauer ordered a switch of positions it would have looked even more like a political farce to the foreign press. Anyway, in view of Germany's overwhelming superiority in the new racing formula introduced that year, such a move would have been completely

The wrong winner. Dick Seaman and Mercedes-Benz on their way to victory in the 1938 German Grand Prix at the Nürburgring. (Daimler AG)

counterproductive if Germany hoped to go on exploiting Grand Prix events as an international showcase for its invincibility. Apart from this, Neubauer probably had quite different things on his mind that day – 24 July 1938 – for in the final stages of the race at the Nürburgring NSKK chief Hühnlein and his deputy SS-*Obergruppenführer* Kraus were badgering him when von Brauchitsch's Mercedes-Benz, which up till then had been ahead of Seaman, caught fire at its second pit stop. After a dramatic fire-fighting and rescue operation von Brauchitsch emerged only slightly singed. Shortly afterwards he was sent back into the race but promptly skidded off the track. He then marched back to the pits to a storm of applause, waving the wrecked car's steering wheel in his hand, and insisted that the bayonet-lock on the steering-column had come loose.

Had the Mercedes-Benz team slipped up and, after the fire caused by careless refuelling, sent their driver back onto the track with an incorrectly fitted steering wheel? Or had the brake pipes been damaged in the fire, thus causing von Brauchitsch's accident? In his memoirs, Neubauer tells how he had to justify himself to the top NSKK brass when such accusations were made following the race. But in the end it all came to nothing. The racing manager, normally so domineering and ranting in his

Up in smoke. Manfred von Brauchitsch's burning ambition to win his home Grand Prix nearly ended in disaster in 1938 when his Mercedes-Benz caught fire during a pit stop (above). The German lost the lead to team-mate Dick Seaman, but continued the race until he crashed his car. Returning to the pits on foot (below), he carried his steering wheel in order to demonstrate that it had not been secured correctly during his pit stop. In this photograph NSKK-Führer Adolf Hühnlein appears to be disputing responsibility for the failure with Mercedes-Benz director Max Sailer. (Daimler AG)

behaviour, may have acted with uncharacteristic humility, but if so this somehow escapes his memory. However, because of all these incidents Neubauer simply did not have the time to turn facts on their head through team manipulation, and to help the second-placed Lang/Caracciola pair to victory in place of Britain's Seaman. As soon as the race ended Hühnlein presented von Brauchitsch to the crowd as the 'moral victor' of the Grand Prix. Then the German racing hero was allowed to pose next to Seaman on the podium for the official honouring of the winner.

Even though Neubauer's memoirs – and, incidentally, von Brauchitsch's too – never tire of assuring us that few people actually took Hühnlein seriously, Neubauer certainly knew how to kowtow to his wishes. On 18 July 1938, six days before the German Grand Prix described above, the representatives of the German works stables were stopping over in Munich. There was a conversation with NSKK officials about taking part in the Grossglockner Race, which, following the annexation of Austria, Hühnlein fervently wished to turn into the greatest mountain race in the world. For this reason it had to be routed along a 20km (12-mile) stretch over the Franz-Josef Pass, regardless of the fact that the racing drivers in their 500bhp monsters would have to negotiate a hair-raisingly narrow and steep descent, not to mention two unlit tunnels of 117m and 311m (128yd and 340yd) respectively. Despite these risks, the Grossglockner Race offered no cash prizes, only the honour of winning. But none of this was a problem for Untertürkheim's racing manager: 'Herr Neubauer gave his immediate agreement to the plan on behalf of Daimler-Benz, and stated that the company would enter its entire team, i.e. its three top drivers. He said he had no concerns about driving through the two tunnels or the steep descent and declared that the Daimler-Benz men would drive over *Knüppeldämme* [tracks of logs laid crosswise] if the *Korpsführer* ordered them to.' Auto Union's racing manager Feuereissen, on the other hand, voiced his opposition to the reckless route, as did his colleagues at BMW, but in this company they had no chance of 'finding a sympathetic ear; at best a pitying smile at their lack of guts.'

To the snobbish stars of motor racing Hühnlein's behaviour may have appeared amusing, even ridiculous. But if so they did not make their attitude public until 1945. In Hühnlein's lifetime these gentlemen were a great deal more accommodating; after all, the NSKK chief was also head of the ONS and as such exerted a direct influence on the regulation of motor racing in Germany and sometimes even abroad, for Hühnlein and Kraus were present at the most important motorcycle and car races in foreign countries. So Germany's racing drivers were under constant observation by NSKK functionaries and informers at every competition they attended.

Georg Meier recalled the Belgian Motorcycle Grand Prix in 1939 on the Spa-Francorchamps road circuit. Treacherous at the best of times, the course was particularly dangerous in the rain. Even the elite of German motorcyclists had second thoughts about entering that year, and with Meier at their head, Ewald Kluge, Heiner Fleischmann and other top riders went to see Hühnlein, but were brusquely dismissed: 'What's got into you? A German racer is not allowed to be afraid! And you of all people, Meier, a sergeant-major in the Wehrmacht!' It was considered a matter of honour for the German motorcycle aces to take part.

The only Grand Prix in history where a non-finisher has stood on the winners' rostrum? In the Germany of 1938 it was NSKK leader Adolf Hühnlein who decided procedure at the Nürburgring – and so Manfred von Brauchitsch appeared alongside race winner Dick Seaman at the victory ceremony. (Daimler AG)

The tone of military command adopted by Hühnlein, the First World War officer and 'old campaigner' of the Nazi movement, admittedly cut more ice in German motorcycling circles than among the racing car stars. For the NSKK leader felt more at home among the *Men in Leather*, to quote the title of a Nazi propaganda film about the two-wheel fraternity and cross-country motorcycling events. German motorcyclists came almost entirely from a lower social background and as works riders earned far less than their successful colleagues in the Silver Arrows. Consider NSKK-*Sturmführer* Ewald Kluge, who joined the Nazi Party on 1 May 1937, was a works rider for DKW, part of Auto Union's extended family, and was reigning European Champion in the 250cc class. In a very successful 1938 season his total income was just 35,507.85 RM. Together with Meier, the 29-year-old Kluge was Germany's highest-earning motorcycle racer. Yet at Mercedes-Benz in 1938 both Hermann Lang and Manfred von Brauchitsch earned at least twice that figure, and probably a great deal more – to say nothing of Rudolf Caracciola. The Silver Arrow drivers were the elite and the avant-garde of National Socialist sport and, in the case of Hans Stuck and Bernd Rosemeyer, also enjoyed the highest protection of the SS. But Caracciola and von Brauchitsch, too, in addition to their obligatory membership of the NSKK, had their own contacts with senior Nazis without, admittedly, having to belong to any other National Socialist organisations.

Rigid controls and intervention by the NSKK leadership were rather what the motorcycle racers had to expect. At the 1938 International Six-Day Event, the most important cross-country fixture in the world, Hühnlein issued specific marching-orders before the 'sporting expedition' to England, exhorting the 43 German entrants in the Six-Day to return home victorious. Even abroad, German colleagues should be greeted with a 'Heil Hitler!' and foreigners with an upraised hand, for 'in salutation the German bows to no one,' as Hühnlein proclaimed. Anyone who did not do what he was told risked being muzzled. After all, success abroad in motorsport was not meant to provoke yet more antipathy against the Nazi regime.

After Hitler's breach of the Munich Agreement in March 1939[1] the motor-racing ambassadors had an even more difficult time whenever they appeared outside Germany. At the Tourist Trophy on the Isle of Man a swastika flag was stolen from the flagpole, which is why an outraged Erwin Kraus made sure that during the races, which took place between

Adolf Hühnlein – here with Georg 'Schorsch' Meier, winner of the 1938 German Grand Prix – preferred the comradeship of motorcycle racers, who weren't generally as sulky as the pampered characters in four-wheeled Grand Prix racing. (Meier)

12 and 16 June, the flags of all other countries should be removed! When 'Schorsch' Meier on his 500cc supercharged BMW became the first foreigner ever to win the Senior Trophy at the British TT – then the most important motorcycle race in the world – *and* on a German machine, the accompanying NSKK brass were on maximum alert against the British press. In a report to Hühnlein, Kraus even translated a passage from the *Isle of Man Weekly Times*: 'If their motorcycles alone can make such a din, what Hell will we go through when the Germans finally let loose with their guns?'

The Nazi functionaries were hoping for a détente but, against strict orders from Kraus, Sergeant-Major Meier made disparaging remarks about the British competitors and their machines. As a member of the Wehrmacht, Meier certainly seems to have been to some extent immune to reprimands from the NSKK. Nonetheless, Kraus wrote on 24 July to the sergeant-major's superiors: 'I have personally made it a point no longer to tolerate any unauthorised speaking in foreign countries by German drivers or German managers, after BMW's manager in England had the audacity to make a speech like the chairman of a war society.' But these problems would very soon resolve themselves. Firstly, the insubordinate Sergeant-Major Meier took a fall while riding in the Swedish Grand Prix, broke his spine in two places and was in plaster for two months. Secondly, the era of great races would in any case be terminated indefinitely from September 1939. From then on, the Germans didn't just talk like 'the chairman of a war society', the acted that way as well.

In the Nazified motorsport world, the boundary between the Party-organised NSKK and the official ONS was unrecognisable from the outset. By virtue of his double function as head of both institutions, Hühnlein was basically responsible for everything that concerned motor racing, advised and assisted by Kraus. Among the initiated, Kraus was known to be pro-Auto Union, whereas the *Korpsführer* posed as non-partisan. As early as 1933 Hühnlein briefly expelled Manfred von Brauchitsch from the NSKK because he had allegedly made unjust accusations against other racing driver members. True, this did not have any very serious consequences for von Brauchitsch; he was allowed to continue racing and was even accepted back into the NSKK.

However, Hühnlein saw a need for regular disciplinary action and for issuing warnings and penalties at national races. But these 'educational measures' usually only affected the younger generation of Silver Arrow drivers: for instance Hanns Geier, driving for Mercedes-Benz, was chastised for allegedly obstructing the faster Hans Stuck in the 1935 German Grand Prix. The fact that Hühnlein chose the venue of the Swiss Grand Prix in Bern to pronounce sentence, shortly after Geier had had a serious accident in practice, certainly created bad feeling, but it was accepted, because it did not pay to get on the wrong side of Hühnlein – especially as the rivals from Daimler-Benz and Auto Union were eying each other suspiciously, and each was trying to get the NSKK boss on their side. At the AVUS Race in 1937, rookie driver Rudi Hasse in a Saxon Silver Arrow caused a tense moment when, in the second qualifying heat, more through inattention than malice aforethought, he caused the closely pursuing Hermann Lang to jam his brakes on. Alfred Neubauer lodged a protest with the ONS and for the final Hasse was hurriedly placed behind Lang on the starting grid.

Hühnlein always had the last word, not least in his speeches in honour of the winner. However, in his memoirs Neubauer comes up with the story that for the authoritarian NSKK leader the presence of drivers' wives and fiancées was always a thorn in his flesh. Despite being banned, the unwelcome ladies agreed with their menfolk that they would take the law into their own hands. Shortly before the start of a race they would rush on to the track and give a smacking kiss to their partners already sitting at the wheel – to wild applause from the crowd.

The fact is that in those days no one could afford either to ignore Hühnlein or to make him look foolish. He even turned up at important races abroad, admittedly never in uniform, but always providing the final court of appeal for his protégés. At the Gran Premio di Tripoli in 1937 Hühnlein once again had to act as mediator between the two German racing stables. Fagioli, who had recently switched to Auto Union, had been obstructed and almost forced off the track by his former stablemate Caracciola while attempting to overtake him. In the words of a report in the Auto Union archives: 'Herr Fagioli was so annoyed that he suddenly ran from our pits to the Mercedes pits shouting for Caracciola. In his excitement he grabbed a hammer and threatened Caracciola with it. Some mechanics quickly jumped in and seized his arms and he dropped the hammer, which fell on to the hands of Zehender [another driver] who was sitting in the Mercedes pits. Fagioli was then brought back to our box, and we made sure he went straight back to the hotel. At the track, Dr Feuereissen immediately reported the incident to *Korpsführer* Hühnlein. The latter took the view that the obstruction should be investigated by the motorsport authorities, and that a request to this effect should be made to the race stewards. This was made in writing at the trackside. Unfortunately the race organiser and responsible sports commissioners had left with Marshall Balbo immediately after the race. We were therefore only able to leave the report with the timekeepers who were present.'

Hühnlein issued written instructions to both stables on how the incident should be handled. With a nice irony, his letter was handed to the Auto Union representatives by Neubauer. It seems that the copy mentioned in the archives has not survived. However, in the papers available we read: 'The *Korpsführer*'s instructions were passed on to Herr Fagioli. The latter happened to be in the hotel, where he had a long discussion with Furmanik, Italy's sports president. We and Furmanik pacified Fagioli, who was in quite a state and kept insisting that Caracciola had tried to kill him. Later on Fagioli calmed down completely and neither the next day nor on

*Marshal Italo Balbo and NSKK leader Adolf Hühnlein illustrate political dress code during
the Gran Premio di Tripoli – don't wear uniform outside your own country because you are
required to appear apolitical. (Kirchberg)*

the journey home did he even mention the matter, nor act in any other
way against the *Korpsführer's* instructions.'

Had he been muzzled by Hühnlein? In the Mercedes-Benz camp people
were saying that Fagioli had *deliberately thrown* the hammer at Caracciola.
This is confirmed, not only in Neubauer's book but also in a letter from
Richard Seaman, who had been an eyewitness. The Englishman, newly
signed up as a works driver for Mercedes-Benz, wrote on 10 May 1937, that
is to say the Monday after the race, giving details of the hammer-throwing
episode. He also reported to his friend, the journalist and photographer
George Monkhouse, on the reaction of Hühnlein, 'who said he would have
Fagioli sacked from the Auto Union team.' But even in his capacity as head
of the ONS and of the NSKK, did Hühnlein really have the influence to
carry out this threat?

Either way, Auto Union were in a fix. To quote from an internal company report: 'There was no on-the-spot investigation by the stewards, nor were our witnesses, the driver or anyone else questioned. The Italian organisers asked us to withdraw our complaint against Caracciola's driving, since Herr Marschall Balbo did not want there to be any unpleasant bickering of that kind at the Tripoli Grand Prix. We told the Italians that we would not withdraw our complaint unless Mercedes-Benz also withdrew their complaint about Herr Fagioli's behaviour after the race. We have not as yet received an official communication of any kind.'

On 23 and 24 May 1937, *ie* one week before the AVUS Race, at which the banked curve was to be opened with a formula-free race, Feuereissen, Auto Union's racing manager, continued his efforts at damage-limitation. Four of his mechanics, responsible in Tripoli for an emergency depot a long way from the pits but right beside the track, gave eyewitness reports 'about the dangerous manner of Caracciola's driving, and described how Fagioli had been obstructed by the Mercedes driver when overtaking, and forced on to the sand beside the track. Fagioli did start the AVUS Race, having been faster even than his stablemate Rosemeyer in the practice laps, but dropped out with gearbox trouble in a preliminary heat.

This was his last outing for Auto Union for a long time. The 39-year-old Italian took a break of more than two months, and only raced for the Zwickau stable in two more events – the Italian Grand Prix on 15 August and the Swiss on 22 August 1937. Was it simply health problems – as was claimed at the time – that made Fagioli take it easy? Was it not also due to the fact that by suspending him, Auto Union could save valuable foreign currency?

On 17 June 1937 the Saxon team's undisputed number one, Bernd Rosemeyer, made a complaint to top management in Chemnitz about the distribution of the bonuses for the AVUS Race. It seems clear that even at Tripoli he only received the same money as Fagioli. However, when it came to matters of finance the racing stars were not the only ones with very sharp ears. The senior management at Auto Union, like their rivals in Daimler-Benz, were constantly occupied with the irksome business of currency and taxation in the remuneration of top foreign drivers. So

Luigi Fagioli's streamlined Auto Union on the new North Curve banking during practice for the AVUS Race in 1937. (Auto Union)

if Rosemeyer, who had by now absolute star status, was irritated, then Auto Union had to make an effort to improve the working atmosphere as rapidly as possible. With a man like Rosemeyer his every wish had to be anticipated. It is a great pity that his personal papers went astray some time during or after the Nazi period.

In the shadow of world politics

In 1936 'blond Bernd' easily won the European Championship and changed the balance of power in Grand Prix racing. His status as Auto Union's undisputed star driver remained unchallengeable in 1937, and on 13 June, immediately after the wipe-out at the AVUS Race, he won the Eifel Race at the Nürburgring, just as he had done the previous year – which is why, immediately afterwards, Heinrich Himmler promoted him

A rare moment: Bernd Rosemeyer displaying SS insignia on his race overalls. After the young German switched from motorcycle racing to Auto Union's Grand Prix team, it did not seem necessary for him to reveal his membership of the black-uniformed Nazi elite in such a way – but this meeting with the Führer in 1937 at the official presentation in front of the Reich Chancellery was a different matter. (Kirchberg)

to SS *Sturmführer* (roughly equivalent to the rank of First Lieutenant). Like Stuck, Rosemeyer enjoyed the protection of the *Reichsführer-SS*, and not without reason; in motorsport, as in other things, the 'black corps' found itself in sharp competition with Hühnlein's rather conservatively run NSKK. This was one reason why, in the political minefield of Hitler's Germany, the motor racing stables were required to adapt smoothly to all sides. For the big cross-country and reliability events Auto Union made the same number of competition cars available 'on loan' to both the NSKK and the SS. In the 1938 season alone each of the Nazi organisations had the use of six DKW and three Wanderer cross-country sports cars. And if the NSKK team's works-maintained BMW 328 sports cars put up a poorer showing than those of the SS racing teams and private BMW drivers (as was the case in the Hamburg City Park Race on 7 May 1939), then Hühnlein sent a letter of complaint to BMW's chief executive Franz Josef Popp in Munich. As regards national and international race entries, the NSKK leader and ONS boss had, in any case, a decisive say in everything, ever since state subsidies from the Reich Ministry of Transport had begun.

It was Hühnlein, too, who gave his approval for German racing cars to make their first and only guest appearance in the American Vanderbilt Cup in 1937. The following year he cancelled the Eifel Race at short notice, because Auto Union was not in a position to put their 3-litre cars, built to the new racing formula, on the starting grid. Earlier, in March 1939, Hühnlein had tried in vain to encourage the Zwickau stable to enter the Grand Prix de Pau in south-west France, together with the Mercedes-Benz team, because, as was argued during a telephone conversation between a senior NSKK officer and Auto Union on the 9th, 'it is absolutely necessary that Auto Union takes part at Pau, since the *Korpsführer* feels it is very important that a demonstration be made at Pau against the efforts to politicise the sport. The fact that Nuvolari [who had just joined Auto Union] is not allowed to enter the Pau race, must not mean that Auto Union cannot go there at all. After all, we have got other drivers and we should think again, and see if we could perhaps enter two cars, driven by Müller and Meier.'

It is certainly a curious notion that Adolf Hühnlein, of all people, should take a stand against 'efforts to politicise' motor racing! It was nevertheless a fact that political tensions in Europe were placing ever greater pressure on international sporting relations. The consequences of the Sudetenland

Crisis of late summer 1938 affected the German teams in the heart of England, on their way to the Grand Prix at Castle Donington, due to take place on 1 October.

On 24 September the talks in Bad Godesberg between Hitler and British prime minister Neville Chamberlain broke down. The German dictator wanted war, but not just yet – so he issued an ultimatum.[2] Even so, the British fleet was placed on alert and France called up its reserves. The two German racing teams, meanwhile, were stranded in the English Midlands, a long way from London, where Auto Union racing manager Feuereissen was holding the fort and keeping his colleague Neubauer posted. The latter was up at Castle Donington with the drivers, mechanics and vehicles of both stables, waiting to see what would happen next. Around noon on 28 September, shortly before the expiry of Hitler's ultimatum, orders came from Germany, which Feuereissen immediately phoned through to Neubauer: pack up and leave England by the fastest possible route; try to get back to the Reich via the Netherlands. If the silver racing cars were threatened with confiscation, they should be set on fire and destroyed to prevent them falling into the hands of the British authorities.

However, there were no such incidents and by about 5.00pm the German expeditionary force reached the ferry at Harwich, where, amidst the throng of other Germans anxious to get home, the news spread that, through Mussolini's mediation, the heads of government of Britain and France would meet Hitler and the Italian dictator the following day. This resulted in the Munich Agreement, announced by Chamberlain and Hitler on 30 September 1938. The last chance for opposition to Hitler within Germany was gone.[3] Chamberlain's desire for peace and fear of war were strong, whence his misguided policy of Appeasement. The territorial demands of the German blackmailer appeared to have been satisfied and now the slogan was 'Peace in our Time'. So on 22 October the British Grand Prix was held after all, with Germany taking part. Nuvolari won it for Auto Union, ahead of the Mercedes-Benzes of Lang and Seaman.

Outside Germany any remaining illusions were shattered on the night of 14–15 March 1939, when the Wehrmacht marched into Czechoslovakia and Hitler incorporated the newly created 'Protectorate of Bohemia and Moravia' into the German Reich. French sports associations cancelled all competitions in Germany or with German participation. Now Hühnlein and

As 'Peace In Our Time' was achieved at Munich, the German 'Silver Arrows' returned for a second visit to Donington Park for the final Grand Prix of 1938. With eventual winner Tazio Nuvolari way ahead, Auto Union's Hermann Paul Müller is seen defending second place from the Mercedes-Benz cars of Dick Seaman and Manfred von Brauchitsch, while poor Arthur Dobson – totally outclassed in his 2-litre ERA – will end up sixth, six laps down. (Sebastian)

the German racing stables had very different problems from the worry that Auto Union's top driver, Nuvolari, was not allowed to enter the Grand Prix in Pau. Mussolini had already forbidden Italian sportsmen from competing in France – a boycott that began as a result of the Spanish Civil War. On 28 March that conflict ended with the capture of Madrid and Franco's final victory, yet Mussolini's sportsmen continued to stay away from events in France. Thus cycling star Gino Bartali was unable to defend his position as winner of the previous year's Tour de France. Nor did Germany or Franco's Spain send any teams. On 25 April *Reichssportführer* Hans von Tschammer und Osten had issued a general ban on German sportsmen competing in France, as a reaction to France's cancellation two days previously of the planned football international between the two countries. And what would happen in motorsport?

In Grand Prix racing the only serious contenders were cars from Germany, Italy (Alfa Romeo, Maserati) and France (Delahaye, Talbot). If the Germans imposed a boycott consistently it would mean the end of appearances by the Silver Arrows. But Adolf Hühnlein was a law unto himself in matters of motorsport and was not obliged to comply with instructions from the *Reichssportführer*; and the racing interests and investments of German motor manufacturers were so great that a boycott would be contrary to their own objectives, particularly as the Nazi regime was continuing to subsidise them. In late April or early May 1939 Hühnlein covered himself by consulting Hitler in person.

Prior to this, on 2 April, Hermann Lang and Manfred von Brauchitsch had driven to a double victory for Mercedes-Benz at the Grand Prix de Pau. The French racing officials went to great lengths to see that the whole event was completely 'non-political', and the British driver Dick Seaman, a reserve for Mercedes-Benz, amused himself by writing to his friend George Monkhouse about four Communists who, on the Saturday before

Lilian Beattie-Seaman visiting her son Richard at his Bavarian chalet in Ambach. She was displeased about Dick's intention to marry a German – Erica Popp, daughter of BMW director Franz Josef Popp, a good friend of Daimler-Benz CEO Wilhelm Kissel. (Daimler AG)

the race, had protested with placards against German cars taking part, but had been immediately locked up. The demonstrators had almost certainly been arrested at the behest of the race organisers.

Seen from today's standpoint one is struck by how loyally sports journalist Charles Faroux, official of the Automobile Club de France and manager of the French Grand Prix, entered the fray on behalf of his German friends. The most powerful figure in French motorsport was open-handed and open-hearted towards his acquaintances at Daimler-Benz AG. The year before, as manager of the Grand Prix de Pau, he had been lent a Mercedes-Benz. Whereas all the other participants' cars, including the Delahaye of the subsequent winner, Dreyfus, were weighed as usual after the practice laps, the Mercedes-Benz did not turn up for this, for Faroux had decreed that the new Silver Arrows only had to be weighed after the race itself. From such small favours is friendship born.

It is quite obvious that in February 1939, when Faroux was guest of honour at the International Car and Motorcycle Exhibition in Berlin, his booking at the prestigious Hotel Adlon was charged to his German friends. It is equally no surprise that since 1937 Hühnlein had actually been an honorary member of the French Automobile Club and made sure that, despite the tense political situation and the boycott of other forms of sport, German drivers and their cars could enter the Le Mans 24 Hours on 18–19 June, as well as the ACF Grand Prix on 9 July. It was probably thanks to Hühnlein's backing that, despite the Mussolini ban, Nuvolari was the only Italian allowed to enter the race. He was, after all, driving for Auto Union and therefore under the German flag! Even the Alfa Romeo stable was on the starting grid in Reims, helped by a ruse that the officials let pass without demur: one of the four cherry-red Italian cars was entered 'privately' by the French driver Raymond Sommer, while the other three were entered by Sommer's Swiss driving colleague, Christian Kautz.

For some time the political omens had been pointing to war, but the race went ahead anyway.

Only German drivers for German racing cars?
Behind the scenes the National Socialist motorsport officials were trying to pull very different strings and ultimately to influence the manning of the racing stables. It was obvious that the universally expected victories

Left: Manfred von Brauchitsch and his new team-mate Luigi Fagioli prepare for practice at the Eifel Race in 1934. (Daimler AG)

Opposite: Achille Varzi and his smart company car – a Horch cabriolet. (Audi AG)

had to be achieved with German drivers at the wheel. That is why, early in 1934, there were frequent enquiries from the Reich Ministry of Transport as to why Daimler-Benz was employing the Italian Fagioli? Chief executive Kissel replied in person: 'One of the chief reasons is that, by engaging such a well-known and proven driver, we want to give our German drivers, and especially the up-and-coming ones, some valuable training. It is well known that for years the Italians and French have been fielding fast, light, single-seat racing cars and so have a wealth of experience with such vehicles. This fact is of particular importance to us, since this is the first time we will be appearing with a completely new lightweight model of racing car, and we are keen to have good prospects of success from the start.'

However, the signing up of foreign drivers not only offended the nationalist sentiments of the functionaries, but was also a threat to the financial situation of the German Reich and its subsidised racing stables. The foreign currency quotas allocated to the racing divisions were extremely tight and, what is more, had to be tapped for numerous international events. But if a foreign guest driver was a genuine star he could be expected to win in a Silver Arrow, and this was important in itself. For one thing it looked good abroad if German cars were driven to victory even by an international celebrity: with

an eye on important export deals as a source of foreign currency, this was a factor not to be underestimated. Furthermore, competitions abroad had the attraction of high starting money and winners' bonuses, providing currency with which their foreign drivers could be paid while still leaving a modest surplus in the Reich's foreign exchange account. Not only that, but the German racing stables could bypass the grasping fingers of Germany's tax authorities by providing their racing stars with hugely expensive company cars as a sort of *quid pro quo*. This was something that Auto Union would live to regret in the case of Varzi, since on the termination of his contract on 31 October 1936 the Italian kept his smart Horch cabriolet firmly in the garage and even demanded further payments.

There were many reasons why there were always financial risks associated with hiring a foreign driver. Thus it was no accident that between 1934 and 1939 the only foreign drivers employed to drive Silver Arrows were the Italians Fagioli, Varzi and Nuvolari, the Monegasque Chiron, the Swiss Kautz, the Romanian-born but Paris-based Zehender and the Englishman Dick Seaman.

To begin with Adolf Hühnlein was critical of the signing up of foreign professionals: 'German drivers in German machines!' was his principle. Yet he hardly raised any open objections at all when it came to hiring Italian experts, though the high fees they were paid sometimes proved an issue. Big names in international motor racing refused to be fobbed off with Reichsmarks, since outside the Reich German money had little value. But if men such as Fagioli, Varzi and Nuvolari wanted to be paid exclusively in Italian lire this would far exceed the currency quotas of the racing divisions. So in order to come to some kind of financial settlement, a form of mixed calculation was necessary. At big races abroad there was the chance to pull in much-needed foreign currency in the form of starting money and winners' bonuses and thus to pay off the foreign pros without any trouble.

As a rule a works driver for Auto Union collected 90 per cent of the starting money and bonuses. German drivers could not be paid in foreign currency but had to receive the equivalent amount in Reichsmarks. For top foreign drivers special rules could be applied. Should there not be sufficient foreign currency to cover the agreed fixed salary, the racing stable would try to pay a large part of a foreign driver's earnings in Reichsmarks if they could, depending on his quality and status.

In the case of Nuvolari, who did not join Auto Union until the middle of the 1938 season and was urgently needed as a replacement following Bernd Rosemeyer's death, the total of his gross salary and guaranteed starting money for five races came to 25,000 RM. He would go on to win Grands Prix at Monza and Castle Donington, which provided additional winners' bonuses in sterling and Italian lire. These foreign currency sums far exceeded his basic salary. In addition, on signature of his contract Nuvolari pocketed a 'golden hello' of 20,000 RM, and under currency regulations he was promised a remittance in the 'German-Italian clearing system' – in other words, his income was converted into lire and paid out in Italy – and there were no objections. The direct settlement in lire, francs, pounds or dollars was in fact subject to the narrow restrictions on currency trading in Nazi Germany. Yet in Nuvolari's case there were no problems. Even Hühnlein was delighted with the deal: 'I see in this a great advertisement for German vehicles, if a master of the wheel like Nuvolari, who is after all at the peak of his career, drives a German car.'

By this time the regulations must have been relaxed somewhat. At the beginning of the Silver Arrow era the taxmen kept on knocking at the door. In 1935 not only did an accurate balance sheet of Varzi's foreign

If you can't beat 'em, join 'em! Even NSKK-Führer Adolf Hühnlein approved of the 'golden hello' Tazio Nuvolari received for signing a contract with Auto Union. (Kirchberg)

currency account have to be maintained by Auto Union, but there were even painstakingly detailed accounts of foreign currency expenditure by each mechanic when working abroad. Even in marginal areas like this one can see the *dirigisme* of the Nazi administration in business and financial policy. In the wake of massive government borrowing to pay for rearmament and national prestige products the country was in the grip of shortages. It was just lucky for the Nazis that they relied on state-sponsored distractions, which – in the case of German racetrack victories – proclaimed the supposed resurgence of national greatness.

However, the successful racing stables were in trouble if they exceeded the currency limits allotted to them. This was the case at Mercedes-Benz at the end of the 1938 season, and was due less to the fact that Dick Seaman was paid too high a salary, than that, although he was driving for Germany, he was paid in foreign currency. Caracciola was based in Switzerland and, having by now been European Champion three times, had enjoyed this currency privilege since the Silver Arrows had started winning. However, it was a major irritation to Hühnlein. He calculated that in the 1938 season the Mercedes-Benz racing division, in their numerous races abroad, had brought in a good 180,000 RM in foreign currency – a sum that should, in fact, have been enough to pay Caracciola's salary, as well as the much more modest contractual fees of the only foreigner in the stable, Dick Seaman. As it happened the young Englishman lived in a fashionable villa in Ambach on Lake Starnberg and spent his salary, largely paid in Reichsmarks, in Germany. What is more he made Germany his principal residence when, on 7 December 1938, he married a German girl, Erika, the daughter of BMW's chief executive Franz Josef Popp.

Nevertheless, the 180,000 RM-worth of foreign currency earned by the Mercedes-Benz racing division in the 1938 season was not enough. The Untertürkheimers had spent some 50,000 RM in foreign currency over and above that. Hühnlein's calculations led him to the conclusion

Dick Seaman spending his leisure time and German currency at Lake Starnberg near Munich. (Daimler AG)

that if Daimler-Benz had paid Caracciola and Seaman in German marks the group's racing division would have ended with a foreign exchange surplus of exactly 11,600 RM. CEO Kissel attempted to mollify him with a curious alternative calculation. In view of the superiority of the German racing cars, foreign countries had so drastically reduced their starting money and winners' bonuses that in fact far less foreign currency revenue had been due. However, through their wins Caracciola and Seaman had succeeded in bringing in additional currency worth roughly 30,000 RM and 20,000 RM respectively. These sums were considerably higher than the expenditure on the two drivers. It was a bold assertion, yet after the war the two other works drivers from that year, Hermann Lang and Manfred von Brauchitsch, put figures on their own earnings in the 1938 season, and even though they did the calculations independently they came to remarkably similar sums of around 70,000 RM. It should be noted that they gave this information in questionnaires about their Nazi past, before the start of their Denazification tribunals.

Hühnlein's interventions may have been tiresome, but they could not be ignored – which is why the executive floors of the big motor companies sought to justify themselves. In the case of the fees paid to Caracciola and Seaman they seem to have been successful. However, on another occasion Hühnlein's veto ensured that Auto Union had to abandon the idea of again signing up their Swiss driver Christian Kautz – albeit none too successful up till then – for the 1939 season.

Occasionally there was also trouble with the German drivers regarding the hiring of foreigners. When, at the start of the 1935 season at the Tunis Grand Prix, Auto Union's then racing manager Willy Walb entered the newly-signed Achille Varzi as the only Auto Union driver, Hans Stuck wrote to Walb: 'It doesn't matter to me whether Varzi drives an old car or a new one, with old or new brakes, to win or just as a trial – what interests me as a German is merely the fact that a German firm gets a foreigner to drive its car in the first race abroad.' To avoid this kind of unpleasantness, it was necessary for the German racing teams, like the Nazis themselves, to rely at an early stage on national self-sufficiency – specifically at the wheels of their Silver Arrows. And this is exactly what both Auto Union and Mercedes-Benz did when, year after year, they went out in search of promising young racing drivers who were worth signing up.

In search of new heroes

On 24 October 1934 Auto Union commenced the first of what were called 'racing car trial drives' at the Nürburgring. These trials were not of the vehicles but of young German candidate drivers – twelve novices per trial – who had usually been picked out for higher things following their success in motorcycle or sports car racing. Some of them were works drivers from the group-owned DKW motorcycle stable. Two racing cars were made available for the trials, firstly on the short 6km southern loop, and the next day on the 22.8km northern loop. It must be remembered that not one of these young men had ever sat in an Auto Union car before, or had ever experienced the completely unfamiliar handling of this unique 350bhp mid-engined machine. But amazingly the trials were completed without any accidents, and three of the 'examinees' went on to the next stage of selection.

In the end Walb decided that only two should be given contracts, and on 11 December 1934 he informed the board: 'My personal impression was that Simons drove with a lot of determination to be picked for our

Hans Stuck testing the Auto Union at Monza in 1935. As the pool of top drivers was quite small, the German companies initiated test sessions to assess talented rookies, pre-season at Monza and post-season at the Nürburgring. (Porsche AG)

team at all costs. Pietsch drove with a much lighter touch and Rosemeyer's superiority was downright casual. Since we have the greatest interest in Pietsch and since he is a younger driver and an employee of the company, we want to have him in the team. So we have recommended hiring both Pietsch and Rosemeyer. We should remember that all the drivers will have to improve their times by about one minute, and it is doubtful whether Simons will ever reach this speed.' Paul Pietsch, then 25 years old, was not to fulfil Auto Union's expectations in the 1935 season; on the other hand Rosemeyer, only two years older, proved to be a godsend – even without the direct protection of his SS chums.

Hans Simons entered Auto Union's young driver trials for the second time in October 1935. Shortly beforehand, director von Oertzen had received a telephone-call from the Reich Ministry of Propaganda in Berlin: 'Today Herr Dr Mahlo called on behalf of the Minister, Dr Goebbels, and spoke in very friendly terms about Herr Simons, who is currently working in the DKW customer service department in Berlin. He stated that Dr Goebbels had expressed the wish that Simons should be given another opportunity for a trial in our racing car [...] I would therefore recommend that S. be called in for the young driver trials at the Nürburgring.'

However, despite all his efforts Simons failed again. There may be some comfort in the fact that not even favouritism at the highest level of the Nazi regime could automatically make someone into a successful racing driver. As Dr Peter Lang, elder son of Mercedes-Benz driver Hermann Lang, put it more than six decades later in a TV interview: 'Out on the track they were on their own. They had no Party manual to help them.' But the Nazis certainly tried, so did the SS, and this resulted in a number of disasters for the racing stables.

Unlike Auto Union, Mercedes-Benz were somewhat late in trying to discover new German talent by means of a selection process based on trial drives. On 9 October 1936, the same day that Auto Union's third successive young driver trials were completed, the Untertürkheim racing division summoned no less than 27 candidates to the Nürburgring. However, their test drives were not to be carried out in Grand Prix racing cars but in perfectly ordinary production cars. In the very first lap one Karl Hoffelner from Munich crashed. According to Neubauer he was 'a member of the SS' who had been recommended to him 'as a good driver in various touring cars'. The next accident ended in a fatality when, in the third lap, at about

11:15am, 25-year-old Hermann Schmitz turned his 2.3-litre production car over on the Carousel straight. In his report, Neubauer noted of the dead man: 'Comes from the Untertürkheim factory (Salzer's department), rode motorcycles for 5 years and cars for 1½ years. Nothing else known.' The trial drives were then suspended, and Neubauer added a brief note on the dispatch of the body. '9 October to crematorium.' Henceforth, the Mercedes-Benz racing division would limit itself to a manageable number of already experienced candidates, who would be put straight into proper racing cars.

The Auto Union racing division also received frequent recommendations from political quarters of talents with well-known names. Aspiring drivers Huschke von Hanstein and Robert 'Bobby' Kohlrausch belonged to the SS and at the start of the 1938 season were given their chance to take part in trials for the works team, at Monza from 12 to 19 March and at the Nürburgring from 10 to 14 May. They both failed. After the Monza results Feuereissen had noted on 29 March: 'Herr Kohlrausch put up the worst showing in the car.' On the short version of the Monza course the SS-*Hauptsturmführer* had braked sharply before a right-hand bend and damaged the racing car's radiator when he skidded into a tree; and on the full Grand Prix course he did not achieve even passable times before he headed for the pits without warning and confessed that 'in a bend the pressure was so great that he did not himself know how he had held on to the car. He had got rather a shock from this and wanted to take a bit of a break. The same afternoon he requested not to drive any more and in the hotel that evening he told me he had imagined driving would be easier and for that reason was sensibly, for the moment, withdrawing from further drives. His morale was pretty low but asked me to ask the board to let him drive a few laps again on the Nürburgring, because he knew the course there very well and it would be a better measure of his ability.'

Feuereissen's verdict is devastating, but he also knew, of course, about the political pressure, which required a decision that was both diplomatic and non-committal. In his view even the second trial for Kohlrausch on the Nürburgring would produce a negative result. However, 'I would nevertheless propose, provided it fits in with our programme, that he be given another opportunity, in trial drives during May, to drive 3–5 laps on the Nürburgring. Given Kohlrausch's good relations with the senior ranks of the SS, I hope that by giving him some additional drives on the Nürburgring we will put a stop to any possible complaints.' Bobby Kohlrausch was indeed invited to the trial, but he did not get a chance to drive because two cars had been severely damaged in accidents involving other test candidates.

SS-*Obersturmführer* Fritz Huschke von Hanstein got a little closer to earning a place in the Saxon racing stable: 'In von Hanstein's case I had the same feeling as at Monza, that he drives with an innocent simplicity, without realising what he himself is doing,' wrote Feuereissen, summarising his observations. He reported a conversation with the driver 'in which he informed me that due to an earlier crash he had a physical affliction, and that his right shoulder-joint had been shattered, so that today he can only raise his right arm a little way. In this conversation I had the impression that the urge to become a racing driver is perhaps not strong enough in him to remove all his inhibitions.' To make matters worse, he came off the track twice: 'After two crashes I therefore took the opportunity to have a word with him and advised him to resign voluntarily, since in view of his arm I could not take the responsibility of letting him go on driving. By then I had also consulted the doctor, who confirmed to me that that arm is not fully functional. I got the impression that Herr von Hanstein understood completely and I drove off on Friday, much relieved.'

Shattered hopes

Feuereissen seems not have been impressed by political connections when it came to judging driving talent. The racing cars with engines of nearly 500bhp were already difficult enough to control, but to handle them faultlessly at competition speeds required truly exceptional ability. In October 1935, while Goebbels' protégé Hans Simons was failing in his second attempt, Feuereissen's momentous choice fell upon three fairly unremarkable talents. The most promising candidate was Rudolf Heydel, a young employee of the in-house test department. In the first trials for the coming season, held at Monza, he was immediately allowed to take the wheel – and on 4 February 1936 had a fatal accident.

Candidate number two was Ernst von Delius. After Heydel was killed the 24-year-old Ernst immediately took his place and as early as 7 June entered his first Grand Prix in Barcelona, coming fourth ahead of his friend and exemplar Bernd Rosemeyer. A year later von Delius too was dead. At the German Grand Prix on 26 July 1937 he engaged in a bitter duel with Seaman, the British rookie with Mercedes-Benz, almost collided with him, spun off the track and died the same evening from serious injuries.

The third candidate on Feuereissen's list was Rudolf Hasse, bespectacled and unimpressive-looking, who spoke with a broad Saxon accent and had risen to the rank of commandant of the volunteer fire-brigade in his home town of Mittweida. He was already 29 years old and a safe pair of hands. In the absence of Caracciola and Rosemeyer he even won the Belgian Grand Prix in 1937. Yet this solid Saxon was never really one of the racetrack elite, which is why, in the Second World War, he drew the short straw and was despatched to the Eastern Front. He died in a field-hospital on 12 August 1942.

His friend Ulrich Bigalke, who failed the young driver trials in October 1936, belonged to the innermost circle of the Auto Union racing division. He attended every event, at home and abroad, wrote reports, took photographs and, most importantly, filmed with a movie-camera. With Wolfgang Staudte, who became a well-known director after the war, he produced films for Auto Union and never gave up his ambition to become a racing driver. On 20 May 1939 he finally made it, coming sixth in the

Left: Little Ernst von Delius posing with his big Auto Union during practice for the German Grand Prix in 1936. The 24-year-old youngster got his break when another candidate, Rudolf Heydel, was killed during pre-season trials at Monza. Just a year later it was von Delius who crashed fatally, during the 1937 German Grand Prix. (Audi AG)

Opposite: Rudolf Caracciola showing the Führer Mercedes-Benz's 1938 world record contender. Racing for Nazi Germany and living in Switzerland was no problem for a big shot like 'Caratsch' as long as he was available for propaganda. During the Second World War prudent Rudi changed his mind – and switched his German passport for a Swiss one. (Daimler AG)

Eifel Race on the Nürburgring, behind Hasse but ahead of Müller, who was actually the team's number two. But at that time there were too few races and too many drivers with Auto Union.

At the end of August it still looked as if the 29-year-old Bigalke might travel as a reserve driver to Brazil, with Nuvolari and Müller. In Rio the Gavea Race had been specially postponed to allow time for the German racing cars to be shipped over. But on 1 September 1939 the German invasion of Poland changed everything. And a man like Bigalke was, as ever, at the forefront of the action: 'Instead of sitting behind the wheel of a racing car he was now in one of our fighter-planes, flying over to Britain,' wrote the *Völkischer Beobachter* on 6 November 1940. 'With him went his camera, and it was natural that this man gave himself wholeheartedly, as he had done all his life, when the call came. When we heard the news that Ulrich Bigalke had not returned from a flight over enemy territory we were very silent and thought about this good comrade.'

It was not the great heroes of motor racing who went off to fight for *Führer, Volk und Vaterland* in the Second World War. Caracciola, Stuck, von Brauchitsch and Lang were too popular – and too clever – to allow themselves to be sacrificed in the front line. They were only heroes in their

own cause. They were much more valuable to the Nazis giving lectures to the troops, recalling heroic racetrack battles and providing entertainment and diversion, just as they had done in the golden age of the silver national racing cars. And with the same skill that had seen them through their Grand Prix races they survived the terrible war unscathed, masters of the art of survival. Caracciola, in any case, wanted only peace and quiet, his money, and the freedom to enjoy his life. He remained in Switzerland and finally became a citizen of the Helvetic Confederation. But none of this was known to the young German soldiers who idolised their racing drivers and who, from 1939 onwards, with every new intake of recruits, were driven into a criminal war.

In 1941 the East Prussian Educational Publishing Society published a novel for young people by Hans Reh entitled *On Speeding Axles – the Story of a Racing Driver*. It was a book that propagated the deceitful man-machine synthesis so dear to the Nazis, and their model of the racing driver willing to sacrifice his life. It was based on the fictitious career of one

Bernd Rosemeyer is hidden somewhere within this crowd of young people seeking his autograph. But the photograph looks less innocent when one considers how German boys identified with their racing heroes but were utterly misled by an ideology that was bound up with warmongering. (Kirchberg)

Horst Riemer, who rose from unemployment during the Weimar period to become – thanks to the Nazis and their enthusiasm for motorsport – a successful racing driver and European Champion, and above all a loyal and courageous soldier. Things had come full circle: it is no coincidence that between 1933 and 1939 the NSKK had trained more than 187,000 sports- and technology-mad young men in its motorsport schools and prepared them for motorised duties in the event of war. In the archives of Auto Union AG there have survived, from the years before 1939, numerous spontaneous and completely unsolicited letters of application from enthusiastic young men who declared themselves 'fully available', wanted at all costs to become racing drivers, and in all seriousness – but oblivious of punctuation – made the most absurd claims: 'My whole life my thoughts my young being I might say my entire life I want to make a gift of to you.' It was from such naïvely dedicated youths that the Nazis produced the human material they needed for their great campaign of conquest and plunder.

Notes

1 On 30 September 1938 Britain, France and Italy signed an agreement with Hitler in Munich ceding the predominantly German-speaking Sudetenland region of western Czechoslovakia to Germany. Hitler gave assurances that he had no further territorial ambitions in Europe and was privately astonished that British prime minister Neville Chamberlain believed him. In March 1939, having threatened the Czech government with the destruction of Prague by bombing, Hitler was able to invade and occupy the country unopposed.

2 Although the Munich Agreement has come to symbolise the failure of the Appeasement policy, the real damage had been done a few days earlier at Bad Godesberg. Chamberlain arrived with a plan he assumed Hitler would accept: 1) The Sudetenland would be ceded to Germany without a plebiscite; and 2) Czechoslovakia's defence treaties with the USSR and France would be dissolved and replaced by an international guarantee of Czech neutrality. But Hitler was determined to wipe Czechoslovakia off the map. He upped the ante and demanded that the Sudetenland be *occupied* by German troops, not later than 1 October. That was what Chamberlain described in protest as Hitler's 'ultimatum'. On 23 September, while the talks were still in progress, news came that the Czech armed forces had mobilised. The talks ended with Chamberlain still apparently believing that Hitler could be trusted, but a few days later Britain and France would betray Czechoslovakia in the vain hope of buying Hitler off.

3 In the weeks running up to Munich and the invasion of Czechoslovakia, a plot to depose Hitler and put him on trial had been hatched among senior German military, political and diplomatic personnel, led by Ludwig Beck, chief of the army general staff. They considered that an armed invasion against Czech resistance, with Britain and France probably taking Czechoslovakia's side, was madness. However, the Munich Agreement cut the ground from under their feet. Beck later played a part in the Stauffenberg Plot to assassinate Hitler in 1944, and when it failed he committed suicide.

CHAPTER SEVEN

IDOLS OF
THEIR ERA

The playful ease with which Bernd Rosemeyer performed in his brief but rapid racing career was unusual in the circumstances prevailing in Germany, and it was for precisely that reason that he swiftly rose to become the regime's most popular showcase sportsman. In his very first season with Auto Union the young daredevil earned the respect of established competitors, and at the end of that year even won his first Grand Prix, on the Masaryk circuit in Czechoslovakia.

In his home town of Lingen, on the river Ems in northern Germany, letters of congratulation were composed with every new victory and copied elsewhere: 'On Monday, in the school playground, we talked only about you. Everywhere you heard "Bernd Rosemeyer came in first." Even in class people talked about you. One of the pupils in our class told this story: "In the summer I was down on Lake Constance. I heard someone mention the name Rosemeyer. I said I knew the racing driver well. Everyone was amazed and asked me lots of questions. One of the three Bavarians said: 'He's a credit to your wee town up there'." Finally, we would like to ask a great favour of you: it would give us great pleasure if sometime you could come and talk to our class about your experiences. You would find us all very appreciative listeners. With the German salute, Heil Hitler! Class 1A of the Evangelical Elementary School.'

The journal *Heimatlese* ('Home Harvest'), published by the National Socialist Teachers' Association for the Weser-Ems District, provided

Is this what friends are for? Ferdinand Porsche and Bernd Rosemeyer with some uniformed guests. They were all members of the SS. Rosemeyer sooner, Porsche later. By chance? Opportunism? Conviction? Who knows. (Audi AG)

Bernd Rosemeyer, the German winner of the Coppa Acerbo, is mobbed by Italian youngsters.
The fascist officer on the left is ex-driver Giuseppe Furmanik, a senior functionary in
Mussolini's state-run motoring organisation.

handouts every month for use in schools. In April 1938 – three months
after his fatal accident – the subject for classroom teaching was Bernd
Rosemeyer. As pedagogical enrichment material, the journal recommended
the 'magnificent book' by Ernst Hornickel, which 'even 14-year-olds can
race through with enthusiasm.' Its title was *How much do you know about
Rosemeyer?* In a book published two years earlier called *Report on the Making
of a Champion*, Hornickel opened with a poetic maxim from the Prussian
military reformer, Field-Marshall Gneisenau:

'Let the weakling, fearful, dither;
who fights for higher things must dare,
he must choose 'twixt life and death.
Let the roaring breakers thunder,
Should you safely land or founder,
Always hold the wheel yourself!'

Rosemeyer, winner of the 1936 German Grand Prix, is honoured by Korpsführer Hühnlein. Interestingly, the trophy is adorned with a Mercedes-Benz racing car silhouette – didn't they expect an Auto Union triumph? (Audi AG)

Beside this he proudly placed a photograph with the caption: 'Bernd Rosemeyer, the happy victor, with the *Führer*'s prize in his hand.'

A dream couple

On 13 July 1936 Rosemeyer married aviatrix Elly Beinhorn,[1] 29 years old and at the time no less famous than himself. She had undertaken long solo flights to Africa, North America and Asia; she had toured giving lectures about her foreign travels and great adventures. She was tomboyish and self-assured, an example to the young. Since 1933 the Nazi organisation for teenage girls, the *Bund Deutscher Mädel*, had included an Elly Beinhorn Group. It is possible that this resolute young pilot was not such a dedicated Nazi as Hanna Reitsch,[2] another famous female flyer, five years her junior; nonetheless, she was a woman who knew how to adapt herself to the style of the Third Reich. Victor Klemperer summed matters up when

Left: The wedding of the year: Elly Beinhorn and Bernd Rosemeyer married two weeks before the 1936 German Grand Prix. The bride is talking with women leaders of the BDM (Bund Deutscher Mädel), the Nazi organisation for teenage girls. This particular BDM delegation was named after the famous aviatrix and therefore attended the wedding. (Kirchberg)

Opposite: Elly Beinhorn-Rosemeyer celebrating her husband's victory in the 1936 Italian Grand Prix at Monza. (Sebastian)

he wrote: 'A note for my university colleagues: the mutual relationship between Goebbel's style and the memoirs of the aviatrix Elly Beinhorn, *My Husband the Racing driver*, offers an extremely interesting field of enquiry for a seminar.'

Rosemeyer took Elly Beinhorn by storm. These were exciting times. No sooner had he won his first Grand Prix than he began wooing her. He then broke an ankle skiing, got severe food-poisoning from some oysters when dining out, went into a sanatorium to recover from the ensuing jaundice, and while there made plans for the wedding.

Just 13 days into the dream marriage Rosemeyer won the German Grand Prix at the Nürburgring and set his sights on winning the European Championship. Shortly afterwards, in strict secrecy, his wife equipped herself with a Messerschmitt Taifun aircraft for a record flight and on 6 August completed the round-trip flight Berlin–Damascus–Cairo–Athens–Berlin in 24 hours. To quote the *Biographical Dictionary of the Third Reich* published in 2002: 'Like her first husband Bernd Rosemeyer, Elly Beinhorn was eagerly taken up and promoted by National Socialist propaganda as the prototype of the young German generation. As an example for the

youth of Germany and a popular ambassador of an able new German nation also successful in sport, she exactly suited the image they wanted to project.'

In a period of state censorship the *vox populi* was responsible for frequent and remarkable whisper-campaigns. Scarcely four months before her marriage to Rosemeyer the famous girl pilot was the focus of such intense speculation that on 24 February 1936 a 'strictly confidential' memorandum was issued to the press by Goebbels' Ministry of Propaganda: 'Rumours are circulating that Elly Beinhorn has been arrested for espionage and shot in [the North German town of] Celle. These rumours are complete nonsense.' Only four months later we read in the secret 'Reports on Germany' of the German Social Democratic Party (SPD), then in exile in Prague: 'The rumours continued even when events were reported in the press, in which the allegedly dead woman took part.'

In those days there was little time for silent reflection; but long after the Second World War Beinhorn did apologise: 'We all lived in an atmosphere of apparently high activity – and we, i.e. our husbands, were the heroes of that era. Hundreds of thousands of people in every country in Europe loved and admired them.' Constantly en route between Grand Prix races, record runs, trips abroad and a little bit of private life, Rosemeyer's career was indeed played out at racing speed – which may not have left him much time for reflection. What is more, the year 1937 dealt him a number of blows in his private life, when first his mother died, then soon afterward his brother was killed in a road accident, then finally his friend and stablemate Ernst von Delius had a fatal accident in the German Grand Prix. Yet a man like Rosemeyer seemed able to put it all to one side and radiate a boundless optimism as he sped on from victory to victory. Almost incidentally, at the end of that year he became a proud father.

Was he really guilty of nothing more than political naïvety and lack of interest? 'Anyone who knew him, knows how proud he was to be a member of the SS,' noted Hans Bretz in his biography of Rosemeyer, published shortly after the driver's death in 1938. 'He knew that, as a racing driver, he was fighting on behalf of a community of men for whom the final and

The remains of Ernst von Delius's Auto Union after his high-speed crash, caused by a mishap while trying to overtake Dick Seaman's Mercedes-Benz. The young German died in hospital from his severe injuries. (Sebastian)

Bernd Rosemeyer and NSKK convoy in the centre of Zwickau in 1936. (Kirchberg)

supreme commitment of their life and skill also meant the final and supreme fulfilment of their existence. So, as a sportsman and a fighter, he embraced his mission and always served it with loyalty and devotion!'

Even in those days Bretz was not just anybody. Born in 1897 in the village of Hörschhausen in the Moselle, he was a member of the NSKK, knew all the drivers and racing stables, attended all the big races in Germany and abroad, and wrote assiduously for the daily and specialist press, sometimes on the payroll of Daimler-Benz, all the while praising his *Führer* and the merging of the ADAC and other motoring associations into the Nazi-dominated German Automobile Club (DDAC). At the end of the war he quickly involved himself in the forefront of German motorsport. In 1949 he became vice-president of the re-founded ADAC and from 1964 until his death in 1972 he served as president of this most powerful of German motor clubs.

So was Bretz mistaken when he wrote in the late 1930s that when, following his victory in the Grosser Preis von Deutschland in 1936, Bernd Rosemeyer received the *Führer*'s Prize 'he was equally delighted with his

The Auto Union crew awaiting events before the Vanderbilt Cup race in 1937. On this occasion the men in uniform are American race officials. (Sebastian)

promotion […] to SS *Sturmführer*', announced by *Reichsführer*-SS Himmler the same day?

Yet this did not prevent Rosemeyer from allowing himself to be seen with a Jewish acquaintance in his hometown of Lingen. This story was told in 2001 by Bernhard Hanauer, a refugee from Nazi Germany, who described a chance meeting with Rosemeyer at Lingen railway station: 'We were friends, but as a Jew at that time I didn't dare approach him.' Yet Rosemeyer apparently had no inhibitions; he spontaneously went over to Hanauer and said: 'What's up with you? Don't you know me any more?'

On a propaganda trip to the USA

The fact that the Auto Union and Mercedes-Benz works teams had no problem with the anti-Semitic ideology of their Nazi motor racing officials is shown by the negotiations over the only race the Silver Arrows entered in the USA. At that meeting on 19 April 1937 in Berlin the two American motorsport representatives were happy to accede to the request of the ONS for a ban on 'political protests' against the appearance of the German racing teams at the Vanderbilt Cup in New York at the end of June. A record of the meeting in the Auto Union archives sums up the conversation: 'Mr Abbott stated that the Germans would without doubt be greeted with great enthusiasm by the organisers and by the Christian community, especially

German-Americans, and could count on a gala reception. In addition, he would arrange for the police to take all precautionary measures to ensure that from the moment they landed, up to the start of the race, any incidents would be avoided. Such incidents could only originate among New York's Jews, whipped up by the press. However, all good Americans would distance themselves from this Jewish posturing, just as they had always done. He and his company, and everyone concerned with the race, had rejected the Jewish machinations in the strongest terms. This was confirmed by Mr Sparrow, who sharply condemned the incitement by the press.' As a 'protection against acts of sabotage' the German embassy hired the famous Pinkerton detective agency, which assisted in guarding the Silver Arrows on the Roosevelt Raceway at night.

The appearance of the German cars on the starting grid was followed by the American press with great, but critical, interest. The race on 2 July 1937 ended in a victory for Bernd Rosemeyer and was grist to the Nazi propaganda mill. Auto Union's racing manager Dr Feuereissen noted: 'The German ambassador told me repeatedly that our appearance in America had done a great service

How the west was won. The grid at the Vanderbilt Cup race in 1937, with eventual winner Bernd Rosemeyer between Rudolf Caracciola (12) and American Rex Mays in his Alfa Romeo (14). (Daimler AG)

to Germany, and also said that our reception by the American public had been extraordinarily good, far better than could have been imagined.' During the entire expedition, not a single 'unfriendly act against Germany' had been recorded. People had been delighted by 'the very nice custom of hoisting the national flag of the leading car during the race. Rosemeyer was leading for 76 laps, and Caracciola was ahead for another eight, so for 84 laps and at the finish of the race the swastika flag was seen on the winner's mast. […] The German ambassador told me he was so pleased that he had immediately sent a telegram to the *Führer*, reporting Germany's victory.'

Elly Beinhorn also remarked at the time: 'This victory in the USA was – as far as public recognition is concerned – my husband's greatest success.' Nor did she fail to mention another, very special honour: 'The reception we got in Bremerhaven was already enough to give an idea of what was awaiting us in Berlin. To his particular delight and satisfaction my husband received the news that in recognition of his victory the *Reichsführer*-SS had promoted him to *Hauptsturmführer*.'

Back home in Germany! Bernd Rosemeyer's arrival in Berlin after his victory in the Vanderbilt Cup race. This success earned him another promotion up the SS hierarchy. (Porsche AG)

Certified Aryan

Within a week of their wedding the famous Beinhorn-Rosemeyer couple had already discovered what it meant to hold a senior rank in the SS. On 20 July 1936, just six days before the German Grand Prix, the Head of the SS *Sippenamt* (office for racial investigation) sent a warning letter to Rosemeyer, then still an *Obersturmführer*: 'The *Reichsführer*-SS has only granted your request on condition that those documents still missing be supplied retrospectively.' The racing driver's *Ahnentafel*, or table of ancestry, still lacked 12 birth certificates and seven marriage certificates, while in the case of his wife as many as 25 of each certificate proving her Aryan descent were absent. This was important because, 'by order of the *Reichsführer*-SS, officers of the SS must provide evidence of Aryan ancestry back to the year 1750. You are requested to complete the appropriate documentation.' This was followed by a further warning, before the preoccupied racing driver replied on 24 February 1937: 'To the Head of the SS Central Office for Race and Settlement: In reply to your letter of 2nd inst. I have to inform you that my wife and I regret we are no longer able to produce the additional documents for the *Ahnentafel*, since the parish registers containing the missing entries can no longer be located or else have been destroyed. However, I am available to make an oral declaration to you on this matter at any time, subject to a prior appointment by telephone. Heil Hitler!'

The SS bureaucrats reacted on 11 March with another warning letter, to which Rosemeyer replied on 22 April to say that he was still unable to submit his fully certified ancestry. The next warning, dated 27 September, gave the racing driver a final date of 1 October for the information to be supplied. His secretary immediately requested a postponement, since 'Herr Rosemeyer is away training in London'.

On 2 October, at Castle Donington, the busy Rosemeyer won the last Grand Prix of the 1937 season, which was also the final race in the 750kg class. Then, from 25 to 27 October, during the Reich Record Week, he set up three world records and 12 further 'best class performances'. In doing so he exceeded the magic 400kph mark for the first time, on the Frankfurt–Heidelberg autobahn. Over one kilometre with a flying start, in a 545bhp record car, he clocked an average of 406.32kph (252.52mph); and over a mile the figure was 406.285kph (252.507mph).

Bernd Rosemeyer about to break the magic 400kph in October 1937. The Reich's Record Week at the Frankfurt–Heidelberg autobahn proved to be a dramatic clash between the two big German car manufacturers. Auto Union dominated, Mercedes-Benz ended up in technical disgrace – a bitter defeat that had to be rectified as swiftly as possible. (Sebastian)

The following day, after he had covered a distance of 5km at a record average speed of 404.6kph (251.4mph), Auto Union staff had to help the half-fainting driver out of the car. The team medic, Dr Gläser, noted his extremely high pulse. When phoning his wife, Rosemeyer tried to find an explanation for his collapse: 'I just don't know what it was. Gläser and our people think it was some kind of poisoning, because fumes and all sorts of stuff gets trapped in the completely enclosed cockpit; I thought it was simply the effect of the speed.' These record runs brought the 1937 season to an end.

On 10 November Rosemeyer received another reminder from the SS Central Office for Race and Settlement. Two days later Elly Beinhorn-Rosemeyer gave birth to a baby son, who was christened Bernd, after his father.

On 14 January 1938 Rosemeyer sent a registered letter to the SS *Sippenamt*: 'Enclosed I am sending you the completed documentation for the *Ahnentafel*, as well as the *Ahnentafel* itself.' He signed it with a 'Heil Hitler!' However, when typing in his rank he mistakenly put 'SS-*Obersturmführer*', then crossed out '*Ober-*' and substituted '*Haupt-*' in his own handwriting. Also in his own hand he added a PS: 'With the best will possible I cannot provide more than this, and hope that it will do. B.R.' Just two weeks later Bernd Rosemeyer was dead.

Mercedes-Benz mobilises

During the Reich's Record Week, to which so much attention was paid by press, public and Party, the Mercedes-Benz racing division, in sharp contrast to Auto Union, committed some embarrassing errors. Even the redesigned aerodynamic bodywork of Untertürkheim's record car still produced too much lift, rather as it had done in the AVUS Race in May 1937. In order to avoid this, and achieve near-record speeds in excess of 375kph (233mph), the fitters cut a slit in the aluminium cladding. The result was that during a test run, when Hermann Lang was driving at about 350kph the bonnet came loose. The 12-cylinder record challenger was hastily returned to the factory for another overhaul. Three days later, on 28 October, Caracciola appeared in a car with modified streamlining. However, he failed to beat the best performances of Rosemeyer and Auto Union.

Daimler-Benz immediately tried to keep this awkward setback within bounds: the company made sure that the official ONS film about the 1937 season made no mention of the Reich Record Week that had been such a success for Auto Union. Thereafter successful efforts were made, even before the opening of the Berlin Motor Show in February 1938, to carry out record runs on the Frankfurt–Heidelberg autobahn. In fact the ONS had decided not hold another Reich Record Week until autumn 1938, but Hühnlein gave Daimler-Benz his approval for some 'internal factory tests', during which, in some cases, world records might be set – whereupon Auto Union, feeling they had been duped, applied for permission to take part in these 'test-runs'.

On 21 January 1938 Auto Union racing manager Feuereissen spoke to Hühnlein, who began by ranting about Auto Union's 'Jewish advertising methods' in the magazine *Leipziger Illustrierte*: 'In the course of the conversation the *Korpsführer* calmed down again and said to me I ought to know very precisely who our personal friends were, and who were our personal enemies. The route we ought to take was that of performance.' Thus Mercedes-Benz enjoyed a better relationship with the top men in the Nazi hierarchy. But Auto Union had the opportunity to hold their own in the hurriedly arranged record runs: 'The *Korpsführer* went on to say that the companies themselves are responsible for deciding how far they can go in this speed-auction.' This meant that on the very first day of the Berlin Car and Motorcycle Exhibition they would be allowed to go for new records. Hühnlein merely wanted to be

Seeking revenge, Rudolf Caracciola and Mercedes-Benz start their successful attack on Bernd Rosemeyer's Auto Union class world record in the early morning of 28 January 1938. (Daimler AG)

in a position to inform Hitler in good time, in other words at least an hour before he made his speech officially opening the exhibition.

Readings from the engine test-beds were unambiguous: the 12-cylinder Mercedes-Benz power unit could by now deliver 736bhp, whereas the 16-cylinder Auto Union engine, despite further modifications, could not get beyond 560bhp. Ferdinand Porsche, who was now once more working for the competition in Untertürkheim, offered the harassed Saxons a new *Stufengebläse* (special blower) for the supercharger, but manufacturing it would take too long and his quote of 10,000 RM was too expensive anyway. The shortfall in horsepower would have to be compensated for by improved aerodynamics, which were tested in a wind tunnel at the Zeppelin factory in Friedrichshafen. Meanwhile all work was suspended on the racing cars for the Grand Prix formula due to come into force for the start of the 1938 season: the duel for prestige on the Reich autobahn was more important. The Untertürkheimers also needed to be able to present Hitler with a new world record for the opening of the Berlin Motor Show. The racing divisions of both corporations were standing with guns at the ready and glaring at each other on the Frankfurt autobahn. As soon as the wintry conditions permitted, Untertürkheim would be off chasing Rosemeyer's best time. On the morning of 28 January 1938 that moment came.

At 8:12am Caracciola set off in the modified record car on the outward leg towards Darmstadt. Despite temperatures around freezing point and frost on the carriageway, the silver projectile raced over the measured section at speeds up to 431.7kph (268.3mph). At 8:45am Caracciola began the return leg and increased the speed at times to 436.8kph (271.4mph). In the middle of both transits, each with a flying start, an average of 432.7kph (268.9mph) was achieved over the measured kilometre and 432.4kph (268.7mph) over the mile.

The last journey

Caracciola's record run was followed closely at Auto Union, and Rosemeyer was swiftly ordered on to the Reichsautobahn. While his streamlined vehicle was being readied for the start he had time to drive along the 14km sealed-off section in a private car and inspect it with chief designer Eberan von Eberhorst. Shortly after 11am he clambered into the tight cockpit of the Auto Union car, whose engine had to be warmed up by a drive out

Bernd Rosemeyer immediately set out to win back his world record from Caracciola. Inevitably it seemed to be a matter of honour who would be the one to give the German nation and its Führer the best performance. (Sebastian)

Above: Rosemeyer's last run. This photograph caused hysteria in Germany because it appeared that Auto Union had sent out its best driver in a damaged car, but in fact the illusion of distorted bodywork on the car's flank was caused by reflections. (Audi AG)

Left: Neither an official investigation was made nor a definitive reason given for Rosemeyer's fatal crash. The German hero appeared to have been killed by a simple twist of fate, struck by a gusting side wind. (Audi AG)

Opposite: The official obituary presented a rare picture of Bernd Rosemeyer wearing his SS uniform. The tone of the text anticipates things to come in the Second World War – heroic death as sacrifice for the German nation. (Remling)

to the turning-point and back. Although the engine would not reach full revs at this stage, the timekeepers noted a maximum speed of 429.9kph (267.1mph) on the return run. Rosemeyer only had to gain a few tenths of a kilometre to beat his rival Caracciola. The strongly rising wind did not worry the driver or his support team.

At 11:40 sharp Rosemeyer started the outward leg of his record attempt. At Kilometre 8.8, level with a cleared track through the forest near Mörfelden, his car was struck by a violently gusting side wind and forced on to the grass verge. Rosemeyer tried to steer out of it, and braked as well, but at a speed of around 400kph (250mph) not even the best driver of his era had any chance of bringing the yawing Silver Arrow back under control. The projectile turned over twice and finished up a total wreck on a bank at the edge of the forest, just short of Kilometre 9.2.

'The incomprehensible, the unbelievable had happened. Bernd Rosemeyer lay without a sound under the trees of the German forest,

overwhelmed by the primeval forces of nature when putting his skill to the ultimate test – A fighter's destiny!' In these poetic words racing manager Feuereissen apostrophised Rosemeyer's last drive in the book of remembrance for the driver's grieving widow. Young Siegfried slain in the forest. The SS mounted a guard of honour round his coffin as a state funeral was prepared in Berlin for the nation's greatest sporting idol, the cost of which, 2,622.10 RM, was shared by the SS and Auto Union. Elly Beinhorn-Rosemeyer would not be robbed of her glory; full of pride and satisfaction she adorned the final pages of her book of remembrance with quotations from the letters of condolence from all the top Nazis. There were words of comfort from Göring, Goebbels, Himmler, Hess, Ribbentrop, Lutze (chief of staff of the SA), Bouhler and Todt – but in pride of place was a personal message from Hitler himself: 'May the thought that he died doing his duty for the honour of Germany soothe your profound pain.'

Among the Nazis' names only one was missing: Hühnlein's sympathy was unwelcome. For the rest of her life Rosemeyer's widow would blame him for her husband's death. It was Hühnlein who first facilitated the record run for Mercedes-Benz, to which, in the battle for fame and honour, Rosemeyer and Auto Union had been obliged to respond. Hühnlein had his own way of dealing with this personal snub, by initially preventing the erection of a memorial at the site of the accident.

The unnecessary death of a sporting hero exposed the core motivation of all the racetrack risk-taking during the age of Nazi dictatorship: vanity and the urge to gain status in a subtle system of favouritism and dependency. Thus the last of Rosemeyer's record runs was really the outcome of a constant struggle for respect and reward, for contracts and subsidies. With every victory and every defeat the competing corporations and their highly paid stars became more implicated in the process of give and take. They were not only fighting for a market share and export opportunities, but were courting the favours of the regime. And just like the regime, they did not hesitate to gamble with human lives for the sake of *Führer, Volk und Vaterland*.

Hitler himself summed it up three weeks after the racing idol's fatal

Even in death poor Bernd was used for Nazi purpose: at Frankfurt his coffin was guarded by SS troopers, and the funeral at Berlin's Dahlem cemetery was largely arranged and directed by SS and NSKK officials. (Sebastian)

Bernd Rosemeyers Leiche wurde zuerst im Hause der ⚡⚡ in Frankfurt am Main aufgebahrt, wo seine Kameraden — die Totenwache Rosemeyer war ⚡⚡-Hauptsturmführer — hielten.

Die Beerdigung in der Stille des Dahlemer Waldfriedhofs war außerordentlich feierlich. Ein Ehrensturm der Leibstandarte Adolf Hitler gab dem berühmten deutschen Rennfahrer das letzte Geleit (rechts).

Zur Beerdigung erschienen nicht nur seine Kameraden von der Auto-Union (rechts erblicken wir im weißen Oyeral zwischen Walfried Winkler und Hans Kahrmann die beiden Auto-Union-Rennfahrer Herm. P. Müller und R. Hasse).

Der Sarg wurde sodann in einem Sonderwagen nach Berlin überführt

und in der Kapelle des Dahlemer Waldfriedhofs feierlich aufgebahrt, wo ⚡⚡-Führer die Totenwache hielten.

Von nun ab aber werden ein ⚡⚡-Sturm und ein Motor-Lehrsturm des NSKK. Bernd Rosemeyers Namen tragen als ein ewiges Vermächtnis.

2 P.B.Z., 4 Weltbild, 3 Schirner, 3 Buttner, 1 Preßephoto, 1 Hoffmann, 1 Scherl.

accident when, at the opening of the IAA in Berlin on 18 February, he delivered a remarkable eulogy: 'For all of us it is painful to know that one of the very best and most courageous of those pioneers in the international recognition of German engine and vehicle manufacturing, Bernd Rosemeyer, had to lose his life so young. But he and all the men who, in those tough races, sit at the wheel of our cars or ride our motorcycles, are fighting with us to give bread, wages and reward to the German working man, who then converts them into other values.'

Those who went along with the Nazis in the end had to play by their rules: Elly Beinhorn-Rosemeyer was not allowed to publish her book about her late husband until she had provided the Reich Chamber of Literature with complete evidence of her Aryan ancestry. On 13 August 1938 the widow sent various birth, death and marriage certificates to the SS Central Office of Race and Settlement, which six days later began a 'further investigation of the test of ancestry', before the head of the *Sippenamt* confirmed, on 13 September 1938: 'In the year 1937 SS-*Hauptsturmführer* Bernd Rosemeyer, SS-No. 214.952 submitted documents providing proof of ancestry for his wife Elly, *née* Beinhorn, born 30.5.1907 in Hanover, up to and including all her grandparents.' The book *My Husband the Racing driver* reached the bookshops in time for Christmas 1938, and achieved sales of over 300,000. Copies were still being eagerly bought well into the Second World War. In 1955 and again in 1987 revised editions appeared, conscientiously purged of earlier references to Hitler, Himmler and their henchmen – and, of course, omitting their messages of condolence at the time.

Considerably earlier, Victor Klemperer had had something to say about Elly Beinhorn's language and conduct during the Nazi dictatorship. From a philological standpoint, he found the book fascinating and on 1 July 1945 noted in his diary: 'Everything about this not unattractive book is interesting and characteristic of its time, especially its style – the deliberately bluff heartiness, which comes to the fore whenever emotion is expressed, whether tacitly or overtly. Here is the Nazi style in its ideal form; Goebbels learned from it and others learned from him. It has the trappings and the emotional stance of the Third Reich – except that, in a purely sporting context, [...] it does not sound as unpleasant as in high politics; the blend here is more naïve and less toxic. Of course, behind the style is the attitude: sport is heroism, it is magnificent, even more magnificent than soldiering.'

The end of an epoch

At a stroke, Rosemeyer's death altered the balance of power between the German racing stables. Auto Union had to justify itself in the face of accusations that it may have been to blame for the loss of its top driver. Reflections of light in photographs of the last record run suggested that there had been negligence in allowing the car to start with bodywork that seemed to have been dented by the side-wind, and an exact replica of the aerodynamic bodywork was built in Zwickau in order to prove that these accusations were based on an optical illusion. All of this brought the development of Auto Union's vehicles for the new formula to a complete halt, which meant that Mercedes-Benz dominated almost the entire Grand Prix season.

For Auto Union's racing division Rosemeyer was irreplaceable, both as a man and a driver, and nerves were raw. After the team's pitiful showing in the first outing of the season, at Reims, the board lodged complaints with the NSKK, the ONS and the propaganda ministry in an effort to muzzle the journalist Eberhard Hundt for his allegedly tendentious reporting. But none of their protests had any effect. And they became superfluous at the end of the season, when Auto Union's new star driver Tazio Nuvolari won the Grands Prix at Monza and Castle Donington.

With Rosemeyer's death the nation had lost a sporting idol – and National Socialism one of its most radiant protagonists, who had distracted people from the miseries of daily life under the compulsion and repression of the state, precisely because he seemed so different from the uniformed representatives of the would-be master-race and their appallingly vulgar Party bosses. A man like Rosemeyer was irreplaceable. Even Himmler seemed to realise that and in February 1938 was not especially keen to see Max Schmeling join the SS.[3] Not even Germany's idol of the boxing ring – who a few months later would be knocked out by Joe Louis in the first round – possessed an aura that approached Rosemeyer's. Perhaps this was precisely symptomatic of the Nazi state, whose ideology relied so strongly on the cult of death and heroic self-sacrifice.

The glow left by the departed Rosemeyer provided a role model for young, courageous imitators – especially those from the ranks of quite ordinary *Volksgenossen*, the ones who were now being sent off to the Front. At Auto Union the great Nuvolari was joined by the rookie driver Hermann

Hermann Paul Müller, pictured in 1937, should have won the 1939 European Championship in his Auto Union, but for the outbreak of the Second World War. However, NSKK-Führer Adolf Hühnlein declared Mercedes-Benz driver Hermann Lang to be European Champion. Müller managed to win the 250cc Motorcycle World Championship in 1955, aged 45. (Audi AG)

Paul Müller in regular race assignments. Müller was born in Bielefeld in 1909, the son of a talented chef, and earned his first racing laurels on a motorcycle, as had Georg Meier, a year younger, who was signed up by Auto Union for the 1939 season. A policeman and later a professional soldier, Meier had made his name as a successful cross-country motorcyclist, before BMW gave him a chance in late 1937 to compete in circuit races on the new supercharged 500. And 'Schorsch', as the seemingly rather gormless Bavarian was always known, immediately succeeded in holding his own against established international competitors. In 1938, his first full season, he even won the European Motorcycle Championship. He was seen as the coming man and in 1939, though continuing to ride two-wheelers for BMW, he also took to the track in racing cars for Auto Union.

Müller, Meier and their Swabian opposite number at Mercedes-Benz, Hermann Lang, all came from humble backgrounds and rose socially through their success in motorsport. However, Meier was different in that, as a member of the Wehrmacht, he was not allowed to join the Nazi Party,

Visiting the Führer but not joining his party. As a soldier in the German army, Georg 'Schorsch' Meier (right), 1938 European 500cc Champion and the first foreign winner of the Isle of Man Senior TT in 1939, did not need to sign up with the NSDAP, NSKK or SS. (Meier)

nor did he have to belong to the NSKK in order to drive in races. 'They kept on pesterin' me, but I didn't join,' Meier recalled in 1998, a few months before he died. 'In England in 1939, on the way to the Tourist Trophy on the Isle of Man, I was able to talk to some Jewish emigrants from Berlin. They knew what was goin' on, all right. So I always stayed in the Wehrmacht, didn't have to join the Party. OK, I was never promoted any higher, so by the end of the war I must've bin the most senior sergeant in the Wehrmacht. But I think I did the right thing.'

A man with ambition
Meanwhile Hermann Lang did everything differently but, in the eyes of the Nazi dictatorship, by no means wrongly. And he had come up the hard way. 'Hermännle' – little Hermann – was 14 in 1923, the year of hyperinflation, when his father died and his mother was left to bring up four boys alone. His elder brothers were both killed in motorcycle accidents, Albert in 1928 and Karl in 1930. Hermann himself had a serious crash in a race but carried

on with his hobby. In 1931, at the age of 22, he became German Hill-Climb Champion in the sidecar combination class, and from then on earned his living racing as a works rider for the Standard company, until he lost his job in the Slump. He was out of work for six months, then scraped a living as a part-time engine driver on a narrow-gauge railway in a gravel-pit, until in the middle of 1933 the young Swabian's dream came true and he was 'hired by Daimler'.

Once the Nazis had taken power everything improved for Hermann Lang: 'I had a job again, doing the work I was trained for! The joy of being allowed to work can only be judged by someone condemned to unemployment. What had happened? How come I was in work again? The German people had been given a destiny by a man who snatched the country from defeat and humiliation and began to build a new Reich – Adolf Hitler! For me, and indeed for millions, this meant an end to unemployment.'[4] So Lang

Fulfilling a dream. At one time unemployed, working-class Hermann Lang got his chance at the Daimler-Benz factory in Untertürkheim and eventually became a Grand Prix driver. Wasn't such a rise only possible in Hitler's reborn Germany? Lang certainly subscribed to that view, as did many other Germans. (Daimler AG)

wrote in his memoirs, co-authored by Hans-Günter Wolf, a journalist in the Daimler-Benz press office, and published in 1943, in the middle of the Second World War. The 6th Army had surrendered in Stalingrad, German cities were being bombed night and day, and Lang, the popular racing driver, lent his name to a book meant to distract people from the gloom of the present, filled with jingoistic patriotism and declarations of support for Hitler and his acolytes.

Nine years later Germany's post-war economic miracle was in full swing, and Lang was once more racing for Mercedes. The Second World War had cost him the best years of his career, but in 1952 he won the Le Mans 24 Hours in a Mercedes-Benz 300SL. It was then that a cleaned-up version of his memoirs appeared as, with the help of his co-author, he took stock once more and carefully left rather a lot of things unmentioned. His eulogy of Hitler, his encounters with Party chiefs and his praise for National Socialism were, needless to say, expunged.

'They were great times,' Lang recalled, looking back on the years 1934–5. As an engine fitter in the racing division, not only had he maintained Fagioli's Silver Arrow, but on cross-country trips he had driven the transporter carrying the priceless machines from Untertürkheim to racing assignments all over Europe. Lang and his fellow mechanics were a seasoned team, and they got to see the big wide world. And in 1935, when he was actually promoted to rookie driver in the works stable, he remained on the closest terms with his workshop colleagues. Lang remembered his origins, which is why his former workmates always kept him fully updated on technical innovations to the racing cars. He also discovered which engine had produced a few extra horsepower on the test-bed. It is the eternal story of a man who wants to get to the top.

Neither Caracciola nor von Brauchitsch, the two established gentleman-drivers in the Mercedes-Benz stable, really took the little mechanic with the Swabian accent very seriously. The spiteful jibes of his upper-crust team colleagues – 'Champagne for us, and a beer for Herr Lang' – are legendary. 'Poor ol' Lang was always havin' the piss taken by Caracciola and Brauchitsch. They treated him rotten,' Georg Meier recalled. 'And when I came along the two of 'em always used to say: "Here comes the Sergeant".'

In test-drives at Monza at the beginning of the 1935 season Lang outshone experienced rivals like Bobby Kohlrausch and the motorcyclist

Hans Soenius. On 16 June he was given his first chance to compete for Mercedes-Benz, in the Eifel Race on the Nürburgring. But in the rain he skidded on the wet surface and came off the track. However, some NSKK men heaved his car out of the ditch so that he was able to carry on and end in fifth place. Admittedly, however, he was far behind the two drivers battling for the lead. Not until close to the finish did Caracciola manage to push Auto Union's new rookie, Rosemeyer, into second place.

Little Hermann drove respectably but still had a lot to learn, and for the moment he was obliged to go right to the bottom of the pecking-order at Mercedes-Benz. Hanns Geier, one place above Lang in the internal ranking, had a bad accident in the Swiss Grand Prix which put an end to his career, so that Lang moved up to become the official reserve driver in the 1936 season. In his races he never stood on the winner's podium, but he did gather invaluable experience. In the German Grand Prix at the Nürburgring he made a big impression when, after Rosemeyer's first pit stop, he led the field for a while until he broke the little finger of his right hand when changing gear and had to be replaced by Caracciola, who had already pulled his own car out of the race. Despite the pain Lang later took over the car of his team-mate von Brauchitsch, who was also incapacitated, and managed to finish in seventh place.

From the middle of the 1936 season onwards such devotion to duty was of particular value, since the Silver Arrows from Untertürkheim, in contrast to their Saxon rivals, were conspicuous for their poor roadholding and unreliability. But unlike the team's prima donnas, the modest Swabian did not constantly complain about mechanical shortcomings. His reward was quick to follow, as from 1 November Lang was given a racing contract with a fixed gross monthly salary of 600 RM. Even though his share of winners' bonuses and starting money increased his earnings considerably, the fixed element was still ridiculously small in comparison with the sums that Caracciola and von Brauchitsch were pocketing. Nonetheless, the rookie gained in status, because over the year he was certainly no slower and represented much better value for money than the seasoned Chiron, who was signed up by Mercedes-Benz in 1936. For that reason the Monegasque, who anyway had to be paid in foreign currency, was dropped, along with Fagioli, and Lang moved up to number three driver in the Mercedes-Benz stable. As a trained mechanic and fitter he also brought with him a

Hermann and Lydia Lang playing the game and winning. Golden days of youth, success and racing – never mind what was going on away from the track. (Daimler AG)

thorough technical knowledge, which established stars like Caracciola and von Brauchitsch lacked. And because the newly-wed Hermann had just set up home in the Bad Canstatt district of Stuttgart he was always on hand whenever he was required to test and evaluate technical improvements to the racing cars.

At the opening of the 1937 season Lang was allowed to take his young wife Lydia with him to Tripoli. On their way through Italy, the unsophisticated couple had the friendly company of racing manager Alfred Neubauer, who acted as their guide and mentor. Travelling to races was still quite an adventure and pretty exhausting. Trips by air were considered both expensive and risky, even though the Auto Union team once travelled to North Africa by flying boat, and the Daimler-Benz people took a scheduled flight to London. Only Bernd Rosemeyer had, thanks to his wife, developed a taste for flying, and having gained a pilot's licence flew to races in his own light aircraft in 1937. But of course he was the top man in German motorsport. And what about airships? The age of the Zeppelin had come to a sudden end on 7 May 1937 when the *Hindenburg* burst into flames on its approach to Lakehurst airfield near New York, and 34 people lost their lives. The same year German drivers crossed the Atlantic by ship for their one and only fixture in the United States. They also took a steamer across the Mediterranean to Tripoli.

But before that the Langs had to drive in a modest company-owned Mercedes-Benz 170 – with Neubauer in constant attendance – from Stuttgart to Zürich, then over the St Gotthard Pass to Milan and on via

Hermann Lang, winner of the 1938 Tripoli Grand Prix, and wife Lydia surrounded by bigwigs Marshal Italo Balbo, NSKK-Führer Adolf Hühnlein and Daimler-Benz director Max Sailer. (Daimler AG)

Rome to Naples, where they boarded a passenger vessel. The whole journey took about ten days, and in 1937 – especially for ordinary folk like the Langs – provided experiences that people of their kind would otherwise have never dreamed of. But for Hermann and Lydia the really fabulous times would only begin when they reached distant Tripoli.

On the high-speed course in the Libyan desert, Rosemeyer, Caracciola, von Brauchitsch, Stuck and Fagioli engaged in pitiless full-throttle duels at average lap speeds well in excess of 220kph (135mph). The team managers figured this was much too fast: the tyres would quickly wear out. Then, no sooner had a driver taken the lead than his ear-protectors would fly off. The unscheduled pit stops cost time and strained the nerves – and would rob Rosemeyer of certain victory. Three times he had to fit new tyres. Only Lang, with iron discipline, kept to an even speed, which meant that his swift drive was only interrupted by a single well-judged pit stop: four new tyres and a good 200 litres of fuel, all in just over 20 seconds! Practice makes perfect, but for their Swabian mate, good old 'Hermännle', who was really still one of them, the mechanics grafted all the more willingly. And in the end it was enough to give him a clear victory in the Gran Premio di Tripoli! Rosemeyer came in a good ten seconds behind him, with von Delius, Stuck and Fagioli taking the next three places. The date was 9 May 1937; Hermann Lang had won his first Grand Prix and completely surprised Daimler-Benz AG by bringing to an end almost a whole year of races without a single victory. Director Sailer, racing manager Neubauer and NSKK chief Hühnlein were on hand to congratulate him.

A Party member of his own free will

Since 1934 membership of the National Socialist Party had grown to more than five million. So great was the rush to join that an emergency stop was

The best of times: Lang meets the Führer in 1938 at the annual parade at the Reich Chancellery in Berlin. (Daimler AG)

put on enrolment, to prevent the 'Movement' being diluted by an influx of new recruits whose motivations may have been unduly opportunistic. However, on 1 May 1937 this embargo was lifted. Anyone joining at this time would surely have been aware of the nature of National Socialism and the institutional terror it perpetrated in the name of the German people? Nevertheless, hundreds of thousands still took the opportunity to become Party members, and Lang was one of them. On 1 May 1937 the Untertürkheim branch of the NSDAP recorded the admission of Hermann Lang, born 6 April 1909, as member no. 5 646 982.

'My father was mad about his sport and totally non-political,' recalls Peter Lang, one of the racing driver's two sons, 'and once they were out there on the track, they were on their own. No party card would be any help; they had to make it themselves, beat the competition alone.' All the same, a party card would have done Hermann Lang no harm in those days. But why did he join the NSDAP in the first place?

None of the other leading German racing drivers of that period felt it either necessary or useful to become a member of the Party. Nor was anyone in those elite motor racing circles compelled to join. It was enough that the brownshirted bully boys could bask in the reflected glory of the privileged racing stars they had promoted. Rudolf Caracciola moved in the highest echelons of the regime thanks to his success, though he merely acted as a decorative accessory to Hitler and his paladins at the annual ritual of opening the Berlin Car and Motorcycle Exhibition, or at NSKK events in honour of sportsmen. It may have been easier for Caracciola than for others to maintain a certain aloofness, not least because of his Swiss domicile and international reputation as a professional racing driver. His team-mate Manfred von Brauchitsch also knew the top Nazis personally and made use of his acquaintanceship. In return he once collected donations for the Nazi Winter Aid programme. But even the wily von Brauchitsch saw no reason to join the Party. Not even Hans Stuck, a past master in cleverly exploiting personal connections, held a Party card.

Yet to someone like Hermann Lang, who had risen from the very bottom and wanted finally to *be* someone in the great world of motor racing, it was important not to pass up this opportunity. He was only 28 at the time, and despite every obstacle he had worked his way steadily to the top, by being quick on the uptake and always willing to go the extra mile. What was in

Hermann Lang's mind? In a quiet moment, decades later, he was asked precisely that question by Winfried Seidel, a collector and connoisseur of Mercedes-Benz cars. And in his broad Swabian the grand old man of motor racing replied: '*Büeble, mir waret damals stolz drauf!*' ('Listen, boyo, we was proud of it in those days!')

On 18 July 1945 Hermann Lang was arrested by US military police at his holiday home in Beutelsbach, near Waiblingen. He spent the night in the cells of the local courthouse and the next morning was transported to Internment Camp No 74 in Ludwigsburg as an 'automatic arrestee'. At that time fairly high-ranking Party officers ended up behind barbed wire 'automatically', by reason of their rank alone. Lang was charged with having held the senior rank of *Staffelführer* in the NSKK, and for the occupying authorities this was evidence enough that they were dealing with a high-ranking Nazi. The racing driver was certainly no such thing but it took a long time before he was able to convince the officials responsible for his detention. Lang's release was indeed 'recommended' on 13 November 1945, but it was another six months before he was a free man. In his 'application for release' he wrote: 'I am a motor-racing driver and have never engaged in any party-political activity. Membership of the NSKK was a condition of practising motorsport. By reason of my international racing victories (European Champion 1939) I was given honorary ranks in the NSKK, which in turn under the rules of the NSKK required me join the NSDAP. I have never held any office in the Party or any of its associated organisations. I owe my career exclusively to my sporting achievements and not to the NSDAP.'

However, in order to qualify for promotion in the NSKK there is no question of him having had to be a member of the Nazi Party. His far more successful and therefore more prominent team-mates Caracciola and von Brauchitsch reached high rank in the NSKK without belonging to the Party. At the time of joining the NSDAP Lang was only just beginning his international career. His claim in 1945 to have been completely non-political may be correct, but in the immediate post-war years almost all Germans made the same assertion about their conduct during the Nazi period. For the Allies and the German judicial authorities acting under their supervision it was no easy task to distinguish between perpetrators, fellow-travellers and those wrongfully imprisoned. The internment camps were full of such cases. And so it was not until 30 April 1946 that the German-staffed five-man 'Security Examination Committee B' took up the case of Hermann Lang and concluded unanimously: 'Release from detention is recommended.' The decision was passed to the Ministry of State, Lang being designated as a 'fellow-traveller' in an appendix to the application for his release.

But the committee had certainly had difficulty in reaching their verdict, and even frankly admitted to being at a loss. For in response to the question: 'Did the prisoner attend Nazi meetings, did he take part in public demonstrations, wear the Party uniform, Party decorations etc?' it was noted that 'it cannot be immediately answered with a "no", for reasons connected with the particular nature of his profession.' However, plenty of Hermann Lang's contemporaries were prepared to speak up for him. A total of 18 employees of Daimler-Benz AG signed a petition. The document signed on 15 April 1946 is a rather clumsily phrased declaration by the Works Council, described as a 'certificate': 'Regarding Herr Hermann Lang, who is well known to have been a racing driver with the Daimler-Benz Corporation, it is hereby certified that after the questioning of several witnesses his politically nominal membership of the Party and the NSKK is confirmed. He was promoted for propaganda reasons on account of his racing successes, and in our opinion this is not to be interpreted as evidence of guilt.'[5]

But in the 1943 edition of Lang's memoirs we can read how political even a totally non-political person can be: 'Firstly I thank my destiny as a German to be allowed to belong to a nation which owes its place in the world to an unbroken series of great deeds and high achievements in every field, but this most of all in the great age in which our *Führer* Adolf Hitler has helped the German nation to achieve acceptance in its constant striving for recognition and equal rights.' Even in wartime, was a prominent racing driver *compelled* to have stuff like that published under his name? No. Lang was a child of his time. He even accepted that the war had put a temporary end to his motor racing career: 'But I soon realised that more important than the happiness of the individual is the happiness of the whole community, and that the battle that I waged was only a tiny fraction of the gigantic struggle of my beloved Fatherland. And this German victory will also be the greatest of my life, when our homeland will stand radiant in that place in the world which is due to it by virtue of its past, its merits and its calling.'

Can he really have been as clueless as all that when he joined the NSDAP? The card index of NSDAP membership shows that a number of his colleagues also joined on 1 May 1937: no. 5 872 259, August Momberger, contract driver with Auto Union for the 1934 season, later manager of the works sports division and engineer in the racing car testing department; no. 5 955 410, Ewald Kluge, works rider for DKW and European Motorcycle Champion in the 250cc class; no. 5 719 979, Baron Fritz Huschke von Hanstein, a young, well-educated gentleman-driver, who joined the NSKK as early as 1932, as is noted on his SS officer's identity-card with membership number 232 177; and the man who would be his boss after the end of the Nazi period, Dr Ferdinand Porsche, no. 5 643 287. In fact Porsche did not apply for membership until 5 October, but such a prominent figure was gladly granted retrospective admission.

It is possible that Hermann Lang's case was similar. After his arrest in the summer of 1945 the former racing driver stated in a questionnaire for the US authorities that from January 1938 until 'the present' he had been a member of the NSDAP. By joining the Party, Lang was far from being alone in German motorsport circles; nor was there any question of 'compulsory membership'. Motorsport enthusiasts, as much as anyone, knew they were living in 'great times', and they paid tribute to the man who had made their grandiose racing victories possible in the first place.

The fastest race in the world

It was also in May 1937 that Hermann Lang celebrated the first two Grand Prix wins of his career. Tripoli was immediately followed by triumph on the AVUS, in what was to be the greatest motor racing spectacle in the history of the Nazi state.

Back in late 1935 it had been decided in Berlin that the AVUS should be converted into the world's fastest racetrack. The top speed already achieved on the AVUS that year, by Hans Stuck, was a lap average of 260kph (161mph), but the Nazis were planning for even faster times and records. To realise this the two straights at the northern entrance to Berlin's urban motorway, each of more than 10km, were connected by a banked 180° curve. This modified northern curve permitted speeds of roughly 180 to 200kph (112–125mph), in other words nearly twice the speed of the existing unbanked curve. The trade journal *Allgemeine Automobil-Zeitung* noted in its issue of 28 December 1935 that 'the planned conversion of the curve was initiated by a personal suggestion from the *Führer*.' However, because the 1936 Summer Olympics in Berlin were far more important, the rebuilding of the north curve was postponed, so that in the Olympic year, of all years, no AVUS Race could be held.

Berlin's City Engineer, Erich Krey, had never designed a banked curve in his life. The structure he built rose to a height of 12.5m (41ft), with the roadway set at an angle of 44°, its surface, some 18m (59 ft) wide, paved with reddish-brown clinker bricks laid on edge. In wet weather these were pretty slippery, but far more critical was the fact that, unlike all other banked curves known at that time, Key had opted for a straight-line cross-section instead of a concave one. Under the theoretical laws of physics the straight cross-section was meant to ensure that if a driving-

Bernd Rosemeyer on the new North Curve banking at AVUS in his streamlined Auto Union. Politically, this was Germany's most prestigious motoring event of 1937, intended to be the fastest race the world had ever seen. The hopes of the NSKK organisers succeeded, but the German racing heroes were forced to flirt with disaster due to the track's dangerous design. (Audi AG)

line high up was chosen, it would not give any advantage in speed or overtaking. However, in practice it had the result that when a specific speed – determined by the type of car – was exceeded, the centrifugal force no longer pressed the vehicle harder down onto the surface, but instead lifted it abruptly outwards, up to and over the top edge of the banking. The drivers in their hurtling racing cars thus became guinea pigs in a battle against centrifugal force.

On the day of the race, 30 May 1937, there were no less than *50,000* people standing on the area inside the north curve. In all more than 300,000 spectators watched this AVUS Race, which was the first and also – though no one knew it at the time – the last appearance of the Silver Arrows on the reconstructed circuit. In order to ensure that this motor racing spectacle would go down in history as the fastest automobile race of all time, Hühnlein's ONS had specified that the event be run under 'free formula' rules. There was thus no weight limit, which meant that Auto Union and Mercedes could enter not only their Grand Prix machines with their exposed road-wheels, but also their fully enclosed record cars with special engines. True, the streamlined cars weighed in at 200–300kg more, but their aerodynamic bodywork allowed far higher speeds. And that was the decisive criterion on the apparently endless straights of the AVUS.

Nothing and no one could challenge the vast superiority of the two German works teams. Scuderia Ferrari did not even enter its Alfa Romeos, having already had to swallow a depressing defeat in Tripoli. The official explanation was that the Italian machines could not be made ready in time. So, warming up for the start, the only sparring partners for the Silver Arrows were three hopelessly inferior Maseratis. To clarify by just how much their performance fell short, each Italian car was generating a mere 300bhp against almost double that figure on the German side. Mercedes-Benz provided three streamlined cars for Caracciola, von Brauchitsch and Lang, while the British rookie Richard Seaman drove a Grand Prix version W125, *ie* with exposed wheels. Auto Union fielded two fully-enclosed Silver Arrows for Rosemeyer and Fagioli, while von Delius and Hasse each had to settle for a 16-cylinder car in regular Grand Prix racing trim.

It was obvious that on this ultra-high-speed circuit only the streamlined cars stood a chance of winning, but the risk their drivers were exposed to was open to question. For after three days of practice runs it was clear that the Continental tyres would only last one or two laps if a car was driven at full throttle. Bernd Rosemeyer, the alpha male among the German drivers, proved once again to be the fastest, even in this star-studded group. In practice he achieved the top score with an average lap speed of 283.7kph (176.3mph), but in just 20 test laps he suffered four burst tyres. In the process he survived a hair-raising moment when, doing about 370kph (230mph), the tread flew off one of his front tyres. Somehow he contrived to save the situation and came through unharmed. It should be remembered that drivers wore no crash helmets back then, just linen or leather flying caps. Combined with goggles these provided protection against the headwind, but nothing more. Safety belts and fireproof overalls were still completely unheard of. Instead, racing was all about courage and driving skill. Sometimes, however, it was necessary to hold back, in order to win or even simply to survive. Astonishingly the majority of Silver Arrow pilots succeeded in doing this, but in this company of dashing macho types a man like Rosemeyer was obliged to show his equally ambitious rivals who was boss. Sadly, a short time later this attitude would cost him his life.

The story of Hermann Lang ended differently. His presumed defiance of death would become rather more circumspect when faced with extreme conditions like those of the AVUS. During practice the young Swabian had an experience similar to Rosemeyer's, only the fault was not a tyre-burst: 'As a result of a minor defect in the fitting of the bodywork, when my car hit a bump the front lifted – it actually took off. As I lost sight of the road, it struck me in a flash: I mustn't turn the steering wheel, otherwise when the front end came down again the front wheels would be in the wrong position and I would inevitable fly off the track! At that moment I was going at full revs – about 380kph [235mph]. Luckily it ended up OK, but I admit it gave me quite a shock.'

Lang had respect – for risks and for authority – and realised that in view of the critical tyre situation it was impossible to drive a normal race. As soon as a driver stepped on the gas, shreds of rubber would be flying round his ears. Or bits of engine. Theoretically, 90 per cent of each lap could be driven at full throttle, but the power units could not cope with that for more than 200 or perhaps 300km (125–185 miles), equivalent to about half the length of a Grand Prix in those days. Result: in their megalomania the Nazis had dreamed up a racetrack that was much too

Caracciola and his streamlined Mercedes-Benz at AVUS in 1937 in the first of two heats,
which he won after a terrific duel against Rosemeyer. Underlining the political importance
of the 1937 AVUS Race, the Mercedes-Benz cars were adorned with swastikas – something
usually confined to record-breaking on the autobahn. (Daimler AG)

fast for the technical capacity of the cars available at the time. But it was
too late to simply cancel the year's most important sports event in the
nation's capital without losing face.

Almost the entire top echelon of the Nazi government took their places
on the VIP stand, and the silver racing cars taxied up to the start, those
of Mercedes-Benz – though not those of Auto Union – decorated with
swastikas, a practice usually reserved for record runs. Though it had been
decided that the show must go on, the main race was shortened from ten
laps to eight – which ought to be possible at a reduced speed, without risking
the tyres. But no one could tell for sure, because, for safety reasons, none
of the competitors had completed more than five practice laps. In order to
reduce the imponderables still further, the two heats, also scheduled for the
Sunday, would each be limited to seven laps, and their only purpose was to
establish the grid positions for the final. The heats would thus be little more
than demonstration runs, each over in about half an hour.

This was lucky for Lang, as in the second heat he had tyre trouble; but
despite a tyre-change and some unintentional obstruction by Hasse he was
still only 21.7 seconds behind the winner, von Brauchitsch, who though he

never made full demands on the 12-cylinder power unit in his streamlined record Mercedes-Benz still averaged over 258kph (160mph). In the first heat the rivals Caracciola and Rosemeyer merely eyed each other intently, and did not get serious until just before the finish. The fully enclosed Mercedes-Benz with its traditional 8-cylinder racing engine crossed the line seven-tenths of a second ahead of the streamlined Auto Union, whose 16-cyclinder was, according to an internal Zwickau report, only running on '12 or 13 pots', and Rosemeyer was 'soaked in oil'. Caracciola's average speed was just on 250kph (155mph).

To contemporaries and successors this might sound impressive, but if the rivals had been allowed to drive as fast as they knew how very different speeds would have been recorded. To give some idea of this, Rosemeyer's fastest lap in this heat averaged 276.32kph (171.73mph), despite his misfortunes. But in the orgy of noise and hurtling speed, who among the 300,000 or more spectators along the AVUS would have picked up on such precise details and spotted the sham? The important thing was that the men at the wheel made a lot of noise. And in the end, for the public to see a German driver win in a German car was not just a matter of honour, it was a foregone conclusion. That the German happened to be Hermann Lang was coincidence, luck or fate: 'In the main race I had decided I wouldn't act the wild man again,' he noted in his recollection of the final, which saw four Mercedes-Benzes pitted against three Auto Unions and the lone Maserati of Laszlo Hartmann. At the time the NSKK race officials were not interested in the fact that the Hungarian driver was Jewish. The Nazi state needed an international cast for the walk-on parts. At the end of the eight-lap contest Hartmann would be two laps behind. The Germans had the race to themselves.

'Worried about their tyres, none of the drivers wanted to go flat out at first,' Lang confessed, 'until this general waiting-game gave Caracciola a chance to take the others unawares and break away from the field. But Rosemeyer immediately went after him and I followed both of them. One after the other they dropped out. Rosemeyer in the second lap, after which he played no further part in the race, and Caracciola in the third lap, when he was also forced to abandon the race.' And because von Brauchitsch also came to grief with clutch damage Lang was the only one left with a streamlined car intact. Behind him came von Delius in an Auto Union with standard bodywork. 'Once again I crossed the line as winner,' Lang recalled. 'On all sides I heard people talk about me as the coming man. After the race I had the special honour of being congratulated by Reich Minister Dr Goebbels, who had attended the race. *Korpsführer* Hühnlein presented me with a wonderful prize. It was so heavy that two mechanics had to carry it. The *Korpsführer* promoted me there and then to *Obertruppführer* in the NSKK.'

A company without liability

In spite of his two successes early in the 1937 season, Lang was still denied his really big breakthrough. Up to the end of the year he did not win another single race. The unchallenged number one at Mercedes-Benz was still Caracciola, who notched up four victories, including three of the four Grands Prix that counted towards the European Championship. He won back the prestigious title from Rosemeyer, who also drove to four important

Surrounded by Joseph and Magda Goebbels and NSKK bosses Adolf Hühnlein and Erwin Kraus, the 'Nobody' – Hermann Lang – is hailed after the final of the AVUS Grand Prix, which he won at an astonishing average speed of 261.63kph (162.61mph). This was Lang's second successive big win, coming three weeks after his sensational victory at Tripoli. (Daimler AG)

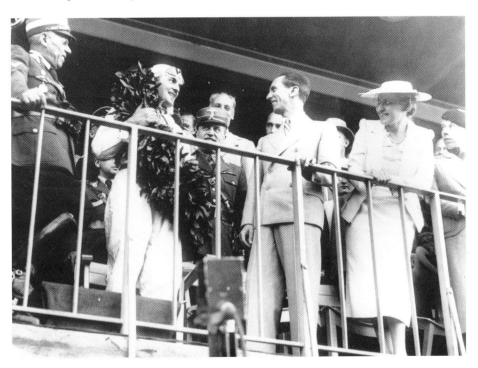

international victories. Yet Lang, the favourite of the race mechanics, had a serious claim to second position within the Mercedes-Benz team hierarchy.

Though under immense pressure, Manfred von Brauchitsch managed to beat Caracciola in the Monaco Grand Prix, but only in the absence of Lang who was ill with a high temperature. Lang was also prevented by angina from entering the Coppa Acerbo, in which von Brauchitsch came second behind Rosemeyer, but he was fit again for Bern and Monza, in both of which he came second to Caracciola. Then on 26 September, in the Masaryk Race, the ambitions of the young Swabian suffered a severe, final setback.

The circuit was situated not far from Brno in Czechoslovakia and ran for 29km along a combination of public highways and streets through a dozen small towns and villages. The width of the track was so tight that overtaking was almost impossible, and at Kilometre 12.6 Lang had a serious accident: 'There was a fast right-hand bend in a bit of forest, bordered by ditches on both sides. The road surface was made of tarmac, but on either side there was a soft verge about a metre wide at the same level. Now, some drivers were in the habit of cutting these corners and driving over the area of soft earth, so that a rut was eventually created along which you could take the bend a bit faster. At the same time there was the problem that the spinning of the rear wheels flung sand and stones onto the tarmac, which in turn meant that a car driving very fast on the tarmac, close to the rut, lost adhesion and skidded sideways.'

In the fifth lap his W125 ran into this gravel, which by now covered the roadway. The car slewed outwards and Lang tried to counteract the skid, but the left front wheel hit a rock and the Silver Arrow overturned and ended up in a ditch, from where quite a large number of spectators were watching the race. Lang was flung out of his driving-seat: 'I was dazed and for a moment couldn't get my bearings. A huge crowd of people gathered, including one man who immediately took me under his wing. He grabbed me by the arm and led me to one side, wishing to spare me from seeing the scene of the accident, for sadly two people were lying dead and twelve were injured – a tragic event, which I only learned about later.'

The man who cared for the shocked and injured driver until an ambulance arrived was probably a fellow ethnic German from the Sudetenland: 'He refused all thanks, saying that he was a German himself and of course he had to help a German driver. Unfortunately we didn't drive straight to the hospital but to the first aid post. Two of the injured were still there; the others had already been shipped off. When I got back in the ambulance at the first aid post some people recognised me; they came up and hurled abuse at me. Since I didn't speak Czech I couldn't explain to them that I felt I was not to blame for the accident, that crashes always had to be expected at races, and that it was the fault of the spectators for exposing themselves to a risk that they had been made aware of.'

The accident occupied Lang for a considerable period. The injured spectators and the relatives of the two dead victims sued him, the Daimler-Benz corporation, and the race organisers. Hermann Lang tells us that case lasted four years and went to appeal twice.

In the summer of 1938 the legal department of Daimler-Benz AG were looking for arguments to put up against the Czech plaintiffs, but the only precedent they could find was a case dating from the 1920s concerning an accident in the Solitude Race caused by a racing driver named Huldreich Heusser. That trial was heard before the Central Criminal Court in Stuttgart and ended in an acquittal for the accused, 'who, as a racing driver, was not in a position to bear responsibility'. But in the view of Daimler-Benz's lawyers there had been much worse accidents which had not led to compensation for the victims among the spectators, or their relatives.

In summer 1938 Lang was confronted with witness statements, but very wisely avoided returning to Czechoslovakia. It could be said that developments in the wider world of politics completely overshadowed the victims' legal action. After 1938 the Masaryk Race was never held again. The Munich Agreement made it possible for the Nazis to annex the Sudetenland region, and then a few months later, on the night of 15 March 1939, the Wehrmacht marched in and occupied the rest of the country, which was renamed 'The Reich Protectorate of Bohemia and Moravia'. And by 1 September, when Germany unleashed its assault on Poland, no one was any longer interested in a lawsuit brought by former Czech citizens against a German company and its racing driver.

However, after the war ended the wheels of justice in Brno began to grind slowly round again. There were actions against the Czech Automobile Club of Moravia-Silesia, against Hermann Lang and against Daimler-Benz AG. On 7 April 1959, in other words almost 22 years after the accident, Daimler-Benz received a demand for payment on behalf of the three seriously injured spectators, Otakar Podaril, his father Adolf Podaril, and Jan Novotny. The company's insurance department asked Alfred Neubauer whether they should accede to this request. The former racing manager replied on 10 April 1959: 'Making a concession in an individual case would be bound to lead automatically, first of all to our acknowledgement of moral guilt, and secondly to creating a precedent under which the other claimants could impose a moral obligation on us.' Neubauer also referred to other accidents, not least to the disaster in the Le Mans 24 Hours on 11 June 1955, when a Mercedes-Benz competition sports car hurtled into a stand and over 80 spectators lost their lives 'but Daimler-Benz AG was never held liable for damages.'

Can a possible act of generosity towards the victims be regarded as an admission of moral guilt? Note that a similar argument would be repeated for a long time in the case of the former prisoners forced to work in the Daimler-Benz factories. That continued until the refusal to make financial compensation began to have a negative impact on the corporation's current business. But that is another story altogether.

Big prizes, big money

'I had built myself a lovely weekend house in the beautiful Rems valley, with a marvellous view over the countryside of Württemberg,' wrote Lang in his personal summing-up of his first full season. He used to get together

Hermann Lang leading Tazio Nuvolari in the 1938 Italian Grand Prix, but he was to lose the fight due to a sick Mercedes-Benz engine. (Sebastian)

regularly with his mates in Cannstadt for a game of skittles, and liked to drink a glass or two of beer or wine – but his income as a racing driver had catapulted him into spheres undreamed of.

To the US military, who interrogated him during his detention in Ludwigsburg, he made statements about his gross income as a racing driver and named figures that were both precise and credible. In 1931, as a successful works rider and employee of the Standard Motorcycle company, he earned 8,000 RM. The following year he was unemployed but managed to achieve an income of between 1,000 and 1,500 RM. Then as a racing car mechanic with Daimler-Benz he received an annual salary of 2,500 RM, and in 1935, as a part-time rookie driver, his pay was 2,600 RM. As late as 1936 his income was still a modest 4,000 RM, in other words not even double what a qualified skilled worker in the company could earn. But thanks to his eye-catching successes in 1937 Lang's income shot up to 60,000 RM! A reader today might just imagine what it would be like if his typical annual salary of 30,000 was, within 12 months, multiplied 15-fold to 450,000. And for our 'Hermännle' the money kept on going up; in 1938 he pocketed 70,000 RM – the same amount as his team colleague von Brauchitsch. In the 1939 season – prematurely ended by the war – Lang enjoyed the unchallenged status of Germany's most successful racing driver, a fact reflected in his total income of 90,000 RM.

As a good Swabian, he naturally invested his newfound wealth in bricks and mortar. Two fine buy-to-let buildings, a large detached home for the family, and a weekend cottage provided financial security and signalled a commitment to his native soil. A man like that was far easier to market as an example to the masses than were Messrs Caracciola and Stuck, with their luxurious chalets in Switzerland and their penchant for sophisticated company.

The two really popular sports idol of those days, Bernd Rosemeyer and Max Schmeling, had perforce dropped out of the picture already – the former through a fatal accident, the latter by being KO'd after just 124 seconds. To make matters worse, just two weeks previously the new national football team with German and Austrian players, put together by Sepp Herberger, had been totally humiliated at the World Cup in France, when it was beaten by Switzerland in a qualifying match and had to quit the tournament. So when it came to sporting success, only the Silver Arrows were left to make an impression.

Manfred von Brauchitsch (46) takes the lead in the 1938 Pescara Grand Prix from Tazio Nuvolari (40). Behind them are Hermann Lang, eventual winner Rudolf Caracciola (his Mercedes-Benz was the only German car to reach the finish), Hermann Paul Müller (Auto Union), Giuseppe Farina in the fastest Alfa Romeo and Rudolf Hasse (Auto Union). The grid had only 12 cars – opposition to the all-conquering 'Silver Arrows' was weakening. (Daimler AG)

New rules, but the same game

However, the 1938 racing calendar was looking extremely thin. The new international formula for racing cars, which was intended to reduce German superiority, had precisely the opposite effect. Mercedes-Benz was more clearly dominant than ever, while Auto Union was in shock following the death of Rosemeyer and was unable to put up any kind of a showing until towards the end of the season. Alfa Romeo, which had now broken away from Scuderia Ferrari, was competing as the Alfa-Corse works team. Soon afterwards it entered a new 3-litre design and from then on, like Maserati, concentrated on building and entering small 1.5-litre racing cars. Due to their lower cost and, not least, the greater equality of opportunity between participants, this *voiturette* class – 'baby-cars', if you like – had for a long time been more popular with international race organisers than the larger formula, which was admittedly spectacular but was all too obviously dominated by the Germans. That is why in 1939 the frustrated Italians would switch to restricting motorsport competitions such as the Tripoli race, the Coppa Ciano, the Coppa Acerbo and the Italian Grand Prix to *voiturettes*.

Against the overwhelming superiority of the German automobile groups not even additional state aid schemes could help, such as were launched first by fascist Italy and then even by democratic France. What the Nazis carried on supposedly in secret but in fact quite obviously the Italians had admittedly been practising since long before 1933, but in the late 1930s the de facto nationalised company Alfa Romeo had gone hopelessly adrift, with endless new models and engines. In any case the injections of state cash were pretty modest in comparison with their German competitors.

In France, from 1934 onwards, a tax charge in favour of national motorsport was levied on every new driving licence. From this and other financial donations the Automobile Club de France had a fund of some 1.5 million francs by 1937. Yet the first bonuses were paid out far too late: Delahaye did not receive its million francs (then equivalent to about 170,000 RM) until 1937; Bugatti was given 40,000 francs in 1938; and in the same year Talbot-Darracq picked up around 600,000 francs of taxpayers' money with which to design and build a 16-cylinder engine under the new 3-litre formula for the season already in progress. Yet neither the power unit nor the chassis was ever used.

Both the financial muscle and the technical potential of the French designers were very limited compared to their German counterparts. A handful of tiny firms were trying in vain to keep pace with the vast resources of the Daimler-Benz and Auto Union groups, not to mention the fact that in democratic France workers were going on strike, and the blockading of suppliers all too often held up the planned building and deployment of French racing cars. The most embarrassing example proved to be that of SEFAC (the initials standing for *Société d'Etudes et de Fabrication d'Automobiles de Course*) which, amidst much excitement and premature laurels, delivered France's national racing car. In its first and only appearance, at the domestic Grand Prix in Reims, the supposed miracle of French engineering genius completed precisely two laps before its engine too went on strike.

It was a further disadvantage that Delahaye and Talbot were relying on big 4.5-litre V12 engines for the new formula that applied from 1938. These had admittedly proved their worth by winning sports car races, but under the formula rules they were not allowed to use a supercharger. The German racing stables, on the other hand, continued to trust their long experience with supercharged engines. Mercedes-Benz and Auto Union developed smaller V12 engines conforming to the new set of rules, since they only had a capacity of 3 litres, but in compensation for that they were allowed to be fitted with superchargers. This format enabled the engineers in Untertürkheim and Zwickau to go on generating more than 480bhp. The fuel consumption, at 70 to 100 litres per 100km depending on the nature of the circuit, was certainly enormous, but the time lost in the necessary pit stops could quickly be made up thanks to the much superior engine performance. The 245bhp French cars, despite their comparatively modest fuel consumption of not more than 40 litres per 100km, had no real chance.

It was all the more ironic then that the first Grand Prix to be run under the new formula, at Pau in south-west France on 10 April 1938, was won by the Jewish driver René Dreyfus in a Delahaye. He was helped by a perhaps lucky, though not underserved, coincidence which admittedly never recurred: the only German car on the grid was the new Mercedes-Benz W154, which at the beginning of the race was driven by Caracciola. True, the Silver Arrow had more horsepower, but it was unable to derive the expected benefit on the narrow town circuit. Dreyfus kept close to Caracciola and actually overtook him. The German took the lead again but then had to go into the pits to refuel while the Delahaye drove straight on. The track was apparently too oily, and surprisingly the faster Mercedes-Benz had no realistic chance of overtaking without risk, as the old racing stories concocted in Untertürkheim tell us to this day. Yet the truth is much more banal: it was due to Caracciola's physical handicap – the hip that was still giving him pain five years after the Monaco

Mercedes-Benz presents Hermann Lang and his W154 to Hitler at the Reich Chancellery after winning the 1938 Tripoli Grand Prix. The Führer appears to be bothered by the noise. (Daimler AG)

accident – combined with a series of technical afflictions, from a faulty clutch
to an unscheduled plug change. Hermann Lang took over the stricken Silver
Arrow and crossed the line in second place, two minutes behind Dreyfus. It was
the first defeat for the German national racing cars in nearly ten months!

Only a few weeks later, in Tripoli on 15 May, the accustomed ranking was
restored. In the absence of Auto Union a secure triple victory was claimed by
Mercedes-Benz in the sequence Lang, Caracciola, von Brauchitsch. Eugenio
Siena was killed when his new Alfa Romeo crashed, and the same fate befell
Laszlo Hartmann in a Maserati. 'In that race two very capable racing colleagues
had to lose their lives,' Lang noted laconically. He himself only just avoided
a collision with a slower competitor, as well as being fortunate to survive a
mishap while refuelling, when the pit crew let petrol slop over his back.

Hermann Lang's 1938 Tripoli win was his second in succession, which was
why he was invited to show the victorious car to Hitler at a special audience
in Berlin. Everything had been arranged by Daimler-Benz director Jakob
Werlin, who was by now also handling the *Führer*'s shareholding in Daimler-
Benz and acting both as General Manager of the Volkswagen plant and
member of its supervisory board. Werlin led Lang into the courtyard of the
Reich Chancellery, where the race mechanics were already waiting. Writing
in 1943, Lang was still filled with delight and gratification: '*Reichsmarschall*
Göring was standing by the car, examining it closely. He was introduced to
me and shook my hand. No sooner had he left than the *Führer* came in. I had
to tell him, too, about Tripoli and the race. The *Führer* wanted to hear what
noise the new engine made, so we started it up. In the courtyard, surrounded
by the walls of tall buildings, it made a roar like a battery of automatic guns
opening fire. As if by magic, all the office windows opened and countless
faces appeared in every one of them. I realised that we racing drivers, too,
owed our fine and proud profession to the *Führer*. From his remarks about
the car and the race I could tell what an expert the *Führer* is in this field.
While the gunfire-like din was going on the *Führer* put his hands over his
ears, but his laugh showed how delighted he was with this German creation.
I was sent on my way with warmest good wishes for the future.'

The last chance
However, that was not enough to enable Lang to win the European
Championship. Only four Grand Prix races counted towards this prize: the

French, German, Italian and Swiss. Von Brauchitsch won in Reims, Seaman at the Nürburgring, Nuvolari in Monza, and Caracciola at the Bremgarten circuit in Switzerland. Once again the title went to Caracciola. In 1938 Lang had unfortunately won the wrong races. Nevertheless, to connoisseurs of the racing scene he was noticeably faster than the seasoned Caracciola, far more reliable than the breakneck von Brauchitsch and, as a German in a German stable, had advantages over Seaman that were not only psychological.

The fact that Lang made his mark in 1939, which would prove to be the last season for the Silver Arrows, came as no surprise. Starting with the very first event, he won five races in succession. On 2 April, in the Grand Prix de Pau, he avenged Daimler-Benz's humiliating defeat the previous year. On 7 May he scored his third successive victory in the Tripoli race, driving – for the first and only time – the 1.5-litre Mercedes-Benz built specially for him and Caracciola under the *voiturette* formula. He celebrated his third win of the season in the Eifel Race on 21 May, when he was once again suitably equipped with a big 3-litre car. Nor did he any longer let himself be

Hermann Lang celebrates his victory at the 1939 Eifel Race. In the final season before the war, the young German won five of the eight races and established a new superiority within the Mercedes-Benz team, Rudolf Caracciola losing his number-one status and sometimes his nerve. (Daimler AG)

While leading the rain-soaked Belgian Grand Prix of 1939, Dick Seaman's Mercedes-Benz left the track, crashed into a tree and caught fire. Seaman tragically sustained severe burns and died from his injuries. In Hermann Lang's memoirs, published in 1943, he expressed outrage at the fact that few people attended Seaman's funeral back in Britain. Perfidious Albion… (Daimler AG)

browbeaten by Stuck and other specialists in mountain events, but chalked up his fourth win of the season in the Kahlenberg mountain road race on 11 June, before going on to win the Belgian Grand Prix on 25 June.

The Belgian event was the first race of the year that actually counted towards the European Championship, as well as the first one run in the rain. Lang emerged victorious, but his British team-mate Dick Seaman suffered a fatal accident. The Briton had been well in front, with a half-minute lead over Lang, when he went off the track in the 22nd lap. His German stablemate spotted the blazing car and made for the pits to tell Alfred Neubauer what had happened. While Dr Richard Gläser, jointly appointed as race doctor by Mercedes-Benz and Auto Union, hurried with Seaman's mechanics to the scene of the accident, Lang returned to the race and victory, narrowly beating Auto Union driver Rudolf Hasse after an unscheduled fuel-stop. Auto Union had already seen three of its own drivers killed over the years – Heydel, von Delius and Rosemeyer – and Seaman was the second Mercedes-Benz fatality, after Otto Merz in 1933.

Lang tells us how Neubauer assessed that Belgian Grand Prix: 'Rich in sacrifice and moments of excitement, this will go down as the greatest day of battle in our racing history. […] We bear this victory home on a shield riddled with holes.' That was the style in those days – full of martial emotion. A great motor race as a prelude to world war. Even in the supposedly non-political journal *Motor und Sport*, Ernst Rosemann wrote in July 1939: 'All-powerful Death stretched out its hand to pluck a young life – a good comrade has left us, snatched from a combative, onward-striving existence: Richard John Beattie Seaman. While we now remember our friend here, German racing drivers and German mechanics will accompany their English comrade to eternal rest in his homeland.' However, it has to be said that in London the German mourners kept almost entirely to themselves.

In spite of everything the dominance of the German racing cars in the 1939 season was more oppressive than ever. In the Eifel Race five Mercedes-Benzes and four Auto Unions were entered against one French Talbot and three Maserati *voiturettes*. At the Belgian Grand Prix, Stuttgart and Saxony each fielded four Silver Arrows, while Alfa Corse put two 3-litre cars on the grid to which were added two Delahayes and a Maserati, all entered by private drivers. Yet what was becoming a tedious routine for international motor racing observers was endlessly eulogised, as ever, by the German press: 'For the fifth time this year Hermann Lang won; another victory for Mercedes-Benz. Lang has had the same run of good luck that other drivers have had before him, but which is not given to them on a plate. It has to be worked for,' pontificated Rosemann, the *Motor und Sport* racing expert who, not possessing a driving licence, had never driven a motor car himself: 'Good luck is always with the strong alone. Currently Hermann Lang is the most powerful personality in motor racing, a man who goes his own way, doggedly upwards, not looking back, trusting in the instrument of his sport, in his machine – and self-confidence like that must finally lead to success. We congratulate Hermann Lang once again. No more need be said!'

But in that brief summer of 1939 all the signs were pointing to war. German pressure on Poland was growing, and it seemed probable that this time Great Britain and France would not meekly submit to Hitler's blackmail and arrogance. Yet there were a few interesting Grand Prix events still to come and Lang seemed within reach of his lifelong goal: to become European Champion! To date he had not lost a single race this season. What is more, his rival Caracciola was showing signs of nerves. At Spa-Francorchamps he skidded in the wet, and in the very first lap at Reims he crashed into the wall of a building.

Time running out. The French Grand Prix at the fast Reims road circuit was one of the few major races to take place in a 1939 season already overshadowed by the threat of war. This is the first lap and the leader, Nuvolari, has already gone through, so that we see second-placed – and eventual winner – Müller (Auto Union) in front of Caracciola (Mercedes-Benz), Meier (Auto Union), Lang (Mercedes-Benz), Stuck (Auto Union) and von Brauchitsch (Mercedes-Benz). (Daimler AG)

It looked as if Lang would drive the last Mercedes-Benz still left in the French Grand Prix to his sixth successive win, when a disastrous engine breakdown turned the outcome of the race on its head. Instead Auto Union celebrated an unexpected double: Hermann Paul Müller won ahead of Schorsch Meier, and NSKK boss Hühnlein showed his penchant for a folksy phrase. If the victors, he said, were now Müller and Meier (the German equivalent of Smith and Jones), then the National Socialist goal of motoring for the common man had been splendidly achieved, and the great sport of motor racing had truly become the people's sport.

In this year of years, what had formerly been the Grosser Preis von Deutschland was renamed the Grosser Preis von Grossdeutschland (the Grand Prix of Greater Germany). Also for the first time that year there was the lure of the title 'Greater German Mountain Champion' which, it should be noted, was given with the Great Mountain Prize of Germany at the end of the Grossglockner race, held in annexed Austria. The Nazis were already building a new national circuit, the Grossdeutschlandring, in the lovely Polenz valley near Pirna, in the region known as 'the Switzerland of Saxony'. Needless to say, it was to be the biggest racetrack in the world, with capacity for one million spectators and parking spaces for 350,000

Volkswagens. The 10km circuit with a track width of over 20m was to be the setting for the next Greater German Grand Prix in 1940, as Adolf Hühnlein announced at the Nürburgring on 23 July.

In this third qualifying race for the 1939 European Championship, Hermann Lang once again put the rest of the field in the shade, and after the second lap over the 22.8km northern loop he was more than 40 seconds ahead when another engine problem put an end to his great performance. Then events followed in rapid succession: Paul Pietsch, driving a Maserati, took the lead for a short time, then Nuvolari in an Auto Union pulled ahead but lost the lead to Caracciola, before Hasse and Müller, thanks to quicker fuel stops, got in front. In increasingly heavy rain, Caracciola fought his way past the Auto Union duo, Hasse skidded off the track and Nuvolari finally dropped out with engine trouble. Thus at the end of a race lasting over four hours, in the treacherous Eifel rain and on an extremely slippery track, Caracciola won with Müller in second place.

The German racing stables had once again barely managed to avoid humiliation: out of four Mercedes-Benzes that started only Caracciola's had survived the chase round the Eifel circuit, while of the five Auto Union

Pointless advertising. Based on a painting by Walter Gotschke, this Daimler-Benz poster praising Caracciola's last victory was presented only days before the outbreak of the Second World War. (Daimler AG)

works drivers only Müller saw the chequered flag. One lap behind the only two Silver Arrows, Paul Pietsch took third place in the new 3-litre Maserati. After the race, Hühnlein was appalled that a good German driver like Pietsch had not been in a Mercedes-Benz or Auto Union car.

The 'Greater German Grand Prix' of 23 July 1939 was the last international sports event during the Nazi Reich for which a Jewish competitor entered. René Dreyfus, then aged 34, piloted his French Delahaye to fourth place, two laps behind Pietsch. The Nazi race officials pretended to be cosmopolitan and peace-loving, just as their carefully angled propaganda would have people believe. Yet just five months previously the Reich Ministry of Transport had issued a confidential instruction ordering the withdrawal of driving licences and vehicle documents from all Jews in Germany. Not only that, but objects made from gold, silver, platinum, as well as pearls and precious stones, had to be handed in by their Jewish owners at 'public purchase-points'. Such was 'legality' and 'normality' in the National Socialist state.

An international motor racing star like Dreyfus, however, could make his guest appearances in Germany unmolested, and there were no objections to him taking his place on the starting grid. Quoted by Nigel Roebuck in *Motor Sport* magazine in March 2005, Dreyfus said: 'It seemed that the Nazis were always particularly nice to me, for some reason. It seems a ridiculous thing to say now – but of course at the time we did not realise what was going on.' So as to be able to go on putting out their nationalist propaganda unobstructed on the international motor racing stage, the Nazi functionaries emphasised their sporting credentials by saying they had nothing against Jewish drivers taking part. Yet scarcely a year later Dreyfus only escaped internment and deportation because he happened to be in the United States for the Indianapolis 500. After that he never returned to France, by then under German occupation.

Time runs out

In July 1939, while the German racing drivers and their admirers were striking camp at the Nürburgring, Great Britain and France failed in their attempt to negotiate a treaty of mutual assistance with Stalin. They had suspicions about the Soviet dictator's territorial ambitions, and so, in Moscow, the Russians suddenly initiated secret talks with Germany. The dance on the edge of a volcano began, while the ill-informed public failed to grasp the fatal drama that was being played out. Only when Ribbentrop flew to Moscow on 23 August did the German-Soviet Non-Aggression Pact become an astonishing, utterly incomprehensible fact. In that brief summer too many people had consoled themselves with false hopes, but now things were getting serious. Yet under Germany's dictatorship the state-controlled mechanisms for suppressing the truth and dazzling the public were still functioning. And still the Silver Arrows raced on triumphantly, trailing behind them an air of well-feigned normality in Hitler's Reich.

On 6 August Hermann Lang won the Grossglockner mountain race. In *Motor und Sport* the egregious Ernst Rosemann had punningly presaged a 'Hermannschlacht' in the Grossglockner pass.[6] In the first of two qualifying heats Hermann Paul Müller beat Hermann Lang with the best time of the day. However, in the second heat, in pouring rain, Lang was able to establish a clear lead and secured overall victory. Nor did the press of the day fail to mention a further important award for the man who now bore the title of Greater German Mountain Champion: 'Hermann Lang earned it [the title] honestly through his performance and because of this performance has been promoted to *Staffelführer* in the NSKK.'

Lang still had a chance of achieving his real objective. The battle for the European Championship that carried such prestige for the German racing stables had to be decided at the Swiss Grand Prix on 20 August. The contest at the Bremgarten circuit near Bern was actually the fourth of the five races that now counted toward the title. Yet by the beginning of August it was clear that the finale at the Gran Premio d'Italia could not take place: the Italians had not finished rebuilding the Monza circuit and cancelled their Grand Prix at short notice. That a German driver would once again be European Champion was clear anyway: the only question that remained was which German.

By today's standards the rules for awarding championship points were rather odd, though clearly defined: the winner of a qualifying race got one point, second place received two, third three, fourth four and all the other starters either four, five, six or seven points depending on the distance covered. This even applied to cars that dropped out. Drivers who did not enter every race were penalised with a blanket eight points for each missed start. Thus up to the 1938 season the European Championship crown went to the driver who, under this formula, collected the *fewest* points. In 1935 the winner was Caracciola, in 1936 Rosemeyer, and in 1937 as well as in 1938 Caracciola again. However, for the 1939 season this points system was changed at the instigation of the International Sporting Committee of the AIACR.

The evaluation system used in France was taken as the most suitable model for the new set of rules. There the winner of a race was awarded ten points, second place got six points, third five points, fourth four points and fifth three points. All other positions, and drivers who did not finish, were allocated one point. The champion was therefore the participant with the *highest* number of points at the end of the season. Curiously, however, the CSI and the AIACR decided *not* to officially introduce this maximum points system for the 1939 season. The odd result of this indecision was that just before the final qualifying race, the Swiss Grand Prix on 20 August, it was not at all clear under which criteria the European Championship should be awarded.

The situation was even more complicated by the fact no less than three German drivers attended the final in Bern with a chance of claiming the title: Lang and Caracciola, with one victory and two retirements each, and Müller, who had chalked up a win, a second place and only one retirement, and thus went to Switzerland as the provisional champion – under both the old and the new scoring systems!

To make matters worse the Swiss organisers had somewhat modified the rules for their Grand Prix, doubtless out of concern for the lack of public interest in the face of total German domination. In order to lure the Alfa Romeo team of Farina and Biondetti to Bern, a preliminary heat had been specially scheduled for *voiturette* racing cars. In the big 3-litre class Mercedes-Benz and Auto Union had a second heat to themselves. Only after these two races of 20 laps over a short distance, totalling 145.6km (which in dry conditions could be covered in less than an hour), did the two classes join up for the final in what was the real Swiss Grand Prix – 30 laps totalling 218.4km. Instead of the normal race duration of 2½ hours non-stop on the Bremgarten circuit, each starter now really only had to concentrate on two sprint races, one of which determined the grid position in the other. Instead of tactical calculation the Mercedes-Benz drivers went flat out from the start, since it was obvious to Lang and Caracciola that, regardless of whether they were rated under the old or the new system, only a victory in the 30-lap final would secure the European

Championship. Their rivals in Auto Union knew that under the new rules Müller needed to come at least second, while if the old system applied a fourth place would suffice.

On the Sunday of the race Lang won the heat for the big car class ahead of Caracciola and von Brauchitsch. Nuvolari, in fourth place, was the best of the Auto Union quartet, whose performance suffered from a wrong choice of tyres. Müller, still hoping for the European Championship, was only seventh across the line in the preliminary heat. A good description of these events is provided by Karl Kudorfer, who had been in the Auto Union press office since the beginning of the year, having previously worked as a PR man for Daimler-Benz from 1935 to 1938. On the evening of 20 August he phoned this report through to Zwickau: 'In the very first heat all the MB drivers were unquestionably faster than the Auto Union drivers. [...] The tyre defects on the Auto Union cars were very noticeable. You see, we had used the same 19-inch tyres as in practice, when they proved themselves thoroughly serviceable. But despite the fact that today was less hot and the tyres were not worn down, suddenly bits of tread began to fly off, which was as inexplicable to the Continental people as it was to us. MB and the others drove on 22-inch tyres. After the first lap it began to rain and because of the tyre defects that had occurred Auto Union also decided to use 22-inch tyres wherever possible. However, since not enough *gesommerte* ('summer-treated') 22-inch tyres were available, these could only be fitted to Stuck's and Nuvolari's cars.'

Only two sets of run-in, or 'summer-treated', 22-inch wet-weather tyres were available to Auto Union for the decisive final race in Bern. So why wasn't one of those sets fitted to Müller's car, since he was most likely to win the title? Well Nuvolari got a set because he was number one in the Saxon stable, with an appropriate contractual guarantee, and at Bremgarten he was, anyway, the fastest Auto Union man. And Hans Stuck got a set because he enjoyed preferential treatment thanks to his political friends in the SS. The shrewd Karl Kudorfer did not need to make special mention of that. He probably knew it was so from his own experience, having been a member of the NSDAP since 1923.

At this point it is necessary to refer to a note dated 28 June 1939 on an internal discussion between Auto Union's racing division and chief executive Carl Werner, in which the drivers to be entered for the Swiss Grand Prix were nominated. Racing manager Feuereissen proposed, 'in case only three cars can be made ready [...] for practical reasons, a team of Nuvolari-Müller-Hasse. Herr Dir. Werner decided against that, taking account of the wish expressed by the *Reichsführer*-SS [Himmler], which A.U. cannot go against, that in this case we should enter Nuvolari-Stuck-Müller.'

As it turned out, in the principal race Lang immediately stormed into the lead in the rain, while Caracciola stuck close behind Farina's little Alfa Romeo for lap after lap. When 'Caratsch' finally succeeded in overtaking, Lang was on his guard and fended off the attacks by his stablemate. As the track dried out the lap speeds got faster and faster; Caracciola did not let go, and the usually all-powerful racing manager Neubauer did not make the slightest attempt to impose stable discipline on the two rivals. No signal came from the pits, no indication that they should hold their positions and bring the race safely home. No, Caracciola was to get his chance to become European Champion again with a victory – provided the right points system was applied.[7]

Müller had meanwhile been able to work his way up to fourth position behind the leading Mercedes-Benz trio of Lang-Caracciola-Brauchitsch – even though, at the start, he had performed an involuntary 360° pirouette on the rain-soaked cobbled surface and consequently had a massive deficit to make up. Or could it be that he had simply been waved through by his Auto Union colleagues who had rushed ahead?[8]

And so the racing drivers and their strategists fought bitterly, on the track, in the pits and behind the scenes, for the positions that would be decisive in gaining the championship honours. However, they could not really be sure what the European racing officials would later decide around their green baize table. At all events Lang did not indulge in little games. With or without permission he kept Caracciola at arm's length and won the race, while Müller solidly defended his fourth place right to the finish.

Thus the fourth and last Grand Prix that counted toward the 1939 European Championship ended without it being possible to announce the name of the new title-holder. Was it Hermann Lang or Hermann Paul Müller? Though the contemporary press was well aware of the dilemma journalists in the Greater German Reich were unable to comment on it, since at the daily press conference on 19 August – the day before the Swiss Grand Prix – they had been instructed not to indulge in speculation about the new European Champion, 'since the question of the points-system is still in dispute.' It is in retrospect remarkable that just 11 days before the German assault on Poland, the Nazi censors were still concerned about the minutiae of sports reportage! On 1 September 1939 the world would have very different things to worry about.

Because of the war the autumn conference of the AIACR in Paris was cancelled, without a decision having been taken to change or retain the old method of awarding points in Grand Prix races. Nor did it announce who was European Champion for 1939, so both Müller and Lang went away empty-handed. But for the German Silver Arrows, unbeaten once again, the season could not yet be filed quietly away.

Adolf Hühnlein personally decided who should be European Champion. At the autumn meeting of the ONS he named Hermann Lang as the new title-holder. The official announcement was made a few days later in a press release to the German dailies, on 30 November 1939. At the time, the

The world is at war, but Germany still has to celebrate its successful racing heroes of the 1939 season. After being honoured by NSKK-Führer Adolf Hühnlein, the prominent drivers were interviewed by a radio commentator who is seen with (from left) Heiner Fleischmann, Hermann Lang, Hans Stuck and Ewald Kluge. After the war, some of these men would claim that they had never worn a Nazi uniform. (Reuss)

The grid for the 1939 Belgrade Grand Prix comprised only five cars. On the front row were the Mercedes-Benz cars of Manfred von Brauchitsch (6) and Hermann Lang (2), on the second row the Auto Unions of Hermann Paul Müller and Tazio Nuvolari (not visible), and on his own at the back Bosko Milenkovic in his completely outdated Bugatti. It was 3 September 1939 – three days into Second World War. (Daimler AG)

fact that Lang had been made European Champion by order of the Nazi Party did not upset anyone at Daimler-Benz. Had he not won the most races anyway? And it was traditional that, where there was any doubt in a sporting decision, Hühnlein, and probably most of the other ONS officials, favoured Untertürkheim more strongly than its Saxon competitor.

More than six decades after this remarkable award, Hermann Paul Müller's aged widow Mariele declared: 'We were cheated.' But in that autumn of 1939 no one complained – neither Hermann Paul Müller and his wife, nor the board of Auto Union. What would have been the point? Hühnlein had awarded the European Championship title from his position of absolute authority. He required neither justification nor a tally of points. Besides, as well as his larger number of victories NSKK-*Staffelführer* Lang had by then reached a considerably higher rank than NSKK-*Truppführer* Müller, and was, furthermore, a member of the NSDAP – QED.

The final duel

It was Sunday afternoon, 3 September 1939, two days after the German invasion of Poland. The competing racing teams of Daimler-Benz and Auto Union were still in Belgrade for a race at the invitation of the Royal Yugoslavian Automobile Club. The trucks had arrived from Untertürkheim the previous Tuesday, their rivals from Zwickau not until Wednesday evening. Two racing cars from each company were prepared for practice and for the race. That year would be the last opportunity for the Silver Arrows to take to the grid. Grand Prix racing was going out of style.

On Thursday 31 August the first practice runs had begun on a short 3km course through Belgrade's inner city. Hermann Lang made the best time, and Manfred von Brauchitsch was just 4/10ths of a second slower. Hermann Paul Müller was another 9/10ths behind. Tazio Nuvolari, the driver of the second Auto Union car, had not yet arrived.

On Friday 1 September the correspondent of the German daily *Neues Tageblatt* cabled Stuttgart: 'In the early hours of this morning, the German racing teams currently in Belgrade received information on German radio about the latest political events in their homeland and listened together to the words of the *Führer*.' Those words were: 'Since 5:45am we have been returning fire. Germany is at war with Poland.'

Should the German racing stables pack up and set off for home? As always on foreign assignments the NSKK was represented by an impressive number of officials. From the German embassy they received the instruction to remain 'in view of the friendly relations with Yugoslavia'. On Friday afternoon the racing cars were back doing their practice laps. But Nuvolari had still not showed up.

On Saturday, too, practice continued, though the official Auto Union report noted laconically that Mercedes-Benz driver von Brauchitsch was 'still drunk

from the previous evening' and completed his laps under the influence of alcohol. Meanwhile, Nuvolari had arrived in Belgrade by train that morning.

On Sunday 3 September von Brauchitsch was missing at breakfast in the hotel. By now the radio had announced Britain's declaration of war on the German Reich. Alfred Neubauer made a dash for the Belgrade aerodrome and prevented von Brauchitsch from flying back to Switzerland. The driver returned to the racetrack.

Shortly before 5pm local time all four German cars taxied on to the grid as planned. They were joined by just one other participant, Yugoslav amateur Bosko Milenkovic in an old Bugatti T51. He came last in the 50-lap race, a full 19 laps behind the others.

Once again the German competitors pursued each other relentlessly. A stone thrown up from the road shattered Lang's driving-goggles, and his car was taken over by reserve driver Walter Bäumer. Von Brauchitsch, in the second Mercedes-Benz, spun off as he was being chased by Nuvolari and Müller, but set off again in pursuit. After 65 minutes the racing spectacle was over, with Nuvolari beating von Brauchitsch to the final flag, but at the trackside the contest continued: Mercedes-Benz proposed lodging a protest against Nuvolari for an alleged violation of the rules at a pit stop, at which Auto Union threatened counter-measures, accusing von Brauchitsch of accepting 'non-permissible assistance'. Not until late in the evening did peace reign between the competitors, and then

Opposite: It is nearly 4pm on raceday and Manfred von Brauchitsch, surrounded by strong-armed mechanics, awaits the order to get in his car. Earlier that day the German racing hero had tried to catch a flight to Switzerland but Alfred Neubauer caught him and brought him back. (Daimler AG)

Right: Tazio Nuvolari won the fierce, final fight between the two German racing teams. Days afterwards Auto Union and Mercedes-Benz officials had nothing better to do but argue about the outcome. (Audi AG)

Lang lost in Belgrade – he had to retire when a stone smashed his goggles. (Daimler AG)

only under pressure from the officials. Several days later the companies' racing divisions were still exchanging letters on the matter with NSKK chief Hühnlein – small-mindedness, egotism, ambition, vanity and self-justification predominated, right to the bitter end.

Thus did the brief era of the Silver Arrows draw to a close. Europe was at war. No Grand Prix races would be held for many years, and there would be no more encounters between the cars from Untertürkheim and Zwickau – even though both teams continued to receive subsidies from the Nazis until well into 1941.

Truth and fiction

They would have been delighted to go on racing even in wartime. On 11 January 1940 Max Sailer reported 'in strict confidence' to his board about a meeting in Merano, in the Italian Tyrol, between representatives of Mercedes-Benz, Auto Union, Alfa Romeo and Adolf Hühnlein, together with the latter's loyal lieutenant, von Bayer-Ehrenburg, and their Italian opposite numbers, Furmanik and Filippini. A joint 'calendar of sports fixtures' was drawn up, which actually included Grand Prix races at Monza and on the new Grossdeutschland circuit. According to Hühnlein, Hitler and his foreign minister von Ribbentrop placed great importance on 'continuing with

They kept racing for as long as possible. The complete BMW factory team receives its instructions for the 1940 Mille Miglia from NSKK-Führer Adolf Hühnlein. (BMW AG)

sport in spite of the war'. Foreign currency would even be released for the purpose. The Reich Foreign Minister suggested holding races in Slovakia,[9] in the Protectorate of Bohemia and Moravia, in Hungary, Yugoslavia and Romania. Unfortunately Belgium and Switzerland could not be considered 'because of the political and economic situation', likewise Sweden, despite an initial 'willingness'. Sailer remained sceptical, fearing that if insufficient money flowed in and no new cars could be built 'all the great success of the last few years might in given circumstances be wiped out at a stroke.' But on 24 January 1940, at Hühnlein's request, Wilhelm Kissel decided to resume preparations, though agreeing on 15 March to a strict economy programme, which two days previously Hühnlein had imposed on companies engaged in motor racing. Once again the CEO of Daimler-Benz AG was bowing to the now very different demands of the Nazi regime. It was no coincidence that Kissel belonged to the NSDAP and the SS, and even a benevolent historian like Neil Gregor cannot avoid attributing him with 'a certain sympathy for the regime and its ideology'. The fact is, however, that on 18 July 1942 Wilhelm Kissel took his own life. Whether it was from despair at the death of his son in action or for other reasons, must remain a matter for speculation.

As it was, the course of the war put an end to all plans for further appearances of the Silver Arrows. The last race in which Germany took part was held on 28 April 1940. The NSKK, jointly with BMW AG, entered a team for the Mille Miglia, which was run on a circuit near Brescia. The BMW team was made up largely of men from the NSKK but also included the Italian Count Lurani and SS-*Hauptsturmführer* Fritz Huschke von Hanstein. The latter was a political choice, since the SS, which had previously sponsored von Hanstein's drives in a black-painted BMW 328 with the registration-number SS-333, wanted to be fittingly represented at this spectacular foreign event. The 29-year-old baron was in fact winning the Mille Miglia in a silver BMW 328 works coupé, but shortly before the end of the race his NSKK colleague Walter Bäumer took over the wheel. Was this due to von Hanstein's 'exhaustion', or did Hühnlein's corps want to have a share in the victory? It is a fact that von Hanstein's racing overalls sported the runic symbol of the SS, while the photograph of Bäumer as victor was subsequently retouched so that his racing outfit bore a resplendent NSKK logo.

Walter Bäumer died in a road accident on 29 June 1941, but after the war Huschke von Hanstein would be seen again on racetracks all over the world – as were so many drivers from the Nazi age of motor racing. Through luck, skill and the help of good friends, the great majority of the gentlemen involved in pre-war German motorsport survived the Second World War.

Huschke von Hanstein was a personal friend of the young Ferry Porsche. They both took a delight in technology, racing and fast cars, and coincidentally both belonged to the SS. The former Auto Union racing manager Dr Feuereissen even wrote a testimonial for von Hanstein, which is how he

Hühnlein's heroes. There was strong political influence from the SS for Huschke von Hanstein (left) to drive a works BMW in the 1940 Mille Miglia. He won with his rather faster team-mate, Walter Bäumer (right), whose NSKK logo was later doctored on to this photograph. (Reuss)

landed a job in 1950 with the Porsche company in Stuttgart's Zuffenhausen district. The baron, who was still racing, built a reputation for the little VW-based Porsche 365 among a 'better class' of people. Soon it was considered chic to drive a Porsche. The thoroughly likeable and jovial von Hanstein rose to become a respected representative of German motorsport the world over. After serving as Porsche's racing manager he took up senior positions in the AvD (Automobile Club of Germany) and the World Automobile Federation.

The fact that in Zuffenhausen he met some colleagues from his past only became public knowledge when the former Waffen-SS *Oberbannführer* Joachim Peiper was forced by public pressure to give up the job he had held with Porsche since 1957. At one time Peiper had been a member of Himmler's personal staff, was for a while in command of a unit on the Eastern Front, and after the war, in what was known as the Malmédy Trial, was condemned to death for his responsibility for the massacre of Belgian civilians in the wake of the Ardennes offensive. The sentence was commuted to life imprisonment, but Peiper was granted early release in 1956 and joined Porsche the following year. Right across post-war German society a remarkable network of friendships had been maintained from the time of the Nazi dictatorship, and this was particularly true in the supposedly non-political world of motor racing. The members of this privileged fraternity simply changed horses.

Before the Nazis arrived on the scene racing in motor cars was something for the elite; it had been popularised during the Nazi dictatorship, then after 1945 had returned to the hands of the 'better classes' – hands which, of course, had remained clean. One of von Hanstein's best friends was Prince Paul von Metternich. The prince was also a Spanish grandee, Duca de Portella, Conde de Castillejo, Count von Königswart, a major landowner in the Tirol, and Grand Prior of the Order of Lazarus in Germany. He had fought for Franco in the Spanish Civil war, and had played his part against the 'Communist menace' outside Madrid and at the capture of Toledo and Barcelona. After the war he started to drive in races, became President of the AvD and finally head of the FIA, the international motor racing federation. Incidentally, the FIA President today is Max Mosley, lawyer, one-time owner of a Formula One racing team – and a son of the former leader of the British Union of Fascists, the late Sir Oswald Mosley.

After 1945 everything picked up very quickly. It had to. Questions about the past were not encouraged, and only a year after the end of the war motor races were again being organised in Germany, despite petrol rationing, driving bans and the suspicions of Allied occupation forces. Soon new racetracks had to be sought, since the public had begun to turn up in droves, in search of distraction from everyday post-war austerity. In Nürnberg, the former Reich Party Arena was used for a motorcycle race on 18 May 1947, to advertise the resurgent two-wheel industry in the Franconia region. Now called the Norisring, the circuit remains in use to this day.

Many of the great racing heroes of the Nazi era appeared here and elsewhere. Stuck, von Brauchitsch, Meier, Müller – even Hermann Lang, who was admittedly still locked in Denazification proceedings and was eventually classified as a 'fellow-traveller'. On 26 May 1948 he was sentenced by a tribunal in Stuttgart to pay a fine of 1,000 RM[10] as a 'penance', but on 30 July protested against this judgement 'since I cannot see why someone should be condemned for driving cars and motorcycles very fast in races – which was the real reason for my honorary promotions.' The wheels of justice grind slowly. The sentencing authority at the Central Denazification Tribunal for Northern Württemberg informed Lang on 2 June 1950 that the penalty would by reduced to 219.45 Deutschmarks, payable as from 1 July 1950 in monthly instalments of 50 DM with a final instalment of 69.45 DM. 'In view of the low level of political involvement and the losses suffered by the accused, the court costs represent hardship. In due consideration of the circumstances it therefore seemed justifiable to reduce the costs owed and to allow payment by instalments.'

On 29 December 1947 Lang's former racing manager, Alfred Neubauer, was also classified as a 'fellow-traveller' by the tribunal for Stuttgart North, and fined just 100 RM. On 11 February 1948 Neubauer appealed against this decision with a detailed written submission. His promotion to NSKK *Oberscharführer* was, he said, 'honorary' and 'was only due to the fact that the *Werkssturm* (factory unit) of the NSKK in Daimler-Benz AG, to which I was recruited against my will as a supporting member, felt it incumbent upon them to give special recognition to my services as manager of our racing team that had been victorious for so many years.' Thereupon the higher tribunal overruled the decision on 5 April 1948 and cancelled the proceedings against Neubauer.

The former Mercedes-Benz racing manager returned to his traditional place of work – as did all the other leading contenders in Hitler's motor racing battles. At a conference of the Motoring Press Club, held from 8 to 10 March 1949 in Burscheid at the invitation of the Goetze company, Neubauer asked for permission to show the last Daimler-Benz racing film made in the Nazi period under the title 'Victory – Record – Championship'. He wanted to show it 'in its international version to this small private gathering', which included, as it had before 1945, Messrs Bretz, Doerschlag, Rosemann and other old friends. Nothing had changed. 'I have in fact found out,' Neubauer explained, 'that particularly in the British Zone, many sports films with a National Socialist background are shown with no criticism at all, because of course recent events cannot simply be erased.'

The former editor and assiduous journalist Hans Bretz, looking back in 1937 on ten years of the Nürburgring, could still recall with enthusiasm that 'in 1933, through the liberating and revivifying deeds of the *Führer*, German motorsport received a boost which removed at a stroke all the obstacles with which it had had to battle till then!' He went on to rejoice that 'from a multiplicity of clubs […] a single club has been formed: the Deutsche Automobil-Club (DDAC).' It was Bretz who became the first vice-president of the re-founded ADAC in 1949 and finally served as the

Nothing to offer but blood, sweat and tales – Alfred Neubauer during the 1955 British Grand Prix at Aintree. Ten years after the Second World War the German 'Silver Arrows' of Mercedes-Benz were back again in what was now called Formula 1, with their former opponents from Auto Union far away and forgotten in communist East Germany. The time was ideal for writing silver-tinted legends about the good old days of racing that really weren't influenced by the Nazis… (Daimler AG)

unchallenged President of Germany's most powerful motoring organisation from 1964 until his death in 1972.

In the post-war period Bretz described the work of the once Nazified ADAC as 'without doubt a deliberate demonstration against the high-handed and partisan role of the NSKK in national and international motoring'; but in 1938, when writing for Daimler-Benz AG, he had sung a very different tune, praising National Socialist sports policy 'which, constantly aiming for the highest goals, has attempted and achieved ever new and greater performances! It is to the credit of the leader of German motorsport, *Korpsführer* Hühnlein, that these internal and external conditions have been created, firstly through the reorganisation of the German club structure, which found expression in the creation of the *Deutsches Automobil-Club*, then most of all in the concentrated power, which the *Nationalsozialistische Kraftfahrkorps* [NSKK] has won for itself under his leadership. Among the men of the Corps, motorsport is no longer chiefly a striving for personal success but rather an untiring battle for the success and honour of the nation!'

The name of another campaigner for German motor racing and for the Nürburgring can be found to this day in the ranks of the honorary citizens of the town of Ahrweiler near the Eifel racetrack: that of NSKK chief Adolf Hühnlein. This mark of distinction has never been officially withdrawn from Hühnlein, as the website of the Old Ahrweiler Society tells us, 'since under our constitution honorary citizenship only lapses on the death of the recipient.'

Notes

1 Elly Beinhorn-Rosemeyer (1907–2007), the daughter of a Hanover businessman, obtained her pilot's licence at age 21, and soon qualified for stunt flying and flying on instruments only. She made her first long-distance flight, to Central Africa, in 1931. On the return flight she crash-landed near Timbuktu and was missing for many days. In 1933 she won the Hindenburg Cup for a 19,000-mile flight that took her across the Himalayas and Australia to South America. After the war she continued to fly and won further trophies. She wrote a number of books including *A Girl Flies Alone* (1932), *My Husband the Racing Driver* (1938) and her 1978 memoirs, *Solo Flight: My Life*.

2 Hanna Reitsch (1912–79) was born in Silesia, the daughter of an ophthalmologist. As a glider pilot she set a number of records, then in 1938 became the Luftwaffe's first female test-pilot. She tested an early helicopter (1938) and the first German jet fighters (1944). A fervent admirer of Hitler, she was the first woman to be awarded the Iron Cross (1st and 2nd Class). She was among the last people to see Hitler alive in the Bunker in April 1945, when she offered to fly him to safety. Interned by the Americans for 15 months she was released without charge in 1947. She wrote two autobiographies, in 1951 and 1978.

3 A proposal that Schmeling should join the SS was turned down by Himmler because 'a man of such high standing in sport as Schmeling can be more use to the German people if he belongs to neither the SS, nor the SA, the NSKK or any other Party organisation.'

4 Quoted from Hermann Lang, *Vom Rennmonteur zum Europameister* ('From Race Mechanic to European Champion'), Munich, 1943.

5 The Denazification Tribunal heard statements from the racing driver's closer friends and acquaintances and reached the conclusion: 'Lang never bothered with politics and never did anything in the National-Socialist cause. The office of *Staffelführer* in the NSKK was conferred on him by reason of his achievements as a racing driver. He is described as a calm and always helpful person. [...] Lang was very popular among his work colleagues, because of his modest and helpful nature, which he retained despite his fame. In his working environment he never said anything that would lead one to conclude that he had National-Socialist sympathies; he simply lived for his work.'

6 In 9 AD, the Roman army on the Rhine suffered a devastating defeat at the hands of the German tribal leader Arminius (Herrmann). Known also as the Battle of the Teutoberg Forest, this *Hermannschlacht* ('Hermann's battle') became an iconic event in German history and was the subject of a famous play by the 19th-century author Heinrich von Kleist.

7 The author notes that on 27 May 1939, hardly a week after Lang's victory in the Eifel Race, Caracciola had complained in a letter to Kissel (CEO of Daimler-Benz) about poor support from the racing team: 'I see little chance of the situation changing at all. Starting with Herr Sailer [the board member with direct responsibility for the racing division] through Neubauer, down to the mechanics, there is an obsession with Lang. Herr Neubauer admitted frankly to Herr von Brauchitsch that he was standing by the man who has good luck, and whom the sun shines on.' Caracciola, whose vanity had been deeply wounded, nonetheless attempted to water down his verbal insults. 'None of this is intended as an attack on Lang, whom I respect as a driver.' However, Caracciola felt compelled to add: 'I really enjoy racing and want to go on driving for a long time. However, this presupposes that I fight with the same weapons as my stablemates. Yet this will hardly be possible in the future, as almost all the mechanics and engine specialists in the racing division are on Lang's side, because he is from Württemberg [*ie* a local]. So they will of course do their best for him, not only in their work, but in the factory as a whole. Under these circumstances, much as I regret doing so, I have to tell you that I am placing my post at your disposal. You will understand my feelings. I have always represented the Mercedes star with the greatest commitment, and have always found you generous and sympathetic. With Heil Hitler and best wishes, I remain yours faithfully, Rudolf Caracciola.' It is interesting to compare Caracciola's griping with Dick Seaman's last letter to his friend George Monkhouse, dated 14 June 1939, in which he says that Lang was not in fact a 'sulky child', like his other colleagues in the Mercedes-Benz stable.

8 An internal works report on Müller's race performance dated 23 August 1939 notes: 'Chassis good. Car shook twice. Roadholding in the race outstanding, even in rain and on slippery surface. [...] Engine tired. From the start of the race Müller had the feeling the engine was going to break down. Idling speed did not work below 3,000 revs. This meant that in addition to his underperforming engine he lost time on every bend.'

9 When Germany invaded Czechoslovakia in March 1939 Hitler drove a wedge between the Czechs and the Slovaks, well aware of the antipathy between the two nations, forced into an uncomfortable marriage in 1918. A separate pro-Nazi puppet state of Slovakia was forcibly set up under the arch-conservative Monsignor Tiso. Though the two countries were reunited in 1945, the 'Velvet Revolution' of the early 1990s led to a second, more amicable divorce.

10 The Reichsmark remained the legal currency of Germany for some time after the war ended. Then, on 20 June 1948, as part of the Marshall Plan, the three Western occupying powers (USA, Britain and France) introduced a new currency in their zones, the Deutschmark (DM). Wages and salaries were paid on a ratio of 1 DM to 1 RM, but savings could only be converted at 10 RM to 1 DM. In 1949 the three Western zones become the German Federal Republic.

CHAPTER EIGHT

EPILOGUE

It is 14 November 1998, a cold, wet Saturday. Time is not on our side. We have an hour to record our piece for television. Maximum. It won't be enough to get a complete impression of him, but we can at least tape an interview while everyone in the Untertürkheim plant is getting geared up for *Stars and Cars*, the annual presentation of the Mercedes-Benz factory's Formula One and other motorsport teams before a large audience. We are here to celebrate Mika Häkkinen's first World Championship title in the latest Silver Arrow. Outside, the V10 power unit is being noisily warmed up in the McLaren; inside, a legend enters the conference room – 93-year-old Manfred von Brauchitsch, almost the last survivor of a distant epoch, a little man who talks very loudly and with great emphasis, still believing that this is the way to impress everyone. 'The racing game in those days just can't be compared with what it's like today,' he begins, sounding like an officer lecturing his men. 'It's something else. It's still about four wheels, a car and speed, but the connection between driver and car is completely different. You've no idea of the energy and physical force we had to apply to the car, the steering wheel and the gear lever. Well of course, there must have been a reason why our hands were always bleeding after a race.'

Once into his stride, he simply bubbles with effervescent enthusiasm: 'We always used to say to each other, either you'll get chucked out, or you won't, but in racing, you were always being flung out, actually.' Manfred von Brauchitsch, at least, has always landed on his feet, throughout his

Last man standing. Manfred von Brauchitsch survived all the political systems that came to grip Germany. The all-time luckiest survivor of Grand Prix racing, he lived long enough to become a legend in his lifetime. (Daimler AG)

long life. An irrepressible little gnome with the wisdom of age, whose blue eyes still gleam. 'Y'know, I've always been a survivor. My life has spanned seven epochs – the Kaiser's empire, First World War, Weimar Republic, Nazi period, Second World War, GDR and Federal Republic.' He has outlived nearly all his former colleagues. And got on the wrong side of many of them. But what does that matter, when you're well over 90? Von Brauchitsch has the privilege of still being able, at the end of a long life, to pose as a legend. He works on his myth. And now, at this late date, he is once more in the service of the Untertürkheim star.

What really went on back then in the Eifel Race on 3 June 1934? Did the W25 really tip the scales at four pounds over the permitted 750kg in a race that wasn't run to the 750kg formula? Did that truly mean it couldn't run at the Nürburgring? If so, they would have been well and truly 'lacquered' (stuffed), as, it will be recalled, von Brauchitsch is reported to have said on the eve of the race. Then all through the night the white paint was rubbed off and the next day they won. It is just a bit odd that none of the contemporary chroniclers seems to have noticed this birth of the Silver Arrows. The garrulous von Brauchitsch did not consider it necessary to

Manfred von Brauchitsch, who spent his post-war years in East Germany, in 1994 at the former Mercedes-Benz Museum within the Untertürkheim factory. (Daimler AG)

mention this extraordinary incident in his earlier biographies, and even former Daimler-Benz mechanics have publicly expressed doubts. What sacrilege. In the end von Brauchitsch may have preferred to opt for the legend. Which is why, to this day, Mercedes-Benz fitters and company historians are still scratching the white paint from the Silver Arrow.

However, there is another legend that he *has* swept away. It is not true that he was the 'eternal loser'. Being able to hold the steering wheel in the fastest racing cars of the age was a privilege that every man dreamed of at the time and one that he has lived off ever since. Caracciola was more successful, Rosemeyer was the absolute genius at the wheel, Lang the irritating *arriviste* and uncomfortably quick competitor, and Stuck was the *grand seigneur*. But after them, at the very least, came Manfred von Brauchitsch. Anyway, he survived them all and what is more won first prize on many occasions: the AVUS in 1932, the Eifel Race in 1934, Monaco in 1937, Reims in 1938. Still pretty impressive, even though most of the headlines proclaimed his spectacular defeats: can anyone have lost the German Grand Prix on the Nürburgring more dramatically than he did to Nuvolari in 1935, with two tyre-bursts in the last 10km? Nothing is impossible: in 1938 there was a no less spectacular exit when his car and overalls caught fire in the pits but he eventually drove on, only to go off the track finally whilst in pursuit of his team-mate Seaman. Did the bayonet lock on the steering wheel of his W154 really come loose? Question after question. But who is interested in the answers today, even if this time they are correct?

'We were glad that our racing cars were still more or less functioning and we could drive again in the next race. But that was one of the many little deceptions we practised in those days,' mused the legend. 'We rather let ourselves be dictated to by a small clique. Men who dressed up like clowns, with bowties, riding-boots and black or brown breeches. To me that world seemed thoroughly crooked.' Yet with every success he actually made the Nazi regime a little bit more popular. Perhaps unintentionally. But it was a good life. And with the successes came promotion. He ended up as a *Sturmführer* in the NSKK.

'I never moved in political circles or got involved in politics,' said von Brauchitsch, also referring to his time in Communist East Germany, the GDR. 'Maybe I told a few lies. But basically I was always honest.' In East Germany he was in great demand, something that after 1945 he soon ceased to be in the West. His attempted comebacks as a racing driver failed, and his time as sports president of the AvD was a short-lived episode. Instead he began to make contacts in the GDR. He staged test-drives with the Johannisthal Racing Collective, then paid visits to the GDR skiing championships in Oberhof, and finally he acted as West Germany's representative at the preparations for the 1951 Communist International Youth Festival in East Berlin. Contacts with the former Soviet Occupation Zone intensified: he signed appeals by the Socialist Unity Party (the only political party recognised in the GDR) against the remilitarisation of Germany, and his autobiography *Kampf um Meter und Sekunden* ('Fighting for Metres and Seconds') was published in East Berlin in 1953 by the state publishing house, Verlag der Nation. He received the sum of 75,000 West German Deutschmarks for it, allegedly at the instigation of the East German president, Walter Ulbricht. 'Full throttle into the wrong bend!' screamed the headlines in the Federal Republic.

On 8 May 1953 von Brauchitsch was arrested at his villa on Lake Starnberg on suspicion of preparing an act of high treason. 'When people ask me about it today, then the route that led me to solitary confinement in Stadelheim gaol is very interesting. It was an experience I went through deliberately. It was incomprehensible to everyone, including my warders, why I was locked up there.' He was released on parole after several months' detention, but before his trial could begin he absconded to the GDR. In the West it became known as 'the Brauchitsch Case', and media interest intensified even more when his first wife, Gisela, committed suicide.

The title of his second autobiography to appear in the GDR was *Ohne Kampf, kein Sieg* ('No Victory Without Struggle'). It was another readable piece of recent history, especially when compared with Neubauer's collection of anecdotes. The legend smiles at this observation, flattered. But the time for our TV interview has long since run out. Manfred von Brauchitsch is urgently required for the reception with Mika Häkkinen and David Coulthard. It's a wrap. He quickly signs a few autographs. One last question: what exactly happened just before the start of the Belgrade Grand Prix in 1939, three days after the German invasion of Poland, when he was fetched back from an aircraft that was about to take off for Switzerland? 'Well, as you know, my friend Rudolf Caracciola lived in Switzerland.' Now all the men from the Mercedes-Benz press office are arriving. A last quick question: 'Herr von

Brauchitsch, was it all worth it…?' But it's too late. Time's up. They have come to take him – and his legend – to the stage, to join Mika and David.

On 5 February 2003 Manfred von Brauchitsch died at his home in Gräfenwarth. He was 97. Five days later a remarkable announcement of his death appeared in the *Frankfurter Allgemeine Zeitung*. On the left-hand side was a last word of greeting from his second wife Liselotte to motorsport officials and participants: 'The heart of a fighter has ceased to beat. […] His achievements as a racing driver and his work for sport as an instrument of peace will never be forgotten.'

Right next to this, on the right-hand half of the page, DaimlerChrysler had placed its advertisement in the same format: 'Manfred von Brauchitsch was an influential member of the Mercedes-Benz racing team in the Silver Arrow era of the 1930s who, with his skill and his enthusiastic commitment, made a decisive contribution to the success of the legendary Silver Arrows. […] Manfred von Brauchitsch will always be remembered as an exceptional racing driver.'

The truth lies somewhere in between – and that is true not only of Manfred von Brauchitsch but also of every other hero of Hitler's motor racing battles.

A classic scene – Manfred von Brauchitsch at the Nürburgring in 1934. (Daimler AG)

BIBLIOGRAPHY

Sources

AU = Sächisches Staatsarchiv Chemnitz, Bestand Auto Union AG
 (*Saxony State Archive, Chemnitz, collection of Auto Union AG*)

BArch = Bundesarchiv Berlin (*German Federal Archives*)

BArch (ehem. BDC) RS-Akte von Hanstein (*von Hanstein papers*)

BArch (ehem. BDC) NSDAP-Zentralkartei (*Central register of the NSDAP*)

BArch (ehem. BDC) RS-Akte Kohlrausch (*Kohlrausch papers*)

BArch (ehem. BDC) RS-Akte Rosemeyer (*Rosemeyer papers*)

BArch (ehem. BDC) RKK Hans Stuck (*Stuck papers*)

BArch NS 19/1057 Persönlicher Stab – Reichsführer-SS, Unterlagen betr. Hans Stuck (*Personal staff of the Reichsführer-SS [Heinrich Himmler], papers concerning Hans Stuck*)

BArch NS 24 Nationalsozialistisches Kraftfahrkorps (*National Socialist Drivers Corps*)

DC = Konzernarchiv DaimlerChrysler AG (*Corporate archives of Daimler Chrysler AG*)

DC Bestand Kissel, Rennen 12.24 (*Kissel collection, races*)

DC Bestand Kissel, Rennen 12.25 (*Kissel collection, races*)

DC Bestand Kissel, Rennen 12.28 (*Kissel collection, races*)

DC Bestand Lang 226/2 (*Lang collection*)

DC Bestand Werlin, 5.56 (*Werlin collection*)

DC Bestand Werlin, 7 (*Werlin collection*)

Generallandesarchiv Karlsruhe GLA Abt. 480, Nr. 11122, Bd. 1 und 2: 'Entschädigungssache Alan A. Robert (fr. Adolf Rosenberger)'
(*General Provincial Archives, Karlsruhe, documents from the compensation lawsuit of Alan A.Robert (formerly Adolf Rosenberger)*)

Staatsarchiv Ludwigsburg StAL Bestand EL 902/20 AZ.37/12/26024 – (*State Archives, Ludwigsburg, papers from the Denazification tribunal of Hermann Lang*)

Staatsarchiv Ludwigsburg StAL Bestand EL 902/20 AZ. 37/16/10835 – Spruchkammerakte Alfred Neubauer (*State Archives, Ludwigsburg, papers from the Denazification tribunal of Alfred Neubauer*)

Staatsarchiv Ludwigsburg StAL Bestand FL 300/33 BüRest S2682 – Entschädigungsverfahren Adolf Rosenberger gegen Porsche (*State Archives, Ludwigsburg, compensation proceedings, Adolf Rosenberger vs Porsche*)

Staatsarchiv Ludwigsburg StAL Bestand EL 902/20 Az: 37/6/5671 – Spruchkammerakte Els Voelter (*State Archives, Ludwigsburg, papers from the Denazification tribunal of Els Voelter*)

Staatsarchiv Ludwigsburg StAL Bestand EL 902/20 Az: 37/1/6680 – Spruchkammerakte Dr. Richard Voelter (*State Archives, Ludwigsburg, papers from the Denazification tribunal of Dr Richard Voelter*)

Amtsgericht Starnberg AZ 32/3340 – Spruchkammerakte Manfred von Brauchitsch (*Starnberg District Court, papers from the Denazification tribunal of Manfred von Brauchitsch*)

Books

Tobias Aichele, *Huschke von Hanstein. Der Rennbaron*, Cologne 1999

Götz Aly, *Hitlers Volksstaat. Raub, Rassenkrieg und nationaler Sozialismus*, Frankfurt am Main 2005

Bernard P. Bellon, *Mercedes in Peace and War: German Automobile Workers, 1903-1945*, New York/Oxford 1990

Wolfgang Benz (Hg.), *Legenden, Lügen, Vorurteile*. Ein Wörterbuch zur Zeitgeschichte, Munich 1992

Wolfgang Benz, *Geschichte des Dritten Reiches*, Munich 2000

John Bentley/Ferry Porsche, *We at Porsche*, G.T.Foulis 1977

Manfred von Brauchitsch, *Kampf um Meter und Sekunden*, East Berlin 1953

Manfred von Brauchitsch, *Ohne Kampf kein Sieg*, Berlin (GDR) 1964

Hans Bretz, "Zehn Jahre Nürburgring GmbH" in: *Jahrbuch des Kreises Ahrweiler 1938*

Hans Bretz, *Mannschaft und Meisterschaft. Eine Bilanz der Grand-Prix-Formel 1934-1937*, published by Daimler-Benz AG, Stuttgart/Cologne 1938

Hans Bretz, *Bernd Rosemeyer. Ein Leben für den deutschen Sport*, Berlin 1938

Hans Bretz, *50 Jahre ADAC. Im Dienste der Kraftfahrt*, Munich/Frankfurt am Main 1953

Michael Burleigh, *The Third Reich – A New History*, London 2000

Gianni Cancellieri/Cesare de Agostini/Martin Schröder, *Auto Union – Die großen Rennen 1934-1939*, Hanover 1979

Rudolf Caracciola, *Mein Leben als Rennfahrer*, Berlin 1939

Rudolf Caracciola/Oskar Weller, *Rennen - Sieg - Rekorde!*, Stuttgart 1943

Adriano Cimarosti, *Autorennsport*, Berne 1979

Uwe Day, *Silberpfeil und Hakenkreuz*. Autorennsport im Nationalsozialismus, Berlin 2005

William Court, *Grand Prix Requiem*. A celebration of motor racing greats who paid speed's ultimate price, Patrick Stephens Limited, Sparkford 1992

Cameron C. Earl, *Quick Silver. A facsimile of B.I.O.S. Report No. 1755 Investigation into the development of German Grand Prix Racing Cars between 1934 and 1939 (including a description of the Mercedes World´s Land Speed Record Contender)*. First published by HMSO in 1948, Reprinted with a new introduction by Karl E. Ludvigsen, London 1996

Hans-Rüdiger Etzold/Ewald Rother/Thomas Erdmann, *Auto Union. Im Zeichen der vier Ringe, 1873-1945*, Band 1, Ingolstadt 1992

Richard von Frankenberg, *Die großen Fahrer unserer Zeit*, 1st edition, Stuttgart 1956

Richard von Frankenberg, *Die großen Fahrer von einst*, 2nd edition, Stuttgart 1967, p115, [First impression 1966]

Uwe Fraunholz, *Motorphobia. Anti-automobiler Protest in Kaiserreich und Weimarer Republik*, Göttingen 2002

Norbert Frei, *Vergangenheitspolitik. Die Anfänge der Bundesrepublik und die NS-Vergangenheit*, Munich 1996

Norbert Frei (Hg.), *Hitlers Eliten nach 1945*, Munich 2003

Neil Gregor, *Daimler-Benz in the Third Reich*, Yale University Press 1998

Sebastian Haffner, *Germany: Jekyll & Hyde. 1939 – An Eye-Witness Analysis of Nazi Germany*, Libris 2005

Sebastian Haffner, *Geschichte eines Deutschen. Die Erinnerungen 1914-1933*, Munich 2002 [1st impression of the revised and enlarged paperback edition]

Sebastian Haffner, *Defying Hitler,* tr. Oliver Pretzel, Orion, London 2003

Beatrice und Helmut Heiber (Hg.), *Die Rückseite des Hakenkreuzes. Absonderliches aus den Akten des Dritten Reiches*, Munich 1993

Emmy Herzog, *Leben mit Leo. Ein Schicksal im Nationalsozialismus*, Münster 2000

Christopher Hilton, *Hitler's Grands Prix in England. Donington 1937 and 1938*, Haynes, Sparkford 1999

Dorothee Hochstetter, *Motorisierung und 'Volksgemeinschaft'. Das Nationalsozialistische Kraftfahrkorps (NSKK) 1931-1945*, Munich 2005

Ernst Hornickel, *Wer wußte das von Rosemeyer? Ein Tatsachenbericht aus dem Werden eines Meisters*, Stuttgart 1937

Ernst Hornickel, *Das sind unsere Rennfahrer*, Stuttgart 1940

Ian Kershaw, *The Hitler Myth: Image and Reality in the Third Reich*, Oxford 2001

Ian Kershaw, *Hitler 1889-1936: Hubris*, Allen Lane 1998

Ian Kershaw, *Hitler 1936-1945: Nemesis*, Allen Lane 2000

Peter Kirchberg, *Grand-Prix-Report Auto Union 1934 bis 1939*, 2nd edition, East Berlin 1984

Victor Klemperer, *Und so ist alles schwankend. Tagebücher Juni bis Dezember 1945*, Berlin 1996

Victor Klemperer, *I Shall Bear Witness: The Diaries of Victor Klemperer 1933-41*, London 1999

Victor Klemperer, *To the Bitter End: the Diaries of Victor Klemperer 1942-45*, London 2000

Victor Klemperer, *The Language of the Third Reich*, Continuum 2006

Volker Kluge, *Max Schmeling. Eine Biographie in 15 Runden*, Berlin 2004

Ulrich Kubisch/Gert Rietner, *Die AVUS im Rückspiegel. Rennen, Rekorde, Rückstaus*, Berlin (West) 1987

Hermann Lang, *Vom Rennmonteur zum Europameister*, Munich 1943

Hermann Lang, *Vom Rennmonteur zum Meisterfahrer*, Munich/Ulm 1952

Karl Ludvigsen, *Mercedes-Benz Racing Cars*, Bond, Parkhurst & Bond 1974

Tatiana Metternich, *An der Rennstrecke. Erinnerungen an Paul Fürst Metternich*, Munic/Berlin 1995

Günther Molter, *Rudolf Caracciola. Titan am Volant*, Stuttgart 1995

Hans Mommsen/Manfred Grieger, *Das Volkswagenwerk und seine Arbeiter im Dritten Reich*, Düsseldorf 1996

George C. Monkhouse, *Mercedes-Benz Grand Prix Racing 1934-1955*, New Cavendish 1983

Horst Mönnich, *BMW. Eine deutsche Geschichte*, Vienna/Darmstadt 1989

Horst Mönnich, *BMW. Eine deutsche Geschichte*, new enlarged and revised edition, Munich 2004

Kurt Möser, *Geschichte des Autos*, Frankfurt am Main, 2002

Valerio Moretti, *When Nuvolari Raced…*, Veloce 1994

Valerio Moretti, *Grand Prix Tripoli 1925-1940*, Automobilia 1994

Fabian Müller, *Ferdinand Porsche*, Berlin 1999

Alfred Neubauer (with Harvey T. Rowe), *Speed Was My Life*, Barrie & Rockliff 1960

Alfred Neubauer (with Harvey T. Rowe), *Männer, Frauen und Motoren*, Hamburg 1958

Alfred Neubauer (with Harvey T. Rowe), *Herr über 1000 PS: Erinnerungen des Rennleiters*, Hamburg 1959

Harry Niemann/Wilfried Feldenkirchen/Armin Hermann (Hg.), *Die Geschichte des Rennsports* (series of historical essays from the DaimlerChrysler archives), Vol. 5, Bielefeld 2002

Chris Nixon, *Racing the Silver Arrows. Mercedes-Benz versus Auto Union 1934-1939*, Osprey 1986

Doug Nye/Geoffrey Goddard, *Dick & George. The Seaman-Monkhouse Letters, 1936-1939*, Palawan 2002

Reinhard Osteroth, *Ferdinand Porsche. Der Pionier und seine Welt*, Hamburg 2004

Werner Oswald, *Deutsche Autos*, Bd. 2, 1920-1945, new edition, Stuttgart 2001

Hans Pohl/Stephanie Habeth/Beate Brüninghaus, *Die Daimler-Benz AG in den Jahren 1933 bis 1945. Eine Dokumentation*, Stuttgart/Wiesbaden 1986

Ferry Porsche/Günther Molter, *Ferry Porsche: Cars Are My Life*, Patrick Stephens Limited, Sparkford 1989

Hans Reh, *Der Meisterfahrer. Aus dem Leben Bernd Rosemeyers. Der deutschen Jugend erzählt von Hans Reh*, 3rd impression, Langensalza-Berlin-Leipzig 1941

Hans Reh, *Auf rasenden Achsen. Die Geschichte eines Rennfahrers*, Königsberg 1941

Erich Maria Remarque, *Station am Horizont*, Cologne 1998

Mike Riedner, *Doppelsieg. Der Rennfahrer und Verleger Paul Pietsch*, Stuttgart 1991

Ernst Rosemann, *Um Kilometer und Sekunden. Kämpfer im Rennwagen – Kämpfer für die Nation*, Stuttgart 1941

Elly Beinhorn-Rosemeyer (with Chris Nixon), *Rosemeyer! A New Biography*, Transport Bookman 1986

Karl Heinz Roth, 'Der Weg zum guten Stern des 'Dritten Reichs': Schlaglichter auf die Geschichte der Daimler-Benz AG und ihrer Vorläufer (1890-1945)', in: *Das Daimler-Benz-Buch*, published by the Hamburger Stiftung für Sozialgeschichte des 20. Jahrhunderts, (*Hamburg Foundation for the Social History of the 20th Century*), Nördlingen 1988

Hans Ruesch (with Arno Schmidt), *The Racer*, Ballantine Books (USA) 1955

Reinhard Rürup (Hg.), *1936. Die Olympischen Spiele und der Nationalsozialismus. The Olympic Games and National Socialism*, 2nd impression, Berlin 1999

Adelheid von Saldern, 'Cultural Conflicts, Popular Mass Culture, and the Question of Nazi Success: The Eilenriede Motorcycle Races, 1924-39', in: *German Studies Review* 15 (1992), S. 317-338

Ludwig Sebastian, *Hinter dröhnenden Motoren. Bernd Rosemeyers Monteur erzählt*, Vienna-Heidelberg 1952

Hans Christoph Graf von Seherr-Thoss, *Die deutsche Automobilindustrie. Eine Dokumentation von 1886 bis heute*, Stuttgart 1974

Miranda Seymour, *The Bugatti Queen. In Search of a Motor-Racing Legend*, Simon & Schuster 2004

Olaf Schiller/Peter Kirchberg, *Die Geschichte der Audi Markenzeichen*, Bielefeld 2002

Rainald Schumann, *H.P. Müller. Meister aller Klassen*, Lemgo 2002

Anna Maria Sigmund, *Des Führers bester Freund.* Adolf Hitler, seine Nichte Geli Raubal und der 'Ehrenarier' Emil Maurice – eine Dreiecksbeziehung, Munich 2005

Rainer Simons, *BMW 328. Vom Roadster zum Mythos*, Munich 1996

Paul Simsa, *Hitler, Käfer, Volksbetrug.* Wie Ferdinand Porsche den 'Führer' faszinierte, Wallmoden 2004

Horst Steffens, 'Massensport, Leistungssport und Sportbegeisterung. Der gesellschaftliche Aufstieg des Sports in den 20er Jahren'. In: *Tanz auf dem Vulkan. Die Goldenen 20er in Bildern, Szenen und Objekten.* Accompanying volume to 'Massensport', Mannheim 1994

Peter Stevenson, *Driving Forces. The Grand Prix Racing World Caught in the Maelstrom of the Third Reich*, Bentley Publishing (USA) 2000

Hans Stuck (with Ernst Günther Burgaller), *Motoring Sport*, G.T.Foulis & Co Ltd 1936

Hans Stuck, *Männer hinter Motoren. Ein Rennfahrer erzählt.* Published by the Luftwaffe General Staff, Ic/VIII, Berlin (undated).

Hans Stuck, *Zweimal Hans Stuck. Ein Rennfahrer-Tagebuch*, 2nd impression, Stuttgart 1972

Christoph Studt, Das Dritte Reich in Daten, Munich 2002, p. 199

Hans Joachim Teichler, *Internationale Sportpolitik im Dritten Reich*, Schorndorf 1991

Uwe Timm, *Am Beispiel meines Bruders*, Munich 2005

Erwin Tragatsch, *Das große Rennfahrerbuch*, Berne/Stuttgart 1970

Erwin Tragatsch, *Die großen Rennjahre 1919-1939*, Berne/Stuttgart 1973

Gerd R. Ueberschär/Winfried Vogel, *Dienen und Verdienen. Hitlers Geschenke an seine Eliten*, Frankfurt am Main 1999

Peter Vann and others, *Auto Union GP Race & Record Cars: Their reconstruction and restoration*, Motorbooks International, Wisconsin 2002

Hermann Weiß (Ed.), *Biografisches Lexikon zum Dritten Reich*, Frankfurt am Main. 2002

Hermann Heinz Wille, *PS auf allen Straßen der Welt. Das Buch vom Auto*, Leipzig/Jena/East Berlin 1964

Robert Wistrich, *Who's Who in Nazi Germany*, Weidenfeld & Nicholson 1982

Brock Yates, *Enzo Ferrari, The Man and The Machine*, Doubleday 1991

LIST OF ABBREVIATIONS

ADAC – *Allgemeiner Deutscher Automobil-Club* ('General German Automobile Club')

AIACR – *Association Internationale des Automobile Clubs Reconnu* ('International Association of Recognised Automobile Clubs')

AvD – *Automobilclub von Deutschland* ('Automobile Club of Germany')

AVUS – *Automobil-Verkerhrs- und Übungs-Strasse* ('Motor traffic and practice road')

CEO – Chief Executive Officer

CSI – *Commission Sportive Internationale* ('International Sporting Commission')

DAF – *Deutsche Arbeitsfront* ('German Labour Front')

DDAC – *Der Deutsche Automobil-Club* ('The German Automobile Club')

DM – Deutschmarks

IAA – *Internationale Automobilausstellungen* ('International Automobile Exhibition')

KdF – *Kraft durch Freude* ('Strength Through Joy')

NSDAP – *Nationalsozialistische Deutsche Arbeiterpartei* ('National Socialist German Workers' Party', or Nazi Party)

NSKK – *Nationalsozialistisches Kraftfahrkorps* ('National Socialist Drivers Corps')

ONS – *Oberste Nationale Sportbehörde* ('Supreme National Sports Authority')

RM – Reichsmarks

SA – *Sturmabteilung* ('Assault Unit', usually rendered as 'Stormtroopers')

SPD – *Sozialdemokratische Partei Deutschlands* ('German Social Democratic Party')

SS – *Schutzstaffel* ('Protection Squad')

INDEX